Webster's
Guide to Business
Correspondence

Webster's
Guide to Business
Correspondence

A Merriam-Webster®

Merriam-Webster Inc., Publishers
Springfield, Massachusetts

A GENUINE MERRIAM-WEBSTER

The name *Webster* alone is no guarantee of excellence. It is used by a number of publishers and may serve mainly to mislead an unwary buyer.

A Merriam-Webster® is the registered trademark you should look for when you consider the purchase of dictionaries and other fine reference books. It carries the reputation of a company that has been publishing since 1831 and is your assurance of quality and authority.

Copyright © 1988 by Merriam-Webster Inc.
Philippines Copyright 1988 by Merriam-Webster Inc.

Library of Congress Cataloging in Publication Data
Main entry under title:

Webster's guide to business correspondence.

Includes index.
1. Commercial correspondence. 2. Letter-writing.
3. English language—Business English.
I. Merriam-Webster, Inc.
HF5726.W34   1988   651.7′5   87-31333
ISBN 0-87779-031-0

Printed and bound in the United States of America

91011AG/M949392

Contents

Preface

Webster's Guide to Business Correspondence is a practical guide to more effective business-letter writing. It is designed to be an aid not only to executives, secretaries, and other businesspeople but also to anyone else who writes business-related correspondence. The book offers comprehensive guidance on a variety of topics having to do with business correspondence and is intended to help writers achieve concise, accurate, and effective communication through their letters.

The book is divided into eight chapters, each of which discusses in detail one topic relating to business correspondence. Each chapter is introduced by its own table of contents, listing all of the major sections in the chapter and the number of the page on which each section begins. Cross-references are placed throughout the text to guide the reader from one subject to another related subject. When specific information is needed, the detailed Index will indicate quickly where the desired material is to be found.

The overall organization of the book is designed to take the reader from the simplest and most often asked about aspects of business-letter writing through to the more complex and specialized aspects of the subject. Chapter 1, "Style in Business Correspondence," introduces the reader to the individual parts of the business letter and takes up general questions having to do with the format and appearance of business letters. This chapter includes many line drawings, tables, and facsimiles that illustrate and supplement the information given in the text. Chapter 2, "Forms of Address," is devoted mostly to a 17-page chart that shows the forms of address that are conventionally used for individuals whose offices, ranks, or professions warrant special courtesy. In both of these chapters, attention is given to the modern gender-related problems associated with salutations and forms of address, and the range of available solutions is presented.

Chapters 3, 4, and 5 are concerned with the compositional aspects of letter-writing. These chapters are based on Merriam-Webster's continuous study of the ways in which Americans use their language, and they draw on our extensive citation files which now include more than 13.5 million examples of English words used in context. Chapter 3, "The Mechanics of Writing," covers matters such as punctuation; capitalization; the formation of plurals, possessives, and compounds; and the treatment of abbreviations and numbers. Chapter 4, "Composition and Grammar," explains and illustrates the use of the eight parts of speech and various kinds of phrases, clauses, sentences, and paragraphs. Chapter 5, "Tone in Writing," is designed to help writers choose their words well and to avoid some of the jargon and clichés that can weaken an otherwise effective letter. In each of these chapters, the book offers concise yet comprehensive descriptions of the rules and conventions that writers have developed for themselves to help them produce clear, consistent, and effective prose. In addition, each of these rules includes one verbal illustration or more to demonstrate how the rule or convention works in context. Where these rules and conventions have exceptions, variations, or fine points that readers need to know about, these too are discussed and exemplified.

Chapter 6, "Composing Letters," presents pointers specifically applicable to composing letters. It also includes more than 40 sample letters designed to meet the needs of specific business-related occasions. For each sample letter, there is a facsimile of the finished letter, accompanied by a description of the elements that go into such a letter.

Chapters 7 and 8 take up two more-specialized topics. Chapter 7 is a guide to correspondence with United States government agencies and includes instructions for the handling of classified information in correspondence. Chapter 8 offers advice on the effective use of the postal service.

Like other Merriam-Webster® publications, *Webster's Guide to Business Correspondence* is the product of a collective effort. Dr. Frederick C. Mish, Editorial Director, made major contributions during the initial planning stages of the book. The text draws much of its material from *Webster's Secretarial Handbook,* Second Edition, and *Webster's Standard American Style Manual* and, as such, relies to a great degree on the work done by the writers and editors of those books. The manuscript for the book was prepared by Julie A. Collier, Associate Editor, and was copyedited by James G. Lowe, Senior Editor, and Madeline L. Novak, Associate Editor. The index was prepared by Eileen M. Haraty, Assistant Editor. Proofreading was done by Kathleen M. Doherty and Stephen J. Perrault, Associate Editors; Eileen M. Haraty, Peter D. Haraty, and Daniel J. Hopkins, Assistant Editors; and Kelly L. Tierney, Editorial Assistant. Helene Gingold, Editorial Department Secretary, prepared typewritten facsimiles. The manuscript was typed by Georgette B. Boucher and Barbara A. Winkler, Senior Editorial Typists, under the direction of Gloria J. Afflitto, Head of the Typing Room. Madeline L. Novak, as Editorial Production Coordinator, directed the book through its typesetting stages. Overall project coordination was provided by John M. Morse, Manager of Editorial Operations and Planning.

Webster's
Guide to Business
Correspondence

Chapter 1

Style in Business Correspondence

CONTENTS

The word *style* as applied to business-letter writing encompasses the format of the letter; the punctuation, capitalization, and other mechanical aspects of the writing; grammar and word usage; and the traditional conventions relating to the etiquette of letter-writing, such as proper salutations, closings, and forms of address. This chapter, however, focuses solely on questions of format and general punctuation patterns. For more on punctuation and the details relating to capitalization and other mechanics of writing, see Chapter 3, "Punctuation, Capitalization, and Other Mechanics of Writing." For a discussion of grammar and word usage, see Chapter 4, "Composition and Grammar" and Chapter 5, "Tone in Writing." For a list of forms of address, see Chapter 2, "Forms of Address."

Style in business correspondence, like language itself, is not a static entity. It has changed over the years to meet the varying needs of its users, and it continues to do so. For example, the open-punctuation pattern and the Simplified Letter have recently gained wide popularity, while the closed-punctuation pattern and the Indented Letter, once considered standard formats, are now little used in the United States. In many cases, this process of change had led to the situation in which writers have a range of alternatives available to them regarding aspects of letter-writing style. This chapter and the ones that follow have been written with these alternative acceptable stylings in mind, and, whenever such alternative stylings exist, they are presented and described. If there are reasons to prefer one over another, the reasons are explained; however, in many cases, the choice will be a question of individual taste, and writers will have to use their own judgment to choose among the acceptable styles.

The Business Letter as Image-Maker

All of the elements of business-letter style come together in a letter to produce a tangible reflection on paper not only of the writer's ability and knowledge and the typist's competence, but also of an organization's total image. For example, well-prepared business letters reflect a firm's pride and its concern for quality. On the other hand, poorly prepared correspondence can create such a negative impression on its recipients that they may have second thoughts about pursuing business relationships with the writer or the writer's organization. This is a special consideration for small businesses. The business letter, then, is actually an indicator of overall organizational style, regardless of the size of the firm. Thus, the impression created by attractively and accurately typed, logically oriented, and clearly written letters can be a crucial factor in the success of any business.

A businessperson may devote as much as 50 percent or more of his or her workday to correspondence. This includes planning and thinking out the directions, tone, and content of outgoing letters or reading and acting on incoming letters. Secretaries spend an even higher proportion of their time on correspondence. And all this time costs money. However, if both writer and typist keep in mind the following simple aids to good letter production, the time and money involved will have been well spent:

1. Stationery should be of high-quality paper having excellent correcting or erasing properties.
2. Typing should be neat and accurate with any corrections or erasures rendered invisible.
3. The essential elements of a letter (such as the date line, inside address, message, and signature block) and any other included parts should conform in page placement and format with one of the generally acceptable, up-to-date business-letter stylings (such as the Simplified Letter, the Block Letter, the Modified Block Letter, the Modified Semi-block Letter, or the Hanging-indented Letter).
4. The language of the letter should be clear, concise, grammatically correct, and devoid of padding and clichés.
5. The ideas in the message should be logically oriented, with the writer always keeping in mind the reader's reaction.
6. All statistical data should be accurate and complete.
7. All names should be checked for accuracy of spelling and style.

Letter Balance and Letterhead Design

It has often been said that an attractive letter should look like a symmetrically framed picture with even margins working as a frame for the typed lines that are balanced under the letterhead. But how many letters really do look like framed pictures? Planning ahead before starting to type is the key to letter symmetry. The following steps will help the writer or typist achieve the desired appearance:

1. Estimate the approximate number of words in the letter or the general length of the message by looking over the writer's rough draft or one's shorthand notes, or by checking the length of a dictated source.
2. Make mental notes of any long quotations, tabular data, long lists or footnotes or of the occurrence of scientific names and formulas that may require margin adjustments, a different typeface, or even handwork within the message.
3. Set the left and right margin stops according to the estimated letter length: about one inch for very long letters (300 words or more, or at least two pages), about one and one-half inches for medium-length ones (about 100–300 words), and about two inches for very short ones (100 words or less).
4. Remember that the closing parts of a letter take 10–12 lines (two inches) or more and that the bottom margin will be at least six lines (one inch). Thus you will want to allow at least three inches from the last line of the message to the bottom of the page.
5. Use the scale on the typewriter's page-end indicator or a guide sheet that numbers each line in the margin as a bottom margin warning; or lightly pencil a warning mark on the paper.
6. Single-space within paragraphs; double-space between paragraphs. Very short letters (up to three sentences) may be double-spaced throughout.
7. Set continuation-sheet margins to match those of the first sheet, and carry over at least three lines of the message to the continuation sheet.

With experience, a secretary can easily estimate the overall length of a letter. An inexperienced secretary should refer to a letter placement table such as Table 1 on page 4. As the table suggests, short letters may be typewritten on half-sheets, on Executive-size stationery, or on full-size stationery with wide margins. Some offices, however, use a standard six-inch typing line for all letters on full-size stationery, regardless of length, because it eliminates the need to reset tabs.

Very short letters typed on full-size stationery may create spacing problems. There are three simple ways to handle the extra space involved in these letters:

1. Use the six-inch line but lengthen the space between the date and the inside address, between the complimentary close and the signature, and between the signature and the transcriber's initials or enclosure notations.
2. Use the six-inch line but double-space. Double spacing should be used only in very short letters (about six lines or less, or up to three sentences). If a double-spaced letter contains more than one paragraph,

Table 1
Letter Placement Table
Three Sizes of Stationery

Lines in Letter Body	Words in Letter Body	Number of Blank Lines between Date and Inside Address*	Typewriter Marginal Stops Elite/Pica	Length of Typing Line	
				Inches	Spaces Elite/Pica
Half-sheet Stationery: Assume Letterhead takes 7 vertical lines. (Baronial—center No. 33 for Elite; No. 28 for Pica)					
9–10	60–66	7	15–60/10–50	4	48/40
11–12	67–73	6	15–59/10–50	4	48/40
13–14	74–80	5	15–60/10–50	4	48/40
15–16	81–87	4	15–60/10–50	4	48/40
17–18	88–94	3	15–60/10–50	4	48/40
19–20	95–100	2	15–60/10–50	4	48/40
Executive-size Stationery: Assume Letterhead takes 8 lines. (Monarch—center No. 43, Elite; No. 36, Pica)					
13–14	95–115	8	15–75/10–60	5	60/50
15–16	116–135	7	15–75/10–60	5	60/50
17–18	136–155	6	15–75/10–60	5	60/50
19–20	156–175	5	15–75/10–60	5	60/50
Full-size Stationery: Assume Letterhead takes 9 lines. (Standard—center No. 51, Elite; No. 42, Pica)					
3–5	under 100	7–12	25–75/22–62	4	48/40
6–10	100–200	4–8	20–80/17–67	5	60/50
11–14	175–200	7	15–87/12–72	6	72/60
15–18	201–225	6	15–87/12–72	6	72/60
19–22	226–250	5	15–87/12–72	6	72/60
23–26	251–275	4	15–87/12–72	6	72/60
27–30	276–300**	3	15–87/12–72	6	72/60

*Assume that the date is typed three lines below the last line of the letterhead on all letters.
**Letters consisting of more than 300 words should be two-page letters.

an indented-paragraph format should be used to help distinguish the paragraphs.
3. Use a four-inch or five-inch typing line, setting margins as suggested in Table 1 above.

Letterhead Design

Letterhead designs vary. Some letterheads are positioned at the center of the top of the page, others are laid out across the top of the page from the left to the right margin, and still others are more heavily balanced right or left of the center. Sometimes a company's name and logo appear at the top of the page, while its address and other data are printed at the bottom.

Regardless of layout and design, a typical business letterhead contains all or some of the following elements, with items 2, 3, 5, and 6 being essential:

1. logo
2. full name of the firm, company, corporation, institution, or group
3. full street address
4. suite, room, or building number, if needed—post office box number, if applicable
5. city, state, and zip code
6. area code and telephone number(s)
7. other data (as telex or cable references, branch offices, or products or services offered)

The names of particular departments, plants, groups, or divisions may be printed on the letterhead of extremely large or diversified companies or institutions. Other organizations such as large law firms may have the full names of their partners and staff attorneys all listed on the letterhead. Elaborate letterhead layouts require especially careful letter planning to avoid an unbalanced look. For example, a letterhead with a long list of names on the left side might be best balanced by use of the Modified Block Letter, where the date, reference numbers, and signature appear on the right side of the page.

High corporate officers frequently use a personalized or executive letterhead. Here the standard company letterhead design is supplemented with the name of the office (as "Office of the President") or with the full name and business title of the officer (as "John M. Jones, Jr., President") printed or engraved in small letters one or two lines beneath the letterhead at or near the left margin. The officer's business title may appear on the same line as his or her name if space permits and if both name and title are short, or it may be blocked directly below the name. Executive stationery is often not printed but instead engraved on a better grade of paper than that of the standard, printed company stationery. Executive stationery is also smaller than the standard, as shown in Table 2 on page 7. Envelopes match the paper and are printed with the executive's name and return address.

If you are writing a business letter for an organization that does not have letterhead stationery, you can create a typewritten letterhead. The typewritten letterhead can include all of the elements included in the printed letterhead (listed above) except for the logo; and, as with the printed letterhead, the essential items are (1) the full name of the company, institution, or group; (2) the full street address; (3) the city, state, and zip code; and (4) the area code and telephone number. The elements are centered, each on its own line.

In writing your own personal correspondence, a letterhead, whether printed or typewritten is not required. In this type of correspondence, a three-line heading replaces the letterhead. The correct form for the heading is to put the street address or post-office box number on line 1, the

```
BEDFORD FALLS HISTORICAL ASSOCIATION
         324 Sycamore Street
        Bedford Falls, ST 56789
          (215)-555-7654

                              May 9, 1988
```

Figure 1.1.   Typewritten letterhead

city, state, and zip code on line 2, and the date on line 3. The heading may be positioned six lines from the top of the edge of the paper (or higher or lower) to achieve a good balance and with the longest line flush with the right margin (see Figure 1.38).

Choosing the Right Paper

Paper and envelope size, quality, and basis weight vary according to application. Table 2 on page 7 lists various paper and envelope sizes along with their uses.

Good-quality paper is an essential element in the production of attractive, effective letters. Paper with rag content is considerably more expensive than sulfite bonds. Nevertheless, many business firms use rag-content paper because it suggests the merit and stature of the company. Since the cost of paper has been estimated at less than five percent of the total cost of the average business letter, it is easy to understand why some companies consider high-quality paper to be worth the added expense—at least for certain types of correspondence. In choosing a good grade of paper, one should look for paper that meets the following standards:

1. The paper withstands corrections and erasures without pitting, buckling, or tearing.
2. The paper accepts even and clear typed characters.
3. The paper permits smooth written signatures.
4. The paper performs well with carbons and in copying machines.
5. The paper withstands storage and repeated handling, and its color wears well over a long time.
6. The paper folds easily without cracking or rippling.
7. The paper holds typeset letterhead without bleed-through.

An important characteristic of paper is its fiber direction or grain. Paper grain should be parallel to the direction of the typewritten lines, thus pro-

Table 2
Stationery and Envelope Sizes and Applications

Stationery	Stationery Size	Application	Envelope	Envelope Size
Standard	8½″ × 11″ *also* 8″ × 10½″	general business correspondence	*commercial* No. 6¾ No. 9 No. 10	3⅝″ × 6½″ 3⅞″ × 8⅞″ 4⅛″ × 9½″
			window No. 6¾ No. 9 No. 10	3⅝″ × 6½″ 3⅞″ × 8⅞″ 4⅛″ × 9½″
			airmail No. 6¾ No. 10	3⅝″ × 6½″ 4⅛″ × 9½″
Executive *or* Monarch	7¼″ × 10½″ *or* 7½″ × 10″	high-level corporate officers' correspondence; usually personalized	*regular* *window*	3⅞″ × 7½″ 3⅞″ × 7½″
Half-sheet *or* Baronial	5½″ × 8½″	extremely brief notes	*regular*	3⅝″ × 6½″

viding a smooth surface for clear and even characters, an easy erasing or correcting surface, and a smooth fit of paper against the typewriter platen. Every sheet of paper has a *felt* side, which is the top side of the paper from which a watermark may be read. It is on this side of the sheet that the letterhead should be printed or engraved.

The weight of the paper must also be considered when ordering stationery supplies. *Basis weight,* also called *substance number,* is the weight in pounds of a ream of paper cut to a basic size. Basis 24 is heaviest for stationery; basis 13 is lightest. Table 3 on page 8 illustrates various paper weights according to their specific uses in the office.

The paper used for carbon copies is lighter in weight and is available as inexpensive *manifold* paper, a stronger and more expensive *onionskin,* or a lightweight letterhead with the word COPY printed on it.

Continuation sheets, although blank, must match the letterhead sheet in color, basis weight, texture, size, and quality. Envelopes should match both the first and continuation sheets. Therefore, these materials should be ordered along with the letterhead to ensure a good match.

Letterhead and continuation sheets as well as envelopes should be stored in their boxes to prevent soiling. A small supply of these materials may be kept in the typist's stationery drawer, but it should be arranged carefully so as to protect the materials from wear and tear.

Table 3
Weights of Letter Papers and Envelopes
For Specific Business Correspondence Applications

Application	Basis Weight
Standard *(i.e., corporate correspondence)*	24 *or* 20
Executive	24 *or* 20
Airmail *(for overseas correspondence)*	13
Branch-office *or* salesmen's stationery	20 *or* 16
Form letters	20 *or* 24
Continuation sheets	match basis weight of first sheet
Half-sheets	24 *or* 20

General Punctuation Patterns in Business Correspondence

Like letterhead designs, the choice of general punctuation patterns in business correspondence is usually determined by the organization. However, it is important that specific punctuation patterns be selected for designated letter stylings and that these patterns be adhered to for the sake of consistency and fast output. The two most common patterns are *open punctuation* and *mixed punctuation.* Their increased popularity in recent years is a reflection of the marked trend toward streamlining correspondence, for these patterns have all but totally replaced the older and more complex *closed punctuation* requiring a terminal mark at the end of each element of a business letter—a pattern that was used most often with the now little-used Indented Letter styling.

Open-Punctuation Pattern

Letters using an open-punctuation pattern exhibit the following characteristics:

1. The end of the date line is unpunctuated, although the comma between day and year is retained.
2. The ends of the lines of the inside address are unpunctuated, unless an abbreviation such as *Inc.* terminates a line, in which case the period after the abbreviation is retained.
3. The salutation if used is unpunctuated.
4. The complimentary close if used is unpunctuated.
5. The ends of the signature block lines are unpunctuated.
6. This pattern is always used with the Simplified Letter (see pages 40–41) and is often used with the Block Letter (see pages 42–43).

Mixed-Punctuation Pattern

Letters using a mixed-punctuation pattern exhibit the following characteristics:

The Simplified Letter   The Block Letter

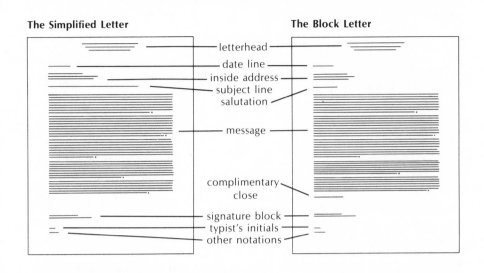

Figure 1.2.   Open-punctuation pattern

1. The end of the date line is unpunctuated, although the comma between the day and year is retained.
2. The ends of the lines of the inside address are unpunctuated unless an abbreviation such as *Inc.* terminates a line, in which case the period after the abbreviation is retained.
3. The salutation is punctuated with a colon.
4. The complimentary close is punctuated with a comma.
5. The end(s) of the signature block line(s) are unpunctuated.
6. This pattern is used with either the Block, the Modified Block, the Modified Semi-block, or the Hanging-indented Letters. (See pages 42–47 and page 39 for facsimiles of these letters.)

As suggested at the beginning of this section, virtually all American business offices today use either the mixed or the open puntuation pattern.

Closed-Punctuation Pattern

Although the closed-punctuation pattern is rarely used in the United States today, it is still employed in some European business correspondence. This pattern exhibits the following characteristics:

1. A period terminates the date line.
2. A comma terminates each line of the inside address except the last, which is ended by a period.

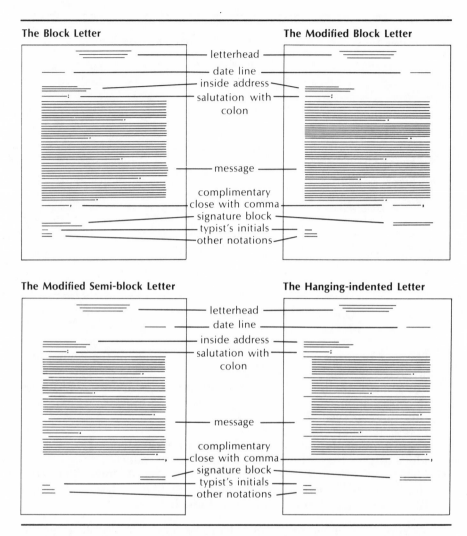

Figure 1.3.   Mixed-punctuation pattern illustrated in four letter stylings

3. A colon punctuates the salutation.
4. A comma punctuates the complimentary close.
5. A comma terminates each line of the signature block except the last, which is terminated by a period.
6. This pattern is used chiefly with the Indented Letter.

It should be pointed out that the illustration of the closed-punctuation pattern is the only description given in this book of the Indented Letter. It is shown here only as a point of information for those who may occasionally encounter it, especially in foreign correspondence.

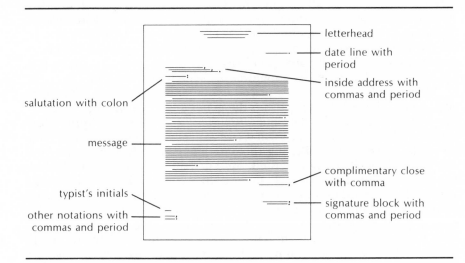

Figure 1.4.   Closed-punctuation pattern with the Indented Letter

The Individual Parts of a Business Letter

The various elements of a business letter are listed below in the order of their occurrence. While asterisked items are essential elements of any letter regardless of its general styling, those items that are unmarked may or may not be included, depending on general styling (as the Simplified Letter or the Block Letter) and on the nature of the letter itself (as general or confidential correspondence):

*date line	attention line	identification initials
reference line	salutation	enclosure notation
special mailing	subject line	carbon copy notation
notations	*message	postscript
on-arrival notations	complimentary close	
*inside address	*signature block	

For a discussion of typewritten letterheads and return addresses, see pages 5–6.

Date Line

The date line may be typed two to six lines below the last line of the printed letterhead; however, three-line spacing is recommended as a standard for most letters. Some office manuals specify a *fixed date line,* positioned three lines below the letterhead in all instances, with extra space added as needed below the date line and elsewhere on the page. Other offices prefer to use a *floating date line,* which may be typed two to six lines below the letterhead, depending on the letter length, space available, and letterhead design. The date line consists of the month, the day, and the year (January 1, 19--), all on one line. Ordinals (such as 1st, 2d, or 24th) should not be used, and the months should not be represented with abbreviations or Arabic numerals. However, the day and the month may be reversed and the comma dropped in United States government correspondence or in British correspondence, where the styling is common (1 January 19--). The date line should never overrun the margin.

The date line is commonly placed in one of four positions, and all are acceptable. The choice depends on the general letter styling or the letterhead layout. Placing the date line *flush with the left margin* is appropriate when using the Block Letter format (see the letter facsimile on pages 42–43 for a full-page view). Placing the date line *flush with the right margin* is appropriate for Hanging-indented, Modified Block, and Modified Semi-block Letters (see pages 39, 44–45, and 46–47). In order to align a date at the right margin, move the typewriter carriage to the right margin and then backspace once for each keystroke (including spaces) that will be required in the typed date. You can then set the tab stops if you are typing several letters that will bear the same date. Centering the date line *directly under the letterhead* or positioning it about *five spaces to the right of center* are other positions that are appropriate when using the Modified Block or Modified Semi-block formats.

Figure 1.5.   Date line blocked flush with the left margin

Figure 1.6.   Date line blocked flush with the right margin

Reference Line

A reference line with file, correspondence, control, order, invoice, or policy numbers is included in a letter when the addressee has specifically requested that correspondence on a subject contain a reference, or when it

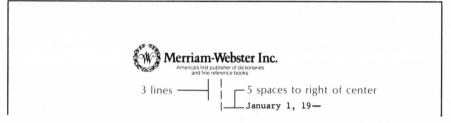

Figure 1.7.   Date line centered directly under the letterhead

Figure 1.8.   Date line positioned about five spaces to the right of dead center

is needed for filing. It may be centered and typed one to four lines below the date, although some offices require that it be typed and single-spaced directly above or below the date to make it less conspicuous. With the Block Letter, the reference line should be aligned flush left. With the Modified Block and the Modified Semi-block Letters, the reference line may be centered on the page or blocked under or above the date line.

reference line blocked left	*reference line blocked right*
January 1, 19--	January 1, 19--
X-123-4	X-123-4
or	*or*
X-123-4	X-123-4
January 1, 19--	January 1, 19--

Figure 1.9.   Reference line blocked with date line to right of dead center

Figure 1.10.   Reference number centered on page, four lines beneath date line

Reference lines on the first sheet must be carried over to the heading of a continuation sheet or sheets. The styling of the date line and the reference line on a continuation sheet should match the one on the first page as closely as possible. For example, if the reference line appears on a line below the date on the first sheet, it should be typed that way on the continuation sheet. The first setup below illustrates a continuation-sheet reference line as used with the Simplified or Block Letter.

    Mr. John B. Jones
    January 1, 19--
    X-123-4
    Page 2

The second example illustrates the positioning of a reference line on the continuation sheet of a Modified Block, a Modified Semi-block, or a Hanging-indented Letter.

    Mr. John B. Jones   January 1, 19--
                                                                          X-123-4

See Figures 1.18 and 1.19 for continuation-sheet facsimiles.

Special Mailing Notations

If a letter is to be sent by any method other than by regular mail, that fact may be indicated on the letter itself as well as on the envelope (see pages 49–57 for details on envelope styling). The all-capitalized special mailing notation such as CERTIFIED MAIL, SPECIAL DELIVERY, or AIR-MAIL (for foreign mail only) in all letter stylings is aligned flush left about four lines below the line on which the date appears, and about two lines above the first line of the inside address. While some organizations prefer that this notation appear on the original and on all copies, others prefer that the notation be typed only on the original. And in many organizations, this notation is omitted no matter how the letter is mailed.

    Vertical spacing (such as between the date line and the special mailing

notation) may vary with letter length; i.e., more space may be left for
short or medium letter lengths.

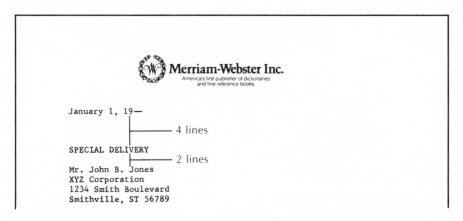

Figure 1.11.   Special mailing notation vis-à-vis inside address and date line

On-arrival Notations

The on-arrival notations that may be included in the letter itself are PER-
SONAL and CONFIDENTIAL. The first indicates that the letter may be
opened and read only by its addressee; the second, that the letter may be
opened and read by its addressee and/or any other person or persons authorized to view such material. These all-capitalized notations are usually
positioned four lines below the date line and usually two but not more
than four lines above the first line of the inside address. They are blocked
flush left in all letter stylings. If a special mailing notation has been used,
the on-arrival notation is blocked one line beneath it. Spacing between the
date line and the on-arrival notation may be increased to as much as six
lines if the letter is extremely brief.

If either PERSONAL or CONFIDENTIAL appears in the letter, it
must also appear on the envelope (see pages 51–53 for envelope styling).

Inside Address

An inside address typically includes the following elements if it is directed
to a particular individual:

1. addressee's courtesy title and full name
2. addressee's business title if required
3. full name of addressee's business affiliation
4. full geographical address

If the letter is addressed to an organization in general, the inside address
typically includes the following elements:

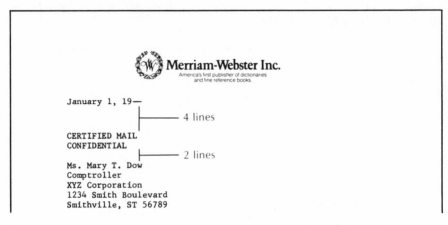

Figure 1.12.   On-arrival notation vis-à-vis date line, special mailing notation, and inside address

1. full name of the firm, company, corporation, or institution
2. individual department name if required
3. full geographical address

The inside address is placed about three to eight but not more than
12 lines below the date. The inside address in the Simplified Letter is
typed three lines below the date. Inside-address page placement in relation to the date may be expanded or contracted according to letter length
or organization policy. The inside address is always single-spaced internally. In most of the letters discussed in this book, the inside address is
blocked flush with the left margin. See pages 37–48 for full-page views.

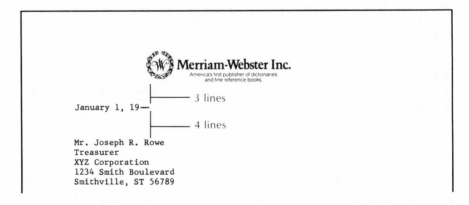

Figure 1.13.   Inside address styling used with the Block Letter

A courtesy title (as *Mr., Ms., Mrs., Miss, Dr.,* or *The Honorable*) should be typed before the addressee's full name, even if a business or professional title (as *Treasurer* or *Chief of Staff*) follows the surname. No courtesy title, however, should ever precede the name when *Esquire* or an abbreviation for a degree follows the name.

Before typing the addressee's full name, the secretary should, if possible, refer to the signature block of previous correspondence from that individual to ascertain the exact spelling and styling of the person's name. This information may also be obtained from printed executive letterhead. A business or professional title, if included, should also match the styling in previous correspondence or in official literature (such as an annual report or a business directory). If an individual holds more than one office (as *Vice President* and *General Manager*) within an organization, the title shown in the signature block of previous correspondence should be copied, or the title of the individual's highest office (in this case, *Vice President*) may be selected. Business and professional titles should not be abbreviated. If a title is so long that it might overrun the center of the page, it may be typed on two lines with the second line indented two spaces.

> Mr. John P. Hemphill, Jr.
> Vice President and Director
>   of Research and Development

Special attention should be paid to the spelling, punctuation, and official abbreviations of company names. Note, for example, whether an ampersand is used for the word *and,* whether series of names are separated by commas, and whether the word *Company* is spelled in full or abbreviated.

The addressee's title may be typed on the same line as the name, separated by a comma. Alternatively, the title may be typed on the second line either by itself or followed by a comma and the name of the organization. Care should be taken, however, to choose a style that will enhance and not detract from the total balance of the letter on the page. The following are acceptable inside-address stylings for business and professional titles:

> Mr. Arthur O. Brown
> News Director
> Radio Station WXYZ
> 1234 Peters Street
> Jonesville, ZZ 56789

> Dr. Joyce A. Cavitt, Dean
> School of Business and Finance
> Stateville University
> Stateville, ST 98765

> Ms. Ann B. Lowe, Director
> Apex Community Theater
> 67 Smith Street
> North Bend, XX 12345

> Mrs. Joyce A. Cavitt
> President, C & A Realty
> Johnson Beach, ZZ 56789

If an individual addressee's name is unknown or irrelevant and the writer wishes to direct a letter to an organization in general or to a unit within that organization, the organization name is typed on line 1 of the inside address, followed on line 2 by the name of a specific department if required. The full address of the organization is then typed on subsequent lines.

XYZ Corporation
Consumer Products Division
1234 Smith Boulevard
Smithville, ST 56789

On the other hand, if an addressee's address is unknown and the writer wishes to send a letter to him or her in care of a third party, the phrase *In care of* (or *c/o*) is used on line 2 before the name of the third party. The percentage sign (%) is a shortcut symbol that can be used, but it is usually not used in formal correspondence.

Street addresses should be typed in full and not abbreviated unless window envelopes are being used (see page 50). Numerals are used for all building, house, apartment, room, and suite numbers except for *One*, which is written out.

One Bayside Drive   6 Link Road   1436 Fremont Avenue

However, when the address of a building is used as its name, the number in the address is written out.

Fifty Maple Street

Numerals are usually used for all numbered street names above *Twelfth*, but numbered street names from *First* through *Twelfth* are usually written out.

19 South 22nd Street   167 West Second   One East Ninth Street
                          Avenue

An alternative, more formal convention calls for writing out all numbered streets up to and including *One Hundredth*.

122 East Forty-second Street   36 East Fiftieth Street

An apartment, building, room, or suite number if required follows the street address on the same line with a comma separating the two.

62 Park Towers, Suite 9   Rosemont Plaza Apartments,
                                     Apartment 117

Note that neither the word *Number* nor its abbreviation *No.* is used between the words *Suite, Apartment,* or *Building* and a following numeral.

Names of cities (except those including the word *Saint,* such as *St. Louis* or *St. Paul*) should be typed out in full, as *Fort Wayne* or *Mount Prospect.* The name of the city is followed by a comma and then by the name of the state and the zip code. Names of states may or may not be abbreviated (the District of Columbia is always styled *DC* or *D.C.*). If a window envelope is being used, the all-capitalized, unpunctuated two-letter Postal Service abbreviation followed by one space and the zip code should be used. If a regular envelope is being used, the name of the state may be typed out in full followed by one space and the zip code, or the two-letter Postal Service abbreviation may be used. Most firms now use the two-letter Postal Service abbreviations on all inside and envelope addresses. See Table 5 on page 52 for a list of these abbreviations.

An inside address should comprise no more than five typed lines. No line should overrun the center of the page. Lengthy organizational names, however, like lengthy business titles, may be carried over to a second line and indented two spaces from the left margin.

Sometimes a single letter will have to be sent to two persons at different addresses, both of whom should receive an original. In these cases, the inside address should consist of two complete sets of names and addresses separated by a line of space. The names should be in alphabetical order unless one person is obviously more important than the other. For salutations used in letters to multiple addressees, see pages 77–85.

For information about styling foreign addresses, see pages 53–55.

Attention Line

If the writer wishes to address a letter to an organization in general but at the same time bring it to the attention of a particular individual, an attention line may be typed two lines below the last line of the inside address and two lines above the salutation if there is one. The attention line is usually blocked flush with the left margin; it must be so blocked in the Simplified and Block Letters. On the other hand, some organizations prefer that the attention line be centered on the page. This placement is acceptable with all letters except the Simplified and the Block. This line should be neither underlined nor entirely capitalized; only its main elements are capitalized. The word *Attention* is not abbreviated. Placement of a colon after the word *Attention* is optional unless the open punctuation pattern is being followed throughout the letter, in which case the colon should be omitted:

Attention Mr. John P. Doe   Attention: Mr. John P. Doe

The salutation appearing beneath the attention line should be "Gentlemen" or "Ladies and Gentlemen" even though the attention line routes the letter to a particular person. Such a letter is actually being written to the organization, so a collective-noun salutation should be used.

Salutation

The salutation—used with all letter stylings except the Simplified—is typed flush with the left margin, two lines beneath the last line of the inside address or two lines below the attention line if there is one. Additional vertical lines of space may be added after the inside address of a short letter which is to be enclosed in a window envelope. The first letter of the first word of the salutation is capitalized, as are the first letters of the addressee's courtesy title and surname. If the mixed-punctuation pattern is being followed in the letter, the salutation is followed by a colon; if open punctuation is being observed, the salutation is unpunctuated.

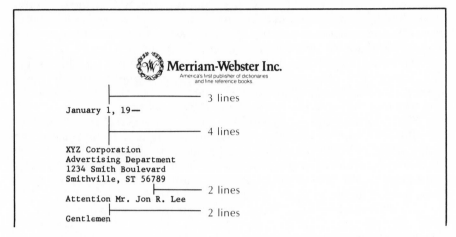

Figure 1.14. Page placement of an attention line in a Block Letter with open punctuation

Only in informal, personal correspondence is the salutation followed by a comma.

One of the most frequently asked questions today is what salutation to use when addressing an organization or when addressing a person whose name and gender are unknown to the letter-writer. Unfortunately, there are no universally accepted forms to use in these situations. Traditionally the salutation "Dear Sir" has been used when the recipient of the letter is to be a particular individual, and "Gentlemen" has been used when the recipient is to be an organization or a group of people within it. However, as it has become more and more likely that the recipients of these letters may be women, many writers—both male and female—have looked for more appropriate salutations. Most commonly, these writers have adopted "Dear Sir or Madam" and "Ladies and Gentlemen" as substitutes for "Dear Sir" and "Gentlemen" respectively; however, these forms do sound awkward to some people. Some writers have used the salutations "Dear People," "Dear Person," "Gentlepeople," "Gentlepersons," and "Dear Sir, Madam, or Ms."; however, there is little evidence that these forms are catching on.

The salutation "To whom it may concern" is another way to begin such a letter; however, it is extremely impersonal and is usually used only when the writer is unfamiliar with both the person and the organization that is being addressed, as when one is addressing a letter of recommendation. In other instances, when a specific organization is being addressed, most writers try to find an alternate salutation.

A different type of salutation now being used to solve the problem of addressing a company or a company officer whose name and sex are unknown is that which simply names the company ("Dear XYZ Company")

or states the title or department of the intended recipient, as in the following examples:

> Dear Personnel Supervisor
> Dear Personnel Department
> Dear XYZ Engineers

The use of this type of salutation has increased markedly in the past several years and is considered acceptable by most businesspeople.

When a letter is addressed to an all-female organization, the salutations "Ladies" or "Mesdames" may be used.

Occasionally a letter writer is faced with an addressee's name that gives no clue as to the addressee's sex. Traditionally in these uncertain cases, convention has required the writer to use the masculine courtesy title in the salutation, as *Mr. Lee Schmidtke, Mr. T. A. Gagnon.* However, some writers prefer to express their uncertainty by using such forms as the following:

> Dear Mr. or Ms. Schmidtke
> Dear Lee Schmidtke

The most convenient way of avoiding the problem of sexual semantics is to use the Simplified Letter styling (see the facsimile on pages 40–41), which eliminates the salutation altogether.

The salutation for a married couple may be styled in the following ways:

> Dear Mr. and Mrs. Hathaway
> Dear Dr. and Mrs. Simpson
> Dear Dr. Smith and Mr. Smith

For more information about choosing appropriate salutations, including salutations for two or more persons and for people with specialized titles, see Chapter 2, "Forms of Address."

Subject Line

A subject line gives the gist of a letter. Its phrasing is necessarily succinct and to the point: it should not be so long as to require more than one line. The subject line serves as an immediate point of reference for the reader as well as a convenient filing tool for the secretaries at both ends of the correspondence.

In the Simplified Letter, which does not include a salutation, the subject line (an essential element) is positioned flush left, three lines below the last line of the inside address. The subject line may be entirely capitalized and not underlined. As an alternative, the main words in the subject line may be capitalized and every word underlined.

If a subject line is included in a letter featuring a salutation, it is frequently positioned flush left, two lines beneath the salutation, and may be entirely capitalized. With the Modified Block and Modified Semi-block styles, however, the subject line may be centered or even indented to

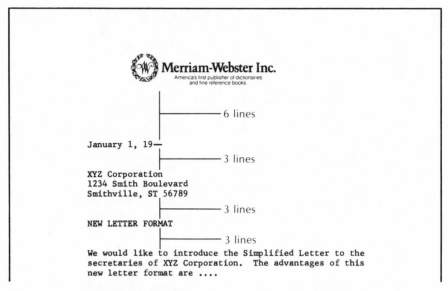

Figure 1.15.   Page placement of the subject line in the Simplified Letter

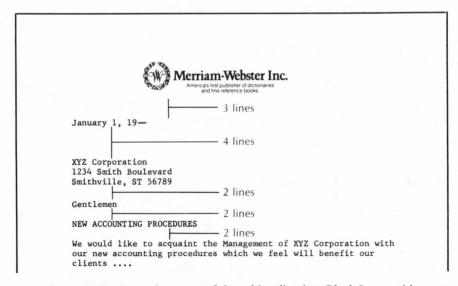

Figure 1.16.   Page placement of the subject line in a Block Letter with open punctuation

match the indention of the paragraphs. Legal correspondence uses the subject line in a variety of positions. Legal correspondence based on letter styles other than the Simplified or Block frequently centers the subject line or positions it at the right. A growing number of law offices prefer to position the subject line two lines above the salutation rather than below it.

The subject line may be entirely capitalized, and the word *subject* may be used to introduce the line. When the word *subject* is used, the subject line may also be capitalized headline-style—that is, with the initial letter of the first word capitalized and with the initial letter of all other words except coordinating conjunctions, articles, and short prepositions also capitalized. The word *reference* is sometimes also used.

SUBJECT: CHANGES IN TRAFFIC ROUTE
Subject: Changes in Traffic Route
Reference: Changes in Traffic Route

The subject-line headings *In re* and *Re* are now seldom used for general office letters; however, they are often used in legal correspondence. Headings should not be used if one is following the Simplified Letter styling.

Care should be taken not to confuse the subject line with the reference line (see pages 12–14). The subject line differs not only in position but also in styling and purpose: the reference line indicates a numerical classification; the subject line identifies the content of the letter.

Message

The body of the letter—the message—should begin two lines below the salutation or two lines below the subject line, if there is one, in all letter stylings except the Simplified Letter, where the message is typed three lines below the subject line.

Paragraphs are single-spaced internally. Double spacing is used to separate paragraphs. If a letter is extremely brief, it may be double-spaced throughout. Paragraphs in such letters should be indented so that they will be readily identifiable.

The first lines of indented paragraphs (as in the Modified Semi-block Letter) should begin five or ten spaces from the left margin; however, the five-space pattern is the most common. With the Hanging-indented Letter, the first lines of the paragraphs are blocked flush left, while subsequent lines are indented five spaces from the left margin. All other letter stylings require flush-left paragraph alignment.

Long quotations should be indented and blocked five to ten spaces from the left and right margins with internal single spacing and top-and-bottom double spacing so that the material will be set off from the rest of the message. Long enumerations should also be indented: enumerations with items requiring more than one line apiece may require single-spacing within each item, followed by double-spacing between items. Tabular data should be centered on the page.

Additional rules for typing letters that have traditionally been observed include the following:

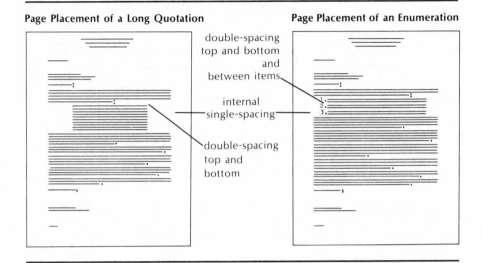

Figure 1.17.   Page placement of items inset within the message

1. Do not divide a word at the end of the first line.
2. Do not divide a word at the end of the last full line of a letter.
3. Do not divide a person's name from his or her courtesy title.

If a letter is long enough to require a continuation sheet or sheets, at least three message lines must be carried over to the next page. The complimentary close and/or typed signature block should never stand alone on a continuation sheet. The last word on a page should not be divided. Continuation-sheet margins should match those of the first sheet. At least six blank lines equaling one inch should be maintained at the top of the continuation sheet.

At the top of every continuation sheet there should be a continuation-sheet heading. The two most common continuation-sheet headings are illustrated in Figures 1.18 and 1.19. The format shown in Figure 1.18 is used with the Simplified and Block Letters. It features a flush-left heading beginning with the page number, followed on the next line by the addressee's courtesy title and full name, and ending with the date on the third line. Some companies prefer that the page number appear as the last line of the continuation-sheet heading, especially if a reference number is included.

Another way to type the heading of a continuation sheet is illustrated in Figure 1.19. In this format, the material is laid out across the page, six lines down from the top edge of the sheet. The addressee's name is typed flush with the left margin, the page number in Arabic numerals is centered on the same line and enclosed with spaced hyphens, and the date is aligned flush with the right margin—all on the same line. This format is often used with the Modified Block, the Modified Semi-block, and the Hanging-indented Letters.

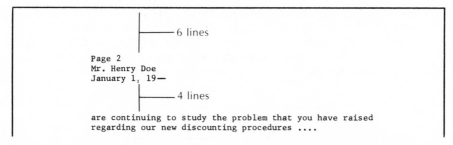

Figure 1.18. Continuation-sheet heading for Simplified and Block Letters

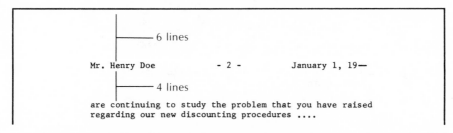

Figure 1.19. Continuation-sheet heading for Modified Block, Modified Semi-block, and Hanging-indented Letters

Complimentary Close

There is no complimentary close in the Simplified Letter. However, a complimentary close is used with all other letter styles. It is typed two lines below the last line of the message. Its page placement depends on the general letter styling being used. With the Block Letter, the complimentary close is blocked flush with the left margin.

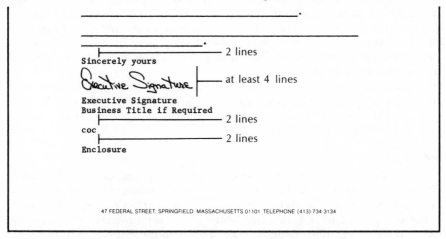

Figure 1.20. Open-punctuation pattern shown in Block Letter format for complimentary close

With the Modified Block, the Modified Semi-block, and the Hanging-indented Letter, the complimentary close may begin at the center or may be aligned directly under the date line (e.g., about five spaces to the right of center, or flush with the right margin) or under some particular part of the printed letterhead. It should never overrun the right margin.

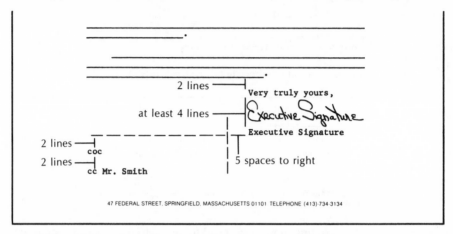

Figure 1.21. Complimentary close five spaces to right of center as in a Modified Block Letter with mixed punctuation

Only the first word of the complimentary close is capitalized. If the open-punctuation pattern is being followed, the complimentary close is unpunctuated. If the mixed-punctuation pattern is being followed, a comma terminates the complimentary close.

The typist should always use the complimentary close that is dictated, because the writer may have a special reason for the choice of phrasing. If the writer does not specify a particular closing, the typist may wish to select the one that best reflects the general tone of the letter and the state of the writer-reader relationship. Table 4 on page 27 lists the most commonly used complimentary closes and groups them according to general tone and degree of formality.

Complimentary closes on letters written over a period of time to a particular person may become gradually more informal and friendly, but they should not revert to a more formal style once an informal pattern has been established.

Signature Block

The first line of the signature block indicates responsibility for the letter. Either the name of the writer or the name of the organization may appear on the first line of the signature block. In the former case, the writer's name is typed at least four lines below the complimentary close; in the latter, the organization name is typed all in capital letters two lines below the complimentary close and the writer's name at least four lines below the organization name.

Table 4
Complimentary Closes Common in Business Correspondence

General Tone & Degree of Formality	Complimentary Close
highly formal—usually used in diplomatic, governmental, or ecclesiastical correspondence to show respect and deference to a high-ranking addressee	Respectfully yours Respectfully Very respectfully
politely neutral—usually used in general correspondence	Very truly yours Yours very truly Yours truly
friendly and less formal—usually used in general correspondence	Most sincerely Very sincerely Very sincerely yours Sincerely yours Yours sincerely Sincerely
more friendly and informal—often used when writer and reader are on a first-name basis but also often used in general business correspondence	Most cordially Yours cordially Cordially yours Cordially
most friendly and informal—usually used when writer and reader are on a first-name basis	As ever Best wishes Best regards Kindest regards Kindest personal regards Regards
British	Yours faithfully Yours sincerely

With the Simplified Letter, the name of the writer is typed entirely in capitals flush left at least five lines below the last line of the message. If the writer's business title is not included in the printed letterhead, it may be typed on the same line as the name entirely in capitals and separated from the last element of the name by a spaced hyphen. Some organizations, however, prefer to use a comma in place of the hyphen. A combination of the two may be used if the title is complex.

JOHN P. HEWETT - DIRECTOR
JOHN P. HEWETT, DIRECTOR
JOHN P. HEWETT - DIRECTOR, TECHNICAL INFORMATION
   or
JOHN P. HEWETT - DIRECTOR
TECHNICAL INFORMATION CENTER

With the Block Letter, the signature block is aligned flush left at least four lines below the complimentary close. Only the first letter of each element of the writer's name is capitalized, and only the first letter of each major element of the writer's business title and department name is capi-

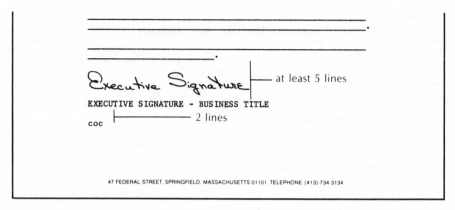

Figure 1.22.   Page placement of signature block in the Simplified Letter

talized if they are included. The business title and the department name may be omitted if they appear in the printed letterhead:

if title and department name are needed for identification	John D. Russell, Director Consumer Products Division
if department name is already printed on the letterhead	John D. Russell Director
if both title and department name appear in printed letterhead	John D. Russell

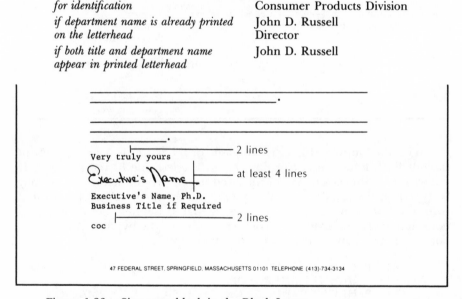

Figure 1.23.   Signature block in the Block Letter

With the Modified Block, the Modified Semi-block, and the Hanging-indented Letters, the signature block begins with the name of the writer typed at least four lines below the complimentary close. The first letter of the first element of each line in the signature block is aligned directly below the first letter of the first element of the complimentary close, unless

this alignment will result in an overrunning of the right margin. In that
case the signature block may be centered under the complimentary close,
as shown in Figure 1.26. Only the first letter of each of the major elements
of the writer's name, title (if used), and department name (if used) is capitalized:

Mrs. Joy L. Tate, Director	Mrs. Joy L. Tate	Mrs. Joy L. Tate
Marketing Division	Director	

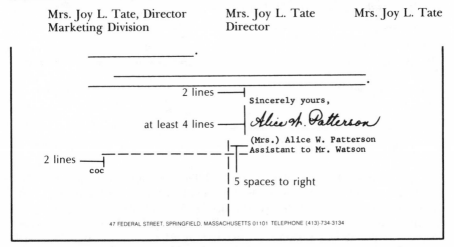

Figure 1.24.   Signature block five spaces to right of center as in a Modified
Block Letter with mixed punctuation

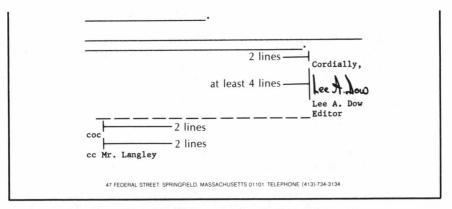

Figure 1.25.   Complimentary close and signature block flush right as in the
Modified Block Letter

If printed letterhead stationery is being used, the name of the firm
should not appear below the complimentary close. If printed letterhead is
not being used, the name of the firm may be typed in capitals two lines
beneath the complimentary close with the first letter of the firm's name
aligned directly underneath and the writer's name typed in capitals and

lowercase at least four lines below the firm's name. The writer's title if needed is typed in capitals and lowercase on a line directly underneath the signature line.

If the company name is long enough to overrun the right margin, it may be centered beneath the complimentary close in the Modified Block and the Modified Semi-block Letters.

Very truly yours,

AJAX VAN LINES, INC.

Samuel O. Lescott

Samuel O. Lescott
Dispatcher

Very truly yours,

JOHNSON AEROSPACE ENGINEERING ASSOCIATES

Sidney C. Johnson

Sidney C. Johnson, Ph.D.
President

Figure 1.26.   Signature block when a printed letterhead is not being used

Regardless of page placement and letter styling, the name of the writer should be typed exactly as it appears in his or her signature. The only exceptions to this rule are the use of *Ms./Mrs./Miss* (as explained in the next paragraph) and the signature of a married woman over the type-written name of her husband preceded by *Mrs.* If applicable, any academic degrees (as *Ph.D.*) or professional ratings (as *P.E.*) that the writer holds should be included after the surname so that the recipient of the letter will know the proper form of address to use in his or her reply.

Typed Signature	*Salutation in Reply*
Francis E. Atlee, M.D.	Dear Dr. Atlee:
Ellen Y. Langford, Ph.D.	Dear Dr. Langford
Dean of Women	*or*
	Dear Dean Langford
Carol I. Etheridge, C.P.A.	Dear Ms. Etheridge
or	
Mrs. Carol I. Etheridge, C.P.A.	Dear Mrs. Etheridge

These academic and professional degrees and ratings need not be repeated in the signature line if they are already included in the printed letterhead, and they are never included in the written signature.

The only titles that may precede a typed signature are *Ms.*, *Mrs.*, and *Miss.* These titles, which may be enclosed in parentheses, are blocked flush left in the Simplified and the Block Letters, and they are aligned with or centered under the complimentary close in the Modified Block, the Modified Semi-block, and the Hanging-indented Letters.

The use of the courtesy title *Ms.* (which usually includes a period even though it is not an abbreviation of any word) has become so widespread that it is now the standard form to use with the name of a woman whose marital status is irrelevant or in doubt. For this reason, there is a marked trend for a woman to omit a courtesy title altogether in the signature line, on the assumption that the recipient will address the reply to "Ms. _____." Only if the writer wishes to show her preference for *Miss* or *Mrs.* will she usually include a courtesy title before her typewritten signature. On the other hand, if the woman's name might be confused with a man's name (as Lee, Lynn, Terry, or Leslie), it is thoughtful to include one of the courtesy titles to help the recipient address a reply. The examples in Figures 1.27 through 1.32 show alternate stylings of the courtesy title with and without the optional parentheses.

Sincerely yours

Joan Conti

Joan Conti
Vice President

Sincerely yours

Joan Conti

Miss Joan Conti
Vice President

Sincerely yours

Joan Conti

Ms. Joan Conti
Vice President

Sincerely yours

Joan Conti

(Miss) Joan Conti
Vice President

Sincerely yours

Joan Conti

(Ms.) Joan Conti
Vice President

Figure 1.27. Signature sylings for unmarried women

Sincerely yours

Joan Conti

Joan Conti
Vice President

Sincerely yours

Joan Conti

Ms. Joan Conti
Vice President

Sincerely yours

Joan Conti

(Ms.) Joan Conti
Vice President

Figure 1.28. Signature stylings for women who consider their marital status irrelevant

Sincerely yours

Joan M. Conti

Joan M. Conti

Sincerely yours

Joan M. Conti

Mrs. Joan M. Conti

Sincerely yours

Joan M. Conti

Ms. Joan M. Conti

Sincerely yours

Joan M. Conti

(Mrs.) Joan M. Conti

Sincerely yours

Joan M. Conti

(Ms.) Joan M. Conti

Figure 1.29. Signature stylings for married women using given name + maiden name initial + husband's surname

Sincerely yours

Joan Conti

Mrs. Robert A. Conti
Vice President

Sincerely yours

Joan Conti

(Mrs. Robert A. Conti)
Vice President

Figure 1.30.   Signature stylings for married women using husband's full name

A widow may use either her first name and her maiden name initial and her late husband's surname with the courtesy title *Mrs.* or *Ms.* enclosed in optional parentheses. She may also use her social signature—her husband's full name with *Mrs.*—although the social signature is not commonly used in business correspondence.

Sincerely yours

Joan M. Conti

Ms. Joan M. Conti

Sincerely yours

Joan M. Conti

(Ms.) Joan M. Conti

Sincerely yours

Joan Conti

Mrs. Robert A. Conti

Figure 1.31.   Signature stylings for widows

A divorcée may use her maiden name if it has been legally regained, along with the courtesy title *Ms.* or *Miss* enclosed in optional parentheses or she may omit the title. She may also use her maiden name and her former husband's surname with *Mrs.*

Sincerely yours

Joan M. Conti

Miss Joan M. Conti

Sincerely yours

Joan M. Conti

Joan M. Conti

Sincerely yours

Joan Conti

Mrs. Matthews Conti

Figure 1.32.   Signature stylings for divorcées

Many married women today use both their maiden and married names in hyphenated form, as "Joan Matthews-Dunn" (or "Mrs. Robert Matthews-Dunn"), with the maiden name usually as the first element of the hyphenated compound. In these cases the handwritten signature may not always match the typewritten name. However, the signature should match the hyphenated name when the signer belongs to a Hispanic culture that traditionally combines maternal and paternal family names with a hyphen, as "Carla Monteiro-Lopez."

On rare occasions a letter may be written and signed by two individuals. In these cases, it is generally best to place the names side by side, with the first name flush left in block styles or beginning slightly left of center in other letter styles in order to leave enough room for two horizontally aligned signatures. If horizontal positioning is not feasible, the names may be placed one under the other.

Very truly yours,

Martin J. Kirchoff   *Sarah K. Wong*
Martin J. Kirchoff   Sarah K. Wong
President   Treasurer

Figure 1.33.   Signature block when two people sign a letter

If the secretary signs a letter for the writer, that person's name is followed by the secretary's initials immediately below and to the right of the surname, or centered under the full name. If the secretary signs a letter in his or her own name for someone else, that individual's courtesy title and surname only are typed directly below.

David R. Robins   *David R. Robins*

Figure 1.34.   Signature when secretary signs the writer's name

Sincerely yours   Sincerely yours   Sincerely yours

Janet A. Smith   *Lee L. Linden*   *Seymour T. Barnes*
(Miss) Janet A. Smith   Lee L. Linden   Seymour T. Barnes
Assistant to Mr. Wood   Secretary to Ms. Key   Assistant to Senator Ross

Figure 1.35.   Signature block when secretary signs as a representative

Identification Initials

The initials of the typist and sometimes those of the writer are placed two lines below the last line of the signature block and are aligned flush left in all letter stylings. Most offices prefer that three capitalized initials be used for the writer's name and two lowercase initials be used for the typist's. There is a marked trend towards complete omission of the writer's initials if the name is already typed in the signature block or if it appears in the printed letterhead. In the Simplified Letter, the writer's initials are usually omitted, and the typist's initials if included on the original are typed in lowercase. Many organizations indicate the typist's initials only on carbons for record-keeping purposes, and they do not show the writer's initials unless another individual signs the letter. The following are common stylings:

FCM/HL	FCM:hl	Franklin C. Mason:
FM/hl	FCM:hol	HL
hol	fcm:hol	
hl	FCM:HL	Franklin C. Mason
	FCM:HOL	HL

A letter dictated by one person (as an administrative secretary), typed by another (as a corresponding secretary), and signed by yet another person (as the writer) may show (1) the writer/signer's initials entirely in capitals followed by a colon and (2) the dictator's initials entirely in capitals followed by a colon and (3) the transcriber/typist's initials in lowercase, as AWM:COC:ds

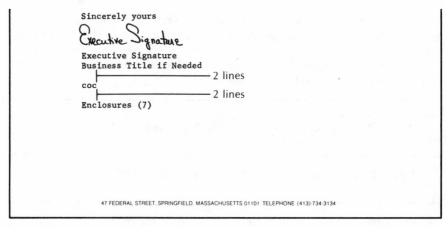

Figure 1.36.   Page placement of identification and enclosure notations

Enclosure Notation

If a letter is to be accompanied by an enclosure or enclosures, one of the following expressions should be aligned flush left and typed one to two lines beneath the identification initials, if there are any, or one to two lines beneath the last line of the signature block, if there is no identification line. The unabbreviated form *Enclosure* is usually preferred.

> Enclosure   *or if more than one*   Enclosures (3)
> enc.   *or*   encl.   *or if more than one*   3 encs.   *or*   Enc. 3

If the enclosures are of special importance, each of them should be numerically listed and briefly described with single-spacing between each item.

> Enclosures: 1. Annual Report (19—), 2 copies
> 2. List of Major Accounts
> 3. Profit and Loss Statement (19—)

The following type of notation then may be typed in the top right corner of each page of each of the enclosures:

Enclosure (1) to Johnson Associates letter No. 1-234-X,
dated January 1, 19—, page 2 of 8

If the enclosure is bound, a single notation attached to its cover sheet will suffice.

When additional material is being mailed separately, a notation such as the following may be used:

Separate mailing: 50th Anniversary Report

Carbon Copy Notation

Carbon copies are now often called *courtesy copies* in view of the widespread use of photocopies; in some offices *c* for *copy* or *pc* for *photocopy* is used instead of the traditional *cc* for *carbon copy*.

A carbon copy notation showing the distribution of courtesy copies to other individuals should be aligned flush left and typed two lines below the signature block if there are no other notations or initials, or two lines below any other notations. If space is very tight, the courtesy copy notation may be single-spaced below the above-mentioned items.

cc   cc: Copy to   Copies to

Multiple recipients of copies should be listed alphabetically. Sometimes only their initials are shown.

cc: WPB
     TLC
     CNR

More often, the individuals' names are shown and sometimes also their addresses, especially if the writer feels that such information can be useful to the addressee.

cc: William L. Carton, Esq.   cc Ms. Lee Jamieson
     45 Park Towers, Suite 1
     Smithville, ST 56789   Copy to Mr. John K. Long

     Dr. Daniel I. Maginnis   Copies to Mr. Houghton
     1300 Dover Drive   Mr. Ott
     Jonesville, ZZ 12345   Mr. Smythe

To save space, the carbon copy notation may group the recipients.

cc Regional Sales Managers

If the recipient of the copy is to receive an enclosure or enclosures as well, that individual's full name and address as well as a description of each enclosure and the total number of enclosed items should be shown in the courtesy copy notation.

cc: Ms. Barbara S. Lee (2 copies, Annual Report)
     123 Jones Street
     Smithville, ST 56789

     Mrs. Sara T. Tufts
     Mrs. Laura E. Yowell

If the first names or initials are given along with the last names, courtesy titles (as *Mr., Mrs., Miss,* and *Ms.*) may be omitted.

  cc: William L. Carton   cc: W.L. Carton
     Daniel I. Maginnis   D.I. Maginnis

Typists usually leave either one or two spaces between the *cc:* and the names that follow. However, if only one name follows the *cc:* and it is given in all initials, the space or spaces may be omitted.

  cc:JBH

If the writer wishes that copies of the letter be distributed without the list of recipients being shown on the original, the blind carbon copy notation *bcc* or *bcc:* followed by an alphabetical list of the recipients' initials or names may be typed on the copies in the same page position as a regular carbon copy notation. The *bcc* notation may also appear in the upper left-hand corner of the copies.

Carbon or courtesy copies are not usually signed. The secretary may type the signature, preceded by the symbol */S/* or */s/*, to indicate that the writer signed the original copy.

Postscript

A postscript is aligned flush left and is typed two to four lines (depending on space available) below the last notation. If the letter's paragraphs are strict-block, the postscript reflects this format. If the paragraphs within the letter are indented, the first line of the postscript is also indented. If the Hanging-indented Letter styling is used, the first line of the postscript is flush left and all subsequent lines are indented five spaces. All postscripts are single-spaced. Their margins conform with those maintained in the letters themselves. The writer should initial a postscript. While it is not incorrect to head a postscript with the initials *P.S.* (for an initial postscript) and *P.P.S.* (for subsequent ones), these headings are redundant and can be omitted.

Letter Styles for Business Correspondence

The following pages contain full-page letter facsimiles of the five most often used business-letter formats—the Simplified Letter, the Block Letter, the Modified Block Letter, the Modified Semi-block Letter, and the Hanging-indented Letter. In addition, the section contains facsimiles of the following letters: the Official Letter Styling on Executive letterhead, the Official Letter Styling on plain bond, and the Half-sheet. Each facsimile contains a detailed description of letter format and styling. At the end of the section is a discussion of time- and money-saving correspondence methods that have gained acceptance in many of today's business offices.

Office of the President

January 1, 19—

Dear Ms. Peterson:

This is a facsimile of the Official Letter Styling often used for personal letters written by an executive, or for letters typed on his own personalized company stationery. The paper size is either Executive or Monarch.

The Official Letter Styling is characterized by the page placement of the inside address: It is typed flush left, two to five lines below the last line of the signature block or below the written signature.

The typist's initials if included are typed two lines below the last line of the inside address. An enclosure notation if needed appears two lines below the typist's initials, or two lines below the last line of the inside address. These notations are also flush left.

A typed signature block is not needed on personalized Executive or Monarch stationery; however, if the writer's signature is either difficult to decipher or if it might be unfamiliar to the addressee, it may be typed four lines below the complimentary close.

Open punctuation and blocked paragraphs may also be used in this letter.

Sincerely,

Ms. Martha Peterson
490 Jones Street
Smithville, ST 56789

47 FEDERAL STREET, SPRINGFIELD, MASSACHUSETTS 01101 TELEPHONE (413)-734-3134

Figure 1.37.   The Official Letter Styling with printed Executive letterhead

                                        4400 Ambler Boulevard
                                        Smithville, ST 56789
                                        January 1, 19—

Dear Bob

This is a facsimile of a letter typed on plain
Executive or Monarch stationery. The basic
format is the same as that of the Official Letter Styling. The block paragraphs and the open
punctuation pattern are illustrated here.

The heading which includes the writer's full
address and the date may be positioned six lines
from the top edge of the page and flush with the
right margin as shown here. Approximately six
vertical lines may be placed after the date line
down to the salutation.

The complimentary close is typed two lines below the last line of the message. The inside
address is flush left, two to five lines below
the last line of the signature block or below
the written signature.

Typist's initials, if included, should be positioned two lines beneath the last line of the
inside address. An enclosure notation or any
other notation if required should be typed two
lines below the typist's initials or two lines
below the last line of the inside address if
there are no initials.

                                        Sincerely

                                        Executive Signature

Mr. Robert Y. Owens
123 East Second Avenue
Jonesville, ST 45678

Figure 1.38.   The Official Letter Styling with plain stationery

Merriam-Webster Inc.
America's first publisher of dictionaries
and fine reference books.

January 1, 19—

Mrs. Althea Nance
Assistant to the President
XYZ Corporation
1234 Smith Boulevard
Smithville, ST 56789

Dear Mrs. Nance:

This is a facsimile of the Hanging-indented Letter which is not ordinarily used
    in general business correspondence but rather in advertising letters as an
    attractive way of catching the reader's eye. Its main feature is the para-
    graph alignment: The first line of each paragraph is aligned flush left,
    but all subsequent lines are indented five spaces from the left margin.
    The paragraphs are single-spaced internally and double-spaced between each
    other. Either the open or the mixed punctuation pattern may be used in the
    Hanging-indented Letter: This facsimile illustrates the mixed pattern.

The date line, usually typed three lines below the last line of the letterhead,
    is aligned flush right. The inside address and salutation are blocked
    flush left. Spacing between these elements parallels that used in the Mod-
    ified Block and the Modified Semi-block Letters.

Continuation sheets must contain at least three message lines, and the last word
    on the first sheet must not be divided. Continuation-sheet headings may be
    blocked left as in the Block Letter or laid out across the top of the page
    as in the Modified Semi-block Letter. Six blank lines are left from the
    top edge of the page to the first line of the heading and four blank lines
    are left before typing the message. Margins and paragraph alignment paral-
    lel those of the first sheet.

The complimentary close and the signature block are aligned under the date.
    Double-spacing is needed between the last message line and the complimenta-
    ry close. At least four lines should be left for the written signature.

Identification initials and enclosure and carbon copy notations are blocked
    flush left at least two lines below the last line of the signature block.
    Postscripts, if needed, are also hanging-indented.

                                    Cordially,

                                    Executive Signature

hg

47 Federal Street, P.O. Box 281, Springfield, MA 01101
Telephone (413) 734-3134

Figure 1.39.   The Hanging-indented Letter

Merriam-Webster Inc.
America's first publisher of dictionaries
and fine reference books

January 1, 19—

Ms. Sarah H. Smith
Director of Marketing
XYZ Corporation
1234 Smith Boulevard
Smithville, ST 56789

SIMPLIFIED LETTER

Ms. Smith, this is the Simplified Letter recommended by the Administrative Management Society. Its main features—block format,
open punctuation, and fewer internal parts—reduce the number of
keystrokes and typewriter adjustments your secretary must make,
thus cutting costs, saving time, and increasing overall letter
output.

The date line is typed six lines below the last letterhead line.
The inside address, also flush left, appears three lines below the
date line. Since the placement of the inside address is designed
for window envelopes, it is suggested that the all-capitalized,
unpunctuated Postal Service State abbreviation be typed after the
city name, followed by one space and the ZIP Code.

The traditional salutation has been dropped and replaced by an un-
headed, all-capitalized subject line typed flush left, three lines
beneath the last inside-address line. The subject line summarizes
the message.

The first message line begins three lines below the subject line.
The first sentence serves as a greeting to the reader. The addressee's name should appear in the first paragraph, preferably in
the first sentence as shown above. Inclusion of the name adds a
personal touch. All paragraphs are blocked flush left, single-
spaced internally, and double-spaced between each other. Tabular
data and numbered lists are also blocked flush left but are set
off from the rest of the message by double-spacing. Long quotations and unnumbered lists should be indented five to ten spaces
from the left and right margins and set off from the rest of the
message by top and bottom double-spacing.

47 FEDERAL STREET. SPRINGFIELD. MASSACHUSETTS 01101 TELEPHONE (413) 734-3134

Figure 1.40.   The Simplified Letter

Ms. Smith
Page 2
January 1, 19—

If a continuation sheet is required, at least three message lines must be carried over. Continuation-sheet format and margins match those of the first sheet. At least six blank lines are left from the top edge of the page to the first line of the heading which is blocked flush left, single-spaced internally, and typically composed of the addressee's courtesy title and name, the page number, and the applicable date. The rest of the message begins four lines beneath the last heading line.

There is no complimentary close in the Simplified Letter, although closing sentences such as "You have my best wishes," and "My best regards are yours" may end the message. The writer's name (and business title if needed) is aligned flush left and typed all in capitals at least five lines below the last message line. Although the Administrative Management Society uses a spaced hyphen between the writer's surname and his business title, some companies prefer a comma. The writer's department name may be typed flush left all in capitals, one line below the signature line.

The identification initials, flush left and two lines below the last line of the signature block, comprise the typist's initials only. An enclosure notation may be typed one line below the identification initials and aligned flush left. Carbon copy notations may be typed one or two lines below the last notation, depending on available space. If only the signature block and/or typist's initials appear before it, the carbon copy notation is typed two lines below.

EXECUTIVE SIGNATURE - BUSINESS TITLE

coc
Enclosures (12)

cc Dr. Alice L. Barnes

Merriam-Webster Inc.
America's first publisher of dictionaries
and fine reference books.

January 1, 19—
X-123-4

XYZ Corporation
Sales Department
1234 Smith Boulevard
Smithville, ST 56789

Attention Mr. John Doe

Gentlemen

SUBJECT: BLOCK LETTER

This is a facsimile of the Block Letter, whose structural parts
are flush left. It may feature either the open or the mixed punctuation pattern: The open pattern is shown here.

The date line is typed two to six lines below the last letterhead
line. Here, it is placed three lines below the letterhead. Account or policy numbers if required are single-spaced and blocked
either above or below the date line.

Placement of the inside address varies by letter length. Here, it
is typed four lines below the date line. If window envelopes are
used, the all-capitalized, unpunctuated Postal Service state abbreviations should be employed. One space intervenes between the
state abbreviation and the ZIP Code. If regular envelopes are to
be used, state names may be typed out in full or abbreviated, depending on organization preference. An attention line if required
is typed two lines below the last inside-address line.

The salutation is typed two lines below the attention line, or two
to four lines below the last inside-address line. The salutation
is "Gentlemen" if the letter is addressed to an organization, even
if there is an attention line directing the letter to a particular
individual within that organization. If the letter is addressed
to an individual whose name is on line 1 of the inside address,
the salutation is "Dear Mr. (or Ms. or Mrs. or Miss) + surname" or
"Dear + first name" depending on the writer/reader relationship.
A subject line, typically all in capitals, may be typed two lines
below the salutation. The subject line is optional.

The first message line is typed two lines below the salutation, or
two lines below the subject line if there is one. The message is

47 FEDERAL STREET, SPRINGFIELD, MASSACHUSETTS 01101 TELEPHONE (413)-734-3134

Figure 1.41.   The Block Letter

XYZ Corporation
Sales Department
January 1, 19—
X-123-4
Page 2

single-spaced internally and double-spaced between paragraphs.
At least three message lines must be carried over to a continuation sheet: At no time should the complimentary close and the
signature block stand alone. The last word on a sheet should not
be divided. The continuation-sheet heading is typed six lines
from the top edge of the page. Account or policy numbers if used
on the first sheet must be included in the continuation-sheet
headings. The message begins four lines below the last line of
the heading.

The complimentary close is typed two lines below the last message
line, followed by at least four blank lines for the written signature, followed by the writer's name in capitals and lowercase.
The writer's business title and/or name of his department may be
included in the typed signature block, if they do not appear in
the printed letterhead.

Identification initials may comprise only the typist's initials if
the same person dictated and signed the letter. These initials
are typed two lines below the last signature-block line. The enclosure notation if used is typed one line below the identification line. The carbon copy notation if needed is placed one or
two lines below any other notations, depending on available space.

Sincerely yours

Executive Signature

Executive Signature
Business Title

coc
Enclosures (2)

cc Mr. Howard T. Jansen

Merriam-Webster Inc.
America's first publisher of dictionaries
and fine reference books.

January 1, 19—

REGISTERED MAIL
PERSONAL

Mr. John Z. Teller
Treasurer
XYZ Corporation
1234 Smith Boulevard
Smithville, ST 56789

Dear Mr. Teller:

This is a facsimile of the Modified Block Letter. It differs from the Block
Letter chiefly in the page placement of its date line, its complimentary close,
and its signature block that are aligned at center, toward the right margin, or
at the right margin. Either the open or the mixed punctuation pattern may be
used: The mixed pattern is illustrated here.

While the date line may be positioned from two to six lines below the last line
of the letterhead, its standard position is three lines below the letterhead,
as shown above. In this facsimile, the date line is typed five spaces to the
right of dead center. If an account or policy number is required, it is blocked
and single-spaced on a line above or below the date.

Special mailing notations and on-arrival notations such as the two shown above
are all-capitalized, aligned flush left, and blocked together two lines above
the first line of the inside address. If used singly, either of these notations
appears two lines above the inside address.

The first line of the inside address is typed about four lines below the date
line. This spacing can be expanded or contracted according to the letter length.
The inside address, the salutation, and all paragraphs of the message are aligned
flush left. The salutation, typed two to four lines below the last line of the
inside address, is worded as it would be in the Block Letter. A subject line if
used is typed two lines below the salutation in all-capital letters and is either
blocked flush left or centered on the page. Underscoring the subject line is also acceptable, but in this case, only the first letter of each word would be capitalized.

The message begins two lines below the salutation or the subject line if there is
one. Paragraphs are single-spaced internally and double-spaced between each other; however, in very short letters, the paragraphs may be double-spaced internally and triple-spaced between each other.

47 Federal Street, P.O. Box 281, Springfield, MA 01101
Telephone (413) 734-3134

Figure 1.42.   The Modified Block Letter

Mr. Teller   - 2 -   January 1, 19—

Continuation sheets should contain at least three message lines. The last
word on a sheet should not be divided. The continuation-sheet heading may be
blocked flush left as in the Block Letter or it may be laid out across the top
of the page as shown above. This heading begins six lines from the top edge
of the page, and the message is continued four lines beneath it.

The complimentary close is typed two lines below the last line of the message.
While the complimentary close may be aligned under some portion of the letterhead, directly under the date line, or even flush with but not overrunning the
right margin, it is often typed five spaces to the right of dead center as
shown here.

The signature line is typed in capitals and lowercase at least four lines below the complimentary close. The writer's business title and department name
may be included if they do not already appear in the printed letterhead. All
elements of the signature block must be aligned with each other and with the
complimentary close.

Identification initials need include only those of the typist, providing that
the writer and the signer are the same person. These initials appear two
lines below the last line of the signature block. An enclosure notation is
typed one line below the identification line, and the carbon copy notation if
required appears one or two lines below any other notations, depending on
space available.

                              Sincerely yours,

                              Executive Signature

                              Executive Signature
                              Business Title

hg
Enclosures (5)

cc Dr. Doe
   Dr. Franklin
   Dr. Mason
   Dr. Watson

Merriam-Webster Inc.
America's first publisher of dictionaries
and fine reference books.

January 1, 19—

Mr. Carroll D. Thompson
Sales Manager
XYZ Corporation
1234 Smith Boulevard
Smithville, ST 56789

Dear Mr. Thompson:

MODIFIED SEMI-BLOCK LETTER

This is a facsimile of the Modified Semi-block Letter. It features a date line aligned either slightly to
the right of dead center or flush right (as shown above).
Its inside address and salutation are aligned flush left,
while the paragraphs of the message are indented five or
ten spaces. Its complimentary close and signature block
are aligned under the date, either slightly to the right
or dead center, or flush right. Identification initials,
enclosure notations, and carbon copy notations are aligned
flush left.

A special mailing notation or an on-arrival notation
if required would have been typed flush left and two lines
above the first line of the inside address. An account or
policy number if needed would have been blocked with the
date, one line above or below it. The page placement of
these elements parallels their positioning in the Modified
Block Letter. An attention line if required is aligned
flush left, two lines below the last line of the inside address. A subject line may be typed in all-capitals two
lines below the salutation and is typically centered on the
page.

The paragraphs are single-spaced internally and
double-spaced between each other unless the letter is extremely short, in which case the paragraphs may be double-
spaced internally and triple-spaced between each other.
Continuation sheets should contain at least three message
lines, and the last word on a sheet should never be divided. The heading for a continuation sheet begins at
least six lines from the top edge of the page and follows the format shown in this letter.

Figure 1.43.   The Modified Semi-block Letter

Mr. Thompson   - 2 -   January 1, 19—

     The complimentary close is typed at two lines below
the last line of the message. The signature line, four
lines below the complimentary close, is aligned with it
if possible, or centered under it if the name and title
will be long. In this case, it is better to align both
date and complimentary close about five spaces to the
right of dead center to ensure enough room for the signature block which should never overrun the right margin.
The writer's name, business title and department name (if
not already printed on the stationery) are typed in capitals and lowercase.

     Although open punctuation may be followed, the mixed
punctuation pattern is quite common with the Modified
Semi-block Letter, and it is the latter that is shown
here.

                         Sincerely yours,

                         Executive Signature

                         Executive Signature
                         Business Title

jml

Enclosures: 2

cc: Dr. Bennett P. Oakley
       Addison Engineering Associates
       91011 Jones Street
       Smithville, ST   56789

     A postscript if needed is typically positioned two
to four lines below the last notation. In the Modified
Semi-block Letter, the postscript is indented five to ten
spaces to agree with message paragraphing. It is not
necessary to head the postscript with the abbreviation
<u>P.S.</u> The postscript should be initialed by the writer.

                             ES

Merriam-Webster Inc.
America's first publisher of dictionaries
and fine reference books.

January 1, 19—

Mr. Ken T. Row
123 Key Place
Smithville, ST   56789

Dear Ken:

This is a facsimile of the half
sheet which is used for the briefest
of notes—those containing one or
two sentences or two very short paragraphs.

The Block, Modified Block, or
Modified Semi-block Letters may be
used, and open or mixed punctuation
may be followed.

Sincerely yours,

Executive Signature

jml

Figure 1.44.   The Half-sheet

Time-saving Correspondence Methods

An increasing number of business offices rely on time-saving and cost-cutting measures for sending out and replying to routine correspondence. Among these methods are the use of form letters and form paragraphs, memorandum forms with detachable reply sections, postal cards, and the writing of marginal notations directly on letters received.

Postal cards Brief messages may be typewritten on standard size (5½ by 3½ inches) postal cards. A message can be fitted on the card if you follow these suggestions:

1. Set the margins for a 4½-inch writing line, which allows half-inch margins at each side. Plan to leave a half-inch margin at the bottom.
2. Type the date on the third line from the top.
3. Omit the inside address.
4. Leave one line of space before the salutation.
5. Leave one line of space before the message.
6. Leave one line of space before the complimentary close and the signature.
7. If necessary, omit one or more of the following: salutation, complimentary close, handwritten signature, identification initials.

Pre-addressed postal cards may also be enclosed with a letter of inquiry to encourage and speed an answer back to your office. You may even type various responses so that the recipient can simply check the appropriate response and mail the card.

Marginal notations The procedure described here is used in many business offices to answer routine queries. The answer to an incoming letter is written at the bottom of the letter, a copy is made for the files, and the original is returned to the sender with the reply written directly on it. Frequently a stamped message or sticker is attached explaining that this speedy reply method is for the customer's convenience.

One variation of this procedure is to stamp on your own letter of inquiry, "Reply here to save time. Photocopy for your files." Or you can enclose a photocopy of your original letter with a request that the recipient simply answer in the margin of the copy and return it to you.

Marginal notations save time and cut costs, and they also reduce the number of file copies. However, they should be used only when such informality is appropriate.

Stylings for Envelope Addresses

The following information may appear on any envelope regardless of its size. Asterisked items are essential and those that are unmarked are optional, depending on the requirements of the particular letter:

*1. The addressee's full name and full geographical address typed approximately in the vertical and horizontal center
2. Special mailing notation or notations typed below the stamp
3. On-arrival notation or notations typed about nine lines below the top left
*4. Sender's full name and geographical address printed or typed in the upper left corner.

The typeface should be block style. The Postal Service does not recommend unusual or italic typefaces.

The address block on a regular envelope should take up no more than 1½″ × 3¾″ of space. There should be ⅝″ of space from the bottom line of the address block to the bottom edge of the envelope. The entire area from the right and left bottom margins of the address block to the right and left bottom edges of the envelope as well as the area under the center of the address block to the bottom center edge of the envelope should be free of print. With regular envelopes, most address blocks are begun about five spaces to the left of horizontal center to admit room for potentially long lines. The address block should be single-spaced. Block styling should be used throughout.

If a window envelope is being used, all address data must appear within the window space, and at least ¼″ margins must be maintained between the address and the right, left, top, and bottom edges of the window space.

Position of Elements

Address-block elements should be styled and positioned as described in the following paragraphs:

First Line If the addressee is an individual, that person's courtesy title and full name are typed on the first line.

>   Mr. Lee O. Idlewild

If an individual addressee's business title is included in the inside address, it may be typed either on the first line of the address block with a comma separating it from the addressee's name, or it may be typed alone on the next line, depending on the length of title and name.

>   Mr. Lee O. Idlewild, President

>   Mr. Lee O. Idlewild
>   President

If the addressee is an organization, its full name is typed on the first line. If a particular department within an organization is specified, its name is typed on a line under the name of the organization.

>   XYZ Corporation
>   Sales Department

Next line The full street address should be typed out (although it is acceptable to abbreviate such designations as *Street, Avenue, Boulevard,* etc.). In mass mailings that will be presorted for automated handling (see pages 54–57), it is correct to capitalize all elements of the address block and to use the unpunctuated abbreviations for streets and street-designations that are recommended by the U.S. Postal Service. Room, suite, apartment, and building numbers are typed immediately following the last element of the street address and are positioned on the same line with it. Building names, if used, are listed on a separate line just above the street address.

A post-office box number, if used, is typed on the line immediately above the last line in order to assure delivery to this point. (The box number precedes the station name when a station name is included.) Both street address and post-office box number may be written in the address, but the letter will be delivered to the location specified on the next-to-last line.

Last line The last line of the address block contains the city, state, and the zip code number. Only one space intervenes between the last letter of the state abbreviation and the first digit of the zip code. The zip code should never be on a line by itself. The zip code is mandatory, as are the all-capitalized, unpunctuated, two-letter Postal Service abbreviations. It is correct, however, to spell the name of a state in full on the letter while using the Postal Service abbreviation on the envelope.

Mr. John P. Smith
4523 Kendall Place, Apt. 8B
Smithville, ST 56789
  or
Mr. John P. Smith
4523 Kendall Pl., Apt. 8B
Smithville, ST 56789

When both post-office box number and street address are included in an address, the zip code should correctly match the location (usually the post-office box) specified in the line just above the last line of the address.

XYZ Corporation
1234 Smith Boulevard
P. O. Box 600
Smithville, ST 56788

If the addressee has indicated a 9-digit zip code on correspondence to you, use the full number to speed delivery to that address.

Cameron Corporation
765 Bay Street, Room III
Smithville, ST 56789-1234

Other elements On-arrival notations such as PERSONAL or CONFIDENTIAL must be typed entirely in capital letters, about nine lines below the

Table 5
Two-letter State Abbreviations for the United States and its Dependencies

Alabama	AL	Kentucky	KY	Oklahoma	OK
Alaska	AK	Louisiana	LA	Oregon	OR
Arizona	AZ	Maine	ME	Pennsylvania	PA
Arkansas	AR	Maryland	MD	Puerto Rico	PR
California	CA	Massachusetts	MA	Rhode Island	RI
Colorado	CO	Michigan	MI	South Carolina	SC
Connecticut	CT	Minnesota	MN	South Dakota	SD
Delaware	DE	Mississippi	MS	Tennessee	TN
District of		Missouri	MO	Texas	TX
Columbia	DC	Montana	MT	Utah	UT
Florida	FL	Nebraska	NE	Vermont	VT
Georgia	GA	Nevada	NV	Virginia	VA
Guam	GU	New Hampshire	NH	Virgin Islands	VI
Hawaii	HI	New Jersey	NJ	Washington	WA
Idaho	ID	New Mexico	NM	West Virginia	WV
Illinois	IL	New York	NY	Wisconsin	WI
Indiana	IN	North Carolina	NC	Wyoming	WY
Iowa	IA	North Dakota	ND		
Kansas	KS	Ohio	OH		

left top edge of the envelope. Any other on-arrival instructions such as *Hold for Arrival* or *Please Forward* may be typed in capitals and lowercase, underlined, and positioned about nine lines from the left top edge of the envelope.

If an attention line is used in the letter itself, it too must appear on the envelope. The attention line must be placed in the address block so that it is directly above the next-to-last line.

XYZ Corporation
Sales Department
Attention Mr. E. R. Bailey
1234 Smith Boulevard
Smithville, ST 56789

A special mailing notation (as CERTIFIED, REGISTERED MAIL, or SPECIAL DELIVERY) is typed entirely in capitals just below the stamp or about nine lines from the right top edge of the envelope. It should not overrun a ½″ margin.

The printed return address (as of a company) may be supplemented by the name of the writer typed in at the top. The return address on a plain envelope should be styled as follows, with the least two blank lines between the return address and the left and top edges of the envelope:

Stephen P. Lemke
123 Ann Street
Jonesville, XX 12345

See Table 2 on page 7 for a chart showing stationery and envelope sizes and applications. See Chapter 8 for detailed treatment of mailing procedures.

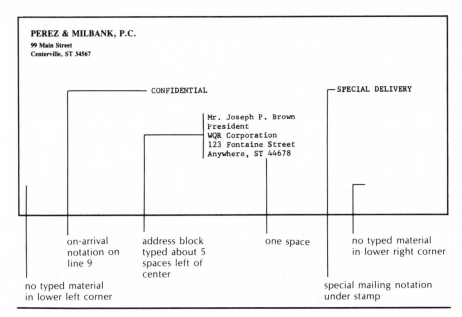

Figure 1.45.   Commercial envelope showing on-arrival and special mailing notations

Foreign Addresses

When typing a foreign address, the secretary should refer first to the return address on the envelope of previous correspondence to ascertain the correct ordering of the essential elements of the address block. Letterhead stationery of previous correspondence may also be checked if an envelope is not available. If neither of these sources is available, the material should be typed as it appears in the inside address of the dictated letter. The following guidelines may be of assistance.

1. All foreign addresses should be typed in English or in English characters. If an address must be in foreign characters (as Russian), an English translation should be inserted between the lines in the address block.
2. Foreign courtesy titles may be substituted for the English, but they are not necessary.
3. The name of the country should be typed in full and in all-capital letters by itself on the last line. Canadian addresses always carry the name CANADA, even though the name of the province is also given.
4. When applicable, foreign postal district numbers should be included. These are positioned either before or after the name of the city, never after the name of the country.

Canadian addresses should adhere to the form requested by the Canada Post for quickest delivery through its automated handling system. As shown in the examples below, the name of the city, fully capitalized, is followed by the name of the province, spelled in full, on one line; the Postal Code follows on a separate line. For mail originating in the United States, CANADA is added on a final line. (Note that capitalization and punctuation differ slightly in French-language addresses.)

Mr. F. F. MacManus	Les Entreprises Optima Ltée
Fitzgibbons and Brown	6789, rue Principale
5678 Main Street	OTTAWA (Ontario)
HALIFAX, Nova Scotia	K1A 0B3
B3J 2N9	CANADA
CANADA	

The Canadian Postal Code consists always of letter-numeral-letter, space, numeral-letter-numeral. Failure to include the correct code number may result in considerable delay in the delivery of mail. When space is limited, the Postal Code may be typed on the same line with the province. In this case, it must be separated from the name of the province by at least two character spaces. The two-letter provincial and territorial abbreviations listed in Table 6 below may also be used when space is limited.

OTTAWA, Ontario K1A 0B3   *or*   OTTAWA, ON K1A 0B3

Table 6
Two-letter Abbreviations for Canadian Provinces

Alberta	AB	Newfoundland	NF	Quebec	PQ
British Columbia	BC	Northwest Territories	NT	Saskatchewan	SK
Labrador	LB	Nova Scotia	NS	Yukon Territory	YT
Manitoba	MB	Ontario	ON		
New Brunswick	NB	Prince Edward Island	PE		

Some samples of foreign corporate abbreviations are shown in Table 7 on page 55.

Addressing for Automation

So that the secretary can take full advantage of the post office's computerized sorting equipment (including new optical character readers that can scan and sort many thousands of pieces of mail an hour), the United States Postal Service recommends that *all* envelopes be addressed properly for automation. All typescript should be clear and easy to read. The basic procedures in addressing envelopes are as follows:

1. Use rectangular envelopes no smaller than $3\frac{1}{2}'' \times 5''$ and no larger than $6\frac{1}{8}'' \times 11\frac{1}{2}''$. There should be good color contrast between the paper and the type impressions.
2. The address should be single-spaced and blocked (straight left margin). The address must be at least $1''$ from the left edge of the enve-

Table 7
Foreign Corporate Abbreviations

A Brief Sampling of Commonly Used Terms

Language	Type of Business	Abbreviation
Danish	Partnership	I/S
	Limited Partnership	K/S
	Limited-liability Company	A/S
	Private Limited-liability Company	Ap/S
Dutch	Private Company	B.V.
	Public Corporation	N.V.
French	Limited-liability Company	SARL
	Corporation	SA
German	Partnership	OHG
	Limited Partnership	KG
	Limited-liability Company	G.m.b.H.
	Corporation	AG
Italian	Corporation	S.p.A.
	Limited-liability Company	S.r.l.
Portuguese	Corporation	SARL
Spanish	Stock Company	SA
	Corporation	S/A
	Company	CIA
Swedish	Joint Stock Company	SA

lope and at least ⅝″ up from the bottom. There should be no print to the right of or below the address.

3. Additional data (as the attention line, account number, or date) should be part of the blocked address. These data should be positioned above the second line from bottom. Envelope addresses should be typed entirely in capital letters without punctuation marks. Use type fonts other than script, italic, or proportionally-spaced fonts. Do not type the address at a slant.

```
C REEVES CORP
ATTN MR R C SMITH
XXX XXXX XX XXX XXX
XXXXXXXX XX XXXXX
```

4. If mail is addressed to occupants of multi-unit buildings, the unit number should appear after the street address on the same line.

```
C REEVES CORP
ATTN MR R C SMITH
186 PARK ST ROOM 960
XXXXXXXX XX XXXXX
```

5. The bottom line of the address should contain the city, state, and zip code number (see Table 5 on page 52).

C REEVES CORP
ATTN MR R C SMITH
186 PARK ST ROOM 960
HARTFORD CT 06106

6. A post-office box number is typed on the line above the last to assure delivery to this point. (Use the zip code for the box number, not for the street address.) The box number precedes the station name.

C REEVES CORP
186 PARK ST
PO BOX 210 LINCOLN STA
HARTFORD CT 06106

7. At least ¼″ should be left between the address and the sides and bottom edges of the opening on window envelopes.

A maximum of 22 strokes or positions is allowed on the last line of an envelope address. The Postal Service suggests the following maximum number of positions:

13 positions for the city
1 space between the city and state
2 positions for the state
1 space between the state and zip code number
5 positions for the zip code number

22 total positions allowed

Many cities exceed the suggested maximum number of 13 positions. The Postal Service suggests that the abbreviations listed in Table 8 below be used to facilitate mail processing.

Table 8
Abbreviations for Street Designators and for Words that Appear Frequently in Place Names

Academy	ACAD	Bottom	BTM	Churches	CHRS
Agency	AGNCY	Boulevard	BLVD	Circle	CIR
Airport	ARPRT	Branch	BR	City	CY
Alley	ALY	Bridge	BRG	Clear	CLR
Annex	ANX	Brook	BRK	Cliffs	CLFS
Arcade	ARC	Burg	BG	Club	CLB
Arsenal	ARSL	Bypass	BYP	College	CLG
Avenue	AVE	Camp	CP	Corner	COR
Bayou	BYU	Canyon	CYN	Corners	CORS
Beach	BCH	Cape	CPE	Court	CT
Bend	BND	Causeway	CSWY	Courts	CTS
Big	BG	Center	CTR	Cove	CV
Black	BLK	Central	CTL	Creek	CRK
Bluff	BLF	Church	CHR	Crescent	CRES

Crossing	XING	Key	KY	Sainte	ST
Dale	DL	Knolls	KNLS	San	SN
Dam	DM	Lake	LK	Santa	SN
Depot	DPO	Lakes	LKS	Santo	SN
Divide	DIV	Landing	LNDG	School	SCH
Drive	DR	Lane	LN	Seminary	SMNRY
East	E	Light	LGT	Shoal	SHL
Estates	EST	Little	LTL	Shoals	SHLS
Expressway	EXPY	Loaf	LF	Shode	SHD
Extended	EXT	Locks	LCKS	Shore	SHR
Extension	EXT	Lodge	LDG	Shores	SHRS
Fall	FL	Lower	LWR	Siding	SDG
Falls	FLS	Manor	MNR	South	S
Farms	FRMS	Meadows	MDWS	Space Flight	
Ferry	FRY	Meeting	MTG	Center	SFC
Field	FLD	Memorial	MEM	Spring	SPG
Fields	FLDS	Middle	MDL	Springs	SPGS
Flats	FLT	Mile	MLE	Square	SQ
Ford	FRD	Mill	ML	State	ST
Forest	FRST	Mills	MLS	Station	STA
Forge	FRG	Mines	MNS	Stream	STRM
Fork	FRK	Mission	MSN	Street	ST
Forks	FRKS	Mound	MND	Sulphur	SLPHR
Fort	FT	Mount	MT	Summit	SMT
Fountain	FTN	Mountain	MTN	Switch	SWCH
Freeway	FWY	National	NAT	Tannery	TNRY
Furnace	FURN	Neck	NCK	Tavern	TVRN
Gardens	GDNS	New	NW	Terminal	TERM
Gateway	GTWY	North	N	Terrace	TER
Glen	GLN	Orchard	ORCH	Ton	TN
Grand	GRND	Palms	PLMS	Tower	TWR
Great	GR	Park	PK	Town	TWN
Green	GRN	Parkway	PKY	Trail	TRL
Ground	GRD	Pillar	PLR	Trailer	TRLR
Grove	GRV	Pines	PNES	Tunnel	TUNL
Harbor	HBR	Place	PL	Turnpike	TPKE
Haven	HVN	Plain	PLN	Union	UN
Heights	HTS	Plains	PLNS	University	UNIV
High	HI	Plaza	PLZ	Upper	UPR
Highlands	HGLDS	Point	PT	Valley	VLY
Highway	HWY	Port	PRT	Viaduct	VIA
Hill	HL	Prairie	PR	View	VW
Hills	HLS	Ranch	RNCH	Village	VLG
Hollow	HOLW	Ranches	RNCHS	Ville	VL
Hospital	HOSP	Rapids	RPDS	Vista	VIS
Hot	H	Resort	RESRT	Water	WTR
House	HSE	Rest	RST	Wells	WLS
Inlet	INLT	Ridge	RDG	West	W
Institute	INST	River	RIV	White	WHT
Island	IS	Road	RD	Works	WKS
Islands	IS	Rock	RK	Yards	YDS
Isle	IS	Rural	R		
Junction	JCT	Saint	ST		

Chapter 2

Forms of Address

CONTENTS

It has already been emphasized that the initial impression created by a letter is vital to the letter's ultimate effectiveness. It follows that the proper use of the conventional forms of address is essential, especially since these forms appear in conspicuous areas of the letter: on the envelope, in the inside address, and in the salutation.

Forms of Address Chart

The following pages contain a chart of alphabetically grouped and listed forms of address for individuals where offices, ranks, or professions warrant special courtesy. (For information about choosing complimentary closes, see page 27.) The main categories in the chart are listed below in the order of their appearance.

Clerical and Religious Orders	Government Officials—Federal
College and University Faculty and Officials	Government Officials—Local
	Government Officials—State
Consular Officers	Military Ranks
Diplomats	Miscellaneous Professional Titles
Foreign Heads of State	United Nations Officials

A special chart headed "Multiple Addressees" immediately follows the Forms of Address Chart, and a more detailed discussion of special titles and abbreviations (such as *Doctor, Esquire, Honorable,* etc.) begins on page 78. For information about the use of gender-neutral salutations, see pages 20–21.

When two or more stylings are shown in the Forms of Address Chart, it should be understood by the reader that the most formal styling appears first. It should also be understood that if the formal address shown for a man in "Sir," the formal address for a woman is "Madam," and vice versa, and that if the informal address for a man is "Mr.," the informal address for a woman is "Mrs.," "Miss," or "Ms.," and vice versa. In cases where this simple equation does not apply, examples for both male and female addresses are given. In all of the examples for female addresses, the courtesy title *Ms.* has been shown; however, the titles *Mrs.* and *Miss* may be freely substituted in all of these cases according to the preference of the recipient if it is known.

Readers will note that approximately half of the positions and ranks in this chart are illustrated with a man's name and half with a woman's name. This is not meant to suggest that any position or rank in this chart is more likely to be held by a man or a woman. On the contrary, it has been assumed that, except in the category of Clerical and Religious Orders, either a man or woman may hold any position or rank included in this chart; however, space limitations in the chart preclude showing examples of both male and female addresses in every instance.

Lack of space has also resulted in the exclusion from the chart of lower-ranking officials such as city water commissioners. Addressing these minor officials should be no problem, however. An official's title appears in the address only if the official *heads* an agency or department; otherwise, only the name of the agency or department is included.

Mrs. Joan R. White, Chairman   Mrs. Joan R. White
Smithville School Board   Smithville School Board

Mrs. Joan R. White
Sheriff, Rockland County

Salutations on letters to minor officials consist of courtesy title + surname. The substitution of a professional title (as "Dear Justice Smith") for the courtesy title is correct only for high-ranking officials such as governors and judges; for military officers; and for certain police and fire officers.

Dear Governor Roy   Dear Chief Roberts
Dear Senator Scott   Dear Sheriff Roberts
Dear Judge Dow   *but also*
Dear Major Smith   Dear Mr. Roberts

Military officers retain their highest rank upon retirement and are addressed in the same way as active officers.

Inside Address Styling	Salutation Styling
Clerical and Religious Orders	

abbot
The Right Reverend John R. Smith, O.S.B.
Abbot of _____

Right Reverend and dear Father
Dear Father Abbot
Dear Father

archbishop
The Most Reverend Archbishop of _____
or
The Most Reverend John R. Smith
Archbishop of _____

Your Excellency

Your Excellency
Dear Archbishop Smith

archdeacon
The Venerable The Archdeacon of _____
or
The Venerable John R. Smith
Archdeacon of _____

Venerable Sir

Venerable Sir
My dear Archdeacon

bishop, Catholic
The Most Reverend John R. Smith
Bishop of _____

Your Excellency
Dear Bishop Smith

bishop, Episcopal
The Right Reverend The Bishop of _____
or
The Right Reverend John R. Smith
Bishop of _____

Right Reverend Sir

Right Reverend Sir
Dear Bishop Smith

bishop, Episcopal, Presiding
The Most Reverend John R. Smith
Presiding Bishop

Most Reverend Sir
Dear Bishop
Dear Bishop Smith

bishop, Protestant (excluding Episcopal)
The Reverend John R. Smith

Reverend Sir
Dear Bishop Smith

brotherhood, member of
Brother John, S.J. *(or other initials for the order)*

Dear Brother John

canon
The Reverend John R. Smith
Canon of _____ Cathedral

Dear Canon Smith

cardinal
His Eminence John Cardinal Smith

Your Eminence
Dear Cardinal Smith

or
His Eminence Cardinal Smith

Your Eminence
Dear Cardinal Smith

or if also an archbishop
His Eminence John Cardinal Smith
Archbishop of _____
or
His Eminence Cardinal Smith
Archbishop of _____

Your Eminence
Dear Cardinal Smith

Your Eminence
Dear Cardinal Smith

Inside Address Styling	Salutation Styling
chaplain, college or university—see COLLEGE AND UNIVERSITY FACULTY AND OFFICIALS	
clergyman, Protestant	
The Reverend Amelia R. Smith	Dear Ms. Smith
or if having a doctorate	
The Reverend Dr. Amelia R. Smith	Dear Dr. Smith
dean (of a cathedral)	
The Very Reverend John R. Smith	Very Reverend Sir
_____ Cathedral	Dear Dean Smith
or	
Dean John R. Smith	Very Reverend Sir
_____ Cathedral	Dear Dean Smith
monsignor, domestic prelate	
The Right Reverend Monsignor John R. Smith	Right Reverend and dear Monsignor
or	Smith
The Rt. Rev. Msgr. John R. Smith	Dear Monsignor Smith
monsignor, papal chamberlain	
The Very Reverend Monsignor John R. Smith	Very Reverend and dear Monsignor
or	Smith
The Very Rev. Msgr. John R. Smith	Dear Monsignor Smith
mother superior (of a sisterhood)	
The Reverend Mother Superior	Reverend Mother
Convent of _____	Dear Reverend Mother
	My dear Reverend Mother Mary
	Angelica
or	
Reverend Mother Mary Angelica, O.S.D.	Reverend Mother
(or other initials of the order)	Dear Reverend Mother
Convent of _____	My dear Reverend Mother Mary
	Angelica
or	
Mother Mary Angelica, Superior	Reverend Mother
Convent of _____	Dear Reverend Mother
	My dear Reverend Mother Mary
	Angelica
patriarch (of an Eastern Orthodox Church)	
His Beatitude the Patriarch of _____	Most Reverend Lord
pope	
His Holiness the Pope	Your Holiness
	Most Holy Father
or	
His Holiness Pope John	Your Holiness
	Most Holy Father
president, Mormon	
The President	My dear President
Church of Jesus Christ of Latter-day Saints	Dear President Smith
priest, Catholic	
The Reverend Father Smith	Dear Father Smith
or	
The Reverend John R. Smith	Dear Father Smith

Inside Address Styling	Salutation Styling

priest, president (of a college or university)—see COLLEGE AND UNIVERSITY FACULTY AND OFFICIALS

rabbi
Rabbi John R. Smith   Dear Rabbi Smith
   or if having a doctorate
Rabbi John R. Smith, D.D.   Dear Dr. Smith

sisterhood, member of
Sister Mary Angelica, S.C. *(or other initials*   Dear Sister
   of the order)   Dear Sister Mary Angelica

College and University Faculty and Officials

chancellor (of a university)
Dr. Amelia R. Smith   Dear Dr. Smith
Chancellor

chaplain (of a college or university)
The Reverend John R. Smith   Dear Chaplain Smith
Chaplain   Dear Mr. Smith
                                                        Dear Father Smith

dean (of a college or university)
Dean Amelia R. Smith   Dear Dr. Smith
                                                        Dear Dean Smith
  or
Dr. Amelia R. Smith   Dear Dr. Smith
Dean   Dear Dean Smith

instructor
Mr. John R. Smith   Dear Mr. Smith
Instructor

president
Dr. Amelia R. Smith   Dear Dr. Smith
President
  or
President Amelia R. Smith   Dear President Smith

president, priest
The Very Reverend John R. Smith   Dear Father Smith
President

professor, assistant or associate
Dr. Amelia R. Smith   Dear Dr. Smith
Assistant Professor of _____   Dear Professor Smith
                                                        Dear Ms. Smith
  or
Dr. Amelia R. Smith   Dear Dr. Smith
Associate Professor of _____   Dear Professor Smith
                                                        Dear Ms. Smith

professor, full
Professor John R. Smith   Dear Professor Smith
  or
Dr. John R. Smith   Dear Dr. Smith
Professor of _____

Inside Address Styling	Salutation Styling

Consular Officers

consulate, American
The American Consulate
(foreign city, country)
   or if in Latin America or Canada
The Consulate of the United States of America

Salutation: Gentlemen / Ladies and Gentlemen (for first); Gentlemen / Ladies and Gentlemen (for last)

The American Consulate	Gentlemen
(foreign city, country)	Ladies and Gentlemen
or if in Latin America or Canada	
The Consulate of the United States of America	Gentlemen
	Ladies and Gentlemen

consul, American (covers all consular grades such as *Consul, Consul General, Vice-Consul,* and *Consular Agent*)

The American Consul	Sir
(foreign city, country)	Sir or Madam
or if in Latin America or Canada	
The Consul of the United States of America	Sir
	Sir or Madam
or if individual name is known	
Amelia R. Smith, Esq.	Madam
American Consul	Dear Ms. Smith
or if in Latin America or Canada	
Amelia R. Smith, Esq.	Madam
Consul of the United States of America	Dear Ms. Smith

consulate, foreign

The _____ Consulate	Gentlemen
(U.S. city, state, zip code)	Ladies and Gentlemen
or	
The Consulate of _____	Gentlemen
(U.S. city, state, zip code)	Ladies and Gentlemen

consuls, foreign (covers all consular grades)

The _____ Consul	Sir
(U.S. city, state, zip code)	Sir or Madame
or	
The Consul of _____	Sir
(U.S. city, state, zip code)	Sir or Madame
or if individual name is known	
The Honorable John R. Smith	Sir
_____ Consul	Dear Mr. Smith

Diplomats

ambassador, American

The Honorable Amelia R. Smith	Madam
American Ambassador	Dear Madam Ambassador
or if in Latin America or Canada	
The Honorable Amelia R. Smith	Madam
Ambassador of the United States of America	Dear Madam Ambassador
or	
The Honorable John R. Smith	Sir
American Ambassador	Dear Mr. Ambassador
or if in Latin America or Canada	
The Honorable John R. Smith	Sir
Ambassador of the United States of America	Dear Mr. Ambassador

Inside Address Styling	Salutation Styling

ambassador, foreign

His Excellency John R. Smith
Ambassador of _____
 or
Her Excellency Amelia R. Smith
Ambassador of _____

Excellency
Dear Mr. Ambassador

Excellency
Dear Madame Ambassador

chargé d'affaires ad interim, American

Amelia R. Smith, Esq.
American Chargé d'Affaires ad interim
 or if in Latin America or Canada
Amelia R. Smith, Esq.
United States Chargé d'Affaires ad Interim

Madam
Dear Ms. Smith

Madam
Dear Ms. Smith

chargé d'affaires ad interim, foreign

Mr. John R. Smith
Chargé d'Affaires ad Interim of _____
 or
Ms. Amelia R. Smith
Chargé d'Affaires ad Interim of _____

Sir
Dear Mr. Smith

Madame
Dear Ms. Smith

chargé d'affaires (de missi), foreign

Ms. Amelia R. Smith
Chargé d'Affaires of _____
 or
Mr. John R. Smith
Chargé d'Affaires of _____

Madame
Dear Ms. Smith

Sir
Dear Mr. Smith

minister, American

The Honorable John R. Smith
American Minister
 or if in Latin America or Canada
Minister of the United States of America
 or
The Honorable Amelia R. Smith
American Minister
 or if in Latin America or Canada
The Honorable Amelia R. Smith
Minister of the United States of America

Sir
Dear Mr. Minister

Dear Mr. Minister

Madam
Dear Madam Minister

Madam
Dear Madam Minister

minister, foreign

The Honorable Amelia R. Smith
Minister of _____
 or
The Honorable John R. Smith
Minister of _____

Madame
Dear Madame Minister

Sir
Dear Mr. Minister

Foreign Heads of State: A Brief Sampling

---

premier

His Excellency John R. Smith
Premier of _____
 or
Her Excellency Amelia R. Smith
Premier of _____

Excellency
Dear Mr. Premier

Excellency
Dear Madame Premier

Inside Address Styling	Salutation Styling
president of a republic	
Her Excellency Amelia R. Smith	Excellency
President of ⸺	Dear Madame President
or	
His Excellency John R. Smith	Excellency
President of ⸺	Dear Mr. President
prime minister	
His Excellency John R. Smith	Excellency
	Dear Mr. Prime Minister
or	
Her Excellency Amelia R. Smith	Excellency
	Dear Madame Prime Minister

Government Officials—Federal

---

attorney general	
The Honorable Amelia R. Smith	Dear Madam Attorney General
The Attorney General	
or	
The Honorable John R. Smith	Dear Mr. Attorney General
The Attorney General	
cabinet officer (other than attorney general)	
The Honorable John R. Smith	Sir
Secretary of ⸺	Dear Mr. Secretary
or	
The Secretary of ⸺	Sir
or	Dear Mr. Secretary
The Honorable Amelia R. Smith	Madam
Secretary of ⸺	Dear Madam Secretary
cabinet officer, former	
The Honorable Amelia R. Smith	Dear Ms. Smith
chairman of a (sub) committee, U.S. Congress (stylings shown apply to House of Representatives & Senate)	
The Honorable John R. Smith	Dear Mr. Chairman
Chairman	Dear Senator Smith
Committee on ⸺	
United States Senate	
or	
The Honorable Amelia R. Smith	Dear Madam Chairman
Chairman	Dear Senator Smith
Committee on ⸺	
United States Senate	
chief justice—see SUPREME COURT, FEDERAL; STATE	
commissioner	
if appointed	
The Honorable Amelia R. Smith	Dear Madam Commissioner
Commissioner	Dear Ms. Smith
or	
The Honorable John R. Smith	Dear Mr. Commissioner
Commissioner	Dear Mr. Smith
if career	
Ms. Amelia R. Smith	Dear Ms. Smith
Commissioner	

Inside Address Styling	Salutation Styling

congressman—see REPRESENTATIVE, U.S. CONGRESS

director (as of an independent federal agency)
The Honorable John R. Smith   Dear Mr. Smith
Director
_____ Agency

district attorney
The Honorable Amelia R. Smith   Dear Ms. Smith
District Attorney

federal judge
The Honorable John R. Smith   Sir
Judge of the United States District   My dear Judge Smith
Court of the _____ District   Dear Judge Smith
of _____

justice—see SUPREME COURT, FEDERAL; STATE

librarian of congress
The Honorable Amelia R. Smith   Madam
Librarian of Congress   Dear Ms. Smith

postmaster general
The Honorable John R. Smith   Sir
The Postmaster General   Dear Mr. Postmaster General
    or
The Honorable Amelia R. Smith   Madam
The Postmaster General   Dear Madam Postmaster General

president of the United States
The President   Mr. President
The White House   My dear Mr. President
                                                        Dear Mr. President

    or
The Honorable Amelia R. Smith   Madam President
President of the United States   My dear Madam President
The White House   Dear Madam President

president of the United States (former)
The Honorable John R. Smith   Sir
(local address)   Dear Mr. Smith

president-elect of the United States
The Honorable Amelia R. Smith   Dear Madam
President-elect of the United States   Dear Ms. Smith

press secretary to the President of the United States
Mr. John R. Smith   Dear Mr. Smith
Press Secretary to the President
of the United States

Inside Address Styling	Salutation Styling
representative, United States Congress	
The Honorable Amelia R. Smith	Madam
United States House of Representatives	Dear Representative Smith
or for local address	
The Honorable Amelia R. Smith	Dear Ms. Smith
Representative in Congress	
representative, United States Congress (former)	
The Honorable John R. Smith	Dear Mr. Smith
(local address)	
senator, United States Senate	
The Honorable Amelia R. Smith	Madam
United States Senate	Dear Senator Smith
senator-elect	
The Honorable John R. Smith	Dear Mr. Smith
Senator-elect	
(local address)	
senator (former)	
The Honorable Amelia R. Smith	Dear Senator Smith
(local address)	
speaker, United States House of Representatives	
The Honorable	Sir
The Speaker of the House of Representatives	
or	
The Honorable Speaker of the House	Sir
of Representatives	
or	
The Honorable John R. Smith	Sir
Speaker of the House of Representatives	Dear Mr. Speaker
	Dear Mr. Smith
speaker, United States House of Representatives (former)	
The Honorable Amelia R. Smith	Madam
(local address)	Dear Madam Speaker
special assistant to the President of the United States	
Mr. John R. Smith	Dear Mr. Smith
supreme court, associate justice	
Mr. Justice Smith	Sir
The Supreme Court of the United States	Mr. Justice
	My dear Mr. Justice
	Dear Mr. Justice Smith
or	
Ms. Justice Smith	Madam
The Supreme Court of the United States	Madam Justice
	My dear Madam Justice
	Dear Madam Justice

Inside Address Styling	Salutation Styling
supreme court, chief justice	
The Chief Justice of the United States	Sir
The Supreme Court of the United States	My dear Mr. Chief Justice
	Dear Mr. Chief Justice
	or
	Madam
	My dear Madam Chief Justice
	Dear Madam Chief Justice
or	
The Chief Justice	Sir
The Supreme Court	My dear Mr. Chief Justice
	Dear Mr. Chief Justice
	or
	Madam
	My dear Madam Chief Justice
	Dear Madam Chief Justice
supreme court, retired Justice	
The Honorable Amelia R. Smith	Madam
(local address)	Dear Justice Smith
territorial delegate	
The Honorable Amelia R. Smith	Dear Ms. Smith
Delegate of _____	
House of Representatives	
undersecretary of a department	
The Honorable John R. Smith	Dear Mr. Smith
Undersecretary of _____	
vice president of the United States	
The Vice President of the United States	Madam
United States Senate	My dear Madam Vice President
	Dear Madam Vice President
or	
The Honorable John R. Smith	Sir
Vice President of the United States	My dear Mr. Vice President
Washington, DC zip code	Dear Mr. Vice President

Government Officials—Local

alderman	
The Honorable John R. Smith	Dear Mr. Smith
	Dear Alderman Smith
or	
Alderman John R. Smith	Dear Mr. Smith
	Dear Alderman Smith
city attorney (includes city counsel, corporation counsel)	
The Honorable Amelia R. Smith	Dear Ms. Smith
councilman—see ALDERMAN	
county clerk	
The Honorable John R. Smith	Dear Mr. Smith
Clerk of _____ County	

Inside Address Styling	Salutation Styling

county treasurer—see COUNTY CLERK

judge
The Honorable Amelia R. Smith
Judge of the _____ Court of _____

Dear Judge Smith

mayor
The Honorable John R. Smith
Mayor of _____

Sir
Dear Mayor Smith

selectman—see ALDERMAN

Government Officials—State

---

assemblyman—see REPRESENTATIVE, STATE

attorney (as commonwealth's attorney, state's attorney)
The Honorable Amelia R. Smith
(title)

Dear Ms. Smith

attorney general
The Honorable John R. Smith
Attorney General of the State of _____
  or
The Honorable Amelia R. Smith
Attorney General of the State of _____

Sir
Dear Mr. Attorney General

Madam
Dear Madam Attorney General

clerk of a court
Amelia R. Smith, Esq.
Clerk of the Court of _____

Dear Ms. Smith

delegate—see REPRESENTATIVE, STATE

governor
The Honorable John R. Smith
Governor of _____
  or in some states
His Excellency, the Governor of _____

Sir
Dear Governor Smith

Sir
Dear Governor Smith

governor (acting)
The Honorable Amelia R. Smith
Acting Governor of _____

Madam
Dear Ms. Smith

governor-elect
The Honorable John R. Smith
Governor-elect of _____

Dear Mr. Smith

governor (former)
The Honorable Amelia R. Smith

Dear Ms. Smith

judge, state court
The Honorable John R. Smith
Judge of the _____ Court

Dear Judge Smith

judge/justice, state supreme court—see SUPREME COURT, STATE

Inside Address Styling	Salutation Styling
lieutenant governor	
The Honorable Lieutenant Governor of _____	Madam
or	
The Honorable Amelia R. Smith	Madam
Lieutenant Governor of _____	Dear Ms. Smith
representative, state (includes assemblyman, delegate)	
The Honorable John R. Smith	Sir
House of Representatives (or The State	Dear Mr. Smith
Assembly or The House of Delegates)	
secretary of state	
The Honorable Secretary of State of _____	Madam
or	
The Honorable Amelia R. Smith	Madam
Secretary of State of _____	Dear Madam Secretary
or	
The Honorable John R. Smith	Sir
Secretary of State of _____	Dear Mr. Secretary
senate, state, president of	
The Honorable John R. Smith	Sir
President of the Senate of the State	Dear Mr. Smith
(or the Commonwealth) of _____	Senator
senator, state	
The Honorable Amelia R. Smith	Madam
The Senate of _____	Dear Senator Smith
speaker, state assembly, house of delegates, or house of representatives	
The Honorable John R. Smith	Sir
Speaker of _____	Dear Mr. Smith
supreme court, state, associate justice	
The Honorable Amelia R. Smith	Madam
Associate Justice of the Supreme Court	Dear Justice Smith
of _____	
supreme court, state, chief justice	
The Honorable John R. Smith	Sir
Chief Justice of the Supreme Court of _____	Dear Mr. Chief Justice
or	
The Honorable Amelia R. Smith	Madam
Chief Justice of the Supreme Court of _____	Dear Madam Chief Justice
supreme court, state, presiding justice	
The Honorable Amelia R. Smith	Madam
Presiding Justice _____ Division	Dear Madam Justice
Supreme Court of _____	
or	
The Honorable John R. Smith	Sir
Presiding Justice	Dear Mr. Chief Justice
_____ Division	
Supreme Court of _____	

Inside Address Styling	Salutation Styling
	Military Ranks

admiral (coast guard, navy)—see also REAR ADMIRAL, VICE ADMIRAL

Admiral John R. Smith, USCG (or USN)	Dear Admiral Smith
or	
ADM John R. Smith, USCG (or USN)	Dear Admiral Smith

airman

| AMN Amelia R. Smith, USAF | Dear Airman Smith |

airman basic

| AB John R. Smith, USAF | Dear Airman Smith |

airman first class

| A1C Amelia R. Smith, USAF | Dear Airman Smith |

brigadier general (air force, army, marine corps)

Brigadier General John R. Smith, USAF (or USMC)	Dear General Smith
or	
BG John R. Smith, USAF (or USA)	Dear General Smith
or	
Brig. Gen. John R. Smith, USMC	Dear General Smith

cadet (U.S. Air Force Academy, U.S. Military Academy)

| Cadet Amelia R. Smith | Dear Cadet Smith |

captain (air force, army, coast guard, navy, marine corps)

Captain John R. Smith, USAF (or USA or USCG or USN or USMC)	Dear Captain Smith
or	
CPT John R. Smith, USAF (or USA)	Dear Captain Smith
or	
CAPT John R. Smith, USCG (or USN)	Dear Captain Smith
or	
Capt. John R. Smith, USMC	Dear Captain Smith

chief petty officer (coast guard, navy)

Chief Petty Officer Amelia R. Smith, USCG (or USN)	Dear Ms. Smith
or	
CPO Amelia R. Smith, USCG (or USN)	Dear Ms. Smith

chief warrant officer W4 (army)

Chief Warrant Officer W4 John R. Smith	Dear Mr. Smith
or	
CWO4 John R. Smith	Dear Mr. Smith

colonel (air force, army, marine corps)

Colonel Amelia R. Smith, USAF (or USA or USMC)	Dear Colonel Smith
or	
COL Amelia R. Smith, USAF (or USA)	Dear Colonel Smith
or	
Col. Amelia R. Smith, USMC	Dear Colonel Smith

Inside Address Styling	Salutation Styling
commander (coast guard or navy)	
Commander John R. Smith, USCG (or USN)	Dear Commander Smith
or	
CDR John R. Smith, USCG (or USN)	Dear Commander Smith
corporal (army)—see also LANCE CORPORAL	
Corporal Amelia R. Smith, USA	Dear Corporal Smith
or	
CPL Amelia R. Smith, USA	Dear Corporal Smith
ensign (coast guard, navy)	
Ensign John R. Smith, USCG (or USN)	Dear Ensign Smith
	Dear Mr. Smith
or	
ENS John R. Smith, USCG (or USN)	Dear Ensign Smith
	Dear Mr. Smith
first lieutenant (air force, army, marine corps)	
First Lieutenant Amelia R. Smith, USAF	Dear Lieutenant Smith
(or USA or USMC)	
or	
1LT Amelia R. Smith, USAF (or USA)	Dear Lieutenant Smith
or	
1st. Lt. Amelia R. Smith, USMC	Dear Lieutenant Smith
first sergeant (army, marine corps)	
First Sergeant John R. Smith, USA (or USMC)	Dear Sergeant Smith
or	
1SG John R. Smith, USA	Dear Sergeant Smith
or	
1st. Sgt. John R. Smith, USMC	Dear Sergeant Smith
general (air force, army, marine corps)—see also BRIGADIER GENERAL, LIEUTENANT GENERAL, MAJOR GENERAL	
General Amelia R. Smith, USAF (or USA or USMC)	Dear General Smith
or	
GEN Amelia R. Smith, USAF (or USA)	Dear General Smith
or	
Gen. Amelia R. Smith, USMC	Dear General Smith
gunnery sergeant (marine corps)	
Gunnery Sergeant John R. Smith, USMC	Dear Sergeant Smith
or	
Gy. Sgt. John R. Smith, USMC	Dear Sergeant Smith
lance corporal (marine corps)	
Lance Corporal Amelia R. Smith, USMC	Dear Corporal Smith
or	
L/Cpl. Amelia R. Smith, USMC	Dear Corporal Smith
lieutenant (coast guard, navy)—see also FIRST LIEUTENANT, SECOND LIEUTENANT	
Lieutenant John R. Smith, USCG (or USN)	Dear Mr. Smith
or	
LT John R. Smith, USCG (or USN)	Dear Mr. Smith

Inside Address Styling	Salutation Styling
lieutenant colonel (air force, army, marine corps)	
Lieutenant Colonel Amelia R. Smith, USAF (or USA or USMC)	Dear Colonel Smith
or	
LTC Amelia R. Smith, USAF (or USA)	Dear Colonel Smith
or	
Lt. Col. Amelia R. Smith, USMC	Dear Colonel Smith
lieutenant commander (coast guard, navy)	
Lieutenant Commander John R. Smith, USCG (or USN)	Dear Commander Smith
or	
LCDR John R. Smith, USCG (or USN)	Dear Commander Smith
lieutenant general (air force, army, marine corps)	
Lieutenant General Amelia R. Smith, USAF (or USA or USMC)	Dear General Smith
or	
LTG Amelia R. Smith, USAF (or USA)	Dear General Smith
or	
Lt. Gen. Amelia R. Smith, USMC	Dear General Smith
lieutenant junior grade (coast guard, navy)	
Lieutenant (j.g.) John R. Smith, USCG (or USN)	Dear Mr. Smith
or	
LTJG John R. Smith, USCG (or USN)	Dear Mr. Smith
major (air force, army, marine corps)	
Major Amelia R. Smith, USAF (or USA or USMC)	Dear Major Smith
or	
MAJ Amelia R. Smith, USAF (or USA)	Dear Major Smith
or	
Maj. Amelia R. Smith, USMC	Dear Major Smith
major general (air force, army, marine corps)	
Major General John R. Smith, USAF (or USA or USMC)	Dear General Smith
or	
MG John R. Smith, USAF (or USA)	Dear General Smith
or	
Maj. Gen. John R. Smith, USMC	Dear General Smith
master sergeant (air force, army)	
Master Sergeant Amelia R. Smith, USAF (or USA)	Dear Sergeant Smith
or	
MSGT Amelia R. Smith, USAF	Dear Sergeant Smith
or	
MSG Amelia R. Smith, USA	Dear Sergeant Smith
midshipman (coast guard and naval academies)	
Midshipman John R. Smith	Dear Midshipman Smith
petty officer (coast guard, navy)	
Petty Officer Amelia R. Smith, USCG (or USN)	Dear Ms. Smith
or	
PO Amelia R. Smith, USCG (or USN)	Dear Ms. Smith

Inside Address Styling	Salutation Styling
private (army, marine corps)	
Private John R. Smith, USA (or USMC)	Dear Private Smith
or	
PVT John R. Smith, USA	Dear Private Smith
or	
Pvt. John R. Smith, USMC	Dear Private Smith
private first class (army)	
Private First Class Amelia R. Smith, USA	Dear Private Smith
or	
PFC Amelia R. Smith, USA	Dear Private Smith
seaman (coast guard, navy)	
Seaman John R. Smith, USCG (or USN)	Dear Seaman Smith
or	
SMN John R. Smith, USCG (or USN)	Dear Seaman Smith
seaman first class (coast guard, navy)	
Seaman First Class Amelia R. Smith, USCG (or USN)	Dear Seaman Smith
or	
S1C Amelia R. Smith, USCG (or USN)	Dear Seaman Smith
second lieutenant (air force, army, marine corps)	
Second Lieutenant John R. Smith, USAF (or USA or USMC)	Dear Lieutenant Smith
or	
2LT John R. Smith, USAF (or USA)	Dear Lieutenant Smith
or	
2nd Lt. John R. Smith, USMC	Dear Lieutenant Smith
senior master sergeant (air force)	
Senior Master Sergeant Amelia R. Smith, USAF	Dear Sergeant Smith
or	
SMSGT Amelia R. Smith, USAF	Dear Sergeant Smith
sergeant (air force, army)—see also FIRST SERGEANT, GUNNERY SERGEANT, MASTER SERGEANT, SENIOR MASTER SERGEANT, SERGEANT MAJOR, STAFF SERGEANT, TECHNICAL SERGEANT	
Sergeant John R. Smith, USAF (or USA)	Dear Sergeant Smith
or	
SGT John R. Smith, USAF (or USA)	Dear Sergeant Smith
sergeant major (army, marine corps)	
Sergeant Major Amelia R. Smith, USA (or USMC)	Dear Sergeant Major Smith
or	
SGM Amelia R. Smith, USA	Dear Sergeant Major Smith
or	
Sgt. Maj. Amelia R. Smith, USMC	Dear Sergeant Major Smith
specialist (army; covers all classes of specialists)	
Specialist Fourth Class John R. Smith, USA	Dear Specialist Smith
or	
S4 John R. Smith, USA	Dear Specialist Smith

Inside Address Styling	Salutation Styling
staff sergeant (air force, army)	
Staff Sergeant Amelia R. Smith, USAF (or USA)	Dear Sergeant Smith
or	
SSGT Amelia R. Smith, USAF	Dear Sergeant Smith
or	
SSG Amelia R. Smith, USA	Dear Sergeant Smith
technical sergeant (air force)	
Technical Sergeant John R. Smith, USAF	Dear Sergeant Smith
or	
TSGT John R. Smith, USAF	Dear Sergeant Smith
vice admiral (navy)	
Vice Admiral Amelia R. Smith, USN	Dear Admiral Smith
or	
VADM Amelia R. Smith, USN	Dear Admiral Smith
warrant officer (army; covers all classes of warrant officers)	
Warrant Officer W1 John R. Smith, USA	Dear Mr. Smith
or	
WO1 John R. Smith, USA	Dear Mr. Smith
any rank not listed	
full title + full name + comma + abbreviation of branch of service	Dear + rank + surname

Miscellaneous Professional Titles	
attorney	
Ms. Amelia R. Smith, Attorney-at-Law	Dear Ms. Smith
or	
Amelia R. Smith, Esq.	Dear Ms. Smith
certified public accountant	
Amelia R. Smith, C.P.A.	Dear Ms. Smith
dentist	
John R. Smith, D.D.S.	Dear Dr. Smith
or	
Dr. John R. Smith	Dear Dr. Smith
engineer	
John R. Smith, P.E.	Dear Mr. Smith
physician	
Amelia R. Smith, M.D.	Dear Dr. Smith
or	
Dr. Amelia R. Smith	Dear Dr. Smith
veterinarian	
John R. Smith, D.V.M.	Dear Dr. Smith
or	
Dr. John R. Smith	Dear Dr. Smith

Inside Address Styling	Salutation Styling
United Nations Officials	

representative, American (with ambassadorial rank)
| The Honorable Amelia R. Smith | Madam |
| United States Permanent Representative to the United Nations | Dear Madam Ambassador |

or

| The Honorable John R. Smith | Sir |
| United States Permanent Representative to the United Nations | Dear Mr. Ambassador |

representative, foreign (with ambassadorial rank)
His Excellency John R. Smith	Excellency
Representative of _____ to the United Nations	My dear Mr. Ambassador
	Dear Mr. Ambassador

or

Her Excellency Amelia R. Smith	Excellency
Representative of _____ to the United Nations	My dear Madame Ambassador
	Dear Madame Ambassador

secretary-general
Her Excellency Amelia R. Smith	Excellency
Secretary-General of the United Nations	My dear Madam (*or* Madame) Secretary-General
	Dear Madam (*or* Madame) Secretary-General

or

His Excellency John R. Smith	Excellency
Secretary-General of the United Nations	My dear Mr. Secretary-General
	Dear Mr. Secretary-General

undersecretary
| The Honorable John R. Smith | Sir |
| Undersecretary of the United Nations | Dear Mr. Smith |

Multiple Addressees (See also discussion on pages 78–85.)

Inside Address Styling	Salutation Styling
two or more men with same surname	
Mr. Arthur W. Jones	Gentlemen
Mr. John H. Jones	
or	*or*
Messrs. A. W. and J. H. Jones	
or	Dear Messrs. Jones
The Messrs. Jones	
two or more men with different surnames	
Mr. Angus D. Langley	Gentlemen *or* Dear Mr. Langley and
Mr. Lionel P. Overton	Mr. Overton
or	*or*
Messrs. A. D. Langley and L. P. Overton	Dear Messrs. Langley and Overton
or	
Messrs. Langley and Overton	
two or more married women with same surname	
Mrs. Arthur W. Jones	Mesdames
Mrs. John H. Jones	
or	*or*
Mesdames A. W. and J. H. Jones	Dear Mesdames Jones
or	
The Mesdames Jones	
two or more unmarried women with same surname	
Miss Alice H. Danvers	Ladies
Miss Margaret T. Danvers	
or	*or*
Misses Alice and Margaret Danvers	
or	Dear Misses Danvers
The Misses Danvers	
two or more women with same surname but whose marital status	
is unknown or irrelevant	
Ms. Alice H. Danvers	Dear Ms. Alice and Margaret Danvers
Ms. Margaret T. Danvers	
two or more married women with different surnames	
Mrs. Allen Y. Dow	Dear Mrs. Dow and Mrs. Frank
Mrs. Lawrence R. Frank	
or	*or*
Mesdames Dow and Frank	Mesdames *or* Dear Mesdames Dow
	and Frank
two or more unmarried women with different surnames	
Miss Elizabeth Dudley	Ladies *or* Dear Miss Dudley and
Miss Ann Raymond	Miss Raymond
or	*or*
Misses E. Dudley and A. Raymond	Dear Misses Dudley and Raymond
two or more women with different surnames but whose marital status	
is unknown or irrelevant	
Ms. Barbara Lee	Dear Ms. Lee and Ms. Key
Ms. Helen Key	

Special Titles, Designations, and Abbreviations

Doctor

If *Doctor* or its abbreviation *Dr.* is used before a person's name, academic degrees (as *D.D.S., D.V.M., M.D.,* or *Ph. D.*) are not included after the surname. The title *Doctor* may be typed out in full or abbreviated in a salutation, but it is usually abbreviated in an envelope address block and in an inside address in order to save space. When *Doctor* appears in a salutation, it must be used in conjunction with the addressee's surname.

> Dear Doctor Smith   *not*   Dear Doctor
> *or*
> Dear Dr. Smith

If a woman holds a doctorate, her title should be used in business-related correspondence even if her husband's name is also included in the letter.

> Dr. Ann R. Smith and Mr. James O. Smith
> Dear Dr. Smith and Mr. Smith

If both husband and wife are doctors, one of the following patterns may be followed.

> Dr. Ann R. Smith and
>   Dr. James O. Smith

> Ann R. Smith, M.D.
> James O. Smith, M.D.

> The Drs. Smith

> Drs. Ann R. and James O. Smith

> The Doctors Smith

> *formal salutation*
> My dear Doctors Smith

> *informal salutation*
> Dear Drs. Smith
> Dear Doctors Smith

Address patterns for two or more doctors associated in a joint practice are.

> Drs. Francis X. Sullivan and
>   Philip K. Ross

> Francis X. Sullivan, M.D.
> Philip K. Ross, M.D.

> *formal salutation*
> My dear Drs. Sullivan and Ross

> *informal salutation*
> Dear Drs. Sullivan and Ross
> Dear Doctors Sullivan and Ross
> Dear Dr. Sullivan and Dr. Ross
> Dear Doctor Sullivan and
>   Doctor Ross

Esquire

The abbreviation *Esq.* for *Esquire* is often used in the United States after the surnames of professional persons such as attorneys, architects, professional engineers, and consuls, and also of court officials such as clerks of court and justices of the peace. *Esquire* may be written in addresses and signature lines but not in salutations. It is used regardless of sex. Some people, however, object to the use of *Esquire* as a title for a woman professional, and one should follow the recipient's wishes, if they are known, in this regard. Alternative forms may then be used, such as "Amy Lutz, Attorney at Law" or "Amy Lutz, P.E."

In Great Britain *Esquire* is generally used after the surnames of people who have distinguished themselves in professional, diplomatic, or social circles. For example, when addressing a letter to a British surgeon or to a high corporate officer of a British firm, one should include *Esq.* after his surname, both on the envelope and in the inside address. Under no circumstances should *Esq.* appear in a salutation. This rule applies to both American and British correspondence. If a courtesy title such as *Dr., Hon., Miss, Mr., Mrs., or Ms.* is used before the addressee's name, *Esquire* or *Esq.* is omitted.

The plural of *Esq.* is *Esqs.* and is used with the surnames of multiple addressees.

Carolyn B. West, Esq. American Consul	Dear Ms. West
Samuel A. Sebert, Esq. Norman D. Langfitt, Esq. *or* Sebert and Langfitt, Esqs. *or* Messrs. Sebert and Langfitt Attorneys-at-Law	Gentlemen Dear Mr. Sebert and Mr. Langfitt Dear Messrs. Sebert and Langfitt
Simpson, Tyler, and Williams, Esqs. *or* Scott A. Simpson, Esq. Annabelle W. Tyler, Esq. David I. Williams, Esq.	Dear Ms. Tyler and Messrs. Simpson and Williams
British Jonathan A. Lyons, Esq. President	Dear Mr. Lyons

Honorable

In the United States, *The Honorable* or its abbreviated form *Hon.* is used as a title of distinction (but not rank) and is accorded elected or appointed (but not career) government officials such as judges, justices, congressmen, and cabinet officers. Neither the full form nor the abbreviation is ever used by its recipient in written signatures, letterhead, business or visiting cards, or in typed signature blocks. While it may be used in an envelope address block and in an inside address of a letter addressed to him or her, it is never used in a salutation. *The Honorable* should never appear before a surname standing alone: there must always be an intervening first name, an initial or initials, or a courtesy title. A courtesy title should not be added, however, when *The Honorable* is used with a full name.

The Honorable John R. Smith	*not* The Honorable Smith
The Honorable J. R. Smith	
The Honorable J. Robert Smith	*and not* The Honorable Mr. John R.
The Honorable Mr. Smith	Smith
The Honorable Dr. Smith	

The Honorable may also precede a woman's name:

The Honorable Jane R. Smith
The Honorable Mrs. Smith

However, if the woman's full name is given, a courtesy title should not be added. When an official and his wife are being addressed, his full name should be typed out.

The Honorable John R. Smith and Mrs. Smith	*or* The Honorable and Mrs. John R. Smith
	Dear Mr. and Mrs. Smith

The stylings "Hon. and Mrs. Smith" and "The Honorable and Mrs. Smith" should *never* be used. If, however, the official's full name is unknown, the styling is:

The Honorable Mr. Smith and Mrs. Smith

If a married woman holds the title and her husband does not, her name appears first on business-related correspondence addressed to both persons. However, if the couple is being addressed socially, the woman's title may be dropped unless she has retained her maiden name for use in personal as well as business correspondence.

business correspondence
The Honorable Harriet M. Johnson and Mr. Johnson	Dear Mrs. (*or* Governor, etc.) Johnson and Mr. Johnson

social correspondence
Mr. and Mrs. Robert Y. Johnson	Dear Mr. and Mrs. Johnson

business correspondence and maiden name retained
The Honorable Harriet A. Ott and Mr. Robert Y. Johnson	Dear Ms. Ott and Mr. Johnson

social correspondence
Ms. Harriet A. Ott Mr. Roger Y. Johnson	Dear Ms. Ott and Mr. Johnson

If space is limited, *The Honorable* may be typed on the first line of an address block, with the recipient's name on the next line.

The Honorable
John R. Smith
  and Mrs. Smith

When *The Honorable* occurs in a running text or in a list of names in such a text, the *T* in *The* is then lowercased.

A speech by the Honorable Charles H. Patterson, the American Consul in Athens

In informal writing such as newspaper articles, the plural forms *the Honorables* or *Hons.* may be used before a list of persons accorded the distinction. However, in official or formal writing either *the Honorable Messrs.* placed before the entire list of surnames or *the Honorable* or *Hon.* repeated before each full name in the list may be used.

formal
. . . was supported in the motion by the Honorable Messrs. Clarke, Goodfellow, Thomas, and Harrington.
. . . met with the Honorable Albert Y. Langley and the Honorable Frances P. Kelley.
informal
. . . interviewed the Hons. Jacob Y. Stathis, Samuel P. Kenton, William L. Williamson, and Gloria O. Yarnell—all United States Senators.

Jr. and Sr.

The designations *Jr.* and *Sr.* may or may not be preceded by a comma, depending on office policy or writer preference; however, one styling should be selected and adhered to for the sake of uniformity.

John K. Walker Jr.   *or*   John K. Walker, Jr.

Jr. and *Sr.* may be used in conjunction with courtesy titles, academic degree abbreviations, or professional rating abbreviations.

Mr. John K. Walker[,] Jr.	John K. Walker[,] Jr., Esq.
General John K. Walker[,] Jr.	John K. Walker[,] Jr., M.D.
The Honorable John K. Walker[,] Jr.	John K. Walker[,] Jr., C.A.M.

Madam and Madame

The title *Madam* should be used only in salutations of highly impersonal or high-level governmental and diplomatic correspondence. The title may be used to address women officials in other instances only if the writer is certain that the addressee is married. The French form *Madame* is recommended for salutations in correspondence addressed to foreign diplomats and heads of state. See Forms of Address Chart for examples.

Mesdames

The plural form of *Madam, Madame,* or *Mrs.* is *Mesdames,* which may be used before the names of two or more married women associated to-

gether in a professional partnership or in a business. It may appear with
their names on an envelope and in the inside address, and it may appear
with their names or standing alone in a salutation. (See also the Multiple
Addressees Chart, page 77.)

Mesdames T. V. Meade and P. A. Tate	Dear Mesdames Meade and Tate
Mesdames Meade and Tate	Mesdames
Mesdames V. T. and A. P. Stevens	Dear Mesdames Stevens
The Mesdames Stevens	Mesdames

Messrs.

The plural abbreviation of *Mr.* is *Messrs.* It is used before the surnames of
two or more men associated in a professional partnership or in a business.
Messrs. may appear on an envelope, in an inside address, and in a salutation when used in conjunction with the surnames of the addressees; however, this abbreviation should never stand alone.

Messrs. Archlake, Smythe, and Dabney	Dear Messrs. Archlake, Smythe, and Dabney
Attorneys-at-law	Gentlemen
Messrs. K. Y. and P. B. Overton	Dear Messrs. Overton
Architects	Gentlemen

Messrs. should never be used before a compound corporate name formed
from two surnames such as *Lord & Taylor* or *Woodward & Lothrup,* or from
a corporate name like *H. L. Jones and Sons.* For correct use of *Messrs. + The
Honorable* or *+ The Reverend,* see pages 81 and 84–85, respectively.

Misses

The plural form of *Miss* is *Misses,* and it may be used before the names of
two or more unmarried women who are being addressed together. It may
appear on an envelope, in an inside address, and in a salutation. Like
Messrs., Misses should never stand alone but must occur in conjunction
with a name or names. (For a complete set of examples in this category,
see the Multiple Addressees Chart, page 77.)

Misses Hay and Middleton	Dear Misses Hay and Middleton
Misses D. L. Hay and H. K. Middleton	Ladies
Misses Tara and Julia Smith	Dear Misses Smith
The Misses Smith	Ladies

Professor

If used only with a surname, *Professor* should be typed out in full; however, if used with a given name and initial or a set of initials as well as a
surname, it may be abbreviated to *Prof.* It is, therefore, usually abbrevi-

ated in envelope address blocks and in inside addresses, but typed out in salutations. *Professor* should not stand alone in a salutation.

Prof. Florence C. Marlowe	Dear Professor Marlowe
Department of English	Dear Dr. Marlowe
	Dear Miss Marlowe
	Mrs. Marlowe
	Ms. Marlowe
	but not
	Dear Professor

When addressing a letter to a professor and his wife, the title is usually written out in full unless the name is unusually long.

Professor and Mrs. Lee Dow	Dear Professor and Mrs. Dow
Prof. and Mrs. Henry Talbott- Smythe	Dear Professor and Mrs. Talbott- Smythe

Letters addressed to couples of whom the wife is the professor and the husband is not may follow one of these patterns:

business correspondence	
Professor Diana Goode and Mr. Goode	Dear Professor Goode and Mr. Goode
business or social correspondence	
Mr. and Mrs. Lawrence F. Goode	Dear Mr. and Mrs. Goode
if wife has retained her maiden name	
Professor Diana Falls Mr. Lawrence F. Goode	Dear Professor (*or* Ms.) Falls and Mr. Goode

When addressing two or more professors—male or female, whether having the same or different surnames—type *Professors* and not *"Profs."*:

Professors A. L. Smith and C. L. Doe	Dear Professors Smith and Doe Dear Drs. Smith and Doe Dear Mr. Smith and Mr. Doe Dear Messrs. Smith and Doe Gentlemen
Professors B. K. Johns and S. T. Yarrell	Dear Professors Johns and Yarrell Dear Drs. Johns and Yarrell Dear Ms. Johns and Mr. Yarrell
Professors G. A. and F. K. Cornett The Professors Cornett	*acceptable for any combination* Dear Professors Cornett Dear Drs. Cornett *if males* Gentlemen *if females* Ladies or Mesdames *if married* Dear Mr. and Mrs. Cornett Dear Professors Cornett Dear Drs. Cornett

Reverend

In formal or official writing, *The* should precede *Reverend;* however, *The Reverend* is often abbreviated to *The Rev.* or just *Rev.,* especially in unofficial or informal writing, and particularly in business correspondence where the problem of space on envelopes and in inside addresses is a factor. The typed-out full form *The Reverend* must be used in conjunction with the clergyman's full name, as in the following examples:

> The Reverend Philip D. Asquith
> The Reverend Dr. Philip D. Asquith
> The Reverend P. D. Asquith

The Reverend may appear with just a surname only if another courtesy rule intervenes:

> The Reverend Mr. Asquith
> The Reverend Professor Asquith
> The Reverend Dr. Asquith

The Reverend, The Rev., or *Rev.* should not be used in the salutation, although any one of these titles may be used on the envelope and in the inside address. In salutations, the following titles are acceptable for clergymen: *Mr.* (or *Ms., Miss, Mrs.*), *Father, Chaplain,* or *Dr.* See the Forms of Address Chart under the section entitled "Clerical and Religious Orders" for examples. The only exceptions to this rule are salutations in letters addressed to high prelates of a church (as bishops, monsignors, etc.). See the Forms of Address Chart. When addressing a letter to a clergyman and his wife, the typist should follow one of the following stylings:

> The Rev. and Mrs. P. D. Asquith
> The Rev. and Mrs. Philip D. Asquith
> The Reverend and Mrs. P. D. Asquith
> The Reverend and Mrs. Philip D. Asquith
> Dear Mr. (*or, if having a doctorate,* Dr.) and Mrs. Asquith
>   *but never*
> Rev. and Mrs. Asquith

Two clergymen having the same or different surnames should not be addressed in letters as "The Reverends" or "The Revs." or "Revs." They may, however, be addressed as *The Reverend* (or *The Rev.*) *Messrs.* or *The Reverend* (or *The Rev.*) *Drs.,* or the titles *The Reverend, The Rev.,* or *Rev.* may be repeated before each clergyman's name.

> The Reverend Messrs. S. J. and   The Rev. S. J. Smith and
>   D. V. Smith   The Rev. D. V. Smith
> The Rev. Messrs. S. J. and   Rev. S. J. Smith and
>   D. V. Smith   Rev. D. V. Smith
> The Reverend Messrs. Smith
> The Rev. Messrs. Smith

When writing to two or more clergymen having different surnames, the following patterns are acceptable:

The Reverend Messrs. P. A. Francis
  and F. L. Beale
The Rev. Messrs. P. A. Francis
  and F. L. Beale
The Rev. P. A. Francis
The Rev. F. L. Beale

In either situation, the following salutations are acceptable:

Gentlemen
Dear Mr. and Mrs. Smith
Dear Messrs. Smith
Dear Mr. Francis and Mrs. Beale
Dear Father Francis and Father Beale

In formal texts, "The Reverends," "The Revs.," and "Revs." are not acceptable as collective titles (as in lists of names). *The Reverend* (or *Rev.*) *Messrs.* (or *Drs.* or *Professors*) may be used, or *The Reverend* or *The Rev.* or *Rev.* may be repeated before each clergyman's name. If the term *clergyman* or the expression *the clergy* is mentioned in introducing the list, a single title *the Reverend* or *the Rev.* may be added before the list to serve all of the names. While it is true that "the Revs." is often seen in newspapers and in catalogs, this expression is still not recommended for formal, official writing.

... were the Reverend Messrs. Jones, Smith and Bennett, as well as ...
Among the clergymen present were the Reverend John G. Jones,
  Mr. Smith, and Dr. Doe.
Prayers were offered by the Rev. J. G. Jones, Rev. Mr. Smith,
  and Rev. Dr. Doe.

Second, Third

These designations after surnames may be styled as Roman numerals (I, III, IV) or as ordinals (2nd / 2d, 3rd / 3d, 4th). Such a designation may or may not be separated from a surname by a comma, depending on office policy or writer preference.

Mr. Jason T. Johnson III (*or* 3rd *or* 3d)
Mr. Jason T. Johnson, III (*or* 3rd *or* 3d)

Sequence of Abbreviations and Initials

The proper order of occurrence of initials representing academic degrees, religious orders, and professional ratings that may appear after a name and that are separated from each other by commas is as follows: (1) religious orders (as *S.J.*); (2) theological degrees (as *D.D.*); (3) academic degrees (as *Ph.D.*); (4) honorary degrees (as *Litt.D.*) (5) professional ratings (as *C.P.A.*).

Initials that represent academic degrees (with the exception of *M.D.*, *D.D.S.*, and other medical degrees) are not commonly used in addresses, and two or more sets of such letters appear even more rarely. Only when the initials represent achievements in different fields that are relevant to one's profession should more than one set be used. On the other hand, initials that represent earned professional achievements (such as *C.P.A., C.A.M., C.P.S.,* or *P.E.*) are often used in business addresses. When any of these sets of initials follow a name, however, the courtesy title *(Mr., Mrs., Ms., Miss, Dr.)* is omitted.

Nancy Robinson, P.L.S.
Mary R. Lopez, C.P.A.
John R. Doe, M.D., Ph.D.
Chief of Staff
Smithville Hospital

John R. Doe, J.D., C.M.C.
The Rev. John R. Doe, S.J., D.D.,
   LL.D.
Chaplain, Smithville College

Chapter 3

The Mechanics of Writing

CONTENTS

The English writing system uses certain conventional devices to help clarify the structure and meaning of words and sentences. Punctuation marks, capital letters, italics, and quotation marks are all mechanical devices employed in a variety of ways to help writers express their messages in an unambiguous way. The formation of plurals, possessives, and compounds and the treatment of abbreviations and numbers are aspects of the language in which these mechanical devices are frequently used and often in very specialized ways. This chapter is designed to help writers make effective use of the mechanical devices of the language to convey information in their letter writing.

Punctuation

Punctuation marks are used in the English writing system to help clarify the structure and meaning of sentences. They separate groups of words for meaning and emphasis; they convey an idea of the variations in pitch, volume, pauses, and intonation of the spoken language; and they help avoid contextual ambiguity. In many cases, the relationship between punctuation and grammatical structure is such that the choice of which mark of punctuation to use is clear and unambiguous. In other cases, however, the structure of a sentence may be such that it allows for several patterns of punctuation. In cases like these, varying notions of correctness have grown up, and two writers might, with equal correctness, punctuate the same sentence quite differently. In this section, in situations where more than one pattern of punctuation may be used, each is explained. If there are reasons to prefer one over another, the reasons are presented;

however, in many cases, using punctuation marks requires the exercise of individual judgment and taste.

This section focuses on general uses of punctuation marks. For detailed information about the punctuation of specific elements in a business letter, see Chapter 1, "Style in Business Correspondence," especially the section on General Punctuation Patterns in Business Correspondence, beginning on page 8.

Ampersand

The ampersand represents the word *and,* and its function is to replace the word when a shorter form is desirable. The ampersand is usually not used in regular text in correspondence; however, it is an acceptable substitute for *and* in some situations.

1. The ampersand is used in the names of companies but not in the names of agencies that are part of the federal government.

    > American Telephone & Telegraph Co.
    > Dow Jones & Company, Inc.
    > Occupational Safety and Health Administration
    > Securities and Exchange Commission

    NOTE: In styling corporate names, writers often try to reproduce the form of the name preferred by the company (taken from an annual report or company letterhead). However, this information may not be available and, even if it is available, can lead to apparent inconsistencies in the letter if several corporate names are used. If this is the case, choose one styling, preferably the one with the ampersand, and use it in all corporate names that include *and.*

2. When ampersands are used with abbreviations in general correspondence, spaces are often left around the ampersand. Writing which makes extensive use of abbreviations, such as technical writing, more commonly omits the spacing.

    > Such loans may be available at your bank or S & L.
    > The R&D budget looks adequate for the next fiscal year.

3. When an ampersand is used between the last two elements in a series, the comma is omitted.

    > the law firm of Shilliday, Fraser & French

Apostrophe

1. The apostrophe is used to indicate the possessive case of nouns and indefinite pronouns. For details regarding this use, see pages 150–153.

2. Apostrophes are sometimes used to form plurals of letters, numerals, abbreviations, symbols, and words referred to as words. For details regarding this use, see pages 146 and 149–150.

3. Apostrophes mark omissions in contractions made of two or more words that are pronounced as one word.

> didn't   you're   o'clock

4. The apostrophe is used to indicate that letters have been intentionally omitted from the spelling of a word in order to reproduce a perceived pronunciation or to give a highly informal flavor to a piece of writing.

> "Head back to N'Orleans," the man said.
> Get 'em while they're hot.
> dancin' till three

NOTE: Sometimes words are so consistently spelled with an apostrophe that the spelling with the apostrophe becomes an accepted variant.

> fo'c'sle for *forecastle*
> bos'n for *boatswain*
> rock 'n' roll for *rock and roll*

5. Apostrophes mark the omission of numerals.

> class of '88   politics in the '90s

NOTE: Writers who use the apostrophe for styling the plurals of words expressed in numerals usually avoid the use of the apostrophe illustrated in the second example above. Either they omit the apostrophe that stands for the missing figures, or they spell the word out.

> 80's *or* eighties *but not* '80's

6. Apostrophes are used to produce the inflected forms of verbs that are made of numerals or individually pronounced letters. Hyphens are sometimes used for this purpose also.

> 86'ed our proposal
> OK'ing the manuscripts

7. An apostrophe is often used to add an *-er* ending to an abbreviation, especially if some confusion might result from its absence. Hyphens are sometimes used for this purpose also. If no confusion is likely, the apostrophe is usually omitted.

> 4-H'er   AA'er   CBer   DXer

8. The use of apostrophes to form abbreviations (as *ass'n* for *association* or *sec'y* for *secretary*) is avoided in most formal writing.

Brackets

1. Brackets enclose editorial comments, corrections, clarifications, or other material inserted into a text, especially into quoted matter.

> This was the first time since it became law that the Twenty-first Amendment [outlining procedures for the replacement of a dead or incapacitated President or Vice President] had been invoked.

> He wrote, "I am just as cheerful as when you was [sic] here."

2. Brackets set off insertions that supply missing letters.

   "If you can't persuade D[israeli], I'm sure no one can."

3. Brackets enclose insertions that take the place of words or phrases that were used in the original version of a quoted passage.

   The report, entitled "A Decade of Progress," begins with a short message from President Stevens in which she notes that "the loving portraits and revealing accounts of [this report] are not intended to constitute a complete history of the decade.... Rather [they] impart the flavor of the events, developments, and achievements of this vibrant period."

4. Brackets enclose insertions that slightly alter the form of a word used in an original text.

   The magazine reported that thousands of the country's children were "go[ing] to bed hungry every night."

5. Brackets are used to indicate that the capitalization or typeface of the original passage has been altered in some way.

   As we point out later, "The length of a quotation usually determines whether it is run into the text or set as a block quotation.... [L]ength can be assessed in terms of number of words, the number of typewritten or typeset lines, or the number of sentences in the passage."

   They agreed with and were encouraged by her next point: "In the past, many secretaries have been placed in positions of responsibility *without being delegated enough authority to carry out the responsibility.*" [Italics added.]

   NOTE: The use of brackets to indicate altered capitalization is optional in most situations. It is required only in cases where meticulous handling of original source material is crucial.

6. Brackets function as parentheses within parentheses.

   The company was incinerating high concentrations of pollutants (such as polychlorinated biphenyls [PCBs]) in a power boiler.

7. Brackets are used in combination with parentheses to indicate units contained within larger units in mathematical copy. They are also used in chemical formulas.

   $$x + 5[(x+y)(2x-y)]$$ $$NH_4[Cr(NH_3)_2(SCN)_4] \cdot H_2O$$

8. No punctuation mark (other than a period after an abbreviation) precedes bracketed material within a sentence. If punctuation is required, the mark is placed after the closing bracket.

   The report stated, "If we fail to find additional sources of supply [of oil and gas], our long-term growth will be limited.

9. When brackets enclose a complete sentence, the required punctuation should be placed within the brackets.

   [The results of years of anti-inflation policies are slow growth, a slightly higher unemployment rate, and lower consumer prices.]

10. No space is left between brackets and the material they enclose or between brackets and any mark of punctuation immediately following. In typewritten material, two spaces precede an opening bracket and follow a closing bracket when the brackets enclose a complete sentence.

```
Judging from its economic statistics, the country could
stand a dose of reflation.  [The results of years of
anti-inflation policies are slow growth, a slightly
higher unemployment rate, and lower consumer prices.]
However, its people seem determined to stick with
austerity.
```

Colon

The colon is a mark of introduction. It indicates that what follows it—whether a cause, a phrase, or even a single word—is linked with some element that precedes it. For information on capitalizing the first word following a colon, see paragraphs 7 and 8 under Beginnings, page 126.

1. With phrases and clauses A colon introduces a clause or phrase that explains, illustrates, amplifies, or restates what has gone before.

The sentence was poorly constructed: it lacked both unity and coherence.

Throughout its history, the organization has combined a tradition of excellence with a dedication to human service: educating the young, caring for the elderly, assisting in community-development programs.

Disk cartridges provide high-density storage capacity: up to 16 megabytes of information on some cartridges.

Time was running out: a decision had to be made.

2. A colon directs attention to an appositive.

The question is this: where will we get the money?

He had only one pleasure: eating.

3. A colon is used to introduce a series. The introductory statement often includes a phrase such as *the following* or *as follows.*

The conference was attended by representatives of five nations: England, France, Belgium, Spain, and Portugal.

Anyone planning to participate should be prepared to do the following: spend all day in a conference session, discuss your company's role in the community, and participate in a conference evaluation.

NOTE: Opinion varies regarding whether a colon should interrupt the grammatical continuity of a clause (as by coming between a verb and its objects). Although many writers avoid this practice and use a full independent clause before the colon, the interrupting colon is common. It is especially likely to be used before a lengthy and complex list, in which case the colon serves to set the list distinctly apart from the normal flow of running text. With shorter or less complex lists, the colon is usually not used.

Our programs to increase profitability include: continued modernization of our manufacturing facilities; consolidation of distribution terminals; discontinuation of unprofitable retail outlets; and reorganization of our personnel structure, along with across-the-board staff reductions.

Our programs to increase profitability include plant modernization, improved distribution and retailing procedures, and staff reductions.

Our programs to increase profitability include the following: continued modernization of our manufacturing facilities; consolidation of distribution terminals; discontinuation of unprofitable retail outlets; and reorganization of our personnel structure, along with across-the-board staff reductions.

4. A colon is used like a dash to introduce a summary statement following a series.

Accounting, home computing, tax laws, investments: she discusses them all.

5. **With quotations** A colon introduces lengthy quoted material that is set off from the rest of a text by indentation but not by quotation marks.

Roy Gaines, executive director of Public Speaking Incorporated, has this to say about speaking to a group:

The best way to get jitters under control is to prepare thoroughly. Get some experience. Get up on stage a few times. Find out what your audience is interested in, know your subject backward and forward, and do research to brighten your talk with anecdotes, jokes, and examples.

Gaines adds that he often mulls over his own speeches late at night while walking the family dog.

6. A colon may be used before a quotation in running text, especially when (1) the quotation is lengthy, (2) the quotation is a formal statement or is being given special emphasis, or (3) the quotation is an appositive.

Said Murdoch: "The key to the success of this project is good planning. We need to know precisely all of the steps that we will need to go through, what kind of staff we will require to accomplish each step, what the entire project will cost, and when we can expect completion."

The inscription reads: "Here lies one whose name was writ in water."

In response, he had this to say: "No one knows better than I do that changes will have to be made soon."

7. **Other uses** A colon separates elements in page references, bibliographical and biblical citations, and fixed formulas used to express ratios and time.

Journal of the American Medical Association 48:356
Springfield, Mass.: Merriam-Webster Inc.
John 4:10
8:30 a.m.
a ratio of 3:5

8. A colon separates titles and subtitles (as of books).

The Great Cookie Jar: Taking the Mysteries Out of the Money System

9. A colon is used to join terms that are being contrasted or compared.

The budget shows an unfavorable difference in research : advertising dollars

10. A colon punctuates the salutation in a business letter using the mixed-punctuation pattern. For more on this use of the colon, see pages 19–20.

Dear Mrs. Wright: Dear Product Manager:
Dear Laurence: Ladies and Gentlemen:
                                     Dear Sir:

11. A colon punctuates memorandum and government correspondence headings and subject lines in general business letters. For more on this use of the colon, see pages 21–23.

TO: VIA:
SUBJECT: REFERENCE:

12. A colon separates writer/dictator/typist initials in the identification lines of business letters. For more on this use of the colon, see pages 33–34.

WAL:jml
WAL:WEB:jml

13. A colon separates carbon-copy or blind carbon-copy abbreviations from the initials or names of copy recipients in business letters. For more on this use of the colon, see pages 35–36.

cc:RSP
   JES
bcc:MWK
    FCM

14. With other marks of punctuation A colon is placed outside quotation marks and parentheses.

There's only one thing wrong with "Harold's Indiscretion": it's not funny.
I quote from the first edition of *Business English* (published in 1985):

15. Spacing In typewritten material, two spaces follow a colon used in running text, bibliographical references, publication titles, and letter or memorandum headings.

The answer is simple: don't go.
SUBJECT: Project X

16. No space precedes or follows a colon when it is used between numerals.

9:30 a.m.   a ratio of 2:4

17. No space precedes or follows a colon in a business-letter identification line or in a carbon-copy notation that indicates a recipient designated by initials. Two spaces follow a colon in a carbon-copy notation that indicates a recipient designated by a full name.

FCM:hg   cc:FCM

cc: Mr. Johnson

Comma

The comma is the most frequently used punctuation mark in the English writing system. Its most common uses are to separate items in a series and to set off syntactical elements within sentences. This section explains the most common aspects of the comma, listed under the following headings:

Between Main Clauses
With Compound Predicates
With Subordinate Clauses and
    Phrases
With Appositives
With Introductory and
    Interrupting Elements
With Contrasting Expressions
With Items in a Series
With Compound Modifiers

In Quotations, Questions, and
    Indirect Discourse
With Omitted Words
With Addresses, Dates, and
    Numbers
With Names, Degrees, and Titles
In Correspondence
Other Uses
With Other Marks of Punctuation

1. Between main clauses A comma separates main clauses joined by a co-ordinating conjunction (as *and, but, or, nor, for,* and sometimes *so* and *yet*). For use of commas with clauses joined by correlative conjunctions, see paragraph 24 below.

> She knew very little about him, and he volunteered nothing.
>
> We will not respond to any more questions on that topic this afternoon, nor will we respond to similar questions at any time in the future.
>
> His face showed disappointment, for he knew that he had failed.
>
> The acoustics in this hall are good, so every note is clear.
>
> We have requested this information many times before, yet we have never gotten a satisfactory reply.

2. When one or both of the clauses are short or when they are closely related in meaning, the comma is often omitted.

> We have tested the product and we are pleased.
>
> We hadn't realized it but none of the shipments were arriving on time.

NOTE: In punctuating sentences such as the ones illustrated above, writers have to use their own judgment regarding whether clauses are short enough or closely related enough to warrant omitting the comma. There are no clear-cut rules to follow; however, factors such as the rhythm, parallelism, or logic of the sentence often influence how clearly or smoothly it will read with or without the comma.

3. Commas are sometimes used to separate main clauses that are not joined by conjunctions. This styling is especially likely to be used if the clauses are short and feature obvious parallelism.

> One day you are a successful corporate lawyer, the next day you are out of work.

> The city has suffered terribly in the interim. Bombs have destroyed most of the buildings, disease has ravaged the population.

NOTE: Using a comma to join clauses that are neither short nor obviously parallel is usually called *comma fault* or *comma splice* and it is usually desirable to avoid such a construction. In general, clauses not joined by conjunctions are separated by semicolons.

4. If a sentence is composed of three or more clauses, the clauses may be separated by either commas or semicolons. Clauses that are short and relatively free of commas can be separated by commas even if they are not joined by a conjunction. If the clauses are long or heavily punctuated, they are separated with semicolons, except for the last two clauses which may be separated by either a comma or a semicolon. Usually a comma will be used between the last two clauses only if those clauses are joined by a conjunction. For more examples of clauses separated with commas and semicolons, see paragraph 5 under Semicolon in this section.

> The pace of change seems to have quickened, the economy is uncertain, the technology seems sometimes liberating and sometimes hostile.

> The policy is a complex one to explain; defending it against its critics is not easy, nor is it clear the defense is always necessary.

5. **With compound predicates** Commas are not usually used to separate the parts of a compound predicate.

> The chairman tried to explain the merger but failed to convince the stockholders.

NOTE: Many writers do use commas to separate the parts of a compound predicate. This is particularly true if the predicate is especially long and complicated, if one part of the predicate is being stressed, or if the absence of a comma could cause even a momentary misreading of the sentence.

> The board helps to develop the financing, new product planning, and marketing strategies for new corporate divisions, and issues periodic reports on expenditures, revenues, and personnel appointments.

> This is an unworkable plan, and has been from the start.

> I try to explain to him what I want him to do, and get nowhere.

6. **With subordinate clauses and phrases** Adverbial clauses and phrases that precede a main clause are usually set off with commas.

> Having made that decision, we turned our attention to other matters.

> To understand the situation, you must be familiar with the background.

> In 1980, the company had its first profitable year.
>
> In addition, staff members respond to queries, take new orders, and initiate billing.

7. If a sentence begins with an adverbial clause or phrase and can be easily read without a comma following it, the comma may be omitted. In most cases where the comma is omitted, the phrase will be short—four words or less. However, the comma can be omitted even after a longer phrase if the sentence can be easily read or seems more forceful that way.

> In January the company will introduce a new line of entirely redesigned products.
>
> If the project cannot be done profitably perhaps it should not be done at all.

8. Adverbial clauses and phrases that introduce a main clause other than the first main clause are usually set off with commas. However, if the adverbial clause or phrase follows a conjunction, two commas are usually used: one before the conjunction and one following the clause or phrase. In some cases three commas are used: one before the conjunction and two more to enclose the clause or phrase. Some writers use only one comma to separate the main clauses.

> His parents were against the match, and had the couple not eloped, their plans for marriage would have come to nothing.
>
> They have redecorated the entire store, but, to the delight of their customers, the store retains much of its original flavor.
>
> We haven't left Springfield yet, but when we get to Boston we'll call you.

9. A comma is not used after an introductory phrase if the phrase immediately precedes the main verb.

> On the filing cabinet lay a bulging portfolio.

10. Subordinate clauses and phrases that follow a main clause or that fall within a main clause are usually not set off by commas if they are restrictive. A clause or phrase is considered restrictive if its removal from the sentence would alter the meaning of the main clause. If the meaning of the main clause would not be altered by removing the subordinate clause or phrase, the clause or phrase is considered nonrestrictive and usually is set off by commas.

> We will be delighted if she decides to stay. [restrictive]
>
> Anyone who wants his or her copy of the book autographed by the author should get in line. [restrictive]
>
> Her new book, which was based on a true story, was well received. [nonrestrictive]
>
> That was a good meal, although I didn't particularly like the broccoli in cream sauce. [nonrestrictive]

11. Commas are used to set off an adverbial clause or phrase that falls between the subject and the verb.

    The weather, fluctuating from very hot to downright chilly, necessitated a variety of clothing.

12. Commas set off modifying phrases that do not immediately precede the word or phrase they modify.

    The hunters, tired and discouraged, headed back to camp.
    We could see the importance, both long-term and short-term, of her proposal.
    The director, burdened with a tight schedule, expanded her staff.

13. Absolute phrases are set off with commas, whether they fall at the beginning, middle, or end of the sentence.

    Our business being concluded, we adjourned for refreshments.
    I'm afraid of his reaction, his temper being what it is.

14. **With appositives** Commas are used to set off a word, phrase, or clause that is in apposition to a noun and that is nonrestrictive.

    The sales manager, Mr. Griffith, is in charge of the meeting.
    We were most impressed by the third candidate, the one who brought a writing sample and asked so many questions.

    NOTE: A nonrestrictive appositive sometimes precedes the word with which it is in apposition. It is set off by commas in this position also.

    A cherished landmark in the city, the Hotel Sandburg has managed once again to escape the wrecking ball.

15. Restrictive appositives are not set off by commas.

    Our account manager Andrea Timmons will be in touch with you.

16. **With introductory and interrupting elements** Commas set off transitional words and phrases (as *finally, meanwhile,* and *after all*).

    Indeed, close coordination between departments can minimize confusion during this period of expansion.
    We are eager to begin construction; however, the necessary materials have not yet arrived.
    The most recent report, on the other hand, makes clear why the management avoids such agreements.

    NOTE: When these words are not used to make a transition, no comma is necessary.

    The materials had finally arrived.

17. Commas set off parenthetical elements, such as authorial asides and supplementary information, that are closely related to the rest of the sentence.

All of us, to tell the truth, were completely amazed by his suggestion.

The president, now in his sixth year with the company, was responsible for the changes in the staff.

NOTE: When the parenthetical element is digressive or otherwise not closely related to the rest of the sentence, it is often set off by dashes or parentheses. For contrasting examples, see paragraph 2 under Dash and paragraph 1 under Parentheses in this section.

18. Commas are used to set off words or phrases that introduce examples or explanations.

He expects to visit three countries this summer, namely, France, Spain, and Germany.

I would like to develop a good, workable plan, i.e., one that would outline our goals and set a timetable for their accomplishment.

NOTE: Words and phrases such as *i.e., e.g., namely, for example,* and *that is* are often preceded by a dash, open parenthesis, or semicolon, depending on the magnitude of the break in continuity created by the examples or explanations. However, regardless of the punctuation that precedes the word or phrase, a comma always follows it. For contrasting examples of dashes, parentheses, and semicolons with these words and phrases, see paragraph 5 under Dash, paragraph 2 under Parentheses, and paragraph 6 under Semicolon in this section.

19. Commas are used to set off words in direct address.

We would like to discuss your account, Mrs. Reid.

The answer, my friends, lies within us.

20. Commas set off mild interjections or exclamations such as *ah* or *oh.*

Ah, weekends—they don't come often enough.

Oh, it was quite a meeting.

21. With contrasting expressions A comma is used to set off contrasting expressions within a sentence.

This project will take six months, not six weeks.

22. Style varies regarding use of the comma to set off two or more contrasting phrases used to describe a single word that follows immediately. Some writers put a comma after the first modifier but not between the final modifier and the word modified. Other writers, who treat the contrasting phrase as a nonrestrictive modifier, put a comma both before and after the phrase.

The harsh, although eminently realistic critique is not going to make you popular.

The harsh, although eminently realistic, critique is not going to make you popular.

This street takes you away from, not toward the capitol building.

This street takes you away from, not toward, the capitol building.

23. Adjectives and adverbs that modify the same word or phrase and that are joined by *but* or some other coordinating conjunction are not separated by a comma.

> a bicycle with a light but sturdy frame
> a multicolored but subdued carpet
> errors caused by working carelessly or too quickly

24. A comma does not usually separate elements that are contrasted through the use of a pair of correlative conjunctions (as *either . . . or, neither . . . nor,* and *not only . . . but also*).

> The cost is either $69.95 or $79.95.
> Neither my secretary nor I noticed the error.
> He was given the post not only because of his diplomatic connections but also because of his great tact and charm.

NOTE: Correlative conjunctions are sometimes used to join main clauses. If the clauses are short, a comma is not added. If the clauses are long, a comma usually separates them.

> Either you do it my way or we don't do it at all.
> Not only did she have to see three salesmen and a visiting reporter during the course of the day, but she also had to prepare for the next day's meeting with the president.

25. Long parallel contrasting and comparing clauses are separated by commas; short parallel phrases are not.

> The more I hear about this new computer, the greater is my desire to obtain one for my office.
> "The sooner the better," I said.

26. With items in a series Words, phrases, and clauses joined in a series are separated by commas. If main clauses are joined in a series, they may be separated by either semicolons or commas. For more on the use of commas and semicolons to separate main clauses, see paragraphs 1, 3, and 4 above and paragraph 5 under Semicolon in this section.

> Pens, pencils, and erasers crowded the drawer.
> Her job required her to pack quickly, to travel often, and to have no personal life.
> He responded patiently while reporters shouted questions, flashbulbs popped, and the crowd pushed closer.

NOTE: Practice varies regarding the use of the comma between the last two items in a series if those items are also joined by a conjunction. In some cases, as in the example below, omitting the final comma (often called the serial comma) can result in ambiguity. Some writers feel that in most sentences the use of the conjunction makes the comma superfluous, and they favor using the comma only when a misreading could result from omitting it. Others feel that it is easier to include the final comma routinely rather than try to consider each sentence separately to decide whether a misreading is possible without the comma. Most reference books, including this one, and most other book-length works of nonfiction use the serial comma. In most other kinds of writing, however, practice is evenly or nearly evenly divided on the use or omission of this comma.

> We are looking for a house with a big yard, a view of the harbor, and beach and docking privileges. [with serial comma]
> We are looking for a house with a big yard, a view of the harbor and beach and docking privileges. [without serial comma]

27. A comma is not used to separate items in a series that are joined with conjunctions.

> I don't understand what this policy covers or doesn't cover or only partially covers.
> I have talked to the president and the vice president and three other executives.

28. When the elements in a series are long or complex or consist of clauses that themselves contain commas, the elements are usually separated by semicolons, not commas. For more on this use of the semicolon, see paragraphs 7 and 8 under Semicolon in this section.

29. **With compound modifiers** A comma is used to separate two or more adjectives, adverbs, or phrases that modify the same word or phrase. For the use of commas with contrasting modifiers, see paragraphs 22 and 23 above.

> She wrote in a polished, professional style.
> The office was lit with a hard, flickering light.

30. A comma is not used between two adjectives when the first modifies the combination of the second adjective plus the word or phrase it modifies.

> a little brown jug
> a small brick building

31. A comma is not used to separate an adverb from the adjective or adverb that it modifies.

> a truly distinctive manner
> running very quickly down the street

32. **In quotations, questions, and indirect discourse** A comma separates a direct quotation from a phrase identifying its source or speaker. If the quotation is a question or an exclamation and the identifying phrase follows the quotation, the comma is replaced by a question mark or an exclamation point.

> Mary said, "I am leaving."
> "I am leaving," Mary said.

Mary asked, "Where are you going?"

"Where are you going?" Mary asked.

"I am leaving," Mary said, "even if you want me to stay."

"Don't do that!" Mary shouted.

NOTE: In some cases, a colon can replace a comma preceding a quotation. For more on this use of the colon, see paragraph 6 under Colon in this section.

33. A comma does not set off a quotation that is an integral part of the sentence in which it appears.

Throughout the session his only responses were "No comment" and "I don't think so."

Just because he said he was "about to leave this minute" doesn't mean he actually left.

34. Practice varies regarding the use of commas to set off shorter sentences that fall within longer sentences and that do not constitute actual dialogue. These shorter sentences may be mottoes or maxims, unspoken or imaginary dialogue, or sentences referred to as sentences; and they may or may not be enclosed in quotation marks. (For more on the use of quotation marks with sentences like these, see paragraph 6 under Quotation Marks. Double, in this section.) Typically the shorter sentence functions as a subject, object, or complement within the larger sentence and does not require a comma. Sometimes the structure of the larger sentence will be styled like actual quoted dialogue, and in such cases a comma is used to separate the shorter sentence from the text that introduces or identifies it. In some cases, where quotation marks are not used, a comma may be inserted simply to mark the beginning of the shorter sentence clearly.

"The computer is down" was the response she dreaded.

He spoke with a candor that seemed to insist, This actually happened to me and in just this way.

The first rule is, When in doubt, spell it out.

When the shorter sentence functions as an appositive in the larger sentence, it is set off with a comma when nonrestrictive and not when restrictive. (For more on restrictive modifiers and appositives, see paragraphs 10, 14, and 15 above.)

He was fond of the slogan "Every man a king, but no man wears a crown."

We had the club's motto, "We make waves," printed on our T-shirts.

35. A comma introduces a direct question regardless of whether it is enclosed in quotation marks or if its first word is capitalized.

I wondered, what is going on here?

The question is, How do we get out of this situation?

36. The comma is omitted before quotations that are very short exclamations or representations of sounds.

> He jumped up suddenly and cried "Yow!"
> When she was done, she let out a loud "Whew!"

37. A comma is not used to set off indirect discourse or indirect questions introduced by a conjunction (such as *that* or *what*).

> Mary said that she was leaving.
> I wondered what was going on there.
> The clerk told me that the book I had ordered had just come in.

38. With omitted words A comma indicates the omission of a word or phrase, especially in parallel constructions where the omitted word or phrase appears earlier in the sentence.

> Common stocks are preferred by some investors; bonds, by others.

39. A comma often replaces the conjunction *that*.

> The road was so steep, we thought surely we would go over the edge.
> The problem is, we don't know how to fix it.

40. With addresses, dates, and numbers A comma is used to set off the individual elements of an address except for zip codes. In current practice, no punctuation appears between a state name and the zip code that follows it. If prepositions are used between the elements of the address, commas are not needed.

> Mrs. Bryant may be reached at 52 Kiowa Circle, Mesa, Arizona.
> Mr. Briscoe was born in Liverpool, England.
> The collection will be displayed at the Wilmington, Delaware, Museum of Art.
> Write to the Bureau of the Census, Washington, DC 20233.
> The White House is located at 1600 Pennsylvania Avenue in Washington, D.C.

NOTE: Some writers omit the comma that follows the name of a state when no other element of an address follows it. This is most likely to happen when a city name and state name are being used in combination to modify a noun that follows; however, retaining this comma is still the more common practice.

> We visited their Enid, Oklahoma plant.
> *but more commonly*
> We visited their Enid, Oklahoma, plant.

41. Commas are used to set off the year from the day of the month. When only the month and the year are given, the comma is usually omitted.

> On October 26, 1947, the newly hired employees began work on the project.

In December, 1903, the Wright brothers finally succeeded in keeping an airplane aloft for a few seconds.

42. A comma groups numerals into units of three to separate thousands, millions, and so on; however, this comma is generally not used in page numbers, street numbers, or numbers within dates. For more on the styling of numbers, see the section on Numbers, beginning on page 175.

a population of 350,000   the year 1986
4509 South Pleasant Street   page 1419

43. With names, degrees, and titles A comma punctuates an inverted name.

Sagan, Deborah J.

44. A comma is usually used between a surname and *Junior, Senior,* or their abbreviations.

Morton A. Williams, Jr.   Douglas Fairbanks, Senior

45. A comma is often used to set off the word *Incorporated* or the abbreviation *Inc.* from the rest of a corporate name; however, many companies elect to omit this comma from their names.

Leedy Manufacturing Company, Incorporated
Tektronics, Inc.
Merz-Fortunata Inc.

46. A comma separates a surname from a following academic, honorary, military, or religious degree or title.

Amelia P. Artandi, D.V.M.   Robert Menard, M.A., Ph.D.
John L. Farber, Esq.   Admiral Herman Washington, USN
Sister Mary Catherine, S.C.

47. In correspondence The comma follows the salutation in informal correspondence and follows the complimentary close in both informal and formal correspondence. In formal correspondence, a colon follows the salutation. For more on this use of the colon, see paragraph 12 under Colon in this section.

Dear Rachel,   Affectionately,   Very truly yours,

48. Other uses The comma is used to avoid ambiguity when the juxtaposition of two words or expressions could cause confusion.

Whatever will be, will be.
To John, Marshall was someone special.
I repaired the lamp that my brother had broken, and replaced the bulb.

49. A comma often follows a direct object or a predicate nominative or predicate adjective when they precede the subject and verb in the sentence. If the meaning of the sentence is clear without this comma, it is often omitted.

> That we would soon have to raise prices, no one disputed.
>
> Critical about the current state of affairs, we might have been.
>
> A disaster it certainly was.

50. With other marks of punctuation Commas are used in conjunction with brackets, ellipsis points, parentheses, and quotation marks. Commas are not used in conjunction with colons, dashes, exclamation points, question marks, or semicolons. If one of these latter marks falls at the same point in a sentence at which a comma would fall, the comma is dropped and the other mark is retained. For more on the use of commas with other marks of punctuation, see the subheading With Other Marks of Punctuation under the heading for those marks of punctuation.

Dash

The dash can function like a comma, a colon, or a pair of parentheses. Like commas and parentheses, dashes set off parenthetic material such as examples; supplemental facts; or appositional, explanatory, or descriptive phrases. Like colons, dashes introduce clauses that explain or expand upon some element of the material that precedes them. The dash is sometimes considered to be a less formal equivalent of the colon and parenthesis, and it does frequently take their place in advertising and other informal contexts. However, dashes may be found in all kinds of writing, including the most formal, and the choice of which mark to use is usually a matter of personal preference.

The dash exists in a number of different lengths. The dash in most general use is the em dash, which is approximately the width of an uppercase M in typeset material. In typewritten material, it is represented by two hyphens. The en dash and the two- and three-em dashes have more limited uses which are explained in paragraphs 13–15 below.

1. **Abrupt change or suspension** The dash marks an abrupt change or break in the structure of a sentence.

   > The board of directors seem happy with the change, but the shareholders—there is the problem.

2. A dash is used to indicate interrupted speech or a speaker's confusion or hesitation.

   > "The next point I'd like to bring up—" the speaker started to say, "I'm sorry. I'll have to stop you there," the moderator broke in.
   >
   > "Yes," he went on, "yes—that is—I guess I agree."

3. **Parenthetic and amplifying elements** Dashes are used in place of other punctuation (such as commas or parentheses) to emphasize parenthetic or amplifying material or to make such material stand out more clearly from the rest of the sentence.

Mail your subscription—now!

In 1976, they asked for—and received—substantial grants from the federal government.

The privately owned consulting firm—formerly known as Aborjaily and Associates—is now offering many new services.

NOTE: When dashes are used to set off parenthetic elements, they often indicate that the material is more digressive than elements set off with commas but less digressive than elements set off by parentheses. For contrasting examples see paragraph 17 under Comma and paragraph 1 under Parentheses in this section.

4. Dashes are used to set off or to introduce defining and enumerating phrases.

The fund sought to acquire controlling positions—a minimum of 25% of outstanding voting securities—in other companies.

The essay dealt with our problems with waste—cans, bottles, discarded tires, and other trash.

5. A dash is often used in place of a colon or semicolon to link clauses, especially when the clause that follows the dash explains, summarizes, or expands upon the clause that precedes it.

The test results were surprisingly good—none of the tested models displayed serious problems.

6. A dash or a pair of dashes often sets off parenthetic or amplifying material introduced by such phrases as *for example, namely, that is, e.g., and i.e.*

After some discussion the motion was tabled—that is, it was removed indefinitely from the board's consideration.

Sports develop two valuable traits—namely, self-control and the ability to make quick decisions.

Not all "prime" windows—i.e., the ones installed when a house is built—are equal in quality.

NOTE: Commas, parentheses, and semicolons are often used for the same purpose. For contrasting examples, see paragraph 18 under Comma, paragraph 2 under Parentheses, and paragraph 6 under Semicolon in this section.

7. A dash introduces a summary statement that follows a series of words or phrases.

Unemployment, strikes, inflation, stock prices, mortgage rates—all are part of the economy.

Once into bankruptcy, the company would have to pay cash for its supplies, defer maintenance, and lay off workers—moves that could threaten its long-term profitability.

8. **With other marks of punctuation** If a dash appears at a point in a sentence where a comma could also appear, the dash is retained and the comma is dropped.

If we don't succeed—and the critics say we won't—then the whole project is in jeopardy.

Our lawyer has read the transcript—all 1200 pages of it—and he has decided that an appeal would not be useful.

Some of the other departments, however—particularly Accounting, Sales, and Credit Collection—have expanded their computer operations.

9. If the second of a pair of dashes appears at a point in a sentence where a period or semicolon would also appear, the period or semicolon is retained and the dash is dropped.

His conduct has always been exemplary—near-perfect attendance, excellent productivity, a good attitude; nevertheless, his termination cannot be avoided.

10. Dashes are used with exclamation points and question marks. When a pair of dashes sets off parenthetic material calling for either of these marks of punctuation, the exclamation point or the question mark is placed inside the second dash. If the parenthetic material falls at the end of a sentence ending with an exclamation point or question mark, the closing dash is not required.

His hobby was getting on people's nerves—especially mine!—and he was extremely good at it.

When the committee meets next week—are you going to be there?—I will present all of the final figures.

Is there any way to predict the future course of this case—one which we really cannot afford to lose?

11. Dashes and parentheses are used in combination to indicate parenthetic material appearing within parenthetic material. Dashes within parentheses and parentheses within dashes are used with about equal frequency.

We were looking for a narrator (or narrators—sometimes a script calls for more than one) who could handle a variety of assignments.

On our trip south we crossed a number of major rivers—the Hudson, the Delaware, and the Patapsco (which flows through Baltimore)—without paying a single toll.

NOTE: If the inner parenthetic element begins with a dash and its closing dash would fall in the same position as the closing parenthesis, the closing dash is omitted and the parenthesis is retained, as in the first example above. If the inner element begins with a parenthesis and its closing parenthesis would coincide with the closing dash, the closing parenthesis and the closing dash are both retained, as in the second example above.

12. En dash En dashes appear only in typeset material, not in typewritten material, and therefore they do not often appear in business correspondence. As a point of information, however, the en dash is shorter than the em dash but slightly longer than the hyphen. Its most frequent uses include as a replacement for a hyphen following a prefix that is added to an open compound, as an equivalent to "(up) to and including" when used between numbers, dates, or other notations to indicate range, as a replacement for the word *to* between capitalized names, and to indicate linkages, such as boundaries, treaties, or oppositions. In all of these uses, a hyphen can be used in typewritten material.

pre–Civil War architecture	1988–89
the New York–Connecticut area	pages 128–34
Washington–Moscow diplomacy	8:30 a.m.–4:30 p.m.

13. **Long dashes** A two-em dash is used to indicate missing letters in a word and, less frequently, to indicate a missing word. A two-em dash is represented in typewritten material by four hyphens.

> Mr. P—— of Baltimore
> That's b——t and you know it.

14. A three-em dash indicates that a word has been left out or that an unknown word or figure is to be supplied. A three-em dash is represented in typewritten material by six hyphens.

> The study was carried out in ———, a fast-growing Sunbelt city.
> We'll leave New York City on the ——— of August.

15. **Spacing** Practice varies as to spacing around the dash. Some publications and some typists insert a space before and after a dash, others do not. Either practice is acceptable.

Ellipsis Points

Ellipsis points is the name most often given to periods when they are used, usually in groups of three, to signal an omission from quoted material or to indicate a pause or trailing off of speech. Other names for periods used in this way include *ellipses, points of ellipsis,* and *suspension points.* Ellipsis points are often used in conjunction with other marks of punctuation, including periods used to mark the ends of sentences. When ellipsis points are used in this way with a terminal period, the omission is sometimes thought of as being marked by four periods. Most of the conventions described in this section are illustrated with quoted material enclosed in quotation marks. However, the conventions are equally applicable to quoted material set as extracts.

NOTE: The examples given below present passages in which ellipsis points indicate omission of material. In most cases, the full text from which these omissions have been made is some portion of the headnote above.

1. Ellipsis points indicate the omission of one or more words within a quoted sentence.

> One book said, "Other names . . . include *ellipses, points of ellipsis,* and *suspension points.*"

2. Ellipsis points are usually not used to indicate the omission of words that precede the quoted portion. However, practice varies on this point, and in some formal contexts, especially those in which the quotation is introduced by a colon, ellipsis points are used.

> The book maintained that "the omission is sometimes thought of as being marked by four periods."
>
> The book maintained: ". . . the omission is sometimes thought of as being marked by four periods."

3. Punctuation used in the original that falls on either side of the ellipsis points is often omitted; however, it may be retained, especially if such retention helps clarify the sentence.

> According to the book, "*Ellipsis points* is the name most often given to periods when they are used . . . to signal an omission from quoted material or to indicate a pause or trailing off of speech."
>
> According to the book, "When ellipsis points are used in this way. . . , the omission is sometimes thought of as being marked by four periods."
>
> According to the book, "*Ellipsis points* is the name most often given to periods when they are used, usually in groups of three, . . . to indicate a pause or trailing off of speech."

4. If an omission comprises an entire sentence within a passage, the last part of a sentence within a passage, or the first part of a sentence other than the first quoted sentence, the end punctuation preceding or following the omission is retained and is followed by three periods.

> That book says, "Other names for periods used in this way include *ellipses, points of ellipsis,* and *suspension points.* . . . When ellipsis points are used in this way with a terminal period, the omission is sometimes thought of as being marked by four periods."
>
> That book says, "*Ellipsis points* is the name given to periods when they are used, usually in groups of three, to signal an omission from quoted material. . . . Other names for periods used in this way include *ellipses, points of ellipsis,* and *suspension points.*"
>
> That book says, "Ellipsis points are often used in conjunction with other marks of punctuation, including periods used to mark ends of sentences. . . . The omission is sometimes thought of as being marked by four periods."

NOTE: The capitalization of the word *The* in the third example is acceptable. When the opening words of a quotation act as a sentence within the quotation, the first word is capitalized, even if that word did not begin a sentence in the original version.

5. If the last words of a quoted sentence are omitted and if the original sentence ends with a period, that period is retained and three ellipsis points follow. However, if the original sentence ends with punctuation

other than a period, the end punctuation often follows the ellipsis points, especially if it helps clarify the quotation.

> Their book said, "Ellipsis points are often used in conjunction with other marks of punctuation. . . ."
>
> He always ends his harangues with some variation on the question, "What could you have been thinking when you . . . ?"

NOTE: Many writers and editors, especially those writing in more informal contexts, choose to ignore the styling considerations presented in paragraphs 4 and 5. They use instead an alternative system in which all omissions are indicated by three periods and all terminal periods that may precede or follow an omission are dropped.

6. Ellipsis points are used to indicate that a quoted sentence has been intentionally left unfinished. In situations such as this the terminal period is not included.

> Read the statement beginning "*Ellipsis points* is the name most often given . . ." and then proceed to the numbered paragraphs.

7. Ellipsis points are used to indicate faltering speech, especially if the faltering involves a long pause between words or a sentence that trails off or is left intentionally unfinished. In these kinds of sentences most writers treat the ellipsis points as terminal punctuation, thus removing the need for any other punctuation; however, practice does vary on this point, and some writers routinely use other punctuation in conjunction with ellipsis points.

> The speaker seemed uncertain how to answer the question. "Well, that's true . . . but even so . . . I think we can do better."
>
> "Despite these uncertainties, we believe we can do it, but . . ."
>
> "I mean . . ." he said, "like . . . How?"

8. Ellipsis points are sometimes used as a stylistic device to catch and hold a reader's attention.

> They think that nothing can go wrong . . . but it does.

9. Each ellipsis point is set off from other ellipsis points, from adjacent punctuation (except for quotation marks, which are closed up to the ellipsis points), and from surrounding text by a space. If a terminal period is used with ellipsis points, it precedes them with no space before it and one space after it.

Exclamation Point

The exclamation point is used to mark a forceful comment. Heavy use can weaken its effect, so it should be used sparingly.

1. An exclamation point can punctuate a sentence, phrase, or interjection.

This is the fourth time in a row he's been late!

No one that I talked to—not even the accounting department!—seemed to know how the figures were calculated.

Ah, those sales figures!

2. The exclamation point replaces the question mark when an ironic or emphatic tone is more important than the actual question.

   Aren't you finished yet!
   Do you realize what you've done!
   Why me!

3. Occasionally the exclamation point is used with a question mark to indicate a very forceful question.

   How much did you say?!
   You did what!?

4. The exclamation point is enclosed within brackets, dashes, parentheses, and quotation marks when it punctuates the material so enclosed rather than the sentence as a whole. It should be placed outside them when it punctuates the entire sentence.

   All of this proves—at long last!—that we were right from the start.
   The dog got the gate open (for the third time!) and ran into the street.
   He shouted, "Wait!" and sprinted toward the train.
   The correct word is "mousse," not "moose"!

5. Exclamatory phrases that occur within a sentence are set off by dashes or parentheses.

   And now our competition—get this!—wants to start sharing secrets.
   The board accepted most of the recommendations, but ours (alas!) was not even considered.

6. If an exclamation point falls at a place in a sentence where a comma or a terminal period could also go, the comma or period is dropped and the exclamation point is retained.

   "Absolutely not!" he snapped.
   She has written about sixty pages so far—and with no help!

   NOTE: If the exclamation point is part of a title, as of a play, book, or movie, it may be followed by a comma. If the title falls at the end of a sentence, the terminal period is usually dropped.

   Marshall and Susan went to see the musical *Oklahoma!*, and they enjoyed it very much.
   They enjoyed seeing the muscial *Oklahoma!*

7. In typewritten material, two spaces follow an exclamation point that ends a sentence. If the exclamation point is followed by a closing bracket, closing parenthesis, or closing quotation marks, the two

spaces follow the second mark. In typeset material, only one space follows the exclamation point.

```
The time is now!  Decide what you are going to do.
She said, "The time is now!"  That meant we had to
decide what to do.
```

The time is now! Decide what you are going to do.

She said, "The time is now!" That meant we had to decide what to do.

Hyphen

1. Hyphens are used to link elements in compound words. For more on the styling of compound words, see the section on Compounds, beginning on page 153.

2. A hyphen marks an end-of-line division of a word when part of the word is to be carried down to the next line.

We visited several showrooms, looked at the prices (it wasn't a pleasant experience; prices in this area have not gone down), and asked all the questions we could think of.

3. A hyphen divides letters or syllables to give the effect of stuttering, sobbing, or halting speech.

S-s-sammy   ah-ah-ah   y-y-es

4. Hyphens indicate a word spelled out letter by letter.

p-r-o-b-a-t-i-o-n

5. A hyphen indicates that a word element is a prefix, suffix, or medial element.

anti-   -ship   -o-

6. A hyphen is used in typewritten material as an equivalent to the phrase "(up) to and including" when placed between numbers and dates. (In typeset material this hyphen is very often replaced by an en dash. For more on the use of the en dash, see paragraph 13 under Dash in this section.)

35-40 years   ages 10-15   1988-89

7. Hyphens are sometimes used to produce inflected forms of verbs that are made of individually pronounced letters or to add an -er ending to an abbreviation; however, apostrophes are more commonly used for this purpose. For more on these uses of the apostrophe, see paragraphs 6 and 7 under Apostrophe in this section.

D.H.-ing for the White Sox   a loyal AA-er

Parentheses

Parentheses enclose supplementary elements that are inserted into a main statement but that are not intended to be part of the statement. For some of the cases described below, especially those listed under the heading "Parenthetic Elements," commas and dashes are frequently used instead of parentheses. (For contrasting examples, see paragraph 17 under Comma and paragraph 2 under Dash in this section.) In general, commas tend to be used when the inserted material is closely related, logically or grammatically, to the main clause; parentheses are more often used when the inserted material is incidental or digressive.

1. **Parenthetic elements** Parentheses enclose phrases and clauses that provide examples, explanations, or supplementary facts. Supplementary numerical data may also be enclosed in parentheses.

> Nominations for the association's principal officers (president, vice president, treasurer, and secretary) were heard and approved at the last meeting.

> Although we liked the applicant (her background, training, and experience were excellent), we weren't ready to hire anyone at that point.

> The company shows good earnings ($3.45 a share vs. $3.05 last year), a strong balance sheet, and a good current yield (7.8%).

2. Parentheses enclose phrases and clauses introduced by expressions such as *namely, that is, e.g.,* and *i.e.* Commas, dashes, and semicolons are also used to perform this function. (For contrasting examples, see paragraph 18 under Comma, paragraph 5 under Dash, and paragraph 6 under Semicolon in this section.)

> In writing to the manufacturer, be as specific as possible (i.e., list the missing or defective parts, describe the nature of the malfunction, and provide the name and address of the store where the unit was purchased).

3. Parentheses set off definitions or translations in the main part of a sentence.

> The company sold off all of its retail outlets and announced plans to sell off its houseware (small appliance) business as well.

> The hotel was located just a few blocks from San Antonio's famous Paseo del Rio (river walk).

4. Parentheses enclose abbreviations synonymous with spelled forms and occurring after those forms, or they may enclose the spelled form occurring after the abbreviation.

> She referred to a ruling by the Federal Communications Commission (FCC).

> They were involved with a study regarding the manufacture and disposal of PVC (polyvinyl chloride).

5. Parentheses often set off cross-references.

> Telephone ordering service is also provided (refer to the list of stores at the end of this catalog).

> The diagram (Fig. 3) illustrates the action of the pump.

6. Parentheses enclose Arabic numerals that confirm a spelled-out number in a general text or in a legal document.

Delivery will be made in thirty (30) days.

The fee for our services is Four Thousand Dollars ($4,000.00), payable to UNCO, Inc.

7. Parentheses enclose the name of a city or state that is inserted into a proper name for identification.

the Norristown (Pa.) State Hospital
the *Tulsa* (Okla.) *Tribune*

8. Some writers use parentheses to set off personal asides.

It was largely as a result of this conference that the committee was formed (its subsequent growth in influence is another story).

9. Parentheses are used to set off quotations, either attributed or unattributed, that illustrate or support a statement made in the main text.

After he had had a few brushes with the police, his stepfather had him sent to jail as an incorrigible ("It will do him good").

10. Other uses Parentheses enclose unpunctuated numbers or letters separating and heading individual elements or items in a series within running text.

We must set forth (1) our long-term goals, (2) our immediate objectives, and (3) the means at our disposal.

11. Parentheses indicate alternative terms.

Please sign and return the enclosed form(s).

12. Parentheses are used in combination with numbers for several other purposes, such as setting off area codes in telephone numbers and indicating losses in accounting.

(413) 256-7899

Operating Profits (in millions)	
Cosmetics	26.2
Food products	47.7
Food services	54.3
Transportation	(17.7)
Sporting goods	(11.2)
Total	99.3

13. With other marks of punctuation If a parenthetic expression is an independent sentence, its first word is capitalized and a period is placed *inside* the last parenthesis. On the other hand, a parenthetic expression that occurs within a sentence—even if it could stand alone as a separate sentence—does not end with a period. It may, however, end with an exclamation point, a question mark, a period after an abbreviation, or a set of quotation marks. A parenthetic expression within a sentence does not require capitalization unless it is a quoted sentence.

> The discussion was held in the boardroom. (The results are still confidential.)
>
> Although several trade organizations worked actively against the legislation (there were at least three paid lobbyists working on Capitol Hill at any one time), the bill passed easily.
>
> After waiting in line for an hour (why do we do these things?), we finally left.
>
> The conference was held in Vancouver (that's in B.C.).
>
> He was totally confused ("What can we do?") and refused to see anyone.

14. If a parenthetic expression within a sentence is composed of two independent clauses, capitalization and periods are avoided. To separate the clauses within the parentheses, semicolons are usually used. If the parenthetic expression occurs outside of a sentence, normal patterns of capitalization and punctuation prevail.

> We visited several showrooms, looked at the prices (it wasn't a pleasant experience; prices in this area have not gone down), and asked all the questions we could think of.
>
> We visited several showrooms and looked at the prices. (It wasn't a pleasant experience. Prices in this area have not gone down.) If salespeople were available, we asked all of the questions we could think of.

15. No punctuation mark (other than a period after an abbreviation) is placed before parenthetic material within a sentence; if a break is required, the punctuation is placed after the final parenthesis.

> I'll get back to you tomorrow (Friday), when I have more details.

16. Parentheses sometimes appear within parentheses, although the usual practice is to replace the inner pair of parentheses with a pair of brackets. (For an example of brackets within parentheses, see paragraph 6 under Brackets in this section.)

> Checks must be drawn in U.S. dollars, (PLEASE NOTE: In accordance with U.S. Department of Treasury regulations, we cannot accept checks drawn on Canadian banks for amounts less than four U.S. dollars ($4.00). The same regulation applies to Canadian money orders.)

17. Dashes and parentheses are often used together to set off parenthetic material within a larger parenthetic element. For details and examples, see paragraph 11 under Dash in this section.

18. **Spacing** In typewritten material a parenthetic expression that is an independent sentence is followed by two spaces. In typeset material, the sentence is followed by one space. In typewritten or typeset material, a parenthetic expression that falls within a sentence is followed by one space.

```
We visited several showrooms and looked at the prices.
(It wasn't a pleasant experience.  Prices in this area
have not done down.)  We asked all the questions we
could think of.
```

We visited several showrooms and looked at the prices. (It wasn't a pleasant experience. Prices in this area have not gone down.) We asked all the questions we could think of.

Period

1. A period terminates a sentence or a sentence fragment that is neither interrogative nor exclamatory.

    Write the letter.
    They wrote the required letters.
    Total chaos. Nothing works.

2. A period punctuates some abbreviations. For more on the punctuation of abbreviations, see the section on Abbreviations, beginning on page 165.

a.k.a.	Assn.	Dr.	Jr.	Ph.D.
fig.	in.	No.	e.g.	ibid.
N.W.	U.S.	Inc.	Co.	Corp.

3. A period is used with an individual's initials. If all of the person's initials are used instead of the name, however, the unspaced initials may be written without periods.

    F. Scott Fitzgerald   Susan B. Anthony
    F.D.R. *or* FDR   T. S. Eliot

4. A period follows Roman and Arabic numerals and also letters when they are used without parentheses in outlines and vertical enumerations.

    I. Objectives
        A. Economy
            1. Low initial cost
            2. Low maintenance cost
        B. Ease of operation
    Required skills are:
        1. Shorthand
        2. Typing
        3. Transcription

5. A period is placed within quotation marks even when it does not punctuate the quoted material.

    The charismatic leader was known to his followers as "the guiding light."
    "I said I wanted to fire him," Henry went on, "but she said, 'I don't think you have the contractual privilege to do that.' "

6. When brackets or parentheses enclose a sentence that is independent of surrounding sentences, the period is placed inside the closing parenthesis or bracket. However, when brackets or parentheses enclose a sentence that is part of a surrounding sentence, the period for the enclosed sentence is omitted.

> On Friday the government ordered a 24-hour curfew and told all journalists and photographers to leave the area. (Authorities later confiscated the film of those who did not comply.)
>
> I took a good look at her (she was standing quite close to me at the time).

7. In typewritten material, two spaces follow a period that ends a sentence. If the period is followed by a closing bracket, closing parenthesis, or quotation marks, the two spaces follow the second mark.

```
Here is the car.  Do you want to get in?
He said, "Here is the car."  I asked if I should get
in.
```

8. One space follows a period that comes after an initial in a name. If a name is composed entirely of initials, no space is required; however, the usual styling for such names is to omit the periods.

> Mr. H. C. Matthews   F.D.R. *or* FDR

9. No space follows an internal period within a punctuated abbreviation.

> f.o.b.   i.e.   Ph.D.   A.D.   p.m.

Question Mark

1. The question mark terminates a direct question.

> What went wrong?
>
> "Who signed the memo?" she asked.

NOTE: The intent of the writer, not the word order of the sentence, determines whether or not the sentence is a question. Polite requests that are worded as questions, for instance, usually take periods, because they are not really questions. Similarly, sentences whose word order is that of a statement but whose force is interrogatory are punctuated with question marks.

> Will you please sit down.
>
> He did that?

2. The question mark terminates an interrogative element that is part of a sentence. An indirect question is not followed by a question mark.

> How did she do it? was the question on everybody's mind.
>
> She wondered, will it work?
>
> She wondered whether it would work.

3. The question mark punctuates each element of an interrogative series that is neither numbered nor lettered. When an interrogative series is numbered or lettered, only one question mark is used, and it is placed at the end of the series.

> Can you give us a reasonable forecast? back up your predictions? compare them with last year's earnings?
>
> Can you (1) give us a reasonable forecast, (2) back up your predictions, (3) compare them with last year's earnings?

4. The question mark indicates uncertainty about a fact.

> Susan O'Hara, advertising vice president(?) of the corporation

5. The question mark is placed inside a closing bracket, dash, parenthesis, or pair of quotation marks when it punctuates only the material enclosed by that mark and not the sentence as a whole. It is placed outside that mark when it punctuates the entire sentence.

> What did Andrew mean when he called the project "a fiasco from the start"?
>
> I had a vacation in 1975 (was it really that long ago?), but I haven't had time for one since.
>
> He asked, "Do you realize the extent of the problem [the housing shortage]?"

6. In typewritten material, two spaces follow a question mark that ends a sentence. If the question mark is followed by a closing bracket, closing parenthesis, or quotation marks, the two spaces follow the second mark. In typeset material, only one space follows the question mark.

> She wondered, will it work? He said he thought it would.
>
> She asked, "Will it work?" He said he thought it would.
>
> She wondered, will it work? He said he thought it would.

7. One space follows a question mark that falls within a sentence.

> Are you coming today? tomorrow? the day after?

Quotation Marks, Double

The following paragraphs describe the use of quotation marks to enclose quoted matter in regular text, to set off translations of words, or to enclose single letters within sentences. For the use of the quotation marks to enclose titles of poems, paintings, or other works, see the section on Capitals, Italics, and Quotation Marks, beginning on page 125.

1. Basic uses Quotation marks enclose direct quotations but not indirect quotations.

> She said, "I am leaving."
>
> "I am leaving," she said, "and I'm not coming back."
>
> "I am leaving," she said, "This has gone on long enough."
>
> She said that she was leaving.

2. Quotation marks enclose fragments of quoted matter when they are reproduced exactly as originally stated.

> The agreement makes it clear that he "will be paid only upon receipt of an acceptable manuscript."
>
> As late as 1754, documents refer to him as "yeoman" and "husbandman."

3. Quotation marks enclose words or phrases borrowed from others, words used in a special way, or words of marked informality when they are introduced into formal writing.

> That kind of corporation is referred to as "closed" or "privately held."
>
> Be sure to send a copy of your résumé, or as some folks would say, your "biodata summary."
>
> They were afraid the patient had "stroked out"—had had a cerebrovascular accident.

4. Quotation marks are sometimes used to enclose words referred to as words. Italic type or underlining is also frequently used for this purpose. For more on this use of italics, see paragraph 4 under Other Uses of Italics, pages 144–145.

> He went through the manuscript and changed every "he" to "she."

5. Quotation marks enclose short exclamations or representations of sounds. Representations of sounds are also frequently set in italic type or underlined. For more on this use of italics, see paragraph 7 under Other Uses of Italics, page 145.

> "Ssshh!" she hissed.
>
> They never say anything crude like "shaddap."

6. Quotation marks enclose short sentences that fall within longer sentences, especially when the shorter sentence is meant to suggest spoken dialogue. Kinds of sentences that may be treated in this way include mottoes and maxims, unspoken or imaginary dialogue, or sentences referred to as sentences.

> Throughout the camp, the spirit was "We can do."
>
> She never could get used to his "That's the way it goes" attitude.
>
> In effect, the voters were saying "You blew it, and you don't get another chance."
>
> Their attitude could only be described as "Kill the messenger."
>
> Another example of a palindrome is "Madam, I'm Adam."

NOTE: Style varies regarding the punctuation of sentences such as these. In general, the force of the quotation marks is to set the shorter sentence off more distinctly from the surrounding sentence and to give the shorter sentence more of the feel of spoken dialogue; omitting the quotation marks diminishes the effect. (For a description of the use of commas in sentences like these, see paragraphs 33 and 34 under Comma in this section.)

The first rule is, When in doubt, spell it out.

They weren't happy with the impression she left: "Don't expect favors, because I don't have to give them."

7. Quotation marks are not used to enclose paraphrases.

> Build a better mouse trap, Emerson says, and the world will beat a path to your door.

8. Direct questions are usually not enclosed in quotation marks unless they represent quoted dialogue.

> The question is, What went wrong?
> As we listened to him, we couldn't help wondering, Where's the plan?
> She asked, "What went wrong?"

NOTE: As in the sentences presented in paragraph 6 above, style varies regarding the use of quotation marks with direct questions; and in many cases, writers will include the quotation marks.

> As we listened to him, we couldn't help wondering, "Where's the plan?"

9. Quotation marks are used to enclose translations of foreign or borrowed terms.

> The term *sesquipedalian* comes from the Latin word *sesquipedalis*, meaning "a foot and a half long."
> While in Texas, he encountered the armadillo ("little armored one") and developed quite an interest in it.

10. Quotation marks are sometimes used to enclose single letters within a sentence.

> The letter "m" is wider than the letter "i."
> Put an "x" in the right spot.
> The metal rod was shaped into a "V."

NOTE: Practice varies on this point. Letters referred to as letters are commonly set in italic type or underlined. (For more on this use of italics, see paragraphs 4 and 5 under Other Uses of Italics, pages 144–145.) Letters often appear in the same typeface as the surrounding text if no confusion would result from the styling.

> a V-shaped blade
> He was happy to get a B in the course.
> How many e's are in her name?

11. **With other marks of punctuation** When quotation marks follow a word in a sentence that is also followed by a period or comma, the period or comma is placed within the quotation marks.

> He said, "I am leaving."
> Her camera was described as "waterproof," but "moisture-resistant" would have been a better description.

NOTE: Some writers draw a distinction between periods and commas that belong logically to the quoted material and those that belong to the whole sentence. If the period or comma belongs to the quoted material, they place it inside the quotation marks; if the period belongs logically to the sentence that surrounds the quoted matter, they place it outside the quotation marks. This distinction was previously observed in a wide range of publications, including U.S. Congressional publications and Merriam-Webster® dictionaries. In current practice, the distinction is made by relatively few writers, although the distinction is routinely made for dashes, exclamation points, and question marks used with quotation marks, as described in paragraph 13 below.

> The package was labeled "Handle with Care".
>
> The act was referred to as the "Army-Navy Medical Services Corps Act of 1947".
>
> Her camera was described as "waterproof", but "moisture-resistant" would have been a better description.
>
> He said, "I am leaving."

12. When quotation marks follow a word in a sentence that is also followed by a colon or semicolon, the colon or semicolon is placed outside the quotation marks.

> There was only one thing to do when he said, "I may not run": promise him a larger campaign contribution.
>
> She spoke of her "little cottage in the country"; she might better have called it a mansion.

13. The dash, question mark, and exclamation point are placed inside quotation marks when they punctuate the quoted matter only. They are placed outside the quotation marks when they punctuate the whole sentence.

> He asked, "When did she leave?"
>
> What is the meaning of "the open door"?
>
> Save us from his "mercy"!
>
> "I can't see how—" he started to say.
>
> He thought he knew where he was going—he remembered her saying, "Take two lefts, then stay to the right"—but the streets didn't look familiar.

14. **Spacing** One space follows a quotation mark that is followed by the rest of a sentence.

> "I am leaving," she said.

15. In typewritten material, two spaces follow a quotation mark that ends a sentence. In typeset material one space follows.

> ```
> He said, "Here is the car."  I asked if I should get
> in.
> ```
>
> He said, "Here is the car," I asked if I should get in.

Quotation Marks, Single

1. Single quotation marks enclose a quotation within a quotation in American (but not British) practice.

   > The witness said, "I distinctly heard him say, 'Don't be late,' and then I heard the door close."

   > The witness said, "I distinctly heard him say, 'Don't be late.' "

   NOTE: When both single and double quotation marks occur at the end of a sentence, the period typically falls *within* both sets of marks.

2. Single quotation marks are sometimes used in place of double quotation marks especially in British usage.

   > The witness said, 'I distinctly heard him say, "Don't be late," and then I heard the door close.'

3. On rare occasions, authors face the question of how to style a quotation within a quotation within a quotation. Standard styling practice would be to enclose the innermost quotation in double marks; however, this construction can be confusing, and in many cases rewriting the sentence can remove the need for it.

   > The witness said, "I distinctly heard him say, 'Don't you say "Shut up" to me.' "

   > The witness said that she distinctly heard him say, "Don't you say 'Shut up' to me."

Semicolon

The semicolon is used in ways that are similar to those in which periods and commas are used. Like a period, the semicolon marks the end of a complete clause, but it also signals that the clause that follows it is closely related to the one that precedes it. The semicolon is also used to distinguish major sentence divisions from the minor pauses that are represented by commas.

1. **Between clauses** A semicolon separates independent clauses that are joined together in one sentence without a coordinating conjunction.

   > Some people are natural leaders in their willingness to accept responsibility and delegate authority with intelligence; others do not measure up.

   > He hemmed and hawed for an hour or more; he couldn't make up his mind.

2. Ordinarily a comma separates main clauses joined with a coordinating conjunction. However, if the sentence might be confusing with a comma in this position, a semicolon is used in its place. Potentially confusing sentences include those with other commas in them or with particularly long clauses.

   > We fear that this situation may, in fact, occur; but we don't know when.

   > In a society that seeks to promote social goals, government will play a powerful role; and taxation, once simply a means of raising money, becomes, in addition, a way of furthering those goals.

As recently as 1978 the company felt the operation could be a successful one that would generate significant profits in several different markets; but in 1981 the management changed its mind and began a program of shutting down plants and reducing its product line.

3. A semicolon joins two statements when the grammatical construction of the second clause is elliptical and depends on that of the first.

In many cases the conference sessions, which were designed to allow for full discussions of topics, were much too long and tedious; the breaks between them, much too short.

4. A semicolon joins two clauses when the seond begins with a conjunctive adverb, as *accordingly, also, besides, consequently, furthermore, hence, however, indeed, likewise, moreover, namely, nevertheless, otherwise, still, then, therefore,* and *thus.* Phrases such as *by the same token, in that case, as a result, on the other hand,* and *all the same* can also act as conjunctive adverbs.

Most people are covered by insurance of one kind or another; indeed, many people don't even see their medical bills.

It won't be easy to sort out the facts of this confusing situation; however, a decision must be made.

The case could take years to work its way through the court system; as a result, many plaintiffs will accept out-of-court settlements.

NOTE: Practice varies regarding the treatment of clauses introduced by *so* and *yet.* Although many writers continue to treat *so* and *yet* as adverbs, it has become standard to treat these words as coordinating conjunctions that join clauses. In this treatment, a comma precedes *so* and *yet* and no punctuation follows them. (For examples, see paragraph 1 under Comma in this section.)

5. When three or more clauses are separated by semicolons, a coordinating conjunction may or may not precede the final clause. If a coordinating conjunction does precede the final clause, the final semicolon is often replaced with a comma. (For the use of commas to separate three or more clauses without conjunctions, see paragraph 4 under Comma in this section.)

Their report was one-sided and partial; it did not reflect the facts; it distorted them.

They don't understand; they grow bored; and they stop learning.

The report recounted events leading up to the incident; it included observations of eyewitnesses, but it drew no conclusions.

NOTE: The choices of whether to use a conjunction and whether to use a semicolon or comma with the conjunction are matters of personal preference. In general, the force of the semicolon is to make the transition to the final clause more abrupt, which often serves to place more emphasis on that clause. The comma and conjunction ease the transition and make the sentence seem less choppy.

6. With phrases and clauses introduced by *for example, i.e.,* **etc.** A semicolon is sometimes used before expressions (as *for example, for instance, that is, namely, e.g.,* or *i.e.*) that introduce expansions or series. Commas, dashes, and parentheses are also used in sentences like these. For contrasting examples, see paragraph 18 under Comma, paragraph 5 under Dash, and paragraph 2 under Parentheses in this section.

> On one point only did everyone agree; namely, that too much money had been spent already.

> We were fairly successful on that project; that is, we made our deadlines and met our budget.

> Most of the contestants had traveled great distances to participate; for example, three had come from Australia, one from Japan, and two from China.

7. In a series A semicolon is used in place of a comma to separate phrases in a series when the phrases themselves contain commas. A comma may replace the semicolon before the last item in a series if the last item is introduced with a conjunction.

> The visitor to Barndale was offered three sources of overnight accommodation: The Rose and Anchor, which housed Barndale's oldest pub; The Crawford, an American-style luxury hotel; and Ellen's Bed and Breakfast on Peabody Lane.

> The schedule calls for orientation and planning sessions in the morning; talks on marketing, long-term investments and tax laws directly after lunch, and an introduction to computer terminology in the late afternoon.

8. When the individual items in an enumeration or series are long or are sentences themselves, they are usually separated by semicolons.

> Among the committee's recommendations were the following: more hospital beds in urban areas where there are waiting lists for elective surgery; smaller staff size in half-empty rural hospitals; review procedures for all major purchases.

9. A semicolon separates items in a list in cases where a comma alone would not clearly separate the items or references.

> (Friedlander 1957; Ballas 1962)
> (Genesis 3:1–19; 4:1–16)

10. With other marks of punctuation A semicolon is placed outside quotation marks and parentheses.

> They referred to each other as "Mother" and "Father"; they were the archetypal happily married elderly couple.

> She accepted the situation with every appearance of equanimity (but with some inward qualms); however, all of that changed the next day.

Virgule

The virgule is known by many names, including *diagonal, solidus, oblique, slant, slash,* and *slash mark.* Most commonly, the virgule is used to represent a word that is not written out or to separate or set off certain adjacent elements of text.

1. **In place of missing words** A virgule represents the word *per* or *to* when used with units of measure or when used to indicate the terms of a ratio.

40,000 tons/year	9 ft./sec.	a 50/50 split
14 gm/100 cc	price/earnings ratio	risk/reward tradeoff

2. A virgule separates alternatives. In this context, the virgule usually represents the words *or* or *and/or*.

alumni/ae	introductory/refresher courses
his/her	oral/written tests

3. A virgule replaces the word *and* in some compound terms.

molybdenum/vanadium steel
in the May/June issue
1973/74
in the Falls Church/McLean, Va., area
an innovative classroom/laboratory

4. A virgule is used, although less commonly, to replace a number of prepositions, such as *at, versus, with,* and *for.*

U.C./Berkeley	parent/child issues
table/mirror	Vice President/Editorial

5. **With abbreviations** A virgule punctuates some abbreviations.

c/o	A/V	d/b/a
A/R	A/1C	S/Sgt
w/	V/STOL	

NOTE: In some cases the virgule may stand for a word that is not represented in the abbreviation (e.g., *in* in *W/O*, the abreviation for *water in oil*).

6. **To separate elements** The virgule is used in a number of different ways to separate groups of numbers, such as elements in a date, numerators and denominators in fractions, and area codes in telephone numbers. For more on the use of virgules with numbers, see the section on Numbers, beginning on page 175.

7. The virgule serves as a divider between lines of poetry that are run in with the text around them. This method of quoting poetry is usually limited to passages of no more than three or four lines. Longer passages are usually set off from the text as extract quotations.

> When Samuel Taylor Coleridge wrote in "Christabel" that "'Tis a month before the month of May,/And the Spring comes slowly up this way," he could have been describing New England.

8. Spacing In general, no space is used between the virgule and the words, letters, or figures separated by it; however, some writers do prefer to place spaces around a virgule used to separate lines of poetry.

Capitals, Italics, and Quotation Marks

Words and phrases are capitalized, italicized or underlined, or enclosed in quotation marks in order to indicate that they have a special significance in a particular context. The section that follows is divided into four parts that describe the kinds of contexts in which capitals, italics, and quotation marks are used. The first part explains the use of capitalized words to begin sentences and phrases. The second explains the use of capitals, italics, and quotation marks to indicate that a word or phrase is a proper noun, pronoun, or adjective. The third and fourth parts explain other uses of capital letters and italics. For other uses of quotation marks, see pages 117–121.

Beginnings

1. The first word of a sentence or sentence fragment is capitalized.

> The meeting was postponed.
> No! I cannot do it.
> Will you go?
> Total chaos. Nothing works.

2. The first word of a sentence contained within parentheses is capitalized. However, a parenthetical sentence occurring inside another sentence is not capitalized unless it is a complete quoted sentence.

> The discussion was held in the boardroom. (The results are still confidential.)
> Although we liked the services they could provide (their banquet facilities were especially good), we could not afford to go there often.
> After waiting in line for an hour (why do we do these things?), we finally left.
> He was totally demoralized ("There is just nothing we can do") and was contemplating resignation.

3. The first word of a direct quotation is capitalized. However, if the quotation is interrupted in midsentence, the second part does not begin with a capital.

> The President said, "We have rejected this report entirely."
> "We have rejected this report entirely," the President said, "and we will not comment on it further."

4. When a quotation, whether a sentence fragment or a complete sentence, is syntactically dependent on the sentence in which it occurs, the quotation does not begin with a capital.

> The President made it clear that "there is no room for compromise."

5. The first word of a sentence within a sentence is usually capitalized. Examples of sentences within sentences include mottoes and rules, unspoken or imaginary dialogue, sentences referred to as sentences, and direct questions. For an explanation of the use of commas and quotation marks with sentences such as these, see paragraphs 34 and 35 under Comma, page 101, and paragraph 6 under Quotation Marks, Double, pages 118–119.

> You know the saying, "Honesty is the best policy."
> The first rule is, When in doubt, spell it out.
> The clear message coming back from the audience was "We don't care."
> My question is, When can we go?
> She kept wondering, how did they get here so soon?

6. The first word of a line of poetry is usually capitalized.

> The best lack all conviction, while the worst
> Are full of passionate intensity.
> —W. B. Yeats

7. The first word following a colon may be either lowercased or capitalized if it introduces a complete sentence. While the former is the usual styling, the latter is also quite common, especially when the sentence introduced by the colon is fairly lengthy and distinctly separate from the preceding clause.

> The advantage of this particular system is clear: it's inexpensive.
> The situation is critical: This company cannot hope to recoup the fourth-quarter losses that were sustained in five operating divisions.

8. If a colon introduces a series of sentences, the first word of each sentence is capitalized.

> Consider the following steps that we have taken: A subcommittee has been formed to evaluate our past performance and to report its findings to the full organization. New sources of revenue are being explored, and relevant organizations are being contacted. And several candidates have been interviewed for the new post of executive director.

9. The first words of run-in enumerations that form complete sentences are capitalized, as are the first words of phrasal lists and enumerations arranged vertically beneath running texts. Phrasal enumerations run in with the introductory text, however, are lowercased.

> Do the following tasks at the end of the day: 1. Clean your typewriter. 2. Clear your desktop of papers. 3. Cover office machines. 4. Straighten the contents of your desk drawers, cabinets, and bookcases.

This is the agenda:
   Call to order
   Roll call
   Minutes of the previous meeting
   Treasurer's report
On the agenda will be (1) call to order, (2) roll call, (3) minutes of the previous meeting, (4) treasurer's report . . .

10. The introductory words *Whereas* and *Resolved* are capitalized in minutes and legislation, as is the word *That* or an alternative word or expression which immediately follows either.

Resolved, That . . .
Whereas, Substantial benefits . . .

11. The first word in an outline heading is capitalized.

  I. Editorial tasks
 II. Production responsibilities
    A. Cost estimates
    B. Bids

12. The first word of the salutation of a letter and the first word of a complimentary close are capitalized.

Dear Mary,	Dear Sir or Madam:	Ladies and Gentlemen:
Gentlemen:	Sincerely yours,	Very truly yours,

13. The first word and each subsequent major word following a SUBJECT or TO heading (as in a memorandum) are capitalized.

SUBJECT: Pension Plans
TO: All Department Heads and Editors

Proper Nouns, Pronouns, and Adjectives

The following paragraphs describe the ways in which a broad range of proper nouns, pronouns, and adjectives are styled—with capitals, italics, quotation marks, or some combination of these devices. In almost all cases, proper nouns, pronouns, and adjectives are capitalized. In many cases, proper nouns are italicized (or underlined in typewritten material) or enclosed in quotation marks in addition to being capitalized. No clear distinctions can be drawn between the kinds of words that are capitalized and italicized, capitalized and enclosed in quotation marks, or simply capitalized, as styling on these points is governed almost wholly by tradition.

The paragraphs that follow are grouped under the following alphabetically arranged headings:

Abbreviations	Derivatives of Proper	Historical Periods
Abstractions and	Names	and Events
Personifications	Geographical and	Hyphenated Compounds
Academic Degrees	Topographical	Legal Material
Animals and Plants	References	Medical Terms
Awards, Honors, and	Governmental, Judicial,	Military Terms
Prizes	and Political Bodies	Numerical Designations

Organizations	Religious Terms	Titles
People	Scientific Terms	Trademarks
Pronouns	Time Periods and Zones	Transportation

1. **Abbreviations** Abbreviated forms of proper nouns and adjectives are capitalized, just as the spelled-out forms would be. For more on the capitalization of abbreviations, see the section on Abbreviations, beginning on page 165.

Dec. for *December*   Wed. for *Wednesday*
Col. for *Colonel*   Brit. for *British*

2. **Abstractions and personifications** Abstract terms, such as names of concepts or qualities, are usually not capitalized unless the concept or quality is being presented as if it were a person. If the term is simply being used in conjunction with other words that allude to human characteristics or qualities, it is usually not capitalized. For more on the capitalization of abstract terms, see paragraph 2 under Other Uses of Capitals, page 143.

a time when Peace walked among us

as Autumn paints each leaf in fiery colors

an economy gripped by inflation

hoping that fate would lend a hand

3. Fictitious names used as personifications are capitalized.

Uncle Sam   Ma Bell   John Bull   Jack Frost
Big Oil squirmed under the new regulations.

4. **Academic degrees** The names of academic degrees are capitalized when they follow a person's name. The names of specific academic degrees not following a person's name are capitalized or not capitalized according to individual preference. General terms referring to degrees, such as *doctorate, master's degree*, or *bachelor's* are not capitalized. Abbreviations for academic degrees are always capitalized.

Martin Bonkowski, Doctor of Divinity
earned her Doctor of Laws degree *or* earned her doctor of laws degree
working for a bachelor's degree
Susan Wycliff, M.S.W.
received her Ph.D.

5. **Animals and plants** The common names of animals and plants are not capitalized unless they contain a proper noun as a separate element, in which case the proper noun is capitalized, but any element of the name following the proper noun is lowercased. Elements of the name preceding the proper noun are usually but not always capitalized. In some cases, the common name of the plant or animal contains a word that was once a proper noun but is no longer thought of as such. In

these cases, the word is usually not capitalized. When in doubt, consult a dictionary. (For an explanation of the capitalization of genus names in binomial nomenclature or of New Latin names for groups above genera in zoology and botany, see paragraphs 67 and 68 below.)

cocker spaniel	lily of the valley	ponderosa pine
great white shark	Hampshire hog	Kentucky bluegrass
Steller's jay	Bengal tiger	Japanese beetle
Rhode Island red	Great Dane	Brown Swiss
black-eyed Susan	wandering Jew	holstein

NOTE: In references to specific breeds, as distinguished from the animals that belong to the breed, all elements of the name are capitalized.

Gordon Setter	Rhode Island Red	Holstein

6. **Awards, honors, and prizes** Names of awards, honors, and prizes are capitalized. Descriptive words and phrases that are not actually part of the award's name are lowercased. (For an explanation of capitalizing the names of military decorations, see paragraph 44 below.)

Academy Award	Emmy
Nobel Prize	Nobel Prize in medicine
Nobel Prize winner	Nobel Peace Prize
Rhodes Scholarship	Rhodes scholar
New York Drama Critics' Circle Award	

7. **Derivatives of proper names** Derivatives of proper names are capitalized when they are used in their primary sense. However, if the derived term has taken on a specialized meaning, it is usually not capitalized.

Roman architecture	Victorian customs	Keynesian economics
an Americanism	an Egyptologist	french fries
manila envelope	pasteurized milk	a quixotic undertaking

8. **Geographical and topographical references** Terms that identify divisions of the earth's surface and distinct areas, regions, places, or districts are capitalized, as are derivative nouns and adjectives.

Chicago, Illinois	the Great Plains
the Middle Eastern situation	the Mariana Trench
the Southwest	the Riviera

9. Popular names of localities are capitalized.

the Big Apple	the Loop	Hell's Kitchen
the Village	the Twin Cities	the Valley

10. Compass points are capitalized when they refer to a geographical region or when they are part of a street name. They are lowercased when they refer to a simple direction.

back East	West Columbus Avenue
out West	down South
east of the Mississippi	traveling north on I-91

11. Nouns and adjectives that are derived from compass points and that designate or refer to a specific geographical region are usually capitalized.

a Southern accent	a Western crop
Northerners	part of the Eastern establishment

12. Words designating global, national, regional, or local political divisions are capitalized when they are essential elements of specific names. However, they are usually lowercased when they precede a proper name or when they are not part of a specific name.

the British Empire	New York City
Washington State	Ward 1
Hampden County	Ohio's Ninth Congressional District
the fall of the empire	the city of New York
the state of Washington	fires in three wards
the county of Hampden	carried her district

   NOTE: In legal documents, these words are often capitalized regardless of position.

the State of Washington	the County of Hampden	the City of New York

13. Generic geographical terms (as *lake, mountain, river, valley*) are capitalized if they are part of a specific proper name.

Crater Lake	Lake Como	Rocky Mountains
the Columbia River	Ohio Valley	Long Island
Great Barrier Reef	Atlantic Ocean	Niagara Falls
Hudson Bay	Strait of Gibraltar	Bering Strait

14. Generic geographical terms preceding names are usually capitalized.

Lakes Mead and Powell	Mounts Whitney and Shasta

   NOTE: When *the* precedes the generic term, the generic term is lowercased.

   the river Thames

15. Generic geographical terms that are not used as part of a proper name are not capitalized. These include plural generic geographical terms that follow two or more proper names and generic terms that are used descriptively or alone.

the Himalaya and Andes mountains	the Missouri and Platte rivers
the Atlantic coast of Labrador	the Arizona desert
the river valley	the Caribbean islands

16. The names of streets, monuments, parks, landmarks, well-known buildings, and other public places are capitalized. However, generic terms that are part of these names (as *avenue, bridge,* or *tower*) are lowercased when they occur after multiple names or are used alone (but see paragraph 17 below.)

Golden Gate Bridge	The Capitol	Rock Creek Park
Eddystone Lighthouse	the Dorset Hotel	Fanueil Hall
the San Diego Zoo	Coit Tower	the Mall
the Pyramids	the Statue of Liberty	Peachtree Street

the Dorset and Drake hotels   Fifth and Park avenues
on the bridge   walking through the park

17. Well-known informal or shortened forms of place names are capitalized.

the Avenue for *Fifth Avenue*
the Street for *Wall Street*
the Exchange for the *New York Stock Exchange*

18. Governmental, judicial, and political bodies Full names of legislative, deliberative, executive, and administrative bodies are capitalized, as are easily recognizable short forms of these names. However, nonspecific noun and adjective references to them are usually lowercased.

United States Congress	the Federal Reserve Board
the Congress	the House
the Federal Bureau of Investigation	the Fed
congressional hearings	a federal agency

NOTE: Practice varies regarding the capitalization of words such as *department, committee,* or *agency* when they are being used in place of the full name of a specific body. They are most often capitalized when the department or agency is referring to itself in print. In most other cases, these words are lowercased.

The Connecticut Department of Transportation is pleased to offer this new booklet on traffic safety. The Department hopes that it will be of use to all drivers.

We received a new booklet from the Connecticut Department of Transportation. This is the second pamphlet the department has issued this month.

19. The U.S. Supreme Court and the short forms *Supreme Court* and *Court* referring to it are capitalized.

The Supreme Court of the United States
the United States Supreme Court
the Supreme Court
the Court

20. Official and full names of higher courts and names of international courts are capitalized. Short forms of official higher court names are often capitalized in legal documents but lowercased in general writing.

The International Court of Arbitration
the United States Court of Appeals for the Second Circuit
the Virginia Supreme Court
the Court of Queen's Bench
a ruling by the court of appeals
the state supreme court

21. Names of city and county courts are usually lowercased.

the Lawton municipal court   police court
the Owensville night court   the county court
small claims court   juvenile court

22. The single designation *court,* when specifically applicable to a judge or a presiding officer, is capitalized.

It is the opinion of this Court that . . .
The Court found that . . .

23. The terms *federal* and *national* are capitalized only when they are essential elements of a name or title.

Federal Trade Commission   National Security Council
federal court   national security

24. The word *administration* is capitalized by some writers when it refers to the administration of a specific United States president. However, the word is more commonly lowercased in this situation. If the word does not refer to a specific presidential administration, it is not capitalized except when it is a part of an official name of a government agency.

the Truman administration   *or*   the Truman Administration
the administration   *or*   the Administration
the Farmers Home Loan Administration
The running of the White House varies considerably from one administration to another.

25. Names of political organizations and their adherents are capitalized, but the word *party* may or may not be capitalized, depending on the writer's preference.

the Democratic National Committee the Republican platform
Tories   Nazis
the Democratic party   *or*   the Democratic Party
the Communist party   *or*   the Communist Party

26. Names of political groups other than parties are usually lowercased, as are their derivative forms.

rightist   right wing   left winger
  but usually   the Left   the Right

27. Terms describing political and economic philosophies and their derivative forms are usually capitalized only if they are derived from proper names.

authoritarianism	nationalism	isolationist
democracy	supply-side economics	civil libertarian
fascism *or* Fascism	social Darwinism	Marxist

28. Historical periods and events The names of conferences, councils, expositions, and specific sporting, historical, and cultural events are capitalized.

the Yalta Conference	the Games of the XXIII Olympiad
the Minnesota State Fair	the Series
the World Series	the San Francisco Earthquake
the Boston Tea Party	the Philadelphia Folk Festival
the Golden Gate International Exposition	

29. The names of some historical and cultural periods and movements are capitalized. When in doubt, consult a dictionary or encyclopedia.

Augustan Age	Renaissance	Stone Age
Prohibition	the Enlightenment	the Great Depression
fin de siècle	space age	cold war *or* Cold War

30. Numerical designations of historical time periods are capitalized only when they are part of a proper name; otherwise they are lowercased.

the Third Reich	Roaring Twenties
seventeenth century	eighties

31. Full names of treaties, laws, and acts are capitalized.

Treaty of Versailles	The Controlled Substances Act of 1970

32. The full names of wars are capitalized. However, words such as *war, revolution, battle,* and *campaign* are capitalized only when they are part of a proper name. Descriptive terms such as *assault, seige,* and *engagement* are usually lowercased even when used in conjunction with the name of the place where the action occurred.

the French and Indian War	the Spanish-American War
the American Revolution	the War of the Spanish Succession
the Revolution of 1688	the Whiskey Rebellion
the Battle of the Bulge	the Battle of the Coral Sea
the Peninsular Campaign	the naval battle of Guadalcanal
the second battle of Manassas	the American and French
the Meuse-Argonne offensive	revolutions
the assault on Iwo Jima	the seige of Yorktown
was in action throughout most of the war	the winter campaign

33. Hyphenated compounds Elements of hyphenated compounds are capitalized if they are proper nouns or adjectives.

Arab-Israeli negotiations
East-West trade agreements
an eighteenth-century poet

Tay-Sachs disease
U.S.-U.S.S.R. détente
American-plan rates

NOTE: If the second element in a two-word compound is not a proper noun or adjective, it is lowercased.

French-speaking peoples
an A-frame house
Thirty-second Street

34. Word elements (as prefixes and combining forms) may or may not be capitalized when joined to a proper noun or adjective. Common prefixes (as *pre-* or *anti-*) are usually not capitalized when so attached. Geographical and ethnic combining forms (as *Anglo-* or *Afro-*) are capitalized; *pan-* is usually capitalized when attached to a proper noun or adjective.

the pro-Soviet faction
un-American activities
Sino-Soviet relations
Pan-Slavic nationalism

post-Civil War politics
Afro-Americans
Greco-Roman architecture
the Pan-African Congress

35. Legal material The names of both plaintiff and defendant in legal case titles are italicized (or underlined in typewritten material). The *v.* for *versus* may be roman or italic. Cases that do not involve two opposing parties have titles such as *In re Watson* or *In the matter of John Watson;* these case titles are also italicized. When the person involved rather than the case itself is being discussed, the reference is not italicized.

Jones v. *Massachusetts*
In re Jones
Smith et al. v. Jones
She covered the Jones trial for the newspaper.

NOTE: In running text a case name involving two opposing parties may be shortened.

The judge based his ruling on a precedent set in the *Jones* decision.

36. Medical terms Proper names that are elements in terms designating diseases, symptoms, syndromes, and tests are capitalized. Common nouns are lowercased.

Duchenne-Erb paralysis
German measles
acquired immunodeficiency
    syndrome
measles

Parkinson's disease
Rorschach test
mumps
herpes simplex

37. Taxonomic names of disease-causing organisms follow the rules established for binomial nonmenclature discussed in paragraph 67 below.

The names of diseases or pathological conditions derived from taxonomic names of organisms are lowercased and not italicized.

> a neurotoxin produced by *Clostridium botulinum*
> nearly died of botulism

38. Generic names of drugs are lowercased; trade names should be capitalized.

> a prescription for chlorpromazine
> had been taking Thorazine

39. Military terms The full titles of branches of the armed forces are capitalized, as are easily recognized short forms of full branch designations.

U.S. Air Force	the Air Force	U.S. Navy
the Navy	U.S. Army	the Army
U.S. Coast Guard	the Coast Guard	U.S. Marine Corps
the Marine Corps	the Marines	the Corps

40. The terms *air force, army, coast guard, marine(s),* and *navy* are lowercased unless they form a part of an official name or refer back to a specific branch of the armed forces previously named. They are also lowercased when they are used collectively or in the plural.

> the combined air forces of the NATO nations
> the navies of the world
> the American army
> In some countries the duty of the coast guard may include icebreaking in inland waterways.

41. The adjectives *naval* and *marine* are lowercased unless they are part of a proper name.

> naval battle   marine barracks   Naval Reserves

42. The full titles of units and organizations of the armed forces are capitalized. Elements of full titles are lowercased when they stand alone.

U.S. Army Corps of Engineers	the corps
the Reserves	a reserve commission
First Battalion	the battalion
4th Marine Regiment	the regiment
Eighth Fleet	the fleet
Cruiser Division	the division
Fifth Army	the army

43. Military ranks are capitalized when they precede the names of their holders, and when they take the place of a person's name (as in direct address). Otherwise they are lowercased.

> General Creighton W. Abrams
> I can't get this rifle any cleaner, Sergeant.
> The major arrived precisely on time.

44. The specific names of decorations, citations, and medals are capitalized.

Medal of Honor	Purple Heart	Silver Star
Navy Cross	Distinguished Service Medal	

45. Numerical designations A noun introducing a reference number is usually capitalized.

Order 704	Flight 409	Form 2E	Policy 118-4-Y

46. Nouns used with numbers or letters to designate major reference headings (as in a literary work) are capitalized. However, nouns designating minor reference headings are typically lowercased.

Book II	Table 3	paragraph 6.1
Volume V	page 101	item 16
Division 4	line 8	question 21

47. Organizations Names of firms, corporations, schools, and organizations and terms derived from those names to designate their members are capitalized. However, common nouns used descriptively or occurring after the names of two or more organizations are lowercased.

Merriam-Webster Inc.	Rotary International
University of Michigan	Kiwanians
Washington Huskies	American and United airlines
played as a Pirate last year	Minnesota North Stars

NOTE: The word *the* at the beginning of such names is capitalized only when the full legal name is used.

48. Words such as *agency, department, division, group,* or *office* that designate corporate and organizational units are capitalized only when they are used with a specific name.

> while working for the Criminal Division in the Department of Justice
> a notice to all department heads

NOTE: Style varies regarding the capitalization of these words when they are used in place of the full name of a specific body. For more on this aspect of styling, see the note following paragraph 18 above.

49. Nicknames, epithets, or other alternate terms for organizations are capitalized.

> referred to IBM as Big Blue
> the Big Three automakers
> trading stocks on the Big Board

50. People The names and initials of persons are capitalized. If a name is hyphenated, both elements are capitalized. Particles forming the initial elements of surnames (as *de, della, der, du, la, ten, ter, van,* and *von*) may or may not be capitalized, depending on the styling of the individual name. However, if a name with a lowercase initial particle begins a sentence, the particle is capitalized.

Thomas De Quincey   E. I. du Pont de Nemours
Sir Arthur Thomas Quiller-Couch   Gerald ter Hoerst
James Van Allen   Heinrich Wilhelm von Kleist
the paintings of de Kooning   De Kooning's paintings are . . .

51. The name of a person or thing can be added to or replaced entirely by a nickname or epithet, a characterizing word or phrase. Nicknames and epithets are capitalized.

Calamity Jane   the Golden Bear   Doctor J.
Bubba Smith   Wilt the Stilt   Attila the Hun
Goose Gossage   Murph the Surf   Meadowlark Lemon
Big Mama Thornton   Dusty Rhodes   Lefty Grove

52. Nicknames and epithets are frequently used in conjunction with both the first and last name of a person. If it is placed between the first and last name, it will often be enclosed in quotation marks or parentheses. However, if the nickname is in general use, the quotation marks or parentheses are often omitted. If the nickname precedes the first name, it is sometimes enclosed in quotation marks, but more often it is not.

Earl ("Fatha") Hines   Joanne "Big Mama" Carner
Mary Harris ("Mother") Jones   Dennis (Oil Can) Boyd
Kissin' Jim Folsom   Mother Maybelle Carter

53. Words of family relationship preceding or used in place of a person's name are capitalized. However, these words are lowercased if they are part of a noun phrase that is being used in place of a name.

Cousin Mercy   Grandfather Barnes
I know when Mother's birthday is.
I know when my mother's birthday is.

54. Words designating languages, nationalities, peoples, races, religious groups, and tribes are capitalized. Descriptive terms used to refer to groups of people are variously capitalized or lowercased. Designations based on color are usually lowercased.

Latin   Canadians   Ibo   Afro-American
Caucasians   Muslims   Christians   Navajo
Bushman (for a nomadic hunter of southern Africa)
bushman (for an inhabitant of the Australian bush)
the red man in America   black, brown, and white people

55. Corporate, professional, and governmental titles are capitalized when they immediately precede a person's name, unless the name is being used as an appositive.

President Roosevelt   Queen Elizabeth   Senator Henry Jackson
Doctor Malatesta   Professor Greenbaum   Pastor Linda Jones

They wanted to meet the new pastor, Linda Jones.

Almost everyone has heard of Chrysler's president, Lee Iacocca.

56. When corporate or governmental titles are used as part of a descriptive phrase to identify a person rather than as a person's official title, the title is lowercased.

Senator Ted Stevens of Alaska   *but*   Ted Stevens, senator from Alaska
Lee Iacocca, president of Chrysler Corporation

NOTE: Style varies when governmental titles are used in descriptive phrases that precede a name.

Alaska senator Ted Stevens   *or*   Alaska Senator Ted Stevens

57. Specific governmental titles may be capitalized when they are used in place of particular individuals' names. In minutes and official records of proceedings, corporate titles are capitalized when they are used in place of individuals' names.

The Secretary of State gave a news conference.

The Judge will respond to questions in her chambers.

The Treasurer then stated his misgivings about the project.

58. Some writers always capitalize the word *president* when it refers to the United States presidency. However, the more common practice is to capitalize the word *president* only when it refers to a specific individual.

It is one of the duties of the President to submit a budget to Congress.

It is one of the duties of the president to submit a budget to Congress.

59. Titles are capitalized when they are used in direct address.

Tell me the truth, Doctor.
Where are we headed, Captain?

60. Pronouns The pronoun *I* is capitalized. For pronouns referring to the Deity, see rule 62 below.

He and I will attend the meeting.

61. Religious terms Words designating the Deity are capitalized.

Allah	God Almighty	the Creator
Jehovah	Yahweh	the Holy Spirit

62. Personal pronouns referring to the Deity are usually capitalized. Relative pronouns (as *who, whom,* and *whose*) usually are not.

God in His mercy
when God asks us to do His bidding
believing that it was God who created the universe

63. Traditional designations of apostles, prophets, and saints are capitalized.

Our Lady   the Prophet   the Lawgiver

64. Names of religions, denominations, creeds and confessions, and religious orders are capitalized, as are adjectives derived from these names. The word *church* is capitalized only when it is used as part of the name of a specific body or edifice or, in some publications, when it refers to organized Christianity in general.

Judaism	Catholicism
the Church of Christ	the Southern Baptist Convention
Apostles' Creed	the Society of Jesus
the Poor Clares	Franciscans
Hunt Memorial Church	a Buddhist monastery
Islamic	the Baptist church on the corner
the Thirty-nine Articles of the Church of England	

65. Names of the Bible or its books, parts, versions, or editions of it and other sacred books are capitalized but not italicized. Adjectives derived from the names of sacred books are variously capitalized and lowercased. When in doubt, consult a dictionary.

Authorized Version	Old Testament	Apocrypha
Talmud	Genesis	Pentateuch
Gospel of Saint Mark	Koran	biblical
talmudic	Koranic	Vedic

66. The names of prayers and well-known passages of the Bible are capitalized.

Ave Maria	the Sermon on the Mount
Ten Commandments	the Beatitudes
the Lord's Prayer	the Our Father

67. Scientific terms Genus names in biological binomial nomenclature are capitalized; species names are lowercased, even when derived from a proper name. Both genus and species names are italicized (or underlined in typewritten material).

Both the wolf and the domestic dog are included in the genus *Canis.*

The California condor *(Gymnogyps californianus)* is facing extinction.

NOTE: When used, the names of races, varieties, or subspecies are lowercased. Like genus and species names, they are italicized.

Hyla versicolor chrysoscelis
Otis asio naevius

68. The New Latin names of classes, families, and all groups above the genus level in zoology and botany are capitalized but not italicized. Their derivative adjectives and nouns in English are neither capitalized nor italicized.

Gastropoda	gastropod
Thallophyta	thallophyte

69. The names, both scientific and informal, of planets and their satellites, asteroids, stars, constellations, groups of stars, and other specific celestial objects are capitalized. However, the words *sun, earth,* and *moon* are usually lowercased unless they occur with other astronomical names. Generic terms that are the final element in the name of a celestial object are usually lowercased.

the Milky Way	Sirius	Ursa Major
Pleiades	Big Dipper	Barnard's star
probes heading for the Moon and Mars		

70. Names of meteorological phenomena are lowercased.

aurora borealis	northern lights	parhelic circle

71. Terms that identify geological eras, periods, epochs, and strata are capitalized. The generic terms that follow them are lowercased. The words *upper, middle,* and *lower* are capitalized when they are used to designate an epoch or series within a period; in most other cases, they are lowercased. The word *age* is capitalized in names such as *Age of Reptiles* or *Age of Fishes.*

Mesozoic era	Quaternary period	Oligocene epoch
Upper Cretaceous	Middle Ordovician	Lower Silurian

72. Proper names forming essential elements of scientific laws, theorems, and principles are capitalized. However, the common nouns *law, theorem, theory,* and the like are lowercased.

Boyle's law	Planck's constant
the Pythagorean theorem	Einstein's theory of relativity

NOTE: In terms referring to popular or fanciful theories or observations, descriptive words are usually capitalized as well.

Murphy's Law	the Peter Principle

73. The names of chemical elements and compounds are lowercased.

hydrogen fluoride
ferric ammonium citrate

74. The names of computer services and data bases are usually trademarks and should always be capitalized. The names of computer languages are irregularly styled either with an initial capital letter or with all letters capitalized. The names of some computer languages are commonly written either way. When in doubt, consult a dictionary.

CompuServe	TeleTransfer	PL/1
Atek	PASCAL *or* Pascal	APL
BASIC	COBOL *or* Cobol	FORTRAN *or* Fortran

75. Time periods and zones The names of the days of the week, months of the year, and holidays and holy days are capitalized.

Easter	Independence Day	June
Tuesday	Yom Kippur	Thanksgiving

76. The names of time zones are capitalized when abbreviated but usually lowercased when written out except for words that are themselves proper names.

CST	central standard time
mountain time	Pacific standard time

77. Names of the seasons are lowercased if they simply declare the time of year; however, they are capitalized if they are personified.

My new book is scheduled to appear this spring.
the sweet breath of Spring

78. Titles Words in titles of books, long poems, magazines, newspapers, plays, movies, novellas that are separately published, and works of art such as paintings and sculpture are capitalized except for internal articles, conjunctions, prepositions, and the *to* of infinitives. The entire title is italicized (or underlined in typewritten material). For the styling of the Bible and other sacred works, see paragraph 65 above.

The Lives of a Cell	*Of Mice and Men*
Saturday Review	*Christian Science Monitor*
Shakespeare's *Othello*	*The Old Man and the Sea*
Gainsborough's *Blue Boy*	the movie *Wait until Dark*

NOTE: Some writers also capitalize prepositions of five or more letters (as *about* or *toward*).

79. An initial article that is part of a title is often omitted if it would be awkward in context. However, when it is included it is capitalized and italicized or underlined. A common exception to this practice regards books that are referred to by an abbreviation. In this case, the initial article is neither capitalized nor italicized.

The Oxford English Dictionary
the 13-volume *Oxford English Dictionary*
the *OED*

80. Practice varies widely regarding the capitalization and italicization or underlining of initial articles and city names in the titles of newspapers. One rule that can be followed is to capitalize and italicize any word that is part of the official title of the paper as shown on its masthead. However, this information is not always available, and even if it is available it can lead to apparent inconsistencies in styling. Because of this, many writers choose one way of styling newspaper titles regardless of their official titles. The most common practice is to italicize the city name but not to capitalize or italicize the initial article.

the *New York Times*	the *Wall Street Journal*
the *Des Moines Register*	the *Washington Post*

81. Some writers choose not to use italics or underlining for titles. They either simply capitalize the words or capitalize them and enclose them in quotation marks.

> the Heard on the Street column in the Wall Street Journal
> our review of "The Lives of a Cell" in last week's issue

82. The first word following a colon in a title is capitalized.

> John Crowe Ransom: An Annotated Bibliography

83. The titles of short poems, short stories, essays, lectures, dissertations, chapters of books, articles in periodicals, radio and television programs, and novellas that are published in a collection are capitalized and enclosed in quotation marks. The capitalization of articles, conjunctions, and prepositions is the same as it is for italicized titles, as explained in paragraph 78 above.

> Robert Frost's "Dust of Snow"
> Katherine Anne Porter's "That Tree"
> John Barth's "The Literature of Exhaustion"
> The talk, "Labor's Power: A View for the Nineties," will be given next week.
> the third chapter of *Treasure Island*, entitled "The Black Spot"
> Her article, "Computer Art on a Micro," was in last month's *Popular Computing*.
> listening to "All Things Considered"
> watching "The Tonight Show"
> D. H. Lawrence's "The Woman Who Rode Away"

84. Common titles of book sections (as a preface, introduction, or index) are capitalized but not enclosed in quotation marks when they refer to a section of the same book in which the reference is made. If they refer to another book, they are usually lowercased.

> See the Appendix for further information.
> In the introduction to her book, the author explains her goals.

85. Practice varies regarding the capitalization of the word *chapter* when it is used with a cardinal number to identify a specific chapter in a book. Most writers capitalize the word, but some do not.

> See Chapter 3 for more details.
> is discussed further in Chapter Four
> *but* in the third chapter

86. The titles of long musical compositions such as operas and symphonies are capitalized and italicized (or underlined in typewritten material); the titles of short compositions are capitalized and enclosed in quotation marks. The titles of musical compositions identified by the nature of the musical form in which they were written are capitalized only.

Verdi's *Don Carlos* "America the Beautiful"
Ravel's "Bolero" Serenade No. 12 in C Minor

87. Trademarks Registered trademarks, service marks, collective marks, and brand names are capitalized.

Band-Aid	Jacuzzi	Kleenex
College Board	Velcro	Realtor
Kellogg's All-Bran	Diet Pepsi	Lay's potato chips

88. Transportation The names of individual ships, submarines, airplanes, satellites, and space vehicles are capitalized and italicized (or underlined in typewritten material). The designations *U.S.S., S.S., M.V.,* and *H.M.S.* are not italicized.

Apollo 11 *Enola Gay*
Mariner 5 *Explorer 10*
Spirit of St. Louis M.V. *West Star*

Other Uses of Capitals

1. Full capitalization of a word is sometimes used for emphasis or to indicate that a speaker is talking very loudly. Both of these uses of capitals are best used very sparingly or avoided altogether in formal writing. Italicization (or underlining) of words for emphasis is more common. For examples of this use of italics, see paragraph 8 under Other Uses of Italics, page 145.

   Results are not the only criteria for judging performance. HOW we achieve results is important also.

   All applications must be submitted IN WRITING before January 31.

   The waiter rushed by yelling "HOT PLATE! HOT PLATE!"

2. A word is sometimes capitalized to indicate that it is being used as a philosophical concept or to indicate that it stands for an important concept in a discussion.

   Many people seek Truth, but few find it.

   the three M's of advertising, Message, Media, and Management

3. Full capitals or a mixture of capitals and lowercase letters or sometimes even small capitals are used to reproduce the text of signs, labels, or inscriptions.

   a poster reading SPECIAL THRILLS COMING SOON

   a Do Not Disturb sign

   a barn with CHEW MAIL POUCH on the side

4. A letter used to indicate a shape is usually capitalized.

   an A-frame house a J-bar V-shaped

Other Uses of Italics

For each of the uses listed below, italic type is used in typeset material (or where it is otherwise available); in typewritten material, underlining is used.

1. Foreign words and phrases that have not been fully adopted into the English language are italicized. The decision whether or not to italicize a word will vary according to the context of the writing and the audience for which the writing is intended. In general, however, any word that appears in the main A–Z vocabulary section of *Webster's Ninth New Collegiate Dictionary* does not need to be italicized.

   > These accomplishments will serve as a monument, *aere perennius*, to the group's skill and dedication.
   > They looked upon this area as a *cordon sanitaire* around the city.
   > After the concert, the crowd headed en masse for the parking lot.
   > The committee meets on an ad hoc basis.

   NOTE: A complete sentence (such as a motto) can also be italicized. However, passages that comprise more than one sentence, or even a single sentence if it is particularly long, are usually treated as quotations; i.e., they are set in roman type and enclosed in quotation marks.

2. Unfamiliar words or words that have a specialized meaning are set in italics, especially when they are accompanied by a short definition. Once these words have been introduced and defined, they do not need to be italicized in subsequent references.

   > *Vitiligo* is a condition in which skin pigment cells stop making pigment.
   > Another method is the *direct-to-consumer* transaction in which the publisher markets directly to the individual by mail or door-to-door.

3. Latin abbreviations are usually not italicized, although the traditional styling has been to italicize them, and some writers still do so.

   > et al.   cf.   e.g.   i.e.   viz.

4. Italic type is used to indicate words referred to as words, letters referred to as letters, or numerals referred to as numerals. However, if the word referred to as a word was actually spoken, it is often enclosed in quotation marks. If the letter is being used to refer to its sound and not its printed form, virgules or brackets can be used instead of italics. And if there is no chance of confusion, numerals referred to as numerals are often not italicized. (For an explanation of the ways in which to form the plurals of words, letters, and numerals referred to as such, see paragraphs 17–19 and 24 under Plurals, pages 149–150.)

   > The panel could not decide whether *data* was a singular or plural noun.
   > *Only* can be an adverb, as in the case of "I *only* tried to help."
   > We heard his warning, but we weren't sure what "other repercussions" meant in that context.

You should dot your *i*'s and cross your *t*'s.

She couldn't pronounce her *s*'s.

He was still having trouble with the /p/ sound.

The first *2* and the last *1* are barely legible.

5. A letter used to indicate a shape is usually capitalized but not set in italics. For more on this use of capital letters, see paragraph 4 under Other Uses of Capitals, page 143.

6. Individual letters are sometimes set in italic type to provide additional typographical contrast. This use of italics is common when letters are used in run-in enumerations or when they are used to identify elements in an illustration.

> providing information about *(a)* typing, *(b)* transcribing, *(c)* formatting, and *(d)* graphics
>
> located at point *A* on the diagram

7. Italics are used to indicate a word created to suggest a sound.

> We sat listening to the *chat-chat-chat* of the sonar.

8. Italics are used to emphasize or draw attention to a word or words in a sentence.

> Students must notify the dean's office *in writing* of all courses added or dropped from their original list.
>
> She had become *the* hero, the one everyone else looked up to.

NOTE: Italics serve to draw attention to words in large part because they are used so infrequently. Writers who overuse italics for giving emphasis may find that the italics lose their effectiveness.

Plurals and Possessives

This section describes the ways in which plurals and possessives are most commonly formed. For some of the questions treated here, various solutions have been developed over the years, but no single solution has come to be universally accepted. In these cases, the range of available solutions is described, and writers must use their own personal judgments to choose among them.

In regard to plurals, consulting a good dictionary will solve many of the problems that are discussed in this chapter. In this regard, the best dictionary to consult is an unabridged dictionary, such as *Webster's Third New International Dictionary*. If such a comprehensive reference book is unavailable the next best thing is a good desk dictionary, such as *Webster's Ninth New Collegiate Dictionary*. Any dictionary that is much smaller than the *Ninth Collegiate* will often be more frustrating in what it fails to show than helpful in what it shows.

In giving examples of plurals and possessives this section uses both *or* and *also* to separate variant forms of the same word. The word *or* is used when both forms of the word are used with approximately equal frequency in standard writing; the form that precedes the *or* is probably slightly more common than the form that follows it. The word *also* is used when one form of the word is much more common than the other; the more common precedes the less common.

Plurals

The plurals of most English words are formed by adding *-s* to the singular. If the noun ends in *-s, -x, -z, -ch* or *-sh,* so that an extra syllable must be added in order to pronounce the plural, *-es* is added to the singular. If the noun ends in a *-y* preceded by a consonant, the *-y* is changed to *-i-* and *-es* is added.

However, many English nouns do not follow this general pattern for forming plurals. Most good dictionaries give thorough coverage to irregular and variant plurals, so they are often the best place to start to answer questions about the plural form of a specific word. The paragraphs that follow describe the ways in which plurals are formed for a number of categories of words whose plural forms are most apt to raise questions.

The symbol → is used throughout this part of this section. In each case, the element that follows the arrow is the plural form of the element that precedes the arrow.

1. **Abbreviations** The plurals of abbreviations are commonly formed by adding *-s* or an apostrophe plus *-s* to the abbreviation; however, there are some significant exceptions to this pattern. For more on the formation of plurals of abbreviations, see paragraphs 1–5 under Plurals, Possessives, and Compounds, page 167.

COLA → COLA's	CPU → CPUs	bldg. → bldgs.
f.o.b. → f.o.b.'s	Ph.D. → Ph.D.'s	p. → pp.

2. **Animals** The names of many fishes, birds, and mammals have both a plural formed with a suffix and one that is identical with the singular. Some have only the *-s* plural; others have only an uninflected plural.

flounder → flounder *or* flounders	mink → mink *or* minks	
quail → quail *or* quails	caribou → caribou *or* caribous	
cow → cows	hen → hens	rat → rats monkey → monkeys
bison → bison	sheep → sheep	shad → shad moose → moose

3. Many of the animals that have both plural forms are ones that are hunted, fished, or trapped, and those who hunt, fish for, and trap them are most likely to use the uninflected form. The *-s* form is especially likely to be used to emphasize diversity of kinds.

   caught four trout
      but
   trouts of the Rocky Mountains

   a place where fish gather
      but
   the fishes of the Pacific Ocean

4. **Compounds and phrases** Most compounds made up of two nouns, whether they appear as one word, two words, or a hyphenated word, are pluralized by pluralizing the final element.

matchbox → matchboxes	spokeswoman → spokeswomen
judge advocate → judge advocates	tree house → tree houses
city-state → city-states	crow's-foot → crow's-feet

5. The plural form of a compound consisting of an *-er* agent noun and an adverb is made by pluralizing the noun element.

hanger-on → hangers-on	looker-on → lookers-on
onlooker → onlookers	passerby → passersby

6. Nouns made up of words that are not nouns form their plurals on the last element.

also-ran → also-rans	ne'er-do-well → ne'er-do-wells
put-down → put-downs	set-to → set-tos
changeover → changeovers	blowup → blowups

7. Plurals of compounds that are phrases consisting of two nouns separated by a preposition are regularly formed by pluralizing the first noun.

aide-de-camp → aides-de-camp	man-of-war → men-of-war
attorney-at-law → attorneys-at-law	lady-in-waiting → ladies-in-waiting
base on balls → bases on balls	coup d'état → coups d'état
power of attorney → powers of attorney	

8. Compounds that are phrases consisting of two nouns separated by a preposition and a modifier form their plurals in various ways.

flash in the pan → flashes in the pan
jack-in-the-box → jack-in-the-boxes *or* jacks-in-the-box
jack-of-all-trades → jacks-of-all-trades
son of a gun → sons of guns
stick-in-the-mud → stick-in-the-muds

9. Compounds consisting of a noun followed by an adjective are regularly pluralized by adding a suffix to the noun.

cousin-german → cousins-german
heir apparent → heirs apparent
knight-errant → knights-errant

NOTE: If the adjective in such a compound tends to be construed as a noun, the compound may have more than one plural form.

attorney general → attorneys general   *or*   attorney generals
sergeant major → sergeants major   *or*   sergeant majors
poet laureate → poets laureate   *or*   poet laureates

10. **Foreign words and phrases** Many nouns of foreign origin retain the foreign plural. However, most of them also have a regular English plural.

> alumnus → alumni
> beau → beaux   *or*   beaus
> crisis → crises
> emporium → emporiums   *or*   emporia
> index → indexes   *or*   indices
> larynx → larynges   *or*   larynxes
> phenomenon → phenomena   *or*   phenomenons
> schema → schemata   *also*   schemas
> seraph → seraphim   *or*   seraphs
> series → series
> tempo → tempi   *or*   tempos

NOTE: A foreign plural may not be used for all senses of a word or may be more commonly used for some senses than for others.

> antenna (on an insect) → antennae
> antenna (on a radio) → antennas

11. Phrases of foreign origin may have a foreign plural, an English plural, or both.

> beau monde → beau mondes   *or*   beaux mondes
> carte blanche → cartes blanches
> hors d'oeuvre → hors d'oeuvres

12. **-ful words** A plural *-fuls* can be used for any noun ending in *-ful,* but some of these nouns also have an alternative, usually less common plural with *-s-* preceding the suffix.

> eyeful → eyefuls
> bucketful → bucketfuls   *or*   bucketsful
> cupful → cupfuls   *also*   cupsful
> tablespoonful → tablespoonfuls   *also*   tablespoonsful

13. **Irregular plurals** A small group of English nouns form their plurals by changing one or more of their vowels.

> foot → feet   man → men   woman → women
> goose → geese   mouse → mice   tooth → teeth
> louse → lice

14. A few nouns have *-en* or *-ren* plurals.

> ox → oxen
> child → children
> brother → brethren

15. Some nouns ending in *-f, -fe,* or *-ff* have plurals that end in *-ves.* Some of these also have regularly formed plurals.

elf → elves	beef → beefs *or* beeves
knife → knives	staff → staffs *or* staves
life → lives	wharf → wharves *also* wharfs

16. **Italic elements** Italicized words, phrases, abbreviations, and letters set within a roman context are variously pluralized with either an italic or roman *s*. A roman *s* is the form most commonly used. If the plural is formed with an apostrophe and an *-s,* the *-s* is almost always roman.

> fifteen *Newsweeks* on the shelf
> answered with a series of *uh-huhs*
> a row of *x*'s

17. **Letters** The plurals of letters are usually formed by the addition of an apostrophe and an *-s,* although uppercase letters are sometimes pluralized by the addition of an *-s* alone.

> p's and q's
> V's of geese flying overhead
> dot your *i*'s
> straight As

18. **Numbers** Numerals are pluralized by adding an *-s,* or, less commonly, an apostrophe and an *-s.*

> two par 5s
> 1970s
> in the 80s
> 1960's
> the mid-$20,000s
> DC-10's

19. Spelled-out numbers are usually pluralized without an apostrophe.

> in twos and threes
> scored two sixes

20. **-o words** Most words ending in an *-o* are pluralized by adding an *-s.* However, some words ending in an *-o* preceded by a consonant have *-s* plurals, some have *-es* plurals, and some have both. When in doubt, consult a dictionary.

> alto → altos
> echo → echoes
> motto → mottoes *also* mottos

21. **Proper nouns** The plurals of proper nouns are usually formed with *-s* or *-es.*

> Bruce → Bruces
> Charles → Charleses
> Hastings → Hastingses
> Velasquez → Velasquezes

22. Proper nouns ending in *-y* usually retain the *-y* and add *-s.*

> February → Februarys
> Mary → Marys

Mercury → Mercurys
  but
Ptolemy → Ptolemies
Sicily → The Two Sicilies
The Rockies

NOTE: Words that were originally proper nouns and that end in *-y* are usually pluralized by changing *-y* to *-i-* and adding *-es,* but a few retain the *-y.*

bobby → bobbies   johnny → johnnies
Jerry → Jerries   Tommy → Tommies
Bloody Mary → Bloody Marys

23. **Quoted elements** Practice varies regarding the plural form of words in quotation marks. Some writers form the plural by adding an *-s* or an apostrophe plus *-s* within the quotation marks. Others add an *-s* outside the quotation marks. Both arrangements look awkward, and writers generally try to avoid this construction.

    too many "probably's" in the statement
    One "you" among millions of "you"s
    a response characterized by its "yes, but"s

24. **Symbols** Although symbols are not usually pluralized, when a symbol is being referred to as a character in itself without regard to meaning, the plural is formed by adding an *-s* or an apostrophe plus *-s.*

    used &'s instead of *and*'s
    his π's are hard to read
    printed three *s

25. **Words used as words** Words used as words without regard to meaning usually form their plurals by adding an apostrophe and a roman *-s.*

    five *and*'s in one sentence
    all those *wherefore*'s and *howsoever*'s

    NOTE: When a word used as a word has become part of a fixed phrase, the plural is usually formed by adding a roman *-s* without the apostrophe.

    oohs and aahs
    dos and don'ts

Possessives

The possessive case of most nouns is formed by adding an apostrophe or an apostrophe plus *-s* to the end of the word.

1. **Common nouns** The possessive case of singular and plural common nouns that do not end in an *s* or *z* sound is formed by adding an apostrophe plus *-s* to the end of the word.

    the boy's mother   at her wit's end   the potato's skin
    men's clothing   children's books   the symposia's themes

2. The possessive case of singular nouns ending in an *s* or *z* sound is usually formed by adding an apostrophe plus -*s* to the end of the word.
An alternate approach, although one less widely accepted, is to add
an apostrophe plus -*s* to the word only when the added -*s* is pronounced. If it isn't pronounced, only an apostrophe is added.

the press's books   the index's arrangement
the boss's desk   the horse's saddle

the audience's reaction   *also*   the audience' reaction
the waitress's duties   *also*   the waitress' duties
the conference's outcome   *also*   the conference' outcome

NOTE: Even those who follow the pattern of adding an apostrophe
plus -*s* to all singular nouns will often make an exception for a multi-
syllabic word that ends in an *s* or *z* sound if it is followed by a word
beginning with an *s* or *z* sound.

for convenience' sake   for conscience' sake
the illness' symptoms   *or*   the illness's symptoms
to the princess' surprise   *or*   to the princess's surprise

3. The possessive case of plural nouns ending in an *s* or *z* sound is
formed by adding only an apostrophe to the end of the word. One
exception to this rule is that the possessive case of one-syllable irregular plurals is usually formed by adding an apostrophe plus -*s*.

horses' stalls   consumers' confidence
geese's calls   mice's habits

4. **Proper names** The possessive forms of proper names are generally
made in the same way as they are for common nouns. The possessive
form of singular proper names not ending in an *s* or *z* sound is made
by adding an apostrophe plus -*s* to the name. The possessive form of
plural proper names is made by adding just an apostrophe.

Mrs. Wilson's store   Utah's capital   Canada's rivers
the Wattses' daughter   the Cohen's house   Niagara Falls' location

5. As is the case for the possessive form of singular common nouns (see
paragraph 2 above), the possessive form of singular proper names
ending in an *s* or *z* sound may be formed either by adding an apostrophe plus -*s* or by adding just an apostrophe to the name. For the sake
of consistency, most writers choose one pattern for forming the possessive of all singular names ending in an *s* or *z* sound, regardless of
the pronunciation of individual names (for exceptions see paragraphs
6 and 7 below). Adding an apostrophe plus -*s* to all such names is
more common than adding just the apostrophe.

Jones's car   *also*   Jones' car
Bliss's statue   *also*   Bliss' statue
Dickens's novels   *also*   Dickens' novels

6. The possessive form of classical and biblical names of two or more syllables ending in *-s* or *-es* is usually made by adding an apostrophe without an *-s*. If the name has only one syllable, the possessive form is made by adding an apostrophe and an *-s*.

   Aristophanes' plays   Achilles' heel   Odysseus' journey
   Judas' betrayal   Zeus's anger   Mars's help

7. The possessive forms of the names *Jesus* and *Moses* are always formed with just an apostrophe.

   Jesus' time   Moses' law

8. The possessive forms of names ending in a silent *-s*, *-z*, or *-x* usually include the apostrophe and the *-s*.

   Arkansas's capital   Camus's *The Stranger*
   Delacroix's painting   Josquin des Prez's music

9. For the sake of convenience and appearance, some writers will italicize the possessive ending when adding it to a name that is in italics. However, most frequently the possessive ending is in roman.

   the U.S.S. *Constitution*'s cannons   the *Mona Lisa*'s somber hues
   Gone With the Wind's ending   *High Noon*'s plot

10. **Pronouns** The possessive case of indefinite pronouns such as *anyone*, *everybody*, and *someone* is formed by adding an apostrophe and an *-s*.

    everyone's   anybody's   everyone's
    everybody's   someone's   somebody's

    NOTE: Some indefinite pronouns usually require an *of* phrase rather than inflection to indicate possession.

    the rights of each   the satisfaction of all
    the inclination of many

11. Possessive pronouns include no apostrophes.

    mine   yours   his   hers
    its   ours   theirs

12. **Phrases** The possessive form of a phrase is made by adding an apostrophe or an apostrophe plus *-s* to the last word in the phrase.

    board of directors' meeting
    his brother-in-law's sidecar
    from the student of politics' point of view
    a moment or so's thought

    NOTE: Constructions such as these can become awkward, and it is often better to rephrase the sentence to eliminate the need for the possessive ending. For instance, the last two examples above could be rephrased as follows:

    from the point of view of the student of politics
    thinking for a moment or so

13. **Words in quotation marks** The possessive form of words in quotation marks can be formed two ways. The apostrophe plus *-s* are placed either inside the quotation marks or outside them. Both arrangements look awkward, and this construction is best avoided.

> the "Today Show"'s cohosts
> the "Grande Dame's" escort
> *but more commonly*
> the cohosts of the "Today Show"
> escort to the "Grande Dame"

14. **Abbreviations** Possessives of abbreviations are formed in the same way as those of nouns that are spelled out. The singular possessive is formed by adding an apostrophe plus *-s* to the abbreviation; the plural possessive, by adding an apostrophe only.

> the AMA's executive committee
> Itek Corp.'s Applied Technology Division
> the Burns Bros.' stores
> the MPs' decisions

15. **Numerals** The possessive form of nouns composed of numerals is made in the same way as for other nouns. The possessive of singular nouns is formed by adding an apostrophe plus *-s;* the possessive form of plural nouns, by adding an apostrophe only.

> 1985's most popular model
> the 1980s' most colorful figure

16. **Individual and joint possession** Individual possession is indicated when an apostrophe plus *-s* is added to each noun in a sequence. Joint possession is most commonly indicated by adding an apostrophe or an apostrophe plus *-s* to the last noun in the sequence. Joint possession may also be indicated by adding a possessive ending to each name.

> Kepler's and Clark's respective clients
> John's, Bill's, and Larry's boats
> Bissell and Hansen's law firm
> Christine and James's vacation home *or* Christine's and James's vacation home

Compounds

A compound is a word or word group that consists of two or more parts that work together as a unit to express a specific concept. Compounds can be formed by combining two or more words (as in *eye shadow, graphic equalizer, farmhouse, cost-effective, blue-pencil, around-the-clock,* or *son of a gun*), by combining word elements (as prefixes or suffixes) with words (as in *ex-president, shoeless, presorted, uninterruptedly,* or *meaningless*), or by combining two or more word elements (as in *supermicro* or *photomicrograph*). Compounds are written in one of three ways: solid (as *cottonmouth*), hyphenated (as *player-manager*), or open (as *field day*).

Some of the explanations that follow make reference to permanent and temporary compounds. Permanent compounds are those that are so commonly used that they have become permanent parts of the language; many of them are entered in dictionaries. Temporary compounds are those created to fit a writer's need at a particular moment. Temporary compounds cannot be found in dictionaries and therefore present particular styling problems.

Self-evident compounds also present styling problems. These are compounds (as *baseball game* or *economic policy*) that are readily understood from the meanings of the words that make them up. Many self-evident compounds, like temporary compounds, are not entered in dictionaries.

In other words, writers faced with having to use compounds cannot rely wholly on dictionaries to guide them in their styling of compounds. They need, in addition, to develop an approach for dealing with compounds that are not in the dictionary.

One approach is simply to leave open any compound that is not in the dictionary. Many writers do this, but there are drawbacks to this approach. A temporary compound may not be as easily recognized as a compound by the reader when it is left open. For instance if you need to use *wide body* as a term for a kind of jet airplane, a phrase like "the operation of wide bodies" may catch the reader unawares. And if you use the open style for a compound modifier, you may create momentary confusion (or even unintended amusement) with a phrase like "the operation of wide body jets."

Another possibility is to hyphenate all compounds that aren't in the dictionary. Hyphenation gives your compound immediate recognition as a compound. But hyphenating all such compounds runs counter to some well-established American practice. Thus you would be calling too much attention to the compound and momentarily distracting the reader.

A third approach is to use analogy to pattern your temporary compound after some other similar compound. This approach is likely to be more complicated than simply picking an open or hyphenated form, and will not free you from the need to make your own decisions in most instances. But it does have the advantage of making your compound less distracting or confusing by making it look as much like other more familiar compounds as possible.

The paragraphs that follow are aimed at helping you to use the analogical approach to styling compounds. You will find compounds listed according to the elements that make them up and the way that they function in a sentence.

This section deals first with compounds formed from whole English words, then compounds formed with word elements, and finally with a small collection of miscellaneous styling conventions relating to compounds. The symbol + in the following paragraphs can be interpreted as "followed immediately by."

Compound Nouns

Compound nouns are combinations of words that function in a sentence as nouns. They may consist of two or more nouns, a noun and a modifier, or two or more elements that are not nouns.

1. **noun + noun** Compounds composed of two nouns that are short, commonly used, and pronounced with falling stress—that is, with the most stress on the first noun and less or no stress on the second—are usually styled solid.

teapot	cottonmouth	birdbath	handmaiden
catfish	sweatband	handsaw	farmyard

2. When a noun + noun compound is short and common but pronounced with equal stress on both nouns, the styling is more likely to be open.

bean sprouts	beach buggy	head louse
fuel oil	duffel bag	dart board

3. Many short noun + noun compounds begin as temporary compounds styled open. As they become more familiar and better established, there is a tendency for them to become solid.

data base	*is becoming*	database
chain saw	*is becoming*	chainsaw
lawn mower	*is becoming*	lawnmower

4. Noun + noun compounds that consist of longer nouns, are self-evident, or are temporary are usually styled open.

wildlife sanctuary	reunion committee
football game	television camera

5. When the nouns in a noun + noun compound describe a double title or double function, the compound is hyphenated.

city-state	dinner-dance	player-manager
decree-law	secretary-treasurer	author-critic

6. Compounds formed from a noun or adjective followed by *man, woman, person,* or *people* and denoting an occupation are regularly solid.

salesman	saleswoman	salesperson	salespeople
congresswoman	handyman	spokesperson	policewoman

7. Compounds that are units of measurement are hyphenated.

foot-pound	man-hour	light-year
kilowatt-hour	column-inch	board-foot

8. **adjective + noun** Most temporary or self-evident adjective + noun compounds are styled open. Permanent compounds formed from relatively long adjectives or nouns are also open.

automatic weapons	modal auxiliary	modular arithmetic
religious freedom	automatic pilot	graphic equalizer
pancreatic juice	minor seminary	white lightning

9. Adjective + noun compounds consisting of two short words may be styled solid when pronounced with falling stress. Just as often, however, short adjective + noun compounds are styled open; a few are hyphenated.

shortcut	longhand	redline	blueprint
yellowhammer	highland	drywall	wetland
dry run	big deal	high gear	long haul
red tape	yellow jacket	red-eye	red-hot

10. **participle + noun** Most participle + noun compounds are styled open, whether permanent, temporary, or self-evident.

frying pan	furnished apartment	shredded wheat
whipped cream	nagging backache	whipping boy

11. **noun's + noun** Compounds consisting of a possessive noun followed by another noun are usually styled hyphenated or open.

crow's-feet	lion's share	fool's gold
cat's cradle	cat's-eye	cat's-paw
stirred up a		
hornet's nest		

NOTE: Compounds of this type that have become solid have lost the apostrophe.

foolscap	menswear	sheepshead

12. **noun + verb + -er; noun + verb + -ing** Temporary compounds in which the first noun is the object of the verb to which the suffix has been added are most often styled open. However, a hyphen may be used to make the relationships of the words immediately apparent. Permanent compounds like these are sometimes styled solid as well.

temporary	gene-splicing	opinion maker	cost-cutting
	risk-taking	career planning	English-speakers
permanent	lifesaver	copyediting	flyswatter
	data processing	bird-watcher	fund-raising
	lawn mower	penny-pinching	bookkeeper

13. **object + verb** Noun compounds consisting of a verb preceded by a noun that is its object are variously styled.

clambake	car wash	face-lift	turkey shoot

14. **verb + object** A few compounds are formed from a verb followed by a noun that is its object. These are mostly older words, and they are solid.

tosspot	breakwater	pinchpenny
cutthroat	carryall	pickpocket

15. **noun + adjective** Compounds composed of a noun followed by an adjective are styled open or hyphenated.

battle royal	consul general	secretary-general
governor-designate	heir apparent	letters patent
sum total	mayor-elect	president-elect

16. **particle + noun** Compounds consisting of a particle (usually a preposition or adverb having prepositional, adverbial, or adjectival force in the compound) and a noun are usually styled solid, especially when they are short and pronounced with falling stress.

downpour	inpatient	outpatient	input
output	throughput	aftershock	overskirt
offshoot	undershirt	crossbones	upkeep

17. A few particle + noun compounds, especially when composed of longer elements or having equal stress on both elements, may be hyphenated or open.

off-season	down payment	off year	cross-fertilization

18. **verb + particle; verb + adverb** These compounds may be hyphenated or solid. Compounds with two-letter particles *(by, to, in, up, on)* are most frequently hyphenated, since the hyphen aids quick comprehension. Compounds with three-letter particles *(off, out)* are hyphenated or solid with about equal frequency. Those with longer particles or adverbs are more often but not always solid.

lay-up	lead-in	run-on	set-to
sit-in	flyby	letup	pileup
shoot-out	show-off	dropout	turnoff
breakthrough	gadabout	giveaway	follow-through

19. **verb + -er + particle; verb + -ing + particle** Except for *passerby*, these compounds are hyphenated.

hanger-on	diner-out	falling-out	runner-up
summing-up	talking-to	goings-on	looker-on

20. **Compounds of three or four elements** Compounds of three or four elements are styled either hyphenated or open. Those consisting of noun + prepositional phrase are generally open, although some are hyphenated. Those formed from other combinations are usually hyphenated.

base on balls	justice of the peace	son of a gun
lily of the valley	jack-of-all-trades	lady-in-waiting
know-it-all	pick-me-up	stick-to-itiveness

21. **letter + noun** Compounds formed from a single letter (or sometimes a combination of them) followed by a noun are either open or hyphenated.

A-frame	B-girl	H-bomb	T-shirt
C ration	D day	I beam	T square
ABO system	J-bar lift	Rh factor	H and L hinge

Compounds That Function as Adjectives

Compound adjectives are combinations of words that work together to modify a noun—that is, they work as unit modifiers. As unit modifiers they should be distinguished from other strings of adjectives that may also precede a noun. For instance, in "a low, level tract of land" or "that long, lonesome road" the two adjectives each modify the noun separately. We are talking about a tract of land that is both low and level and about a road that is both long and lonesome. These are coordinate modifiers.

In "a low monthly fee" or "a wrinkled red necktie" the first adjective modifies the noun plus the second adjective. In other words, we mean a monthly fee that is low and a red necktie that is wrinkled. These are non-coordinate modifiers. But in "low-level radiation" we do not mean radiation that is low and level or level radiation that is low; we mean radiation that is at a low level. Both words work as a unit to modify the noun.

Unit modifiers are usually hyphenated. The hyphens not only make it easier for the reader to grasp the relationship of the words but also avoid confusion. The hyphen in "a call for more-specialized controls" removes any ambiguity as to which word *more* modifies. By contrast, the lack of a hyphen in a phrase like "graphic arts exhibition" gives it an undesirable ambiguity.

1. **Before the noun (attributive position)** Most two-word permanent or temporary compound adjectives are hyphenated when placed before the noun.

tree-lined streets	fast-acting medication
an iron-clad guarantee	a tough-minded negotiator
class-conscious persons	Spanish-American relations
well-intended advice	the red-carpet treatment
a profit-and-loss statement	an input-output device
arrested on a trumped-up charge	a risk-free investment

2. Temporary compounds formed of an adverb (as *well, more, less, still*) followed by a participle (or sometimes an adjective) are usually hyphenated when placed before a noun.

more-specialized controls	a just-completed survey
a still-growing company	a well-funded project
these fast-moving times	a now-vulnerable politician

3. Temporary compounds formed from an adverb ending in -*ly* followed by a participle may sometimes be hyphenated but are more commonly open, because adverb + adjective + noun is a normal word order.

a widely-read feature	internationally-known authors
but more often	
generally recognized categories	a beautifully illustrated book
publicly supported universities	our rapidly changing plans

4. The combination of *very* + adjective is not a unit modifier.

  a very satisfied smile

5. Many temporary compound adjectives are formed by using a compound noun—either permanent or temporary—to modify another noun. If the compound noun is an open compound, it is usually hyphenated so that the relationship of the words is more immediately apparent to the reader.

  the farm-bloc vote   a picture-framing shop
  a short-run printing press a secret-compartment ring
  a tax-law case   ocean-floor hydrophones

6. Some open compound nouns are considered so readily recognizable that they are frequently placed before a noun without a hyphen.

  a high school diploma *or* a high-school diploma
  a data processing course *or* a data-processing course
  a dry goods store *or* a dry-goods store

7. A proper name placed before a noun to modify it is not hyphenated.

  a Thames River marina   a Huck Finn life
  a Korean War veteran   a General Motors car

8. Compound adjectives of three or more words are hyphenated when they precede the noun. Many temporary compounds are formed by hyphenating a phrase and placing it before a noun.

  spur-of-the-moment decisions
  higher-than-anticipated costs

9. Compound adjectives composed of foreign words are not hyphenated when placed before a noun unless they are regularly hyphenated.

  the per capita cost   an a priori argument
  a cordon bleu restaurant   a ci-devant professor

10. Chemical names used as modifiers before a noun are not hyphenated.

  a sodium hypochlorite bleach
  a critic acid solution

11. Following the noun (as a complement or predicate adjective) When the words that make up a compound adjective follow the noun they modify, they tend to fall in normal word order and are no longer unit modifiers. They are therefore no longer hyphenated.

  Controls have become more specialized.
  The company is still growing.
  a statement of profit and loss
  arrested on charges that had been trumped up
  decisions made on the spur of the moment
  They were ill prepared for the journey.

12. Many permanent and temporary compounds keep their hyphens after the noun in a sentence if they continue to function as unit modifiers. Compounds consisting of adjective or noun + participle, adjective or noun + noun + -ed (which looks like a participle), or noun + adjective are most likely to remain hyphenated.

> Your ideas are high-minded but impractical.
> streets that are tree-lined
> You were just as nice-looking then.
> metals that are corrosion-resistant
> tends to be accident-prone

13. Permanent compound adjectives are usually styled as they appear in the dictionary whether they precede or follow the noun they modify.

> The group was public-spirited.
> The problems are mind-boggling.
> is well-read in economics

14. Compound adjectives of three or more words are normally not hyphenated when they follow the noun they modify.

> These remarks are off the record.

15. Permanent compounds of three or more words may be entered as hyphenated adjectives in dictionaries. In such cases the hyphens are retained as long as the phrase is being used as a unit modifier.

> the plan is still pay-as-you-go
> *but*   a plan in which you pay as you go

16. It is possible that a permanent hyphenated adjective may appear alongside a temporary compound in a position where it would normally be open (as "one who is both ill-humored and ill prepared"). It is best to resolve these inconsistencies, either by hyphenating both compounds or leaving both compounds open.

17. When an adverb modifies another adverb that is the first element of a compound modifier, the compound may lose its hyphen. If the first adverb modifies the whole compound, however, the hyphen should be retained.

> a very well developed idea
> a delightfully well-written book
> a most ill-humored remark

18. Adjective compounds that are names of colors may be styled open or hyphenated. Color names in which each element can function as a noun (as *blue green* or *chrome yellow*) are almost always hyphenated when they precede a noun; they are sometimes open when they follow the noun. Color names in which the first element can only be an adjective are less consistently treated; they are often not hyphenated before a noun and are usually not hyphenated after.

blue-gray paint
paint that is blue-gray   *also*   paint that is blue gray
bluish gray paint   *or*   bluish-gray paint

19. Compound modifiers that include a number followed by a noun are hyphenated when they precede the noun they modify. When the modifier follows the noun, it is usually not hyphenated. For more on the styling of numbers, see the section on Numbers, beginning on page 175.

five-card stud   ten-foot pole   twelve-year-old girl
an 18-inch rule *but* a 10 percent raise
a child who is ten years old

20. An adjective that is composed of a number followed by a noun in the possessive is not hyphenated.

a two weeks' wait   a four blocks' walk

Compounds That Function as Adverbs

1. Adverb compounds consisting of preposition + noun are almost always written solid. However, there are a few well-known exceptions.

downtown   downwind   onstage   overseas
upstairs   upfield   offhand   underhand
  but
in-house   off-line   on-line

2. Compound adverbs of more than two words are usually styled open, and they usually follow the words they modify.

every which way   high and dry   off and on
little by little   hook, line, and sinker over and over

3. A few three-word adverbs are homographs of hyphenated adjectives and are therefore styled with hyphens. But many adverbs are styled open even if an adjective formed from the same phrase is hyphenated.

back-to-back (adverb or adjective)
face-to-face (adverb or adjective)
  but
hand-to-hand combat   fought hand to hand
off-the-cuff remarks   spoke off the cuff

Compound Verbs

1. Two-word verbs consisting of a verb followed by an adverb or a preposition are styled open.

get together   run around   run across
set to   run wild   put down
break through   strike out   print out

2. A compound composed of a particle followed by a verb is styled solid.

upgrade   outflank   overcome   bypass

3. A verb derived from an open or hyphenated compound noun—permanent, temporary, or self-evident—is hyphenated.

blue-pencil	double-check	poor-mouth
sweet-talk	tap-dance	water-ski

4. A verb derived from a solid noun is styled solid.

bankroll	roughhouse	mainstream

Compounds Formed with Word Elements

Many new and temporary compounds are formed by adding word elements to existing words or by combining word elements. There are three basic word elements: prefixes (as *anti-, re-, non-, super-*), suffixes (as *-er, -ly, -ness, -ism*), and combining forms (as *mini-, macro-, pseud-, ortho-, -ped, -graphy, -gamic, -plasty*). Prefixes and suffixes are usually attached to existing words; combining forms are usually combined to form new words.

1. prefix + word Except as specified below, compounds formed from a prefix and a word are usually styled solid.

precondition	refurnish	suborder	postwar
interagency	misshapen	overfond	unhelpful

2. If the prefix ends with a vowel and the word it is attached to begins with the same vowel, the compound is usually hyphenated.

anti-inflation	co-owner	de-emphasize	multi-institutional

NOTE: There are many exceptions to this styling (as *cooperate* and *reentry*).

3. If the base word to which a prefix is added is capitalized, the compound is hyphenated.

anti-American	post-Victorian	pre-Columbian	inter-Caribbean

NOTE: The prefix is usually not capitalized in such compounds. But if the prefix and the base word together form a new proper name, the compound may be solid with the prefix capitalized (as *Postimpressionist, Precambrian*).

4. Compounds made with *self-* and *ex-* meaning "former" are hyphenated.

self-pity	ex-wife

5. If a prefix is added to a hyphenated compound, it may be either followed by a hyphen or closed up solid to the next element. Permanent compounds of this kind should be checked in a dictionary.

unair-conditioned	non-self-governing
ultra-up-to-date	unself-conscious

6. In typewritten material, if a prefix is added to an open compound, the prefix is followed by a hyphen. In typeset material, this hyphen is often represented by an en dash. (For more on this use of the en dash, see paragraph 12 under Dash, on pages 106–107.)

ex–Boy Scout   post–coup d'état
ex–Boy Scout   post–coup d'état

7. A compound that would be identical with another word if styled solid is usually hyphenated to prevent misreading.

a multi-ply fabric   re-collect the money   un-ionized particles

8. A compound that might otherwise be solid may be hyphenated if it could be momentarily puzzling (as from consecutive vowels, doubled consonants, or simply an odd combination of letters.)

coed *or* co-ed   overreact *or* over-react
coworker *or* co-worker   interrow *or* inter-row

9. Temporary compounds formed from *vice-* are usually hypenated; however, some permanent compounds (as *vice president* and *vice admiral*) are open.

10. When prefixes are attached to numerals, the compounds are hyphenated.

pre-1982 expenses   post-1975 vintages   non-20th-century ideas

11. Compounds created from combining forms like *Anglo-*, *Judeo-*, or *Sino-* are hyphenated when the second element is an independent word. They are written solid when it is a combining form.

Judeo-Christian   Austro-Hungarian   Sino-Soviet
Italophile   Francophone   Anglophobe

12. Prefixes that are repeated in the same compound are separated by a hyphen.

sub-subheading

13. Some prefixes and initial combining forms have related independent adjectives or adverbs that may be used where the prefix might be expected. A temporary compound with *quasi(-)* or *pseudo(-)* therefore may be written open as modifier + noun or hyphenated as combining form + noun.

quasi intellectual *or* quasi-intellectual
pseudo liberal *or* pseudo-liberal

NOTE: in some cases (as *super, super-*), the independent modifier may not mean quite the same as the prefix.

14. Compounds consisting of different prefixes with the same base word and joined by *and* or *or* are sometimes shortened by pruning the first compound back to the prefix. The missing base word is indicated by a hyphen on the prefix.

> pre- and postoperative care
> anti- or pro-Revolutionary sympathies

15. **word + suffix** Except as noted below, compounds formed by adding a suffix to a word are styled solid.

> Darwinist   fortyish   landscaper   powerlessness

16. Permanent or temporary compounds formed with a suffix are hyphenated if the addition of the suffix would create a sequence of three indentical letters.

> bell-like   will-less   a coffee-er coffee

17. Temporary compounds made with a suffix are often hyphenated if the base word is more than three syllables long, if the base word ends with the same letter the suffix begins with, or if the suffix creates a confusing sequence of letters.

> tunnel-like   American-ness   jaw-wards
> umbrella-like   industry-wide   battle-worthy

18. Compounds made from a number + *odd* are hyphenated whether the number is spelled out or in numerals; a number + *-fold* is solid if the number is spelled out but hyphenated if it is in numerals.

> 20-odd   twenty-odd
> 12-fold   twelvefold

19. Most compounds formed from an open or hyphenated compound + a suffix do not separate the suffix by a hyphen. But such suffixes as *-like, -wide, -worthy,* and *-proof,* all of which are homographs of independent adjectives, are attached by a hyphen.

> good-humoredness   dollar-a-yearism   do-it-yourselfer
> a United Nations-like agency

NOTE: Open compounds often become hyphenated when a suffix is added unless they are proper nouns.

> middle age *but* middle-ager   New Englandism
> tough guy *but* tough-guyese   Wall Streeter

20. **combining form + combining form** Many new terms in technical fields are created by adding combining form to combining form or combining form to a word or word part. Such compounds are generally intended to be permanent, even though many never get into the dictionary. They are regularly styled solid.

Miscellaneous Styling Conventions

1. Compounds that would otherwise be styled solid according to the principles described above are written open or hyphenated to avoid

ambiguity, to ensure rapid comprehension, or to make the pronunciation clearer.

meat-ax	*or* meat ax	bi-level	tri-city
re-utter		umbrella-like	un-iced

2. When typographical features such as capitals or italics make word relationships in a sentence clear, it is not necessary to hyphenate an open compound (as when it precedes a noun it modifies).

a *Chicago Tribune* story   an "eyes only" memo

I've been Super Bowled to death.

a *noblesse oblige* attitude

Abbreviations

Abbreviations are used for a variety of reasons: to save space, to avoid repetition of long words and phrases that may distract the reader, and to reduce keystrokes for typists. In addition, abbreviations are used simply to conform to conventional usage.

Unfortunately, the contemporary styling of abbreviations is to a large extent inconsistent and arbitrary. No set of rules can hope to cover all the possible variations, exceptions, and peculiarities encountered in print. The styling of abbreviations—whether capitalized or lowercased, closed up or spaced, punctuated or unpunctuated—depends most often on a writer's preference or an organization's policy. For example, some companies style the abbreviation for *cash on delivery* as *COD*; others prefer *C.O.D.* or *c.o.d.*

All is not complete confusion, however, and general patterns can be discerned. Some abbreviations (as *e.g., etc., i.e., No.,* and *viz.*) are governed by a strong tradition of punctuation, while others (as *NATO, NASA, NOW, OPEC,* and *SALT*) that are pronounced as words tend to be all-capitalized and unpunctuated. Styling problems can be dealt with by consulting a good general dictionary such as *Webster's Ninth New Collegiate Dictionary,* especially for capitalization guidance, and by the following the guidelines of one's own organization or the dictates of one's own preference. An abbreviations dictionary such as *Webster's Guide to Abbreviations* may also be helpful.

Punctuation

The paragraphs that follow describe a few broad principles that apply to abbreviations in general. However, there are many specific situations in which these principles will not apply. The section on Specific Styling Conventions, beginning on page 182, contains information on these specific situations and on particular kinds of abbreviations.

1. A period follows most abbreviations that are formed by omitting all but the first few letters of a word.

    bull. for *bulletin*   fig. for *figure*
    bro. for *brother*   Fr. for *French*

2. A period follows most abbreviations that are formed by omitting letters from the middle of a word.

    secy. for *secretary*   agcy. for *agency*
    mfg. for *manufacturing*   Mr. for *Mister*

3. Punctuation is usually omitted from abbreviations that are made up of initial letters of words that constitute a phrase or compound word. However, for some of these abbreviations, especially ones that are not capitalized, the punctuation is retained.

    GNP for *gross national product*   PC for *personal computer*
    EFT for *electronic funds transfer* f.o.b. for *free on board*

4. Terms in which a suffix is added to a numeral, such as *1st, 2nd, 3d, 8vo,* and *12mo,* are not abbreviations and do not require a period.

5. Isolated letters of the alphabet used to designate a shape or position in a sequence are not punctuated.

    T square   A 1   I beam   V sign

6. Some abbreviations are punctuated with one or more virgules in place of periods.

    c/o for *care of*   w/o for *without*
    d/b/a for *doing business as*   w/w for *wall to wall*

Capitalization

1. Abbreviations are capitalized if the words they represent are proper nouns or adjectives.

    F for *Fahrenheit*   Nov. for *November*
    NBC for *National*   Brit. for *British*
      Broadcasting Company

2. Abbreviations are usually capitalized when they represent single letters of words that are normally lowercased. There are, however, some very common abbreviations formed in this way that are not capitalized.

    TM for *trademark*   EEG for *electroencephalogram*
    ETA for *estimated time of arrival* FY for *fiscal year*
    CATV for *community*
      antenna television
    a.k.a. for *also known as*   d/b/a for *doing business as*

3. Most acronyms that are pronounced as words, rather than as a series of letters, are capitalized. If they have been assimilated into the lan-

guage as words in their own right, however, they are most often low-ercased.

OPEC	NATO	MIRV	NOW account
quasar	laser	sonar	scuba

Plurals, Possessives, and Compounds

1. Punctuated abbreviations of single words are pluralized by adding -s before the period.

bldgs.	bros.	figs.	mts.

2. Punctuated abbreviations that stand for phrases or compounds are pluralized by adding -'s after the last period.

Ph.D.'s	f.o.b.'s	J.P.'s	M.B.A.'s

3. Unpunctuated abbreviations that stand for phrases or compound words are usually pluralized by adding -s to the end of the abbreviation.

COLAs	CPUs	PCs	DOSs

NOTE: Some writers pluralize such abbreviations by adding -'s to the abbreviation; however, this styling is far less common than the one described above.

4. The plural form of most lowercase single-letter abbreviations is made by repeating the letter. For the plural form of single-letter abbreviations that are abbreviations for units of measure, see paragraph 5 below.

cc. for *copies*	ff. for *and the following ones*
ll. for *lines*	nn. for *notes*
pp. for *pages*	vv. for *verses*

5. The plural form of abbreviations of units of measure is the same as the singular form.

30 sec.	24 ml	20 min.	200 bbl.
30 d.	24 h.	50 m	10 mi.

6. Possessives of abbreviations are formed in the same way as those of spelled-out nouns: the singular possessive is formed by the addition of -'s, the plural possessive simply by the addition of an apostrophe.

the CPUs' memory	most CPUs' memories
Brody Corp.'s earnings	Bay Bros.' annual sale

7. Compounds that consist of an abbreviation added to another word are formed in the same way as compounds that consist of spelled-out nouns.

a Kalamazoo, Mich.-based company
an AMA-approved medical school

8. Compounds formed by adding a prefix or suffix to an abbreviation are usually styled with a hyphen.

> an IBM-like organization
> non-DNA molecules
> pre-HEW years

Specific Styling Conventions

The following paragraphs describe styling practices commonly followed for specific kinds of situations involving abbreviations. The paragraphs are arranged under the following alphabetical headings.

A and An	Degrees	Military Ranks and
A.D. and B.C.	Division of	Units
Agencies, Asssociations,	Abbreviations	Number
and Organizations	Full Forms	Personal Names
Beginning a Sentence	Geographical Names	Saint
Books of the Bible	Latin Words and	Scientific Terms
Company Names	Phrases	Time
Compass Points	Latitude and	Titles
Contractions	Longitude	Units of Measure
Dates	Laws and Bylaws	Versus

1. A and an The choice of the article *a* or *an* before abbreviations depends on the sound with which the abbreviation begins. If an abbreviation begins with a consonant sound, *a* is normally used. If an abbreviation begins with a vowel sound, *an* is used.

> a B.A. degree   a YMCA club   a UN agency
> an FCC report   an SAT score   an IRS agent

2. A.D. and B.C. The abbreviations A.D. and B.C. are usually styled in typeset matter as punctuated, unspaced small capitals; in typed material they usually appear as punctuated, unspaced capitals.

> *in printed material*   41 B.C.   A.D. 185
> *in typed material*   41 B.C.   A.D. 185

3. The abbreviation A.D. usually precedes the date; the abbreviation B.C. usually follows the date. However, many writers and editors place A.D. after the date, thus making their placement of A.D. consistent with their placement of B.C. In references to whole centuries, the usual practice is to place A.D. after the century. The only alternative is not to use the abbreviation at all in such references.

> A.D. 185 *but also* 185 A.D.
> the fourth century A.D.

4. Agencies, associations, and organizations The names of agencies, associations, and organizations are usually abbreviated after they have been spelled out on their first occurrence in a text. The abbreviations are usually all capitalized and unpunctuated.

> EPA   SEC   NAACP   NCAA   USO   NOW

NOTE: In contexts where the abbreviation will be recognized, it may be used without having its full form spelled out on its first occurrence.

5. **Beginning a sentence** Most writers avoid beginning a sentence with an abbreviation that is ordinarily not capitalized. Abbreviations that are ordinarily capitalized, on the other hand, are commonly used to begin sentences.

> Page 22 contains . . . *not* P. 22 contains . . .
> Doctor Smith believes . . . *or* Dr. Smith believes . . .
> OSHA regulations require . . .

6. **Books of the Bible** Books of the Bible are generally spelled out in running text but abbreviated in references to chapter and verse.

> The minister based the sermon on Genesis
> In the beginning God created the heavens and the earth.—Gen. 1:1

7. **Company names** The styling of company names varies widely. Many writers avoid abbreviating any part of a company's name unless the abbreviation is part of the company's official name. However, many other writers routinely abbreviate words such as *Company, Corporation,* and *Incorporated.* Words such as *Airlines, Associates, Fabricators* and *Manufacturing,* however, are spelled out.

> Ginn and Company *or* Ginn and Co.
> The Bailey Banks and Biddle Company *or* The Bailey Banks and Biddle Co.

NOTE: An ampersand frequently replaces the word *and* in official company names. For more on this use of the ampersand, see paragraph 1 under Ampersand, page 88.

8. If a company is easily recognizable from its initials, its name is usually spelled out for the first mention and abbreviated in all subsequent references. Some companies have made their initials part of their official name, and in those cases the initials appear in all references.

> *first reference*   General Motors Corp. released figures today . . .
> *subsequent reference*   A GM spokesperson said . . .
> MCM Electronics, an Ohio-based electronics company . . .

9. **Compass points** Compass points are abbreviated when occurring after street names, though styling varies regarding whether these abbreviations are punctuated and whether they are preceded by a comma. When compass points form essential internal elements of street names, they are usually spelled out in full.

> 2122 Fourteenth Street, NW *or* 2122 Fourteenth Street NW
> *or* 2122 Fourteenth Street, N.W.
> 192 East 49th Street
> 1282 North Avenue

10. **Contractions** Some abbreviations resemble contractions by including an apostrophe in place of omitted letters. These abbreviations are not punctuated with a period.

    sec'y for *secretary*   ass'n for *association*   dep't for *department*

    NOTE: This style of abbreviation is usually avoided in formal correspondence.

11. **Dates** The names of days and months should not be abbreviated in running text. The names of months are not abbreviated in date lines of business letters, but they may be abbreviated in government or military correspondence.

    the December issue of *Scientific American*
    a meeting held on August 1, 1985 *or* a meeting held on Aug. 1, 1985
    general business date line   November 1, 1985
    military date line   1 Nov 1985

12. **Degrees** Except for a few academic degrees with highly recognizable abbreviations (as *A.B., M.S.,* and *Ph.D.*), the names of degrees and professional ratings are spelled out in full when first mentioned in running text. Often the name of the degree is followed by its abbreviation enclosed in parentheses, so that the abbreviation may be used alone later in running text. When a degree or professional rating follows a person's name it is usually abbreviated.

    Special attention is devoted to the master of arts in teaching (M.A.T.) degree.
    Julia Ramirez, P.E.

13. Like other abbreviations, abbreviations of degrees and professional ratings are often unpunctuated. In general, punctuated abbreviations are more common for academic degrees, and unpunctuated abbreviations are slightly more common for professional ratings, especially if the latter comprise three or more capitalized letters.

R.Ph.	P.E.	CLA	CMET
Ph.D.	B.Sc.	M.B.A.	BGS

14. The first letter of each element in abbreviations of all degrees and professional ratings is capitalized. Letters other than the first letter are usually not capitalized.

D.Ch.E.	Litt.D.	M.F.A.	D.Th.

15. **Division of abbreviations** Division of abbreviations at the end of lines or between pages is usually avoided.

    received an M.B.A.   *not*   received an M.B.-
    degree   A. degree

16. **Full forms** When using an abbreviation that may be unfamiliar or confusing to the reader, many writers give the full form first, followed

by the abbreviation in parentheses. In subsequent references just the abbreviation is used.

first reference   At the American Bar Association (ABA) meeting in June . . .

subsequent reference   At that particular ABA meeting . . .

17. **Geographical names** U.S. Postal Service abbreviations for states, possessions, and Canadian provinces are all-capitalized and unpunctuated, as are Postal Service abbreviations for streets and other geographical features when these abbreviations are used on envelopes addressed for automated mass handling.

addressed for automated handling   1234 SMITH BLVD
                                          SMITHVILLE, MN 56789
regular address styling   1234 Smith Blvd.
                                          Smithville, MN 56789

18. Abbreviations of states are often used in running text to identify the location of a city or country. In this context they are set off with commas, and punctuated, upper- and lowercase state abbreviations are usually used. In other situations within running text, the names of states are usually not abbreviated.

John Smith of 15 Chestnut St., Sarasota, Fla., has won . . .
the Louisville, Ky., public library system
Boston, the largest city in Massachusetts, . . .

19. Terms such as *street* and *parkway* are variously abbreviated or unabbreviated in running text. When they are abbreviated, they are usually punctuated.

our office at 1234 Smith Blvd. (*or* Boulevard)
an accident on Windward Road (*or* Rd.)

20. Names of countries are usually spelled in full in running text. The most common exceptions to this pattern are the abbreviations *U.S.S.R.* and *U.S.* (see paragraph 22 below).

Great Britain and the U.S.S.R. announced the agreement.

21. Abbreviations for the names of most countries are punctuated. Abbreviations for countries whose names include more than one word are often not punctuated if the abbreviations are formed from only the initial letters of the individual words.

Mex.	Can.	Scot.
Ger.	Gt. Brit.	U.S. *or* US
U.S.S.R. *or* USSR	U.K. *or* UK	U.A.E. *or* UAE

22. *United States* is often abbreviated when it is being used as an adjective, such as when it modifies the name of a federal agency, policy, or program. When *United States* is used as a noun in running text, it is usu-

ally spelled out, or it is spelled on its initial use and then abbreviated in subsequent references.

U.S. Department of Justice
U.S. foreign policy
The United States has offered to . . .

23. *Saint* is usually abbreviated when it is part of the name of a geographical or topographical feature. *Mount, Point,* and *Fort* are variously spelled out or abbreviated according to individual preference. *Saint, Mount,* and *Point* are routinely abbreviated when space is at a premium. (For more on the abbreviation of *Saint,* see paragraph 35 below.)

St. Louis, Missouri	St. Kitts	Mount McKinley
Mount St. Helens	Fort Sumter	Point Pelee

24. **Latin words and phrases** Words and phrases derived from Latin are commonly abbreviated in contexts where readers can reasonably be expected to recognize them. They are punctuated, lowercased, and usually not italicized.

etc.	i.e.	e.g.	viz	et al.	pro tem.

25. **Latitude and longitude** Latitude and longitude are abbreviated in tabular data but written out in running text.

in a table	lat. 10°20′N *or* lat. 10-20N
in text	from 10°20′ north latitude to 10°30′ south latitude

26. **Laws and bylaws** Laws and bylaws, when first mentioned, are spelled in full. Subsequent references to them in a text may be abbreviated.

first reference	Article I, Section 1
subsequent reference	Art. I, Sec. 1

27. **Military ranks and units** Military ranks are usually given in full when used with a surname only but are abbreviated when used with a full name.

Colonel Howe	Col. John P. Howe

28. In nonmilitary correspondence, abbreviations for military ranks are punctuated and set in capital and lowercase letters. Within the military (with the exception of the Marine Corps) these abbreviations are all-capitalized and unpunctuated. The Marine Corps follows the punctuated, capital and lowercase styling.

in the military	BG John T. Dow, USA
	LCDR Mary I. Lee, USN
	Col. S. J. Smith, USMC
outside the military	Brig. Gen. John T. Dow, USA
	Lt. Comdr. Mary I. Lee, USN
	Col. S. J. Smith, USMC

29. Abbreviations for military units are capitalized and unpunctuated.

USA USAF SAC NORAD

30. Number The word *number,* when used with figures such as *1* or *2* to indicate a rank or rating, is usually abbreviated. When it is, the *N* is capitalized, and the abbreviation is punctuated.

The No. 1 priority is to promote profitability.

31. The word *number* is usually abbreviated when it is part of a set unit (such as a contract number).

Contract No. N-1234-76-57   Publ. Nos. 12 and 13
Policy No. 123-5-X   Index No. 7855

32. Personal names Personal names are not usually abbreviated.

George S. Patterson   *not*   Geo. S. Patterson

33. Unspaced initials of famous persons are sometimes used in place of their full names. The initials may or may not be punctuated.

FDR   *or*   F.D.R.

34. When initials are used with a surname, they are spaced and punctuated.

F. D. Roosevelt

35. Saint The word *Saint* is often abbreviated when used before the name of a saint or when it is the first element of the name of a city or institution named after a saint. However, when it forms part of a surname, it may or may not be abbreviated. In the case of surnames and names of institutions, the styling should be the one used by the person or the institution.

St. Peter   *or*   Saint Peter   St. Cloud, Minnesota
St. John's University   Saint Joseph College
Augustus Saint-Gaudens   Louis St. Laurent

36. Scientific terms In binomial nomenclature, a genus name may be abbreviated with its initial letter after the first reference to it is spelled out. The abbreviation is always punctuated.

first reference   *Escherichia coli*
subsequent reference   *E. coli*

37. Abbreviations for the names of chemical compounds or mechanical or electronic equipment or processes are usually not punctuated.

OCR PCB CPU PBX

38. The symbols for chemical elements are not punctuated.

H Cl Pb Na

39. Time When time is expressed in figures, the abbreviations that follow are most often styled as punctuated lowercase letters; punctuated small capital letters are also common.

    8:30 a.m.   10:00 p.m.   8:30 A.M.   10:00 P.M.

40. In transportation schedules *a.m.* and *p.m.* are generally styled in capitalized, unpunctuated, unspaced letters.

    8:30 AM   10:00 PM

41. Time zone designations are usually styled in capitalized, unpunctuated, unspaced letters.

    EST   PST   CDT

42. Titles The only courtesy titles that are invariably abbreviated in written references are *Mr., Ms., Mrs.,* and *Messrs.* Other titles, such as *Doctor, Representative,* or *Senator,* may be either written out or abbreviated.

    Ms. Lee A. Downs
    Messrs. Lake, Mason, and Nambeth
    Doctor Howe   *or*   Dr. Howe

43. Despite some traditional injunctions against the practice, the titles *Honorable* and *Reverend* are often abbreviated.

        the Honorable Samuel I. O'Leary   *or*   the Hon. Samuel I. O'Leary
        the Reverend Samuel I. O'Leary   *or*   the Rev. Samuel I. O'Leary

44. The designations *Jr.* and *Sr.* may be used in conjunction with courtesy titles, with abbreviations for academic degrees, and with professional rating abbreviations. They may or may not be preceded by a comma according to the writer's preference. They are terminated with a period, and they are commonly only used with a full name.

    Mr. John K. Walker, Jr.
    Dr. John K. Walker, Jr.
    General John K. Walker Jr.
    The Honorable John K. Walker, Jr.
    John K. Walker Jr., M.D.

45. When an abbreviation for an academic degree, professional certification, or association membership follows a name, it is usually preceded by a comma. No courtesy title should precede the name.

    Dr. John Smith   *or*   John Smith, M.D.   *but not*   Dr. John Smith, M.D.
    Katherine Derwinski, CLU
    Carol Manning, M.D., FACPS

46. The abbreviation *Esq.* for *Esquire* is used in the United States after the surname of professional persons such as attorneys, architects, consuls, clerks of the court, and justices of the peace. It is not used, however,

if a courtesy title such as *Dr., Hon., Miss, Mr., Mrs.,* or *Ms.* precedes
the first name. For more on the use of *Esquire,* see pages 78–79.

> Carolyn B. West, Esq.

47. **Units of measure** Measures and weights may be abbreviated in figure
plus unit combinations. However, if the numeral is written out, the
unit should also be written out.

> 15 cu ft   *or*   15 cu. ft.   *but*   fifteen cubic feet
> How many cubic feet does the refrigerator hold?

48. Abbreviations for metric units are usually not punctuated. Abbreviations for traditional units are usually punctuated.

> 14 ml   12 km   22 mi.   8 ft.   4 sec.   20 min.

49. **Versus** *Versus* is usually abbreviated as the lowercase roman letter *v.*
in legal contexts; it is either spelled out or abbreviated as lowercase
roman letters *vs.* in general contexts.

> *in a legal context*   Smith v. Vermont
> *in a general context*   honesty versus dishonesty
>   *or*
>   honesty vs. dishonesty

Numbers

The styling of numbers presents special difficulties to writers because
there are so many conventions to follow, some of which may conflict when
applied to particular passages. The writer's major decision is whether to
write out numbers or to express them in figures, and usage varies considerably on this point. This chapter explains most of the conventions used
in the styling of numbers. A discussion of general principles is followed
by detailed information on specific situations involving numbers.

Numbers as Words or Figures

At one extreme of styling, all numbers, sometimes even including dates,
are written out. This usage is uncommon and is usually limited to procla-
mations, legal documents, and some other types of very formal writing.
At the other extreme, some types of technical writing, such as statistical
reports, contain no written-out numbers except sometimes at the beginning of a sentence.

In general, figures are easier to read than the spelled-out forms of
numbers; however, the spelled-out forms are helpful in certain circumstances, such as in distinguishing different categories of numbers or in
providing relief from an overwhelming cluster of numerals. Most writers
follow one or the other of two common conventions combining numerals

and written-out numbers. The conventions are described in this section, along with the situations that provide exceptions to the general rules.

1. **Basic conventions** The first system requires that a writer use figures for exact numbers that are greater than nine and words for numbers nine and below (a variation of this system sets the number ten as the dividing point). In this system, numbers that consist of a whole number between one and nine followed by *hundred, thousand, million,* etc. may be spelled out or expressed in figures.

> She performed in 22 plays on Broadway, seven of which won awards.
>
> The new edition will consist of 25 volumes which will be issued at a rate of approximately four volumes per year.
>
> The cat show attracted an unexpected two thousand entries.
>
> They sold more than 2,000 units in the first year.

2. The second system requires that a writer use figures for all exact numbers 100 and above (or 101 and above) and words for numbers from one to ninety-nine (or one to one hundred) and for numbers that consist of a whole number between one and ninety-nine followed by *hundred, thousand, million,* etc.

> The artist spent nearly twelve years completing these four volumes, which comprise 435 hand-colored engravings.
>
> The 145 seminar participants toured the area's eighteen period houses.
>
> In the course of four hours, the popular author signed twenty-five hundred copies of her new book.

3. **Sentence beginnings** Numbers that begin a sentence are written out, although some writers make an exception for the use of figures for dates that begin a sentence. It is best to avoid spelled-out numbers that are lengthy and awkward by restructuring the sentence so that the number appears elsewhere than at the beginning and may then be styled as a figure.

> Sixty-two new models will be introduced this year.
> *or*
> There will be 62 new models introduced this year.
>
> Nineteen eighty-seven was our best earnings year so far.
> *or*
> 1987 was our best earnings year so far.
>
> One hundred fifty-seven illustrations, including 86 color plates, are contained in the book.
> *or*
> The book contains 157 illustrations, including 86 color plates.

4. **Adjacent numbers and numbers in series** Generally, two separate sets of figures should not be written adjacent to one another in running text unless they form a series. So that the juxtaposition of unrelated figures will not confuse the reader, either the sentence is restructured

or one of the figures is spelled out. Usually the figure with the written form that is shorter and more easily read is converted. When one of two adjacent numbers is an element of a compound modifier, the first of the two numbers is often expressed in words, the second in figures. But if the second number is the shorter, the styling is often reversed.

original	*change to*
16 ½-inch dowels	sixteen ½-inch dowels
25 11-inch platters	twenty-five 11-inch platters
20 100-point games	twenty 100-point games
78 20-point games	78 twenty-point games
By 1997, 300 more of the state's schools will have closed their doors.	By 1997, three hundred more of the state's schools will have closed their doors.

5. Numbers paired at the beginning of a sentence are usually styled alike. If the first word of the sentence is a spelled-out number, the second, related number is also spelled out. However, some writers and editors prefer that each number be styled independently, even if that results in an inconsistent pairing.

> Sixty to seventy-five copies will be required.
> Sixty to 75 copies will be required.

6. Numbers that form a pair or a series referring to comparable quantities within a sentence or a paragraph should be treated consistently. The style of the largest number usually determines the style of the other numbers. Thus, a series of numbers including some which would ordinarily be spelled out might all be styled as figures. Similarly, figures are used to express all the numbers in a series if one of those numbers is a mixed or simple fraction.

> The three jobs took 5, 12, and 4½ hours, respectively.
> We need four desks, three chairs, fourteen typewriters, and six file cabinets.

7. **Round numbers** Approximate or round numbers, particularly those that can be expressed in one or two words, are often written out in general writing; in technical and scientific writing they are more likely to be expressed as numerals.

> seven hundred people
> five thousand years
> four hundred thousand volumes
>
> *but in technical writing*
> 50,000 people per year
> 20,000 species of fish

8. For easier reading, numbers of one million and above may be expressed as figures followed by the word *million, billion,* and so forth. The figure may include a decimal fraction, but the fraction is not usu-

ally carried past the first digit to the right of the decimal point, and it is never carried past the third digit. If a more exact number is required, the whole amount should be written in figures.

about 4.6 billion years old
1.2 million metric tons of grain
the last 600 million years
$7.25 million
$3,456,000,000
> *but* 200,000 years   *not*   200 thousand years

Ordinal Numbers

1. Ordinal numbers generally follow the styling rules for cardinal numbers. If a figure would be required for the cardinal form of a number, it should also be used from the ordinal form; if the conventions call for a written-out form, it should be used for both cardinal and ordinal numbers. In technical writing, however, ordinal numbers are usually written as figure-plus-suffix combinations. In addition, certain ordinal numbers—for example, those specifying percentiles and latitudinal lines—are conventionally set as figures.

the sixth Robert de Bruce	the 20th century
the ninth grade	the 98th Congress
the 40th parallel	the 12th percentile
the 9th and 14th chapters	the 40th parallel
his twenty-third try	

2. The forms *second* and *third* may be written with figures as *2d* or *2nd, 3d* or *3rd, 22d* or *22nd, 93d* or *93rd, 102d* or *102nd.* A period does not follow the suffix.

Roman Numerals

Roman numerals, which may be written either in capital or lowercase letters, are conventional in the specific situations described below. Roman numerals are formed by adding the numerical values of letters as they are arranged in descending order going from left to right. If a letter with a smaller numerical value is placed to the left of a letter with a greater numerical value, the value of the smaller is subtracted from the value of the larger. A bar placed over a numeral ($\bar{V}$) multiplies its value by one thousand.

1. Roman numerals are traditionally used to differentiate rulers and popes that have identical names.

Elizabeth II	Innocent X
Henry VIII	Louis XIV

2. Roman numerals are used to differentiate related males who have the same name. For more on this use of Roman numerals, see page 85.

James R. Watson II	James R. Watson 2nd *or* 2d

NOTE: Possessive patterns for these names are the following:

| *singular* | James R. Watson III's (*or* 3rd's *or* 3d's) house |
| *plural* | the James R. Watson IIIs' (*or* 3rds' *or* 3ds') house |

3. Roman numerals are used to differentiate certain vehicles and vessels, such as yachts, that have the same name. If the name is italicized, the numeral is italicized also. Names of American spacecraft formerly bore Roman numerals, but Arabic numerals are now used.

> *Shamrock V*
>
> The U.S. spacecraft *Rangers VII, VIII,* and *IX* took pictures of the moon.
>
> On July 20, 1969, *Apollo 11* landed on the moon.

4. Lowercase Roman numerals are often used to number book pages that precede the regular Arabic sequence, as in a foreword, preface, or introduction.

5. Roman numerals are often used in enumerations to list major headings. An example of an outline with Roman-numeral headings is shown on page 187.

6. Roman numerals are found as part of a few established technical terms such as blood-clotting factors, quadrant numbers, designations of cranial nerves, and virus or organism types. Also, chords in the study of music harmony are designated by capital and lowercase Roman numerals. For the most part, however, technical terms that include numbers express them in Arabic form.

> | blood-clotting factor VII | HTLV-III virus |
> | quadrant III | *but* |
> | the cranial nerves II and IX | adenosine 3',5'-monophosphate |
> | Population II stars | cesium 137 |
> | type I error | PL/1 programming language |

Punctuation and Inflection

The paragraphs that follow explain general rules for the use of commas and hyphens in compound and large numbers, as well as the plural forms of numbers. For the styling of specific categories of numbers, such as dates, money, and decimal fractions, see the section on Specific Styling Conventions, beginning on page 182.

1. **Commas in large numbers** In general writing, with the exceptions explained in paragraph 3 below, figures of four digits may be styled with or without a comma; the punctuated form is more common. If the numerals form part of a tabulation, commas are necessary so that four-digit numerals can align with numerals of five or more digits.

> 2,000 case histories   *or less commonly*   1253 people

2. Whole numbers of five digits or more (but not decimal fractions) use a comma to separate three-digit groups, counting from the right.

> a fee of $12,500
> 15,000 units
> a population of 1,500,000

3. Certain types of numbers do not conform to these conventions. Decimal fractions and serial and multidigit numbers in set combinations, such as the numbers of policies, contracts, checks, streets, rooms, suites, telephones, pages, military hours, and years, do not contain commas.

> check 34567   the year 1929
> Room 606   Policy No. 33442
> 1650 hours   page 407

4. Hyphens Hyphens are used with written-out numbers between 21 and 99.

> forty-one   forty-first
> four hundred twenty-two
> the twenty-fifth day

5. A hyphen is used between the numerator and the denominator of a fraction that is written out when that fraction is used as a modifier. A written-out fraction consisting of two words only (as *two thirds*) is usually styled open, although the hyphenated form is also common. Multiword numerators and denominators are usually hyphenated. If either the numerator or the denominator is hyphenated, no hyphen is used between them. For more on fractions, see pages 187–188.

> a two-thirds majority   forty-five hundredths
> three fifths of her paycheck   four five-hundredths
> seven and four fifths

6. Numbers that form the first part of a compound modifier expressing measurement are followed by a hyphen. An exception to this practice is that numbers are not followed by a hyphen when the second part of the modifier is the word *percent*.

> a 5-foot board   an eight-pound baby
> a 28-mile trip   a 680-acre ranch
> a 10-pound weight   a 75 percent reduction

7. An adjective or adverb made from a numeral plus the suffix *-fold* contains a hyphen, while a similar term made from a written-out number is styled solid. (For more on the use of suffixes with numbers, see page 164.)

> a fourfold increase
> increased 20-fold

8. Serial numbers, such as social security or engine numbers, often contain hyphens that make lengthy numerals more readable.

   020-42-1691

9. Numbers are usually not divided at the end of a line. If division is unavoidable, the break occurs only after a comma. End-of-line breaks do not occur at decimal points, and a name with a numerical suffix (as Robert F. Walker III) is not divided between the name and the numeral.

10. **Inclusive numbers** Inclusive numbers—those which express a range—are separated either by the word *to* or by a hyphen or en dash, which serves as an arbitrary equivalent of the phrase "(up) to and including" when used between dates and other inclusive numbers. (The en dash is explained in paragraph 12 under Dash, pages 106–107.)

pages 40 to 98	the fiscal year 1987–1988
pages 40–98	spanning the years 1915 to 1941
pp. 40–98	the decade 1920–1930

    NOTE: Inclusive numbers separated by a hyphen or en dash are not used in combination with the words *from* or *between,* as in "from 1955–60" or "between 1970–90." Instead, phrases like these are written as "from 1955 to 1960" or "between 1970 and 1990."

11. Units of measurement expressed in words or abbreviations are usually used only after the second element of an inclusive number. Symbols, however, are repeated.

    an increase in dosage from 200 to 500 mg
    ten to fifteen dollars
    30 to 35 degrees Celsius
       but
    $50 to $60 million
    45° to 48° F

12. Numbers that are part of an inclusive set or range are usually styled alike: figures with figures, spelled-out words with other spelled-out words. Similarly, approximate numbers are usually not paired with exact numbers.

    from 8 to 108 absences
    five to twenty guests
    300,000,000 to 305,000,000   *not*   300 million to 305,000,000

13. Inclusive page numbers and dates may be written in full (1981–1982) or elided (1981–82). However, inclusive dates that appear in titles and other headings are almost never elided. Dates that appear with era designations are also not elided.

467–68 *or* 467–468	1724–27 *or* 1724–1727
203–4 *or* 203–204	1463–1510
552–549 B.C.	1800–1801

NOTE: Elided numbers are used because they save space. The most commonly used style for the elision of inclusive numbers is based on the following rules:

1. Never elide inclusive numbers that have only two digits: 33–37, *not* 33–7.
2. Never elide inclusive numbers when the first number ends in 00: 100–108, *not* 100–08 *and not* 100–8.
3. In other numbers, omit *only* the hundreds digit from the higher number: 232–34, *not* 232–4.
4. Where the next-to-last digit of both numbers is zero, write only one digit for the higher number: 103–4, *not* 103–04.

467–68 *or* 467–468	203–4 *or* 203–204
1724–27 *or* 1724–1727	1800–1801
550–602	552–549 B.C.
1463–1510	

14. Plurals The plurals of written-out numbers are formed by the addition of *-s* or *-es*.

Back in the thirties these roads were unpaved.

Christmas shoppers bought the popular toy in twos and threes.

15. The plurals of figures are formed by adding *-s*. Some writers prefer to add an apostrophe before the *-s*. For more on the plurals of figures, see paragraphs 18 and 19 under Plurals, page 149, and paragraph 5 under Apostrophe, page 89.

This ghost town was booming back in the 1840s.

The first two artificial hearts to be implanted in human patients were Jarvik-7s.

but also

1's and *7*'s that looked alike

Specific Styling Conventions

The following paragraphs describe styling practices commonly followed for specific types of situations involving numbers. The paragraphs are arranged under the following alphabetical headings:

Addresses	Fractions and Decimal	Ratios
Dates	Fractions	Serial Numbers and
Degrees of Temperature	Money	Miscellaneous
and Arc	Percentages	Numbers
Enumerations and	Proper Names	Time of Day
Outlines		Units of Measurement

1. **Addresses** Arabic numerals are used for all building, house, apartment, room, and suite numbers except for *one*, which is written out.

6 Lincoln Road
1436 Fremont Street
but
One Bayside Drive

NOTE: When the address of a building is used as its name, the number in the address is written out.

Fifty Maple Street

2. Numbered streets have their numbers written as ordinals. There are two distinct conventions for the styling of numbered street names. The first, useful where space is limited, calls for Arabic numerals to denote all numbered streets above Twelfth; numbered street names from First through Twelfth are written out. A second, more formal, convention calls for the writing out of all numbered street names up to and including One Hundredth.

19 South 22nd Street	145 East 145th Street
167 West Second Avenue	122 East Forty-second Street
One East Ninth Street	36 East Fiftieth
in the Sixties (streets from 60th to 69th)	
in the 120s (streets from 120th to 129th)	

NOTE: A disadvantage of the first convention is that the direct juxtaposition of the house or building number and the street number may occur when there is no intervening word such as a compass direction. In these cases, a spaced hyphen may be inserted to distinguish the two numbers, or the second convention may be used and the street number written out.

2018–14th Street
2018 Fourteenth Street

3. Arabic numerals are used to designate interstate, federal, and state highways and, in some states, county roads.

U.S. Route 1 *or* U.S. 1	Massachusetts 57
Interstate 91 *or* I-91	County 213

4. **Dates** Year numbers are styled as figures. However, if a number representing a year begins a sentence, it may be written in full or the sentence rewritten to avoid beginning it with a figure. (For additional examples, see paragraph 3 under Numbers as Words or Figures, page 176.)

1988
1888–96

Fifteen eighty-eight marked the end to Spanish ambitions for the control of England.
or
Spanish ambitions for the control of England ended in 1588 with the destruction of their "Invincible Armada."

5. A year number may be abbreviated, or cut back to its last two digits, in informal writing or when an event is so well-known that it needs no century designation. In these cases an apostrophe precedes the numerals. For more on this use of the apostrophe, see paragraph 5 under Apostrophe, page 89.

> He always maintained that he'd graduated from Korea, Clash of '52.
> the blizzard of '88

6. Full dates (month, day, and year) may be styled in one of two distinct patterns. The traditional styling is the month-day-year sequence, with the year set off by commas that precede and follow it. An alternate styling is the inverted date, or day-month-year sequence, which does not require commas. This sequence is used in U.S. government publications and in the military.

> *traditional style*
> July 8, 1776, was a warm, sunny day in Philadelphia.
> the explosion on July 16, 1945, at Alamaogordo
> *military style*
> the explosion on 16 July 1945 at Alamogordo
> Lee's surrender to Grant on 9 April 1865 at Appomattox

7. Ordinal numbers are not used in expressions of full dates. Even though the numbers may be pronounced as ordinals, they are written as cardinal numbers. Ordinals may be used, however, to express a date without an accompanying year, and they are always used when preceded in a date by the word *the*.

> December 4, 1829
> on December 4th   *or*   on December 4
> on the 4th of December

8. Commas are usually omitted from dates that include the month and year but not the day. Alternatively, writers sometimes insert the word *of* between month and year.

> in November 1805   back in January of 1981

9. Once a numerical date has been given, a reference to a related date may be written out.

> After the meeting on June 6 the conventioneers left for home, and by the seventh the hotel was virtually empty.

10. All-figure dating (as 6-8-85 or 6/8/85) is inappropriate except in the most informal correspondence. It also creates a problem of ambiguity, as it may mean either June 8, 1985, or August 6, 1985.

11. References to specific centuries are often written out, although they may be expressed in figures, especially when they form the first element of a compound modifier.

the nineteenth century
a sixteenth-century painting
but also
20th-century revolutions

12. In general correspondence, the name of a specific decade often takes a short form. Although many writers place an apostrophe before the shortened word and a few capitalize it, both the apostrophe and the capitalization are often omitted when the context clearly indicates that a date is being referred to.

in the turbulent seventies
but also
back in the 'forties
in the early Fifties

13. The name of a specific decade is often expressed in numerals, usually in plural form. (For more on the formation of plural numbers, see paragraphs 14 and 15 under Punctuation and Inflection, page 182.) The figure may be shortened with an apostrophe to indicate the missing numerals, but any sequence of such numbers should be styled consistently. (For more on this use of the apostrophe, see paragraph 5 under Apostrophe, page 89.)

the 1950s and 1960s   *or*   the '50s and '60s
but not
the 1950s and '60s
and not
the '50's and '60's

14. Era designations precede or follow words that specify centuries or numerals that specify years. Era designations are unspaced and are nearly always abbreviated; they are usually printed as small capitals and typed as regular capitals, and they may or may not be punctuated with periods. Any date that is given without an era designation or context is understood to mean A.D. The two most commonly used abbreviations are B.C. (before Christ) and A.D. (*anno Domini,* "in the year of our Lord"). The abbreviation B.C. is placed after the date, while A.D. is usually placed before the date but after a century designation.

1792–1750 B.C.
A.D. 35
the second century A.D.
between 7 B.C. and A.D. 22

15. **Degrees of temperature and arc** In technical writing, figures are generally used for quantities expressed in degrees. In addition, the degree symbol (°) rather than the word *degree* is used with the figure. With the Kelvin scale, however, neither the word *degree* nor the symbol is used with the figure.

a 45° angle
6°40′10″N
32° F
0° C
Absolute zero is zero kelvins or 0 K.

16. In general writing, the quantity expressed in degrees may or may not be written out, depending on the styling conventions being followed. In general, a figure is followed by the degree symbol or the word *degree;* a written-out number is always followed by the word *degree.*

latitude 43°19″N
latitude 43 degrees N
a difference of 43 degrees latitude
The temperature has risen thirty degrees since this morning.

17. **Enumerations and outlines** Both run-in and vertical enumerations are often numbered. In run-in enumerations, each item is preceded by a number (or an italicized letter) enclosed in parentheses. The items in the list are separated by commas if the items are brief and have little or no internal punctuation; if the items are complex, they are separated by semicolons. The entire run-in enumeration is introduced by a colon if it is preceded by a full clause.

We feel that she should (1) increase her administrative skills, (2) pursue additional professional education, and (3) increase her production.

The oldest and most basic word-processing systems consist of the following: (1) a typewriter for keyboarding information, (2) a console to house the storage medium, and (3) the medium itself.

The vendor of your system should (1) instruct you in the care and maintenance of your system; (2) offer regularly scheduled maintenance to ensure that the system is clean, with lubrication and replacement of parts as necessary; and (3) respond promptly to service calls.

18. In vertical enumerations, the numbers are usually not enclosed in parentheses but are followed by a period. Each item in the enumeration begins its own line, which is either flush left or indented. Runover lines are usually aligned with the first word that follows the number, and figures are aligned on the periods that follow them. Each item on the list is usually capitalized if the items on the list are syntactically independent of the words that introduce them. However, style varies on this point, and use of a lowercase style for such items is fairly common. There is no terminal punctuation following the items unless at least one of the items is a complete sentence, in which case a period follows each item. Items that are syntactically dependent on the words that introduce them begin with a lowercase letter and carry the same punctuation marks that they would if they were a run-in series in a sentence.

Required skills include the following:
1. Shorthand

2. Typing
3. Transcription

To type a three-column table, follow this procedure:
1. Clear tab stops.
2. Remove margin stops.
3. Determine precise center of the page. Set a tap stop at center.

The vendor of your system should
1. instruct you in the care and maintenance of your system;
2. offer regularly scheduled maintenance to ensure that the system is clean, with lubrication and replacement parts as necessary; and
3. respond promptly to service calls.

19. Outlines make use of Roman numerals, Arabic numerals, and letters.

I. Editorial tasks
  A. Manuscript editing
  B. Author contact
    1. Authors already under contract
    2. New authors
II. Production responsibilities
  A. Scheduling
    1. Composition
    2. Printing and binding
  B. Cost estimates and bids
    1. Composition
    2. Printing and binding

20. Fractions and decimal fractions In running text, fractions standing alone are usually written out. Common fractions used as nouns are usually styled as open compounds, but when they are used as modifiers they are usually hyphenated. For more on written-out fractions, see page 180.

two thirds of the paint
a two-thirds majority
three thirty-seconds
seventy-two hundredths
one one-hundredth

NOTE: Most writers try to find ways to avoid the necessity of writing out complicated fractions (as *forty-two seventy-fifths*).

21. Mixed fractions (fractions with a whole number, such as 3½) and fractions that form part of a unit modifier are expressed in figures in running text. A *-th* is not added to a figure fraction.

waiting 2½ hours   a ⅞-mile course
1¼ million population   a 2½-kilometer race

NOTE: When mixed fractions are typewritten, the typist leaves a space between the whole number and the fraction. The space is closed up when the number is set in print. Fractions that are not on the typewriter keyboard may be made up by typing the numerator, a virgule, and the denominator in succession without spacing.

22. Fractions used with units of measurement are expressed in figures.

$\frac{1}{10}$ km $\frac{1}{4}$ mile

23. Decimal fractions are always set as figures. In technical writing, a zero is placed to the left of the decimal point when the fraction is less than a whole number. In general writing, the zero is usually omitted.

> An example of a pure decimal fraction is 0.375, while 1.402 is classified as a mixed decimal fraction.
> 0.142857
> 0.2 gm
> received 0.1 mg/kg diazepam i.v.
> *but*
> a .40 gauge shotgun

24. A comma is never inserted in the numbers following a decimal point.

25. Fractions and decimal fractions are usually not mixed in a text.

> 5½ lb. 2⅕ oz.
> 5.5 lb. 2.2 oz.
> *but not*
> 5½ lb. 2.2 oz.

26. Money Sums of money are expressed in words or figures, according to the conventions described under Basic Conventions, page 176. If the sum can be expressed in one or two words, it is usually written out in running text. But if several sums are mentioned in the sentence or paragraph, all are usually expressed as figures. When the amount is written out, the unit of currency is also written out. If the sum is expressed in figures, the symbol of the currency unit is used, with no space between it and the numerals.

> We paid $175,000 for the house.
> My change came to 87¢.
> The shop charged $67.50 for hand-knit sweaters.
> The price of a nickel candy bar seems to have risen to more like forty cents.
> Fifty dollars was stolen from my wallet.
> forty thousand dollars
> fifty-two dollars

27. Monetary units of mixed dollars-and-cents amounts are expressed in figures.

> $16.75 $307.02 $1.95

28. Even-dollar amounts are often expressed in figures without a decimal point and zeros. But when even-dollar amounts are used in a series with or are near to amounts that include dollars and cents, the decimal point and zeros are usually added for consistency. The dollar sign is repeated before each amount in a series or inclusive range; the word *dollar* may or may not be repeated.

The price of the book rose from $7.95 in 1970 to $8.00 in 1971 and then to $8.50 in 1972.

The bids were eighty, ninety, and one hundred dollars.

or

The bids were eighty dollars, one hundred dollars, and three hundred dollars.

29. Sums of money given in round units of millions or above are usually expressed in a combination of figures and words, either with a dollar sign or with the word *dollars*. For more on the handling of round numbers, see paragraphs 7 and 8 under Numbers as Words or Figures, pages 177–178.

> 60 million dollars
> a $10 million building program
> $4.5 billion

30. In legal documents a sum of money is usually written out fully, with the corresponding figures in parentheses immediately following.

> twenty-five thousand dollars ($25,000)

31. Percentages In technical writing, specific percentages are styled as figure plus unspaced percent sign (%). In general correspondence, the percentage number may be expressed as a figure or spelled out, depending on the conventions that apply to it. The word *percent* rather than the symbol is used in nonscientific texts.

technical	*general*
15%	15 percent
13.5%	87.2 percent
	Twenty-five percent of the office staff was out with the flu.
	a four percent increase

32. The word *percentage* or *percent,* used as a noun without an adjacent numeral, should never be replaced by a percent sign.

> Only a small percentage of the staff objected to the smoking ban.

33. In a series or unit combination the percent sign should be included with all numbers, even if one of the numbers is zero.

> a variation of 0% to 10%

34. Proper names Numbers in the names of religious organizations and of churches are usually written out in ordinal form. Names of specific governmental bodies may include ordinals, and these are written out if they are one hundred or below.

> Third Congregational Church
> Seventh-Day Adventists
> Third Reich
> First Continental Congress

35. Names of electoral, judicial, and military units may include ordinal numbers that precede the noun. Numbers of one hundred or below are written out.

> First Congressional District
> Twelfth Precinct
> Ninety-eighth Congress *or* 98th Congress
> Circuit Court of Appeals for the Third Circuit
> United States Eighth Army *or* 8th United States Army

36. Specific branches of labor unions and fraternal organizations are conventionally identified by an Arabic numeral usually placed after the name.

> International Brotherhood of Electrical Workers Local 42
> Elks Lodge No. 61
> Local 98 Operating Engineers

37. Ratios Ratios expressed in figures use a colon, a hyphen, a virgule, or the word *to* as a means of comparison. Ratios expressed in words use a hyphen, or the word *to*.

> a 3:1 chance
> odds of 100 to 1
> a 6-1 vote
> 22.4 mi/gal
> a ratio of ten to four
> a fifty-fifty chance

38. Serial numbers and miscellaneous numerals Figures are used to refer to things that are numbered serially, such as chapter and page numbers, addresses, years, policy and contract numbers, and so forth.

> Serial No. 5274   vol. 5, p. 202
> Permit No. 63709   column 2
> pages 420–515   Table 16

39. Figures are also used to express stock market quotations, mathematical calculations, scores, and tabulations.

> won by a score of 8 to 2 $3\frac{1}{8}$ percent bonds
> the tally: 322 ayes, 80 nays $3 \times 15 = 45$

40. Time of day In running text the time of day is usually spelled out when expressed in even, half, or quarter hours.

> Quitting time is four-thirty.
> The meeting should be over by half past eleven.
> We should arrive at a quarter past five.

41. The time of day is also usually spelled out when it is followed by the contraction *o'clock* or when *o'clock* is understood.

> He should be here by four at the latest.

My appointment is at eleven o'clock.
or
My appointment is at 11 o'clock.

42. Figures are used to delineate a precise time.

The meeting is scheduled for 9:15 in the morning.
Her plane is due at 3:05 this afternoon.
The program starts at 8:30 in the evening.

43. Figures are also written when the time of day is used in conjunction with the abbreviations *a.m. (ante meridiem)* and *p.m. (post meridiem)*. The punctuated lowercase styling for these abbreviations is most common, but punctuated small capital letters are also frequently used. These abbreviations should not be used in conjunction with the words *morning* or *evening;* and the word *o'clock* should not be combined with either *a.m.* or *p.m.*

8:30 a.m.   *or*   8:30 A.M.
10:30 p.m.   *or*   10:30 P.M.
8 a.m.   *or*   8 A.M.
    but
9:15 in the morning
11:00 in the evening
nine o'clock

NOTE: When twelve o'clock is written, it is helpful to add the designation *midnight* or *noon*, as *a.m.* and *p.m.* sometimes cause confusion.

twelve o'clock (midnight)
twelve o'clock (noon)

44. For consistency, even-hour times should be expressed with a colon and two zeros, when used in a series or pairing with any odd-hour times.

He came at 7:00 and left at 9:45.

45. The 24-hour clock system—also called military time—uses no punctuation and is expressed without the use of *a.m., p.m.,* or *o'clock.*

from 0930 to 1100   at 1600 hours

46. Units of measurement Numbers used with units of measurement are treated according to the basic conventions explained in the first part of this section. However, in some cases writers achieve greater clarity by styling all numbers—even those below ten—that express quantities of physical measurement as numerals.

The car was travelling in excess of 80 miles an hour.
The old volume weighed three pounds and was difficult to hold in a reading position.
but also in some general texts

3 hours, 25 minutes
saw 18 eagles in 12 minutes
a 6-pound hammer
weighed 3 pounds, 5 ounces

47. When units of measurement are written as abbreviations or symbols, the adjacent numbers are always figures.

6 cm   67.6 fl oz
1 mm   4′
$4.25   98.6°

48. When two or more quantities are expressed, as in ranges or dimensions or series, an accompanying symbol is usually repeated with each figure.

4″ by 6″ cards
temperature on successive days of 30°, 55°, 43°, and 58°
$400–$500

Chapter 4

Composition and Grammar

CONTENTS

No guide to effective communication can ignore the basic components of discourse: the word, the phrase, the clause, the sentence, and the paragraph. Each of these increasingly complex units contributes to the expression of a writer's ideas.

The simplest component of discourse is the word. The treatment of words in this chapter focuses on their grammatical function in a sentence. For a discussion of the ways in which words convey tone in writing, see Chapter 5, "Tone in Writing." General questions concerning the more complex language components of phrases, clauses, sentences, and paragraphs are also discussed in this chapter. For a discussion of the compositional topics that relate specifically to letter-writing, see Chapter 6, "Composing Letters."

Parts of Speech

Words have traditionally been classified into eight parts of speech: the adjective, adverb, conjunction, interjection, noun, preposition, pronoun, and verb. This classification system is based mainly on a word's inflectional features, its general grammatical functions, and its positioning within a sentence. On the following pages, these parts of speech are listed alphabetically and discussed briefly.

Adjective

An adjective is a word that typically describes or modifies the meaning of a noun. Adjectives serve to point out a quality of a thing named, to indicate its quantity or extent, or to specify a thing as distinct from something else.

Adjectives are often classified by the ways in which they modify or limit the meaning of a noun. The classifications commonly referred to are the following: descriptive adjectives, demonstrative adjectives, indefinite adjectives, interrogative adjectives, possessive adjectives, predicate adjectives, proper adjectives, relative adjectives, and articles.

A *descriptive adjective* describes something or indicates a quality, kind, or condition ("a *sick* person," "a *brave* soldier," "a *new* dress"). The *demonstrative adjectives*, such as *this* and *that*, point to what they modify in order to distinguish it from others. These two are the only adjectives with plural forms ("*this* child," "*these* children"; "*that* house," "*those* houses"). An *indefinite adjective* designates an unidentified or not immediately identifiable person or thing ("*some* books," "*other* hotels"). An *interrogative adjective* conveys the force of a question ("*Whose* office is this?" "*Which* book do you want?"). A *possessive adjective* is the possessive form of a personal pronoun ("*her* idea," "*his* job," "*my* car," "*our* savings plan," "*their* office," "*your* opinion"). A *proper adjective* is derived from a proper noun and takes its meaning from what characterizes the noun. It is usually capitalized ("*Victorian* furniture," "a *Puerto Rican* product," "*Keynesian* economics"). A *relative adjective* introduces an adjectival clause ("at the April conference, by *which* time the report should be finished") or a clause that functions as a noun ("the uncomfortable position of not knowing *which* course she should follow"). An *article* is one of a small group of words (as *a, an,* and *the*) that are used with nouns to limit or give definiteness to the application of a noun ("*a* condominium," "*an* honor," "*the* jetliner").

The following paragraphs describe some other types of adjectives. They also outline situations involving adjectives that are sometimes troublesome for writers.

1. **Absolute adjectives** Some adjectives (such as *prior, maximum, optimum, minimum,* and *first*) admit no comparison under ordinary circumstances (see paragraphs 3 and 4 below), because they represent ultimate conditions. These adjectives are called *absolute adjectives*. Some writers are careful to modify these adjectives with adverbs such as *almost, near,* or *nearly,* rather than *least, less, more, most,* or *very.*

> an almost fatal dose
> at near maximum capacity
> a more nearly perfect likeness

NOTE: Many writers do compare and qualify this type of adjective in order to show connotations and shades of meaning they consider less than absolute.

> a more perfect union
> a less complete account

When in doubt about the comparability of an absolute adjective, one should check the definitions and examples of usage given for the adjective in a dictionary.

2. **Adjective/noun agreement** The number (singular or plural) of a demonstrative adjective *(this, that, these, those)* should agree with that of the noun it modifies.

> these kinds of typewriters   *not*   these kind of typewriters
> those sorts of jobs   *not*   those sort of jobs
> this type of person   *not*   these type of people

3. **Compared with adverbs** Both adjectives and adverbs describe or modify other words; however, adjectives can only modify nouns, while adverbs can modify verbs, adverbs, and adjectives. For more on the differences between adjectives and adverbs, see paragraph 14 below and paragraphs 4–6 under Adverb in this section.

4. **Comparison of adjectives** The main structural feature of an adjective is its ability to indicate degrees of comparison (positive, comparative, superlative) by addition of suffixal endings *-er/-est* to the base word, by addition of *more/most* or *less/least* before the base word, or by use of irregular forms.

positive	*comparative*	*superlative*
clean	cleaner	cleanest
meaningful	more meaningful	most meaningful
meaningful	less meaningful	least meaningful
bad	worse	worst

5. The comparative degree is used to show that the thing being modified has more (or less) of a particular quality than the one or ones to which it is being compared. The superlative degree is used to show that the thing being modified has the most (or least) of a quality out of all of the ones to which it is being compared. The superlative degree is most commonly used when there are more than two things being compared.

> *comparative*
> prices that were higher than those at other stores
> a better report than our last one
> the more expensive of the two methods
> *superlative*
> the highest prices in the area
> the best report so far
> the most expensive of the three methods

6. In general, the comparatives and superlatives of one-syllable adjectives are formed by adding *-er/-est* to the base word. The comparatives and superlatives of adjectives with more than two syllables are formed by adding *more* and *most* or *less* and *least* before the base word. The comparatives and superlatives of two-syllable adjectives are variously formed by adding *-er/-est* to the base word or using *more* and *most* or *less* and *least* before the base word. When in doubt about the inflection of a particular adjective, one should consult a dictionary.

positive	*comparative*	*superlative*
big	bigger	biggest
loose	looser	loosest
empty	emptier	emptiest
narrow	narrower	narrowest
complex	more complex	most complex
concise	less concise	least concise
important	more important	most important
troublesome	less troublesome	least troublesome

7. Some adjectives are ordinarily not compared, because they are felt to represent ultimate conditions. For more on these adjectives, see paragraph 1, above.

8. **Coordinate and noncoordinate adjectives** Adjectives that share equal relationships to the nouns they modify are called *coordinate adjectives* and are separated from each other by commas.

  a concise, coherent essay
  a hard, flickering light

9. When the first of two adjectives modifies the noun plus a second adjective, the result is a pair of *noncoordinate adjectives.* Noncoordinate adjectives are not separated by commas.

  a low monthly fee
  the first warm day

10. **Double comparisons** Double comparisons are considered nonstandard and should be avoided.

  an easier method   *not*   a more easier method
  the easiest solution   *not*   the most easiest solution

11. **Incomplete or understood comparisons** Some comparisons are left incomplete because the context clearly implies the comparison. These are commonly used especially in advertising. It should be understood, however, that the use of incomplete comparisons is often considered careless or illogical in formal writing.

  Get better buys here!
  We have lower prices.

12. **Nouns used as adjectives** Nouns are frequently used to describe other nouns, and in this way they act like adjectives. For more on the use of nouns as modifiers, see paragraph 6 under Noun in this section and the discussion under Compounds That Function as Adjectives, pages 158-161.

13. **Placement within a sentence** Adjectives may occur in the following positions within sentences: (1) preceding the nouns they modify, (2) fol-

lowing the nouns they modify, (3) following the verb *to be* and other linking verbs in the predicate-adjective position, and (4) following some transitive verbs used in the passive voice.

(1) the black hat   a dark, shabby coat
(2) an executive par excellence   painted the room blue
(3) a hat that is black   food that tastes stale
    while I felt sick
(4) a room that was painted blue
    passengers found dead at the crash site

14. Predicate adjectives A predicate adjective modifies the subject of a linking verb (as *be, become, feel, taste, smell, seem*) which it follows.

> She is happy.
> The milk tastes sour.
> The student seems puzzled.

NOTE: Because some linking verbs (as *feel, look, smell, taste*) can also function as active verbs, which can in turn be modified by adverbs, writers are sometimes confused over whether they should use the adverbial or adjectival form of a modifier after the verb. The answer is that an adjective is used if the subject of the sentence is being modified. If the verb is being modified, an adverb is used. (For more examples, see paragraph 5 under Adverb in this section.)

> Your report looks good. [adjective]
> The colors feel right. [adjective]
> The engine smells hot. [adjective]
> They looked quickly at each item. [adverb]
> He felt immediately for his wallet. [adverb]
> She felt the corners carefully for dampness. [adverb]

Adverb

An adverb is a word or combination of words typically serving as a modifier of a verb, an adjective, another adverb, a preposition, a phrase, a clause, or a sentence and expressing some relation of manner or quality, place, time, degree, number, cause, opposition, affirmation, or denial.

Most commonly, adverbs take the form of an adjective with an *-ly* ending added to it *(actually, congenially, madly, really)*. There are many exceptions to this pattern, however. For instance, adverbs based on adjectives ending in *-ly (costly, friendly, likely)* do not include an additional *-ly* ending but take the same form as the adjective. In addition, some adverbs do not end in *-ly (now, quite, too)*.

Adverbs answer such questions as the following: "when?" ("Please reply *at once*"); "how long?" ("This job is taking *forever*"); "where?" ("She works *there*"); "in what direction?" ("Move the lever *upward*"); "how?" ("The staff moved *expeditiously* on the project"); and "to what degree?" ("The book was *very* popular").

1. **Basic uses** Adverbs modify verbs, adjectives, and other adverbs.

> She *carefully* studied the balance sheet.
> She gave the balance sheet *very* careful study.
> She studied the balance sheet *very* carefully.

2. Conjunctive adverbs join clauses or link sentences. (For more on this use of adverbs, see paragraphs 13–15 under Conjunction in this section.)

> You are welcome to join our car pool; *however,* please be ready by 7:00 a.m.
> He thoroughly enjoyed the symposium. *Indeed,* he was fascinated by the presentations.

3. In addition, adverbs may be essential elements of two-word verbs commonly having separate entries in dictionaries.

> Our staff will work *up* the specifications.
> We can work them *up* later.

4. **Compared with adjectives** Adverbs but not adjectives modify action verbs.

> *not*
> He answered very *harsh.*
> *instead*
> He answered very *harshly.*

5. Complements referring to the subject of a sentence and occurring after linking verbs conventionally take adjectives but not adverbs. (For more examples, see paragraph 14 under Adjective in this section.)

> *not*
> He looks *badly* these days.
> The letter sounded *strongly.*
> *instead*
> He looks *bad* these days.
> The letter sounded *strong.*
> *and also*
> He looks *good* these days.
> He looks *well* these days.

NOTE: In the last two examples, either *good* or *well* is acceptable, because both words are here functioning as adjectives in the sense of "healthy."

6. Adverbs but not adjectives modify adjectives and other adverbs.

> *not*
> She looked *dreadful* tired.
> *instead*
> She looked *dreadfully* tired.

7. **Comparison of adverbs** Most adverbs have three different forms to indicate degrees of comparison (positive, comparative, superlative). The positive form is the same as the base word (*quickly, loudly, near*). The comparative form is usually shown by the addition of *more* or *less* before the base word (*more quickly, less quickly*); the superlative form is usually shown by the addition of *most* or *least* (*most quickly, least quickly*). However, a few adverbs (such as *fast, slow, loud, soft, early, late,* and *quick*) may be compared in two ways: by the method described above or by the addition of the suffixal endings *-er/-est* to the base word (*quick, quicker, quickest*). For an explanation of the uses of the comparative and superlative forms, see paragraph 5 under Adjective in this section.

8. As a general rule, one-syllable adverbs use the *-er/-est* endings to show comparison. Adverbs of three or more syllables use *more/most* and *less/ least*. Two-syllable adverbs take either form.

fast	faster	fastest
late	later	latest
easy	easier	easiest
madly	more madly	most madly
happily	more happily	most happily

9. Some adverbs (such as *quite* and *very*) cannot be compared.

10. **Double negatives** A combination of two negative adverbs (such as *not, hardly, never,* and *scarcely*) used to express a single negative idea is considered substandard.

> *not*
> We *cannot* see *hardly* any reason why we should buy this product.
> *instead*
> We *cannot* see any reason why we should buy this product.
> We can see *hardly* any reason why we should buy this product.

11. **Emphasis** Adverbs (such as *just* and *only*) are often used to emphasize other words. A writer should be aware of the various emphases that can result from the positioning of an adverb in a sentence.

> *emphasis on the action itself*
> He *just* nodded to me as he passed.
> *emphasis on timing of the action*
> He nodded to me *just* as he passed.

12. In some positions and contexts, these adverbs can be ambiguous.

> They will only tell it to you.

It is not clear whether this writer means that they will only tell it, not put it in writing, or that they will tell no one else. If the latter interpretation is intended, a slight shift of position would remove the uncertainty.

> They will tell it only to you.

13. **Placement within a sentence** Adverbs are generally positioned as close as possible to the words they modify if such a position will not result in misinterpretation.

> *unclear*
> A project that the board would support *completely* occupied her thinking.

It is unclear whether the writer means "would support completely" or "completely occupied her thinking." The adverb may be moved to another position, or the sentence may be recast, depending on intended meaning.

> *clear*
> A project that the board would *completely* support occupied her thinking.
> *or*
> Her thinking was *completely* occupied with a project that the board would support.

14. When an adverb separates *to* from the verbal element of an infinitive ("hope to really start"), the result is called a split infinitive. For a discussion of split infinitives, see paragraph 32 under Verb in this section.

15. In some cases, adverbs modify an entire sentence rather than a specific word or phrase within the sentence. Such adverbs are referred to as *sentence adverbs,* and their position can vary according to the emphasis one wishes to use.

> *Fortunately* they had already placed their order.
> They *fortunately* had already placed their order.
> They had already placed their order *fortunately.*

16. **Relative adverbs** Relative adverbs (such as *when, where, why*) introduce subordinate clauses. (For more on subordinate clauses, see the section on Clauses, beginning on page 228.)

> They met at a time *when* prospects were good.
> I went into the room *where* they were sitting.
> Everyone knows the reason *why* she did it.

Conjunction

A conjunction is a word or phrase that joins together words, phrases, clauses, or sentences. Conjunctions may occur in many different positions in a sentence, although they ordinarily do not appear at the end of a sentence unless the sentence is elliptical. There are three main types of conjunctions: *coordinating, correlative,* and *subordinating.* In addition to these three types of conjunctions, the English language has transitional adverbs and adverbial phrases called *conjunctive adverbs*. These function as conjunctions even though they are customarily classified as adverbs. A definition and discussion of the three types of conjunctions and of conjunctive adverbs follows. (For information about punctuating sentences with conjunctions, see paragraphs 1–4, 23, and 26–28 under Comma, pages 94–95 and 99–100, and paragraphs 1–5 under Semicolon, pages 121–122.)

Coordinating conjunctions Coordinating conjunctions (such as *and, but, for, or, nor, so,* and *yet*) join together grammatical elements of equal weight. The elements may be words, phrases, subordinate clauses, main clauses, or complete sentences.

1. Coordinating conjunctions are used to join elements, to exclude or contrast, to offer alternatives, or to propose reasons, grounds, or a result.

   joining elements
   She ordered pencils, pens, *and* erasers.
   Sales were slow, *and* they showed no sign of improvement.

   excluding or contrasting
   He is a brilliant *but* arrogant man.
   They offered a promising plan, *but* it had not yet been tested.

   alternative
   She can wait here *or* go on ahead.

   reason or grounds
   The report is useless, *for* its information is no longer current.

   result
   His diction is excellent, *so* every word is clear.

2. A comma is used before a coordinating conjunction linking coordinate clauses, especially when these clauses are lengthy. For more on the use of Commas between clauses, see paragraphs 1–4 under Comma, pages 94–95.

   We encourage applications from all interested persons, *but* we do have high professional standards that the successful applicant must meet.

3. Coordinating conjunctions should link equal grammatical elements—for example, adjectives with other adjectives, nouns with other nouns, participles with other participles, clauses with other equal-ranking clauses, and so on. Combining unequal grammatical elements may result in unbalanced sentences.

   unbalanced (*and* links a participial phrase with an adverbial clause)
   Having become disgusted *and* because he was tired, he left the meeting.

   balanced (*and* links two adjectives)
   Because he was tired *and* disgusted, he left the meeting.
   Having become tired *and* disgusted, he left the meeting.

4. Coordinating conjunctions should not be used to string together excessively long series of elements, regardless of their grammatical equality.

strung-out
We have sustained enormous losses in this division, *and* we have realized practically no profits even though the sales figures indicate last-quarter gains, *and* we are therefore reorganizing the entire management structure as well as cutting back on personnel.

tightened
Because this division has sustained enormous losses and has realized only insignificant profits even with its last-quarter sales gains, we are totally reorganizing its management. We are also cutting back on personnel.

5. The choice of just the right coordinating conjunction for a particular verbal situation is important: the right word will pinpoint the writer's true meaning and intent and will emphasize the most relevant idea or point of the sentence. The following three sentences show increasingly stronger degrees of contrast through the use of different conjunctions:

neutral
He works hard *and* doesn't progress.

more contrast
He works hard *but* doesn't progress.

stronger contrast
He works hard, *yet* he doesn't progress.

6. The coordinating conjunction *and/or* linking two elements of a compound subject often poses a problem: should the verb that follows be singular or plural? A subject comprising singular nouns connected by *and/or* may be considered singular or plural, depending on the meaning of the sentence.

singular
All loss *and/or* damage is to be the responsibility of the sender. [one or the other and possibly both]

plural
John R. Westlake *and/or* Maria A. Artandi are hereby *appointed* as the executors of my estate. [both executors are to act, or either of them is to act if the other dies or is incapacitated]

Correlative conjunctions Correlative conjunctions are coordinating conjunctions that are regularly used in pairs, although they are not placed adjacent to one another.

7. Correlative conjunctions are used to link alternatives and equal elements.

alternatives
Either you go *or* you stay.
He had *neither* looks *nor* wits.

equal elements
Both typist *and* writer should understand the rules of punctuation.
Not only was there inflation, *but* there was *also* unemployment.

8. Because they link equal grammatical elements, correlative conjunctions should be placed as close as possible to the elements they join.

misplaced (joining clause and verb phrase)
Either I must send a telex *or* make a long-distance call.

repositioned (joining two verb phrases)
I must *either* send a telex *or* make a long-distance call.

9. The negative counterpart to *either . . . or* is *neither . . . nor.* The conjunction *or* should not be substituted for *nor,* because its substitution will destroy the negative parallelism. However, *or* may occur in combination with *no.*

not
He received *neither* a promotion *or* a raise.

instead
He received *neither* a promotion *nor* a raise.

also
He received *no* promotion *or* raise.

Subordinating conjunction Subordinating conjunctions join a subordinate or dependent clause to a main clause.

10. Subordinating conjunctions are used to express cause, condition or concession, manner, purpose or result, time, place or circumstance, and alternative conditions or possibilities.

cause
Because she learns quickly, she is doing well in her new job.

condition or concession
Don't call *unless* you have the information.

manner
He looks *as though* he is ill.
We'll do it *however* you tell us to.

purpose or result
She routes the mail early *so that* they can read it.

time
She kept meetings to a minimum *when* she was president.

place or circumstance
I don't know *where* he has gone.
He tries to help out *wherever* it is possible.

conditions or possibilities
It was hard to decide *whether* I should go or stay.

11. The subordinating conjunction *that* introduces several kinds of subordinate clauses, including those used as noun equivalents (such as a subject or an object of a verb or as a predicate nominative).

Yesterday I learned *that* he has been sick for over a week.

12. In introducing subordinate clauses, subordinating conjunctions deemphasize less important ideas in favor of more important ideas. The writer must take care that the point he or she wishes to emphasize is in the main clause and that the points of less importance are subordinated. Notice how differently these two versions strike the reader.

> We were just coming out of the door *when* the building burst into flames.
> *As* we were just coming out of the door, the building burst into flames.

Conjunctive adverb Conjunctive adverbs are transitional adverbs and adverbial phrases that express relationships between two units of discourse (as two main clauses, two complete sentences, or two or more paragraphs). Conjunctive adverbs are classed as adverbs, but they function as conjunctions when they are used as connectives. Some common conjunctive adverbs are listed below.

accordingly	first	incidentally	on the contrary
also	for example	in conclusion	otherwise
anyhow	for instance	indeed	second
anyway	furthermore	in fact	still
as a result	further on	later	that is (to say)
besides	hence	likewise	then
consequently	however	moreover	therefore
e.g.	i.e.	namely	to be sure
finally	in addition	nevertheless	too

13. Conjunctive adverbs are used to express addition, to add emphasis, to express contrast or discrimination, to introduce illustrations or elaborations, to express or introduce conclusions or results, or to orient elements of discourse as to time or space.

addition
This employee deserves a substantial raise; *furthermore,* she should be promoted.

emphasis
He is brilliant; *indeed,* he is a genius.

contrast or discrimination
The major responsibility lies with the partners; *nevertheless,* associates should be competent in decision-making.

illustrations or elaborations
Losses were due to several negative factors; *namely,* inflation, foreign competition, and restrictive government regulation.

conclusions or results
Government overregulation in that country reached a prohibitive level in the last quarter. *Thus,* we are phasing out all of our operations there.

time or space
First, we can remind them that their account is long overdue; *second,* we can say that we must consider consulting our attorneys if they do not meet their obligation.

14. Conjunctive adverbs are usually placed at the beginning of a clause or sentence. When they are placed later in the clause or sentence, additional emphasis is placed on them.

The overdue shipment arrived this morning; *however,* we must point out that it was incomplete.

The overdue shipment arrived this morning; we must point out, *however,* that it was incomplete.

15. The misuse of conjunctive adverbs can lead to a problem known as *comma fault.* When a conjunctive adverb is used to connect two main clauses, a semicolon should be used; a comma will not suffice. (For more on comma fault and punctuation between main clauses, see paragraphs 1–4 under Comma, pages 94–95 and paragraph 5 under Semicolon, page 122.)

comma fault
The company had flexible hours, *however* its employees were expected to abide by their selected arrival and departure times.

repunctuated
The company had flexible hours; *however,* its employees were expected to abide by their selected arrival and departure times.

Interjection

Interjections are exclamatory or interrupting words or phrases that express an emotion. Interjections are usually independent clauses that lack grammatical connection with the rest of the sentence. They often stand alone.

1. Interjections may be stressed or ejaculatory words, phrases, or even short sentences.

Absurd!
No, no!
Get out!
Not now!

2. Interjections may also be so-called "sound" words, such as those representing shouts, hisses, or cries:

Shh! The meeting has begun.
Pssst! Come over here.
Ouch! That hurts.
Ugh! What a horrible flavor.

3. Emphatic interjections expressing forceful emotions use exclamation points.

Fire!
What an awful time we had!

4. Mildly stressed words or sentences may be punctuated with commas and periods.

Ah, that's my idea of a terrific deal.
Well, well, so that's the solution.
Oh, you're probably right.

5. Interjections should be sparingly used in discourse, and then only to signal genuine emotion or for strong emphasis.

Noun

A noun is a word that is the name of something (as a person, animal, place, object, quality, concept, or action). Nouns are used in a sentence as the subject or object of a verb, as the object of a preposition, as a predicate after a linking verb, as an appositive name, or as a name in an absolute construction.

Nouns exhibit these characteristic features: they are inflected for possession; they have number (that is, they are either singular or plural); they are often preceded by determiners (as *a, an, the; this, that, these, those; all, every,* and other such qualifiers; *one, two, three,* and other such numerical quantifiers; *his, her, their,* and other such pronominal adjectives); a few of them still show gender differences (as masculine *host, actor,* feminine *hostess, actress*); and many of them are formed by adding a suffix (such as *-ance, -ist, -ness,* and *-tion*).

1. Basic uses Nouns are used as subjects, direct objects, objects of prepositions, indirect objects, retained objects, predicate nominative, objective complements, and appositives and in direct address.

> *subject*
> The *office* was quiet.
> *direct object*
> He locked the *office.*
> *object of a preposition*
> The file is in the *office.*
> *indirect object*
> He gave his *client* the papers.
> *retained object*
> His client was given the *papers.*
> *predicate nominative*
> Mrs. Adams is the managing *partner.*
> *objective complement*
> They made Mrs. Adams managing *partner.*
> *appositive*
> Mrs. Adams, the managing *partner,* wrote that memorandum.
> *direct address*
> *Mrs. Adams,* may I present Mr. Bonkowski.

2. Compound nouns Because English is not a static and unchanging entity, many of its words undergo styling variations because of the changing preferences of its users. The styling of compound nouns (whether open, closed, or hyphenated) is especially subject to changing usage. No rigid set of rules can cover every possible variation or combination; however, some consistent patterns of usage can be discerned. For a description of these patterns, see the discussion under Compound Nouns, pages 155–158.

3. Indefinite articles with nouns Before a word or abbreviation beginning with a consonant *sound,* the article *a* is used. This is true even if the spelling of the word begins with a vowel.

a BA degree	a COD package	a door
a hat	a human	a union
a one	a U.S. Senator	

4. Before *h-* in an unstressed or lightly stressed first syllable, the article *a* is more frequently used, although *an* is more usual in speech whether or not the *h-* is actually pronounced. Either is acceptable in speech or writing.

a historian *or* an historian
a heroic attempt *or* an heroic attempt
a hilarious performance *or* an hilarious performance

5. Before a word or abbreviation beginning with a vowel *sound,* the article *an* is used. This is true even if the spelling (especially of an abbreviation) begins with a consonant.

an icicle	an orange	an unknown
an hour	an honor	an nth degree
an FCC report	an MIT professor	an Rh factor

6. Nominals Nominals are words or groups of words that function as nouns. Adjectives, gerunds, and infinitives act as nominals. An example of an adjective used as a noun is the word *good* in the phrase "the good die young." Examples of gerunds and infinitives used as nouns are *seeing* in the clause "seeing is believing" and *to see* in the clause "to see is to believe." Noun phrases and noun clauses are also considered to be nominals. For more information about gerunds and infinitives, see paragraphs 12–14 under Verb in this section. For information about noun phrases and noun clauses, see pages 227 and 228 respectively.

7. Nouns used as adjectives A frequent practice in English is to use a noun as an adjective by placing it before another noun (in the attributive position), as in *school board* or *office management.* When nouns are frequently combined in this way, they become familiar compounds like *profit margin, systems analysis, money market, box lunch.* Such compounds provide useful verbal shortcuts (e.g., office management = the management of an office or offices). However, care should be taken not to pile up so many of these noun modifiers that the reader has difficulty sorting out their meanings.

shorter but unclear
Management review copies of the Division II sales department machine parts file should be indexed.

longer but clear
Copies of the machine parts file from the Division II sales department should be indexed before being sent to management for review.

NOTE: Both of these sentences could be made clearer by hyphenating the compound nouns used as adjectives. For complete information about the treatment of this kind of compound, see the discussion under Compounds That Function as Adjectives, pages 158–161.

> Management-review copies of the Division II sales-department machine-parts file should be indexed.

8. Plurals The plurals of nouns are usually indicated by addition of an -s or -es to the base word, although some nouns (such as those of foreign origin) have irregular plurals. For complete information about the formation of plurals, see the discussion under Plurals, pages 146–150.

9. Possessives The possessive case is the only noun case indicated by inflection. Typically, the possessives of nouns are formed by the addition of an apostrophe plus -s to singular nouns or just an apostrophe to plural words ending in -s. For complete information about the formation of possessives, see the discussion under Possessives, pages 150–153.

10. Proper nouns Proper nouns are nouns that name a particular person, place, or thing and distinguish it from other members of the same class. The most obvious feature of proper nouns is that they are almost always capitalized. For complete information about capitalizing proper nouns, see the discussion under Proper Nouns, Pronouns, and Adjectives, pages 127–143.

Preposition

A preposition is a word that combines with a noun, pronoun, or noun equivalent (as a phrase or clause) to form a phrase that usually acts as an adverb, adjective, or noun.

Prepositions are not characterized by inflection, number, case, gender, or identifying suffixes. They can be identified chiefly by their position within sentences and by their grammatical functions. Prepositions may be simple, i.e., composed of only one element (*against, from, near, of, on, out,* or *without*); or they may be compound, i.e., composed of more than one element (*according to, by means of,* or *in spite of*).

1. Basic uses Prepositions are chiefly used to link nouns, pronouns, or noun equivalents to the rest of the sentence. A prepositional phrase is usually adverbial or adjectival in function.

> She expected resistance *on* his part.
> He sat down *beside* her.

2. Conjunctions vs. prepositions The words *after, before, but, for,* and *since* may function as either prepositions or conjunctions. Their position within the sentence identifies them as conjunctions or prepositions. Conjunctions link two words or sentence elements that have the same grammatical function. Prepositions precede a noun, pronoun, noun phrase, or noun equivalent.

conjunction
I was a bit concerned *but* not panicky. (*but* links two adjectives)

preposition
I was left with nothing *but* hope. (*but* precedes a noun)

conjunction
The device conserves fuel, *for* it is battery-powered. (*for* links two clauses)

preposition
The device conserves fuel *for* residual heating. (*for* precedes a noun phrase)

3. **Implied or unknown prepositions** If two words combine idiomatically with the same preposition, that preposition need not be used after both.

> We were antagonistic [*to*] and opposed *to* the whole idea.
> *but*
> We are interested *in* and anxious *for* raises.

4. **Position** Prepositions may occur in the following positions: before nouns or pronouns ("*below* the desk," "*beside* them"); after adjectives ("antagonistic *to*," "insufficient *in*," "symbolic *of*"); and after the verbal elements of idiomatically fixed verb + preposition combinations ("take *for*," "get *after*," "come *across*").

5. There is no reason why a preposition cannot terminate a sentence, especially when it is an integral element in an idiomatically fixed verb phrase.

> His lack of organization is only one of the things I put up *with*.
> What does all this add up to?

6. **Use of *between* and *among*** Despite an unfounded notion to the contrary, the preposition *between* can be used of more than two items. It is especially appropriate to denote a one-to-one relationship, regardless of the number of items. *Between* can be used when the number is unspecified, when more than two are enumerated, and even when only one item is mentioned (but repetition is implied).

> Treaties established economic cooperation *between* nations.
> This is *between* you and me and the lamppost.
> He paused *between* every sentence to clear his throat.

Among is more appropriate where the emphasis is on overall distribution rather than individual relationships.

> There was discontent *among* the peasants.

NOTE: When *among* is automatically chosen for more than two, the results can sound strained.

> The author alternates *among* quotes, clichés, and street slang.

Pronoun

A pronoun is a word that is used as a substitute for a noun or noun equivalent, takes noun constructions, and refers to persons or things named or understood in the context. The noun or noun equivalent for which it substitutes is called the *antecedent*.

Pronouns exhibit all or some of the following characteristic features: case (nominative, possessive, objective); number (singular, plural); person (first, second, third person); and gender (masculine, feminine, neuter). Pronouns are divided into seven major categories, each with its own function. Each pronoun category is listed and described alphabetically in this section.

Demonstrative pronouns The words *this, that, these,* and *those* are classified as pronouns when they function as nouns (they are classified as demonstrative adjectives when they modify nouns; see the discussion under Adjective in this section).

1. Demonstrative pronouns point out the person or thing referred to and distinguish it from others of the same type.

    These are the best cookies I've ever eaten.

    Those are strong words.

2. They also distinguish between a person or thing nearby and one further away.

    This is my desk; *that* is yours.

3. A potentially troublesome situation occurs when a demonstrative pronoun introduces a sentence referring back to something previously mentioned. The reference should be clear and not cloudy:

    cloudy
    The heir's hemophilia, the influence of an unprincipled faith healer on the royal family, devastating military setbacks, general strikes, mass outbreaks of typhus, and repeated crop failures contributed to the revolution. *This* influenced the course of history.

    clear
    None of the participants in the political scandal kept records of what they said or did. *That* is most unfortunate, and it should be a lesson for the future.

4. When demonstrative pronouns are used with the words *kind, sort,* and *type + of +* noun, they should agree in number with both nouns.

    not
    We want *these kind* of *pencils.*

    instead
    We want *this kind* of *pencil.*

    or
    We want *these kinds* of *pencils.*

Indefinite pronouns Indefinite pronouns designate an unidentified or not immediately identifiable person or thing. They are chiefly used as third-person references and do not distinguish gender. Examples of indefinite pronouns are the following: *all, another, any, anybody, anyone, anything, both, each, each one, either, everybody, everyone, everything, few, many, much, neither, nobody, none, no one, other, several, some, somebody, someone, something.*

5. Indefinite pronouns should agree in number with their verb. The following are singular and take singular verbs: *another, anything, each one, everything, much, nobody, no one, one, other, someone, something.*

    Much is being done.
    No one wants to go.

6. The following indefinite pronouns are plural and take plural verbs: *both, few, many, several.*

    Many were called; *few were* chosen.

7. Some indefinite pronouns (such as *all, any, none, some*) present problems because they may be either singular or plural, depending on whether they are used with mass nouns or count nouns (a *mass noun* identifies something not ordinarily thought of in terms of numbered elements; a *count noun* identifies things that can be counted).

    with mass noun
    All of the *property is* entailed.
    None of the *ink was* erasable.
    Not *any* of the *sky was* visible.

    with count noun
    All of our *bases are* covered.
    None of the *clerks were* available.
    Not *any* of the *stars were* visible.

8. The following are singular in form, and as such logically take singular verbs. However, because of their plural connotations, informal speech has established the use of plural pronoun references to them: *anybody, anyone, everybody, everyone, somebody.*

    I knew *everybody* by *their* first names.
    Don't tell *anyone; they* might spread the rumor.

Even in more formal contexts, expressions such as the following are used increasingly, especially as a result of attempts to avoid sexism in language:

    We called *everyone* by *their* first *names.*
    instead of
    We called *everyone* by *his* first *name.*

For more about avoiding sexism in the use of personal pronouns, see paragraph 22 below.

9. In some constructions an apparently singular indefinite pronoun may take a plural verb if the context makes it seem plural. The following two sentences illustrate how a singular indefinite pronoun may take either a singular or plural verb, depending on how the writer interprets *either:*

> *Either* of these pronunciations *is* acceptable.
> *Either* of these pronunciations *are* acceptable.

The conventional choice of verb would be *is,* because the subject of the sentence is the singular pronoun *either.* However, the proximity of the plural word *pronunciations,* together with the possibility of interpreting *either* to mean "one or both," gives the writer or speaker the opportunity to choose either a singular or a plural verb, depending on the interpretation of the subject.

10. The indefinite pronouns *any* and *anyone* are conventionally followed by *other(s)* or *else* when they form part of a comparison of two individuals in the same class.

> *not*
> Helen has more seniority than *anyone* in the firm.
> *instead*
> Helen has more seniority than *anyone else* in the firm.
> *not*
> Our house is older than *any* building on the block.
> *instead*
> Our house is older than *any other* building on the block.

The addition of *else* and *other* in the preceding sentences avoids the logical impossibility that Helen has more seniority than herself or that our house is older than itself. Likewise, it prevents the possible misreading that Helen is not a member of the firm or that our house is not on the block.

11. The antecedent of an indefinite pronoun should be clearly stated, not implied. A good check for a clear reference is to see if there is an antecedent in the sentence that could be substituted for the pronoun.

> *unclear*
> He's the author of a best-selling book on sailing, despite the fact that he's never set foot on *one.*
> *clear*
> He's the author of a best-selling book on sailing, despite the fact that he's never set foot on a sailboat.

12. **Interrogative pronouns** The interrogative pronouns *what, which, who, whom,* and *whose* as well as combinations of these words with the suffix *-ever* are used to introduce direct and indirect questions.

> *Who* is she?
> He asked me *who* she was.

Whom did the article accuse?

She asked *whom* the article accused.

Whoever can that be?

We wondered *whoever* that could be.

Personal pronouns Personal pronouns refer to beings and objects and reflect the person, number, and gender of those antecendents. Examples of personal pronouns are: *he, I, it, she, they, we, you.*

13. Most personal pronouns take different forms for the three cases.

	Nominative	Possessive	Objective
first person singular	I	my, mine	me
first person plural	we	our, ours	us
second person singular	you	your, yours	you
second person plural	you	your, yours	you
third person singular	he	his, his	him
	she	her, hers	her
	it	its, its	it
third person plural	they	their, theirs	them

14. A personal pronoun agrees in person, number, and gender with the word it refers to. However, the case of a pronoun is determined by its function within a sentence. The nominative case is used for a pronoun that acts as a subject of a sentence or as a predicate nominative (but see paragraph 15 below). The possessive case is used for pronouns that express possession or a similar relationship. The objective case is used for pronouns that are direct objects, indirect objects, retained objects, objects of prepositions, or objective complements.

You and *I* thought the meeting was useful.

My assistant and *I* attended the seminar.

Our new candidate will be *you.*

We all had *our* own offices.

The vice president informed my assistant and *me* about the seminar.

She gave *me* the papers.

Just between *you* and *me,* the meeting was much too long.

I was given *them* yesterday.

That makes our new candidate *her.*

15. The nominative case after the verb *to be* (as in "It is I" and "This is she") is considered standard English and is preferred by strict grammarians, but the objective case (as in "It's me") also may be used without criticism, especially in spoken English.

The only candidate left for that job may soon be she.

or

The only candidate left for that job may soon be her.

16. When a personal pronoun occurs in a construction introduced by *than* or *as*, it should be in the nominative case:

> He received a bigger bonus than *she* [did].
> She has as much seniority as *I* [do].

17. The suffixes *-self* and *-selves* combine only with the possessive case of the first- and second-person pronouns *(myself, ourselves, yourself, yourselves)* and with the objective case of the third-person pronouns *(himself, herself, itself, themselves)*. Other combinations (as "hisself" and "theirselves") are considered nonstandard and should not be used.

18. Personal pronouns in the possessive case (such as *your, their, theirs, its*) do not contain apostrophes and should not be confused with similar-sounding contractions (such as *you're, they're, there's, it's*), which do contain apostrophes.

> *possessive personal pronoun*
> Put the camera in *its* case.
> *Whose* camera is it?
>
> *contraction*
> *It's* an expensive camera.
> *Who's* going to go?

19. When one uses the pronoun *I* or *me* with other pronouns or with other people's names, *I* or *me* should be last in the series:

> Mrs. Smith and *I* were trained together.
> He and *I* were attending the meeting.
> The memorandum was directed to Ms. Montgomery and *me*.

20. Some companies prefer that writers use *we* and not *I* when speaking for their companies in business correspondence. *I* is more often used when a writer is referring only to himself or herself. The following example illustrates use of both within one sentence:

> *We* [i.e., the writer speaks for the company] have reviewed the manuscript that you sent to *me* [i.e., the manuscript was sent only to the writer] on June 1, but *we* [a corporate or group decision] feel that it is too specialized a work to be marketable by *our* company.

21. While the personal pronouns *it, you,* and *they* are often used as indefinite pronouns in spoken English, they can be vague or even redundant in some contexts.

> *vague*
> *They* said at the seminar that the economy would experience a third-quarter upturn. (The question is: Who exactly is *they?*)
> *explicit*
> The economists on the panel at the seminar predicted a third-quarter economic upturn.
> *redundant*
> In the graph *it* says that production fell off by 50%.
> *lean*
> The graph indicates a 50% production drop.

22. Forms of the personal pronoun *he* and the indefinite pronoun *one* are the standard substitutes for antecedents whose genders are mixed or irrelevant:

> Present the letter to the executive for *his* approval.
> Each employee should check *his* W-2 form.
> If *one* really wants to succeed, *one* can.

However, many writers today who are concerned about sexism in language recast such sentences, where possible, to avoid generic use of the masculine pronoun:

> Present the letter to the executive for approval.
> All employees should check *their* W-2 forms.
> Each employee should check *his or her* W-2 form.

The phrase *his or her* should be used sparingly, however, as it seems awkward and could certainly become tiresome if used frequently throughout a text. For more on avoiding the generic use of the masculine pronoun, see paragraph 8 above.

23. Reciprocal pronouns The reciprocal pronouns *each other* and *one another* are used in the object position to indicate a mutual action or cross relationship between the members comprised in a plural or compound subject.

> They do not quarrel with *one another*.
> Karen and Rachel spelled *each other* at driving on their trip.

24. Reciprocal pronouns may also be used in the possessive case:

> The two secretaries borrowed *one another's* stationery.
> The president and his vice president depend on *each other's* ideas.

25. Reflexive pronouns Reflexive pronouns express reflexive action or add extra emphasis to the subject of the sentence, clause, or verbal phrase in which they occur. Reflexive pronouns are formed by compounding the personal pronouns *him, her, it, my, our, them,* and *your* with *-self* or *-selves*. Reflexive pronouns are used when an object or subjective complement refers to the same thing as the foregoing noun or noun phrase.

> She dressed *herself*.
> The baby isn't *himself* this morning.
> They asked *themselves* if they were being honest.
> I *myself* am not afraid.
> The cook told Jim to help *himself*.

Relative pronouns The relative pronouns are *that, what, which, who, whom,* and *whose,* as well as combinations of these with *-ever*. They introduce subordinate clauses acting as nouns or modifiers. While a relative pronoun itself does not exhibit number, gender, or person, it does determine the number, gender, and person of elements that follow it in the relative clause because of its implicit agreement with its antecedent. Consider, for instance, the following sentence:

People *who are* ready to start *their* jobs should arrive at 8:00 a.m.

In this sentence, the relative pronoun "who" refers to the plural subject "People," and it acts as the subject of the relative clause "who are ready to start their jobs." Because it refers to a plural word it acts like a plural word within its clause and therefore calls for the plural verb "are" and the plural pronoun "their."

26. The relative pronoun *who* typically refers to persons and some animals; *which,* to things and animals; and *that,* to both beings and things.

   a man who sought success
   a man whom we can trust
   Seattle Slew, who won horse racing's Triple Crown
   a book which sold well
   a dog which barked loudly
   a book that sold well
   a dog that barked loudly
   a man that we can trust

27. Relative pronouns can sometimes be omitted for the sake of brevity.

   The man *whom* I was talking to is the president.
      or
   The man I was talking to is the president.

28. The relative pronoun *what* may be substituted for the longer and more awkward phrases "that which," "that of which," or "the thing which" in some sentences.

   stiff
   He was blamed for *that which* he could not have known.
   easier
   He was blamed for *what* he could not have known.

29. The problem of when to use *who* or *whom* has been blown out of proportion. The situation is very simple: standard written English makes a distinction between the nominative and objective cases of these pronouns when they are used as relatives or interrogatives.

   nominative case
   Who is she?
   Who does she think she is, anyway?
   She thinks she is the one *who* ought to be promoted.
   Give me a list of the ones *who* you think should be promoted.
   objective case
   Whom are you referring to?
   To *whom* are you referring?

He's a man *whom* everyone should know.
He's a man with *whom* everyone should be acquainted.

In speech, however, case distinctions and boundaries often become blurred, with the result that spoken English favors *who* as a general substitute for all uses of *whom* except in set phrases such as "*To whom* it may concern." In speech, then, *who* may be used not only as the subject of the clause it introduces but also as the object of a verb in a clause that it introduces or as an interrogative.

Let us select *who* we think will be the best candidate.
See the manager, Mrs. Keats, *who* you should be able to find in her office.
Who should we tell?

30. *Whom* is commonly used as the object of a preposition in a clause that it introduces; however, the form *who* is commonly used to introduce a question even when it is the object of a preposition:

Presiding is a judge *about whom* I know nothing.
He is a man *for whom* I would gladly work.
  but
Who (rarely *whom*) are you going to listen to?
Who (rarely *whom*) do you work for?

31. While in speech the nominative form *who* can be used in the objective case in certain kinds of sentences, the reverse is not true: the objective form *whom* cannot be used in the nominative case, either in spoken or in written English. One should therefore avoid such usages as "*Whom* do you suppose is coming to the meeting?" which result from a mistaken notion that *whom* is somehow always more correct.

32. The relative pronouns *whoever* and *whomever* follow the same principles as *who* and *whom* in formal writing:

nominative
Tell *whoever* is going to research the case that . . . .
He wants to help *whoever* needs it most.

objective
She makes friends with *whomever* she meets.

NOTE: In speech, however, as with *who* and *whom*, case distinctions become blurred, and *whoever* is used without criticism in most sentences:

Whoever did she choose?

Verb

A verb is a word that is characteristically the grammatical center of a predicate and expresses an act, occurrence, or mode of being. Verbs are inflected for agreement with the subject and for mood, voice, or tense. Verbs typically have rather full descriptive meaning and characterizing quality, but they sometimes are almost completely devoid of these especially when they are used as auxiliary or linking verbs.

Verbs exhibit the following characteristic features: inflection *(help, helps, helping, helped),* person (first, second, third person), number (singular, plural), tense (present, past, future), aspect (time relations other than the simple present, past, and future), voice (active, passive), mood (indicative, subjunctive, imperative), and suffixation (as by the typical suffixal markers *-ate, -en, -ify,* and *-ize*).

Inflection Regular verbs have four inflected forms signaled by the suffixes *-s* or *-es, -ed,* and *-ing.* The verb *help* as shown in the sentence above is regular. Most irregular verbs have four or five forms, as *see, sees, seeing, saw,* and *seen;* and one, the verb *be,* has eight: *be, is, am, are, being, was, were,* and *been.* When one is uncertain about a particular inflected form, one should consult a dictionary that indicates not only the inflections of irregular verbs but also those inflections resulting in changes in base-word spelling.

> blame; blamed; blaming
> spy; spied; spying
> picnic; picknicked; picnicking

A dictionary should also show variant inflected forms.

> bias; biased *or* biassed; biasing *or* biassing
> counsel; counseled *or* counselled; counseling *or* counselling
> diagram; diagramed *or* diagrammed; diagraming *or* diagramming
> travel; traveled *or* travelled; traveling *or* travelling

All of the foregoing forms may be found at their respective main entries in *Webster's Ninth New Collegiate Dictionary.* There are, however, a few rules that will aid one in ascertaining the proper spelling patterns of certain verb forms.

1. Verbs ending in a silent *-e* generally retain the *-e* before consonant suffixes (as *-s*) but drop the *-e* before vowel suffixes (as *-ed* and *-ing*).

> arrange; arranges; arranged; arranging
> hope; hopes; hoped; hoping
> require; requires; required; requiring
> shape; shapes; shaped; shaping

NOTE: A few verbs ending in a silent *-e* retain the *-e* before vowel suffixes in order to avoid confusion with other words.

> dye; dyes; dyed; dyeing *(vs. dying)*
> singe; singes; singed; singeing *(vs. singing)*

2. Monosyllabic verbs ending in a single consonant preceded by a single vowel double the final consonant before vowel suffixes (as *-ed* and *-ing*).

> brag; bragged; bragging
> grip; gripped; gripping
> pin; pinned; pinning

3. Polysyllabic verbs ending in a single consonant preceded by a single vowel and having an accented last syllable double the final consonant before vowel suffixes (as *-ed* and *-ing*).

commit; committed; committing
control; controlled; controlling
occur; occurred; occurring
omit; omitted; omitting

NOTE: The final consonant of such verbs is not doubled when two vowels occur before the final consonant or when two consonants form the ending of the verb.

daub; daubed; daubing
soil; soiled; soiling
help; helped; helping
lurk; lurked; lurking
peck; pecked; pecking

4. Verbs ending in *-y* preceded by a consonant regularly change the *-y* to *-i* before all suffixes except *-ing*.

carry; carried; carrying
marry; married; marrying
study; studied; studying

NOTE: If the final *-y* is preceded by a vowel, it remains unchanged in suffixation.

delay; delayed; delaying
enjoy; enjoyed; enjoying
obey; obeyed; obeying

5. Verbs ending in *-c* add a *-k* when a suffix beginning with *-e* or *-i* is added.

mimic; mimics; mimicked; mimicking
panic; panics; panicked; panicking
traffic; traffics; trafficked; trafficking

NOTE: Words derived from this type of verb also add a *-k* when such a suffix or the suffix *-y* is added to them.

panicky
trafficker

6. Tense, aspect, voice, and mood English verbs exhibit their simple present and simple past tenses by use of two single-word grammatical forms.

simple present = do
simple past = did

7. The future tense is expressed by *shall* or *will* followed by the base form of the verb or by use of the simple present or present progressive forms in a revealing context.

I *shall do* it.
He *will do* it.
I *leave* shortly for New York.
I *am leaving* shortly for New York.

8. Aspect is a property that allows verbs to indicate time relations other than the simple present, past, or future tenses. Aspect covers these relationships:

action occurring in the past and continuing to the present	has seen	*present perfect*
action completed at a past time or before the immediate past	had seen	*past perfect*
action that will have been completed by a future time	will have seen	*future perfect*
action occurring now	is seeing	*progressive*

In contexts that require it, the perfective and the progressive aspects can be combined to yield special verb forms, such as *had been seeing*.

9. Voice enables a verb to indicate whether the subject of a sentence is acting (he *loves* = active voice) or whether the subject is being acted upon (he *is loved* = passive voice).

10. Mood indicates manner of expression. The indicative mood states a fact or asks a question (He *is* here. *Is* he here?). The subjunctive mood expresses condition contrary to fact (I wish that he *were* here). The imperative mood expresses a command or request (*Come* here. Please *come* here).

11. Transitive and intransitive verbs Verbs may be used transitively or intransitively. A *transitive* verb acts upon a direct object.

She *contributed* money.
He *ran* the store.

An *intransitive* verb does not act upon a direct object.

She *contributed* generously.
He *ran* down the street.

NOTE: As in the examples above, many verbs are transitive in one sense and intransitive in another.

Verbals There is another group of words derived from verbs and called *verbals* that deserve added discussion. The members of this group—the gerund, the participle, and the infinitive—exhibit some but not all of the characteristic features of their parent verbs.

12. A gerund is an *-ing* verb form, but it functions mainly as a noun. It has both the active *(seeing)* and the passive *(being seen)* voices. In addition to voice, a gerund's verbal characteristics are as follows: it conveys the notion of a verb—i.e., action, occurrence, or being; it can take an object; and it can be modified by an adverb. In the following sentences, for instance, "Typing" and "driving" are gerunds, "data" and "cars" are their objects, and "daily" and "fast" are adverbs modifying the gerund.

> *Typing* tabular *data daily* is a boring task.
> He liked *driving cars fast.*

NOTE: Nouns and pronouns occurring before gerunds are expressed by the possessive.

> She is trying to improve *her typing.*
> We objected to *their telling* the story all over town.
> We saw the *boy's whipping.* (i.e., the boy being whipped)
> We expected the *senator's coming.* (i.e., his arrival)

13. Participles, on the other hand, function as adjectives and may occur alone ("a *broken* typewriter") or in phrases that modify other words ("*Having broken the typewriter,* she gave up for the day"). Participles have active and passive forms like gerunds.

> *active-voice participial phrase modifying "he"*
> *Having failed to pass the examination,* he was forced to repeat the course.
> *passive-voice participial phrase modifying "he"*
> *Having been failed* by his instructor, he was forced to repeat the course.

NOTE: Participles, unlike gerunds, are not preceded by possessive nouns or pronouns:

> We saw the *boy whipping* his dog. (i.e., we saw the boy doing the whipping)
> We saw the *senator coming.* (i.e., we saw him arrive)

14. Infinitives may exhibit active *(to do)* and passive *(to be done)* voices, and they may indicate aspect *(to be doing, to have done, to have been doing, to have been done)*. Infinitives may take complements and may be modified by adverbs. In addition, they can function as nouns, adjectives, and adverbs in sentences. Examples:

> *noun use*
> *To be known* is *to be castigated.* (subject and predicate nominative)
> He tried everything except *to bypass his superior.* (object of preposition "except")
> *adjectival use*
> They had found a way *to increase profits greatly.* (modifies the noun "way")
> *adverbial use*
> He was too furious *to speak.* (modifies "furious")

NOTE: Although *to* is the characteristic marker of an infinitive, it is not always stated but may be understood:

> He helped [to] complete the marketing report.

15. **Sequence of tenses** If the main verb in a sentence is in the present tense, any other tense or compound verb form may follow it in subsequent clauses, as:

I *realize* that you *are leaving.*	I *realize* that you *will be leaving.*
I *realize* that you *left.*	I *realize* that you *will leave.*
I *realize* that you *were leaving.*	I *realize* that you *will have been leaving.*
I *realize* that you *have been leaving.*	I *realize* that you *can be leaving.*
I *realize* that you *had left.*	I *realize* that you *may be leaving.*
I *realize* that you *had been leaving.*	I *realize* that you *must be leaving.*

16. If the main verb is in the past tense, that tense imposes time restrictions on any subsequent verbs in the sentence, thus excluding use of the present tense, as:

I *realized* that you *were leaving.*	I *realized* that you *would be leaving.*
I *realized* that you *left.*	I *realized* that you *could be leaving.*
I *realized* that you *had left.*	I *realized* that you *might be leaving.*
I *realized* that you *had been leaving.*	I *realized* that you *would leave.*

17. If the main verb is in the future tense, it imposes time restrictions on subsequent verbs in the sentence, thus excluding the possibility of using the simple past tense, as:

He *will see* you because he *is going* to the meeting too.
He *will see* you because he *will be going* to the meeting too.
He *will see* you because he *will go* to the meeting too.
He *will see* you because he *has been going* to the meetings too.
He *will see* you because he *will have been going* to the meetings too.

18. In general, most writers try to maintain an order of tenses throughout their sentences that is consistent with natural or real time, e.g., present tense = present-time matters, past tense = past matters, and future tense = matters that will take place in the future. However, there are two outstanding exceptions to these principles. First, if one is discussing the contents of printed or published material, one conventionally uses the present tense.

In *Etiquette,* Emily Post *discusses* forms of address.
This analysis *gives* market projections for the next two years.
In his latest position paper on the Middle East, the Secretary of State *writes* that . . . .

Second, if one wishes to add the connotation of immediacy to a particular sentence, one may use the present tense instead of the future.

I *leave* for Tel Aviv tonight.

19. The sequence of tenses in sentences which express contrary-to-fact conditions is a special problem frequently encountered in writing. The examples below show the sequence correctly maintained.

If he *were* on time, we *would leave* now.
If he *had been* (not *would have been*) on time, we *would have left* an hour ago.

20. At one time, *shall* was considered the only correct form to use with the first person in simple future tenses *(I shall, we shall)*, while *will* was limited to the second and third persons *(you will, it will, they will)*. Today, however, either of the following forms is considered correct for the first person:

more formal
We *shall give* your request special attention.

less formal
We *will give* your request special attention.

Subject-verb agreement Verbs agree in number and in person with their grammatical subjects. At times, however, the grammatical subject may be singular in form, but the thought it carries—i.e., the notional subject—may have plural connotations. Here are some general guidelines. For discussion of verb agreement with indefinite-pronoun subjects, see paragraphs 5–9 under Pronoun in this section. For discussion of verb number as affected by a compound subject whose elements are joined by *and/or*, see paragraph 6 under Conjunction in this section.

21. Plural and compound subjects take plural verbs even if the subject is inverted.

Both dogs and cats *were* tested for the virus.

Grouped under the heading "fine arts" *are* music, theater, and painting.

22. Compound subjects or plural subjects working as a unit take singular verbs in American English.

Lord & Taylor *has* stores in the New York area.
Cauliflower and cheese *is* my favorite vegetable.
Five hundred dollars *is* a stiff price for a coat.
  but
Twenty-five milligrams of pentazocine *were* administered.

23. Compound subjects expressing mathematical relationships may be either singular or plural.

One plus one *makes* (or *make*) two.
Six from eight *leaves* (or *leave*) two.

24. Singular subjects joined by *or* or *nor* take singular verbs; plural subjects so joined take plural verbs.

A freshman or sophomore *is* eligible for the scholarship.
Neither freshmen nor sophomores *are* eligible for the scholarship.

NOTE: If one subject is singular and the other plural, the verb agrees with the number of the subject that is closer to it.

Either the secretaries or the supervisor *has* to do the job.
Either the supervisor or the secretaries *have* to do the job.

25. Singular subjects introduced by *many a, such a, every, each,* or *no* take singular verbs, even when several such subjects are joined by *and.*

Many an executive *has* gone to the top in that division.
No supervisor and no assembler *is* excused from the time check.
Every chair, table, and desk *has* to be accounted for.

26. The agreement of the verb with its grammatical subject ordinarily should not be skewed by an intervening phrase.

    One of my reasons for resigning *involves* purely personal considerations.
    The president of the company, as well as members of his staff, *has* arrived.
    He, not any of the proxy voters, *has* to be present.

27. The verb *to be* agrees with its grammatical subject and not with its complement.

    His mania *was* fast cars and beautiful women.
    Women in the work force *constitute* a new field of study.

    NOTE: The verb *to be* introduced by the word *there* must agree in number with the subject following it.

    There *are* many complications here.
    There *is* no reason to worry about him.

28. Collective nouns—such as *orchestra, team, committee, family*—usually take singular verbs but can take plural verbs if the emphasis is on the individual members of the unit rather than on the unit itself.

    The committee *has agreed* to extend the deadline.
    but also
    The committee *have been* at odds ever since the beginning.

29. The word *number* in the phrase *a number of* usually takes a plural verb, but in the phrase *the number of* it takes a singular verb.

    A number of errors *were* (also *was*) made.
    The number of errors *was* surprising.

30. A relative clause that follows the expression *one of those/these* + plural noun takes a plural verb in conventional English, but in informal English it may take a singular verb.

    He is one of those executives who *worry* (also *worries*) a lot.
    This is one of those typewriters that *create* (also *creates*) perfect copies.

31. **Linking and *sense* verbs** Linking verbs (as the various forms of *to be*) and the so-called "sense" verbs (as *feel, look, taste, smell,* as well as particular senses of *appear, become, continue, grow, prove, remain, seem, stand,* and *turn*) connect subjects with predicate nouns or adjectives.

    He *is* a vice president.
    He *became* vice president.
    The temperature *continues* cold.
    The future *looks* prosperous.
    I *feel* bad.
    He *remains* healthy.

NOTE: Sense words often cause confusion, in that writers sometimes mistakenly use adverbs instead of adjectives following these words.

not
This perfume smells nicely.
instead
This perfume smells nice.
not
The meat tastes well.
instead
The meat tastes good.

32. Split infinitives A split infinitive is an infinitive that has a modifier between the *to* and the verbal (as in "to really care"). In the past, some grammarians disapproved of this construction, and many people still try to avoid it whenever they can. However, the split infinitive has been around a long time and has been used by a wide variety of distinguished English writers. It can be a useful device if a writer wants to stress the verbal element of an infinitive or express a thought that is most clearly shown with *to* + adverb + infinitive. In some cases where special emphasis on a word or a group of words is desirable, that emphasis cannot be achieved with an undivided infinitive construction. For example, in the phrase "to *thoroughly* complete the financial study" the position of the adverb as close as possible to the verbal element of the whole infinitive phrase strengthens the effect of the adverb on the verbal element. This situation is not necessarily true in the following reworded phrases:

to complete *thoroughly* the financial study
thoroughly to complete the financial study
to complete the financial study *thoroughly*

In other instances, the position of the adverb may actually modify or change the entire meaning.

original
arrived at the office to *unexpectedly* find a new name on the door
recast with new meanings
arrived at the office *unexpectedly* to find a new name on the door
arrived at the office to find a new name on the door *unexpectedly*

NOTE: Very long adverbial modifiers that interrupt an infinitive are clumsy and should be avoided or recast.

clumsy
He wanted to *completely and without mercy* defeat his competitor.
recast
He wanted to defeat his competitor *completely and without mercy*.

33. Dangling participles Dangling participles are participles occurring in a sentence without a normally expected syntactic relation to the rest of the sentence. They are best avoided, as they may create confusion for the reader or seem ludicrous.

dangling
Walking through the door, her coat was caught.

recast
While walking through the door, she caught her coat.
Walking through the door, she caught her coat.
She caught her coat while walking through the door.

dangling
Caught in the act, his excuses were unconvincing.

recast
Caught in the act, he could not make his excuses convincing.

dangling
Having been told that he was incompetent and dishonest, the executive fired the man.

recast
Having told the man that he was incompetent and dishonest, the executive fired him.
Having been told by his superior that he was incompetent and dishonest, the man was fired.

NOTE: Participles should not be confused with prepositions that end in *-ing*—like *concerning, considering, providing, regarding, respecting, touching,* etc.

prepositional usage
Concerning your complaint, we can tell you . . . .
Considering all the implications, you have made a dangerous decision.
Touching the matter at hand, we can say that . . . .

Phrases

A phrase is a brief expression that consists of two or more grammatically related words that may contain either a noun or a finite verb (that is, a verb that shows grammatical person and number) but not both, and that often functions as a particular part of speech with a clause or sentence.

Basic Types

There are seven basic types of phrases.

1. An *absolute phrase* consists of a noun followed by a modifier (such as a participle). Absolute phrases act independently within a sentence without modifying a particular element of the sentence. Absolute phrases are also referred to as *nominative absolutes*.

   He stalked out, *his eyes staring straight ahead.*

2. A *gerund phrase* is a verbal phrase that includes a gerund and functions as a noun.

   Sitting on a patient's bed is bad hospital etiquette.

3. An *infinitive phrase* is a verbal phrase that includes an infinitive and that may function as a noun, adjective, or adverb.

noun
To do that would be stupid.

adjective
This was a performance *to remember*.

adverb
He struggled *to get free*.

4. A *noun phrase* consists of a noun and its modifiers.

The concrete building is huge.

5. A *participial phrase* is a verbal phrase that includes a participle and that functions as an adjective.

Listening all the time with great concentration, she began to line up her options.

6. A *prepositional phrase* consists of a preposition and its object. It may function as a noun, adjective, or adverb.

noun
Out of debt is where we'd like to be!

adjective
Here is the desk *with the extra file drawer*.

adverb
He now walked *without a limp*.

7. A *verb phrase* consists of a verb and any other terms that either modify it or that complete its meaning.

She *will have arrived too late* for you to talk to her.

Usage Problems

1. Usage problems with phrases occur most often when a modifying phrase is not placed close enough to the word or words that it modifies. The phrase "On December 10" in the following sentence, for example, must be repositioned to clarify just what happened on that date.

original
We received your letter concerning the shipment of parts on December 10.

recast
On December 10 we received your letter concerning the shipment of parts.

or
We received your letter concerning the December 10 shipment of parts.

2. A very common usage problem with phrases involves dangling participial phrases. For a discussion of dangling participles, see paragraph 33 under Verb, pages 225–226.

Clauses

A clause is a group of words containing both a subject and a predicate. A clause functions as an element of a compound or a complex sentence. There are two general types of clauses: the *main* or *independent clause* and the *subordinate* or *dependent clause*. The main clause (such as "it is hot") is an independent grammatical unit and can stand alone. The subordinate clause (such as "because it is hot") cannot stand alone. A subordinate clause is either preceded or followed by a main clause.

Basic Types

Like phrases, clauses can perform as particular parts of speech within the total environment of the sentence. There are three basic types of clauses having part-of-speech functions.

1. The *adjective clause* modifies a noun or pronoun and typically follows the word it modifies.

> Her administrative assistant, *who was also a speech writer,* was overworked.
>
> I can't see the reason *why you're upset.*
>
> He is a man *who will succeed.*
>
> Anybody *who opts for a career like that* is crazy.

2. The *adverb clause* modifies a verb, an adjective, or another adverb and typically follows the word it modifies.

> They made a valiant effort, *although the risks were great.*
>
> *When it rains,* it pours.
>
> I'm certain *that he is guilty.*
>
> We accomplished less *than we did before.*

3. The *noun clause* fills a noun slot in a sentence and thus can be a subject, an object, or a complement.

> *subject*
> *Whoever is qualified* should apply.
>
> *object of a verb*
> I do not know *what his field is.*
>
> *object of a preposition*
> Route that journal to *whichever department you wish.*
>
> *complement*
> The trouble is *that she has no ambition.*

Elliptical Clauses

Some clause elements may be omitted if the context makes clear the understood elements:

> I remember the first time [that] we met.
>
> This typewriter is better than that [typewriter is].
>
> When [she is] on the job, she is always competent and alert.

Placement of Clauses

A modifying clause should be placed as close as possible to the word or words it modifies. This placement will give maximum clarity, and it avoids the possibility that the reader will misinterpret written material. If intervening words muddy the overall meaning of a sentence, it should be rewritten or recast.

> *muddy*
> A memorandum is a piece of business writing, less formal than a letter, which serves as a means of interoffice communication.
>
> *recast*
> A memorandum, less formal than a letter, is a means of interoffice communication.

Restrictive and Nonrestrictive Clauses

Clauses that modify are also referred to as *restrictive* or *nonrestrictive*. Whether a clause is restrictive or nonrestrictive has a direct bearing on sentence punctuation. For information about punctuating restrictive and nonrestrictive clauses, see paragraph 10 under Comma, page 96.

1. Restrictive clauses are the so-called "bound" modifiers. They are absolutely essential to the meaning of the word or words they modify, they cannot be omitted without the meaning of the sentences being radically changed, and they are unpunctuated.

   > Women who aren't competitive should not aspire to high corporate office.

   In this example, the restrictive clause "who aren't competitive" limits the classification of women, and thus is essential to the total meaning of the sentence. If, on the other hand, the restrictive clause is omitted as shown below, the classification of women is now not limited at all, and the sentence conveys an entirely different idea.

   > Women should not aspire to high corporate office.

2. Nonrestrictive clauses are the so-called "free" modifiers. They are not inextricably bound to the word or words they modify but instead convey additional information about them. Nonrestrictive clauses may be omitted altogether without the meaning of the sentence being radically changed, and they are set off by commas; i.e., they are both preceded and followed by commas when they occur in mid-sentence.

   > Our guide, who wore a green beret, was an experienced traveler.

   In this example, the nonrestrictive clause "who wore a green beret" does not restrict the classification of the guide; i.e., it does not set him apart from all other guides but merely serves as a bit of incidental detail. Removal of the nonrestrictive clause does not affect the meaning of the sentence:

   > Our guide was an experienced traveler.

Tacked-on *Which* Clauses

Tacking a *which* clause onto the end of a sentence when the clause actually refers to the total idea of the sentence is considered to be a usage fault. It can usually be avoided by recasting the sentence.

tacked-on
The company is retooling, which I personally think is a wise move.
recast
The company's decision to retool is a wise move in my opinion.
    or
I believe that the company's decision to retool is wise.

Sentences

A sentence is a grammatically self-contained unit that consists of a word or a group of syntactically related words and that (1) expresses a statement (declarative sentence); (2) asks a question (interrogative sentence); (3) expresses a request or command (imperative sentence); or (4) expresses an exclamation (exclamatory sentence). A sentence typically contains both a subject and a predicate, begins with a capital letter, and ends with a punctuation mark.

Basic Types

Sentences are classified into three main types on the basis of their clause structure.

1. The *simple sentence* is a complete grammatical unit having one subject and one predicate (either or both of which may be compound).

Paper is costly.
Bond and tissue are costly.
Bond and tissue are costly and are sometimes scarce.

2. The *compound sentence* is made up of two or more main clauses.

I could arrange to arrive late, or I could simply send a proxy.
This commute takes at least forty minutes by car, but we can make it in twenty by train.
A few of the executives had Ph.D.'s, even more of them had B.A.'s, but the majority of them had both B.A.'s and M.B.A.'s.

3. The *complex sentence* combines a main clause with one or more subordinate clauses (subordinate clauses are italicized in the examples).

The committee meeting began *when the business manager and the secretarial staff supervisor walked in.*
Although the city council made some reforms, the changes came so late *that they could not prevent these abuses.*

Construction

The construction of grammatically sound sentences can be achieved by following some general guidelines.

1. Sentence coordination should be maintained by the use of connectives linking phrases or clauses of equal rank. When a connective is used to link phrases or clauses that are not equal, the resulting sentence is ineffective at best, and can be confusing.

   faulty coordination with improper use of "and"
   I was sitting in on a meeting, and he stood up and started a long rambling discourse on a new pollution-control device.

   recast (one clause subordinated)
   I sat in on a meeting during which he stood up and rambled on about a new pollution-control device.

   recast (two sentences)
   I sat in on that meeting. He stood up and rambled on about a new pollution-control device.

   faulty coordination with improper use of "and"
   This company employs a full-time research staff and was founded in 1945.

   recast (one clause subordinated)
   This company, which employs a full-time research staff, was founded in 1945.

   recast (one clause reworded into a phrase)
   Established in 1945, this company employs a full-time research staff.

2. Parallel, balanced sentence elements are necessary in order to achieve good sentence structure. When clauses having unparallel subjects are linked together, the resulting sentence can be unclear.

   unparallel
   The report gives market statistics, but he does not list his sources for these figures.

   parallel
   The report gives market statistics, but it does not list the sources for these figures.

   unparallel
   We are glad to have you as our client, and please call on us whenever you need help.

   parallel
   We are glad to have you as our client and we hope that you will call on us whenever you need help.

   recast into two sentences
   We are glad to have you as our client. Please do call on us whenever you need help.

3. In order for a sentence to read effectively, its elements should be tightly linked together. When sentence elements are strung together by loose or excessive use of *and,* the sentence as a whole can be too lengthy and lacking in logical flow to be readily understood.

faulty coordination/excessive use of "and"
This company is a Class 1 motor freight common carrier of general commodities and it operates over 10,000 tractors, trailers, and city delivery trucks through 200 terminals, and serves 40 states and the District of Columbia.

recast into three shorter, more effective sentences
This company is a Class 1 motor freight common carrier of general commodities. It operates over 10,000 tractors, trailers, and city delivery trucks through 200 terminals. The company serves 40 states and the District of Columbia.

4. The correct choice of a conjunction to link clauses is important in writing an effective sentence. *And* is a general coordinating conjunction which functions to join sentence elements. If a sentence is expressing more than simple linkage, as when one clause is being contrasted with another, or when a reason or result is being expressed, a more specific conjunction should be used. For more on the specific functions of coordinating and subordinating conjunctions, see paragraphs 1–6 and 10–12 under Conjunction, pages 201–202 and 203–204 respectively.

too general
The economy was soft *and* we lost a lot of business.

specific
We lost a lot of business *because* the economy was soft.
The economy was soft, *so* we lost a lot of business.

specific
The soft economy has cost us a lot of business.

5. Unnecessary or unexpected grammatical shifts in a sentence interrupt the reader's thought train and needlessly complicate the material. Some unnecessary grammatical shifts are shown below, along with their improvements:

unnecessary shifts in verb voice
Any information you *can give* us *will be* greatly *appreciated* and we *assure* you that discretion *will be exercised* in its use.

rephrased (note the italicized all-active verb voice)
We *will appreciate* any information that you *can give* us. We *assure* you that we *will use* it with discretion.

unnecessary shifts in person
One can use either erasers or correction fluid to remove typographical errors; however, *you* should make certain that *your* corrections are clean.

rephrased (note that the italicized pronouns are consistent)
One can use either erasers or correction fluid to eradicate errors; however, *one* should make certain that *one's* corrections are clean.
    or
You can use either erasers or correction fluid to eradicate errors; however, *you* should make certain that *your* corrections are clean.

unnecessary shift from phrase to clause
Because of the current parts shortage and *we are experiencing a strike*, we cannot fill any orders now.

rephrased
Because of a parts shortage and a strike, we cannot fill any orders now.
  or
Because we are hampered by a parts shortage and we are experiencing a strike, we cannot fill any orders now.

6. A rational, logical ordering of sentence elements is a writer's best guarantee that the material will be understood. Closely related elements, for example, should be placed as close together as possible for the sake of maximum clarity.

   related elements separated
   We would appreciate your sending us the instructions on copy-editing by mail or cable.

   related elements joined
   We would appreciate your sending us by mail or by cable the copy-editing instructions.

   We would appreciate your mailing or cabling us the copy-editing instructions.

   We would appreciate it if you would mail or cable us the copy-editing instructions.

7. Sentences should form complete, independent grammatical units containing both a subject and a predicate. Exceptions are dialogue or specialized copy where fragmentation may be used for particular reasons (as to reflect speech or to attract the reader's attention).

   incomplete grammatical units
   During the last three years, our calculator sales soared. While our conventional office machine sales fell off.

   complete grammatical units
   During the last three years, our calculator sales soared, but our conventional office machine sales fell off.

   While our conventional office machine sales fell off during the last three years, our calculator sales soared.

   sentences fragmented for special effects in advertising
   See it now. The car for the Nineties . . . A car you'll want to own.

Sentence Length

Sentence length is directly related to the writer's purpose: there is no magic number of words that guarantees a good sentence. For example, an executive covering broad and yet complex topics in a long memorandum may choose concise, succinct sentences for the sake of clarity, impact, fast dictation, and readability. On the other hand, a writer who wants the reader to reflect on what is being said may employ longer, more involved sentences. Still another writer may juxtapose long and short sentences to emphasize an important point. The longer sentences may build up to a climactic and forceful short sentence.

Sentence Strategy

1. **Coordination and subordination** Either coordination or subordination or a mixture of both can be used to create a variety of stylistic writing effects. Coordination links independent sentences and sentence elements by means of coordinating conjunctions, while subordination transforms elements into dependent structures by means of subordinating conjunctions. Coordination tends to promote rather loose sentence structure, which can become a fault; subordination tends to tighten the structure and to emphasize a main clause.

   coordination
   During the balance of 1983, this Company expects to issue $100,000,000 of long-term debt and equity securities *and* may guarantee up to $200,000,000 of new corporate bonds.

   subordination
   While this Company expects to issue $100,000,000 of long-term debt and equity securities during the balance of 1983, it may also guarantee up to $200,000,000 of new corporate bonds.

2. **Interrupting elements** Interrupting the normal flow of discourse by inserting comments can be a useful device to call attention to an aside, to emphasize a word or phrase, to convey a particular tone (as forcefulness), or to make the prose a little more informal. Interrupting elements should be used with discretion; too many of them may distract the reader and disrupt his or her train of thought. The following are examples of effective interrupted sentences:

   an aside
   His evidence, if reliable, could send our client to prison.

   emphasis
   These companies—ours as well as theirs—must show more profits.

   forcefulness
   This, gentlemen, is the prime reason for your cost overruns. I trust it will not happen again?

3. **Parallelism and balance** While interruption breaks up the flow of discourse, parallelism and balance work together toward maintaining an even, rhythmic thought flow. Parallelism means a similarity in the grammatical construction of adjacent phrases and clauses that are equivalent, complementary, or antithetical in meaning.

   These ecological problems are of crucial concern *to* scientists, *to* businessmen, *to* government officials, and *to* all citizens.

   Our attorneys have argued *that* the trademark is ours, *that* our rights have been violated, and *that* appropriate compensation is required.

   He was respected not only *for his intelligence* but also *for his integrity.*

Balance is the juxtaposition and equipoise of two or more syntactically parallel constructions (as phrases and clauses) that contain similar, contrasting, or opposing ideas:

> To err is human; to forgive, divine.
>
> —Alexander Pope

> Ask not what your country can do for you—ask what you can do for your country.
>
> —John F. Kennedy

And finally, a series can be an effective way to emphasize a thought and to establish a definite prose rhythm:

> The thing that interested me . . . about New York . . . was the . . . contrast it showed between the dull and the shrewd, the strong and the weak, the rich and the poor, the wise and the ignorant. . . .
>
> —Theodore Dreiser

4. **Periodic and cumulative sentences** Stylistically, there are two basic types of sentences—the periodic and the cumulative or loose. The periodic sentence is structured so that its main idea or its thrust is suspended until the very end, thereby drawing the reader's eye and mind along to an emphatic conclusion. In the example below, the main point follows the final comma.

> While the Commission would wish to give licensees every encouragement to experiment on their own initiative with new and different means of providing access to their stations for the discussion of important public issues, it cannot justify the imposition of a specific right of access by government fiat.
>
> —*Television/Radio Age*

The cumulative sentence, on the other hand, is structured so that its main point appears first, followed by other phrases or clauses expanding on or supporting it. In the following example, the main point precedes the first comma.

> The solution must be finely honed, lest strategists err too much on the side of sophistication only to find that U.S. military forces can be defeated by overwhelming mass.
>
> —William C. Moore

The final phrase or clause in a cumulative sentence theoretically could be deleted without skewing or destroying the essential meaning of the total sentence. A cumulative sentence is therefore more loosely structured than a periodic sentence.

5. **Reversal** A reversal of customary or expected sentence order is another effective stylistic strategy, when used sparingly, because it injects a dash of freshness, unexpectedness, and originality into the prose.

customary or expected order
I find that these realities are indisputable: the economy has taken a drastic downturn, costs on all fronts have soared, and jobs are at a premium.

reversal

That the economy has taken a drastic downturn; that costs on all fronts have soared; that jobs are at a premium—these are the realities that I find indisputable.

6. **Rhetorical questions** The rhetorical question is yet another device to focus the reader's attention on a problem or an issue. The rhetorical question requires no specific response from the reader but often merely sets up the introduction of the writer's own view. In some instances, a rhetorical question works as a topic sentence in a paragraph; in other instances, a whole series of rhetorical questions may spotlight pertinent issues for the reader's consideration.

What can be done to correct the problem? Two things, to begin with: never discuss cases out of the office, and never allow a visitor to see the papers on your desk.

7. **Variety** As a means of keeping the reader's attention, careful writers try to maintain a balance of different kinds of sentences. For example, they may use a combination of simple, compound, and complex sentences in a paragraph, together with a variey of short and long sentences. Writers also vary the beginnings of their sentences so that every sentence in a paragraph does not begin directly with the subject. Any kind of repetitious pattern creates monotony. Through judicious use of combinations of sentence patterns and the sentence strategies discussed in the preceding pragraphs, a writer can attain an interesting, diversified style.

Paragraphs

The underlying structure of any written communication—be it a memorandum, a letter, or a report—must be controlled by the writer if the material is to be clear, coherent, logical in progression, and effective. Since good paragraphing is a means to this end, it is essential that the writer become adept at using techniques of paragraph development and of transition between paragraphs. While the writer is responsible for the paragraphing system, the secretary still should be able to recognize various kinds of paragraphs and their functions as well as the potential problems that might arise in structuring a logical paragraph system. In this way, the secretary can assist the writer, especially by pointing out possible discrepancies that might result in misinterpretation by the reader or that might detract from the total effect of the communication.

A paragraph is a subdivision in writing that consists of one or more sentences, that deals with one or more ideas, or that quotes a speaker or a source. The first line of a paragraph is indented in reports, studies, articles, theses, and books. However, the first line of a paragraph in business letters and memorandums may or may not be indented, depending on the style being followed. See Chapter 1 for business-letter styling.

Paragraphs should not be considered as isolated entities that are self-contained and mechanically lined up without transitions or interrelationship of ideas. Rather, paragraphs should be viewed as components of larger groups or blocks that are tightly interlinked and that interact in the sequential development of a major idea or cluster of ideas. The overall coherence of a communication depends on this interaction.

Individual paragraphs and paragraph blocks are flexible: their length, internal structure, and purpose vary according to the writer's intention and his own style. For example, one writer may be able to express his point in a succinct, one-sentence paragraph, while another may require several sentences to make his point. Writers' concepts of paragraphing also differ. For instance, some writers think of paragraphs as a means of dividing their material into logical segments with each unit developing one particular point in depth and in detail. Others view paragraphs as a means of emphasizing particular points or adding variety to long passages.

Development of Paragraphs

Depending on the writer's intentions, paragraph development may take any of the following directions:

1. The paragraph may move from the general to the specific.

2. The paragraph may move from the specific to the general.

3. The paragraph may exhibit an alternating order of comparison and contrast.

4. The paragraph may chronicle events in a set temporal order—e.g., from the beginning to the end, or from the end to the beginning.

5. The paragraph may describe something (as a group of objects) in a set spatial order—e.g., the items being described may be looked at from near-to-far, or vice versa.

6. The paragraph may follow a climactic sequence with the least important facts or examples described first followed by a buildup of tension leading to the most important facts or examples then followed by a gradual easing of tension. Other material can be so ordered for effectiveness; for example, facts or issues that are easy to comprehend or accept may be set forth first and followed by those that are more difficult to comprehend or accept. In this way the easier material makes the reader receptive and prepares him to comprehend or accept the more difficult points.

7. Anticlimactic order is also useful when the writer's intent is to persuade the reader. With this strategy, the writer sets forth the most

persuasive arguments first so that the reader, having been influenced in a positive way by that persuasion, moves along with the rest of the argument with a growing feeling of assent.

Effective Paragraphing

The following material outlines some ways of building effective paragraphs within a text.

A topic sentence—a key sentence to which the other sentences in the paragraph are related—may be placed either at the beginning or at the end of a paragraph. A lead-in topic sentence should present the main idea in the paragraph and should set the initial tone of the material that follows. A terminal topic sentence should be an analysis, a conclusion, or a summation of what has gone before it.

A single-sentence paragraph can be used to achieve easy transition from a preceding to a subsequent paragraph (especially when the paragraphs are long and complex), if it repeats an important word or phrase from the preceding paragraph, if it contains a pronoun reference to a key individual mentioned in a preceding paragraph, or if it is introduced by an appropriate conjunction or conjunctive adverb that tightly connects the paragraphs.

1. Since the very first paragraph sets initial tone, introduces the subject or topic under discussion, and leads into the main thrust of a communication, it should be worded so as to immediately attract the reader's attention and arouse interest. These openings can be effective:

   A. a succinct statement of purpose or point of view
   B. a concise definition (as of a problem)
   C. a lucid statement of a key issue or fact

2. These openings, by contrast, can blunt the point of the rest of the material:

   A. an apology for the material to be presented
   B. a querulous complaint or a defensive posture
   C. a rehash of ancient history (as a word-for-word recap of previous correspondence)
   D. a presentation of self-evident facts
   E. a group of sentences rendered limp and meaningless because of clichés

3. The last paragraph ties together all of the ideas and points that have been set forth earlier and reemphasizes the main thrust of the communication. These can be effective endings:

   A. a setting forth of the most important conclusion or conclusions drawn from the preceding discussion
   B. a final analysis of the main problem or problems under discussion
   C. a lucid summary of the individual points brought up earlier

D. a final, clear statement of opinion or position
E. concrete suggestions or solutions if applicable
F. specific questions asked of the reader if applicable

4. The following endings, by contrast, can reduce the effectiveness of a communication:

A. apologies for a poor presentation
B. qualifying remarks that blunt or negate incisive points made earlier
C. insertion of minor details or afterthoughts
D. a meaningless closing couched in clichés

5. The following are tests of good paragraphs:

A. Does the paragraph have a clear purpose? Is its utility evident, or is it there just to fill up space?
B. Does the paragraph clarify rather than cloud the writer's ideas?
C. Is the paragraph adequately developed, or does it merely raise other questions that the writer does not attempt to answer? If a position is being taken, does the writer include supporting information and statistics that are essential to its defense?
D. Are the length and wording of all the paragraphs sufficiently varied, or does the writer employ the same types of locutions again and again?
E. Is the sentence structure coherent?
F. Is each paragraph unified? Do all the sentences really *belong* there; or does the writer digress into areas that would have been better covered in another paragraph or that could have been omitted altogether?
G. Are the paragraphs coherent so that one sentence leads clearly and logically to another? Is easy, clear transition between paragraphs effected by a wise selection of transitional words and phrases which indicate relationships between ideas and signal the direction in which the writer's presentation is moving?
H. Does one paragraph simply restate in other terms what has been said before?

Chapter 5

Tone in Writing

CONTENTS

The tone of a communication is usually set in the first paragraph. It may be formal or informal, neutral or biased, friendly or critical, or it may reflect any number of other feelings and attitudes. Under ordinary circumstances it is maintained throughout the subsequent paragraphs to the end. What kind of tone a writer wishes to establish will depend on several factors. One important factor is the underlying reason or reasons why the letter is being written. Another important factor is the personal attitude of the writer toward the reader and the subject matter. Finally, the content of the material (for instance, whether it is general or technical) will, to some extent, determine the kind of tone a writer can establish.

The Importance of Tone

The effect of the tone of a communication on its reader cannot be overemphasized. A letter, for example, may exhibit well-ordered layout, clean typing, attractive stationery, good sentence structure, correct spelling, and smooth flow from one paragraph to another. It may contain complete, logically presented data. Yet if the tone of the letter is abrupt or rude, the effect of the material on the reader will be negative. The reader's response should therefore be kept in mind at all times. Some principles relevant to tone in general business communications are outlined and discussed briefly in the following paragraphs. For further examples of varying tone in business letters, the reader may consult Chapter 6, where several kinds of letters are illustrated.

A communication should be reader-oriented. The reader's point of view and possible responses should never be forgotten, even when the writer is intent on setting forth his or her objectives. Compare the following two approaches:

abrupt
We have read with interest your article on HDPE pipe in the October 12 issue of *Plastics*. Since our marketing division is preparing a multiclient

study on plastic pipe applications, we will need offprints of the following papers you have written on this subject: . . .

polite
We have read with interest your article on HDPE pipe in the October 12 issues of *Plastics*. Our marketing division is preparing a multiclient study on plastic pipe applications—a study that will not be complete without reference to your outstanding research. We'd therefore be pleased if you'd send us offprints of the following papers you've written on the subject: . . .

A writer's familiarity with the subject matter is not automatically shared by the reader. A writer should neither write down to experts in a given field nor write over the heads of nonexperts. The way information is presented in a communication should be adjusted to the appropriate level of the reader.

Use of the personal pronouns *I, we,* and *you* can go far to personalize a communication, as can common courtesy and tactfulness. An added benefit of all three is that they make the reader feel more involved in the discussion. Passive or impersonal constructions, on the other hand, work against the writer; when overused, they depersonalize a communication and lessen its impact. Compare the following pairs of examples:

impersonal
The enclosed brochure outlining this Company's services may be of interest.

This Company is gratified when its clients offer useful suggestions.

personal
We've enclosed a brochure outlining our services, which we hope will interest you.

We appreciate your taking the time to offer such a useful suggestion.

impersonal
Reference is made to your May 1 letter received by this office yesterday.

Enclosed is the requested material.

It is the understanding of this writer that the contract is in final negotiation stages.

personal
We are referring to your May 1 letter which we received yesterday.

We're enclosing the material you requested.

I understand that the contract is in final negotiation stages.

Originality in Writing Style

The effectiveness and overall output of communications can be markedly increased if one avoids the padding and clichés that can blunt what otherwise might be incisive writing. Unfortunately, these expressions, sometimes called *business static,* have become fixtures in the vocabularies of some writers. Some of the phrases (such as "regret to advise you") are best avoided because they are stale. Others (such as "aforesaid"), while common in legal documents, sound stiff and awkward in general business contexts. Still others (such as "beg to respond") have an antiquated ring. Some expressions (such as "forward on") are redundant, while others (such as "acknowledge receipt of") are too long and unwieldy. One such clumsy phrase, "Enclosed please find," appears all too often in the first line of business letters. True, it is a convenient opener, but it is also stilted and impersonal. An opening such as "We are enclosing" or "Enclosed are" is not only more natural but also more likely to establish a rapport with the customer, client, or other recipient.

These clichéd expressions are all too often used in conspicuous areas of a text: at the very beginning where initial tone is set or at the very end where a summation is made. They are also likely to crop up at the beginning and end of individual sentences and paragraphs where particular ideas and points are being set forth. Their use in these strategic positions works against the writer: a busy reader can become exasperated if it is necessary to wade through superfluous or hackneyed expressions to get at the gist of a communication.

The following is a representative list, in alphabetical order, of expressions that are best avoided by writers seeking more clarity, brevity, and originality in their business communications.

abeyance   *hold in abeyance* This expression sounds stilted in most contexts and can usually be avoided. Compare the following sentences:

> *stilted*
> We are holding our final decision in abeyance.
> *easier*
> We are deferring our final decision.
> We are delaying our final decision.
> We are holding up our final decision.

above   While the use of this word as a noun ("see the above"), an adjective ("the above figure shows"), and as an adverb ("see above") is indeed acceptable, its overuse within one letter can distract a reader. Alternative expressions include the following:

> See the figure on page 27.
> See the figure at the top of the page.
> This figure shows . . .
> See the material illustrated earlier.

above-mentioned   This term is overlong and is often overworked within a single letter.

> *longer*
> The above-mentioned policy . . .
> *shorter*
> This policy . . .

acknowledge receipt of This expression requires 22 keystrokes, but the alternative expression *have received* is a 13-stroke synonym.

> *longer*
> We acknowledge receipt of your check.
>
> *shorter*
> We have received your check.

advise This word has been overworked when meaning "to inform." It can be replaced by either of the shorter verbs *say* or *tell.*

> *longer*
> We regret to advise you that Mrs. Mercer is no longer with the firm.
>
> *shorter*
> We must tell you that Mrs. Mercer is no longer with the firm.
> We're sorry to say that Mrs. Mercer is no longer with the firm.

advised and informed This phrase is redundant, since the two words used here simply repeat each other.

> *redundant*
> He has been advised and informed of our position.
>
> *lean*
> He has been told of our position
> He knows our position.

affix (one's) signature to This expression is padding, and can be reduced to *sign.*

> *padded*
> Please affix your signature to the enclosed documents.
>
> *lean*
> Please sign these documents.
> Please sign the enclosed documents.

aforementioned/aforesaid These words are commonly used in legal documents but sound verbose and pompous in general contexts. The same idea can usually be conveyed by one of the demonstrative adjectives *(this, that, these, those).*

> *verbose*
> The aforementioned company . . .
>
> *natural*
> This company . . .
> The company in question . . .
> The company mentioned earlier . . .
>
> *verbose*
> We must reach a decision regarding the aforesaid dispute.
>
> *natural*
> We must make a decision about this (that) dispute.

amplify to a maximum   This expression may be pared down to *maximize*.

> *padded*
> ... expect all salesmen to amplify to a maximum their sales calls next month.
>
> *lean*
> ... expect all salesmen to maximize their next month's sales calls.

—*see also* REDUCE TO A MINIMUM

and etc.   This phrase is redundant, because *etc.* is the abbreviation of the Latin *et cetera* meaning "and the rest." Omit the *and*.

> *not*
> carbon packs, onionskin, bond, and etc.
>
> *instead*
> carbon packs, onionskin, bond, etc.

and/or   This expression is best restricted to use between two alternatives, where it means "A or B or both." In longer series, such as "A, B and/or C," *and/or* will likely be either vague or unnecessary.

as per   This expression has been overworked when meaning "as," "in accordance with," and "following." It is an unoriginal and formulaic way to begin a letter, paragraph, or sentence.

> *overworked*
> As per your request of ...
> As per our telephone conversation of ...
> As per our agreement ...
>
> *more natural*
> As you requested ...
> According to your request ...
> In accordance with your request ...
> As a follow-up to our telephone conversation ...
> In accordance with our telephone conversation ...
> As we agreed ...
> According to our agreement ...

as regards   This phrase can also be expressed by the terms *concerning* or *regarding*.

> *stiff*
> As regards your complaint ...
> *easier*
> Let's talk about your complaint.

as stated above   This phrase can be more naturally expressed.

> As we have said ...

assuring you that   This is an outmoded participial-phrase ending to a business letter that should not be used.

outmoded
Assuring you that your cooperation will be appreciated, I remain
Sincerely yours

current
I will appreciate your cooperation.
Sincerely yours

as to   This phrase has been as overworked as the phrase *as per*. It can be replaced with *regarding, concerning, about,* or *of*.

overworked
As to your second question . . .

fresher
Regarding your second question . . .
Coming to your second question . . .
Let's look at your second question.

overworked
We have no means of judging as to the wisdom of that decision.

fresher
We cannot (can't) judge the wisdom of that decision.

at all times   This may be shortened to *always*.

longer
We shall be glad to meet with you at all times.

shorter
We'll always be glad to meet with you.
We're always glad to meet with you.

at an early date   This wording is both long and vague. Shorter and clearer alternatives are *immediately* and *by* (date).

at once and by return mail   These terms are repetitious when joined together; either *at once* or *immediately* will suffice.

repetitive
Please send us your check at once and by return mail.

succinct
Please send us your check at once (*or* immediately).

—*see also* RETURN MAIL

attached hereto/attached herewith   These phrases are quite impersonal and may be expressed in more personal ways.

Attached is/are . . .
We are attaching . . .
We have attached . . .
You'll see attached . . .

—*see also* ENCLOSED HEREWITH

at this point in time/at this time   These phrases may be shortened to *now, currently,* or *at (the) present.* Similarly, *at that point in time* and *at that time* may be shortened to *then.*

at this writing   This may be shortened to *now.*

at your earliest convenience   This expression manages to convey nothing more in 28 keystrokes than the alternative *as soon as you can,* which requires only 18 strokes and states the case explicitly. Other alternative expressions include *now, immediately, by* (date), and *within* (number) *days.*

basic fundamentals   This is redundant. Either *the basics* or *the fundamentals* may be substituted.

basis   *on the basis of, on a——basis*   These phrases are somewhat long-winded and can often be avoided.

> *Longer*
> On the basis of what we have seen so far, we project a six-month production schedule.
>
> They accepted the project on the basis of the merits of that view.
>
> We will ship parts on an as-needed basis.
>
> *Shorter*
> From what we have seen so far, we project a six-month production schedule.
>
> They accepted the project because of the merits of that view.
>
> We will ship parts as needed.

However, these phrases are sometimes very useful, and there often is no good way to avoid them.

because   Using a clause beginning with *because* as the subject of a sentence is common in speech but is usually avoided in formal writing.

> *Not*
> Because you have not received the shipment yet does not mean we did not send it.
>
> *Instead*
> The fact that you have not received the shipment yet does not mean we did not send it.

— *see also* REASON IS BECAUSE

beg   *beg to acknowledge, beg to advise, beg to state*   These and other such *beg* combinations sound antiquated. The following may be used instead:

> We acknowledge . . .
> We have received . . .

Thank you for . . .
We're pleased to tell you . . .

brought to our notice   This is long and may be recast as follows:

We note . . .
We notice . . .
We see . . .

contents carefully noted   This expression contributes little or no information and should be omitted.

not
Yours of the 1st received and contents carefully noted.
instead
We've read carefully your June 1 letter.
We've read your June 1 letter.
The instructions in your June 1 letter have been followed.

dated   This word is unnecessary when used in phrases like "your letter dated June 1." The word *dated* may simply be omitted.

your June 1 letter
your letter of June 1

deem (it)   This is a stiff way of saying *think* or *believe*.

stiff
We deem it advisable that you . . .
easier
We think you ought to . . .
We think it advisable that you . . .

demand and insist   These words are redundant when joined together; the use of just one of the following at a time will suffice: *demand* or *insist* or *require*.

despite the fact that   This expression may be pared down to *although* or *though*.

due to/due to the fact that   These are both stiff and may be reduced to *because (of)* or *since*.

duly   This word is meaningless in expressions like "Your order has been duly forwarded," and it can almost always be omitted.

Your order has been forwarded.
We've forwarded your order.

earnest endeavor   This phrase can be cloying when used in sentences such as "It will be our earnest endeavor to serve our customers." It should be replaced with more straightforward phrasing, such as "We shall try to serve our customers."

enclosed herewith/enclosed please find   These are impersonal and stilted expressions. The following are better alternatives:

> We enclose . . .
> We are enclosing . . .
> We have enclosed . . .
> Enclosed is/are . . .

—*see also* ATTACHED HERETO/ATTACHED HEREWITH

endeavor   This is an eight-letter verb that can be replaced by the three-letter verb *try,* which is synonymous and not pompous.

> *pompous and longer*
> We shall endeavor to . . .
>
> *direct and shorter*
> We'll (*or* We shall) try to . . .
> We'll make a real effort to . . .
> We'll make every effort to . . .
> We'll do everything we can to . . .
> We'll do our best to . . .

esteemed   This word can seem overly effusive when used in a sentence like "We welcome your esteemed favor of June 9." This sentence can be recast as follows: "Thank you for your letter of June 9."

favor   This word should never be used in the sense of a letter, an order, a check, or other such item.

finalize/prioritize   The suffix *-ize* is frequently added to nouns and adjectives to coin new words, such as *hospitalize, computerize, familiarize,* and *Americanize.* The *-ize* suffix has been applied in this way for hundreds of years, and most words ending in *-ize* are completely acceptable to nearly everyone. However, some 20th-century coinages of this sort, such as *finalize* and *prioritize,* strike some people as being needless neologisms or bureaucratic gobbledygook. To avoid such objections, replace them with "to put in final form," "to give final approval to," and "to rate (or list) in order of priority."

for the purpose of   This expression may be more succinctly worded as *for.*

> *padded*
> necessary for purposes of accounting
>
> *lean*
> necessary for accounting

forward on   This phrase is redundant, since *forward* alone conveys the meaning adequately.

> *redundant*
> We have forwarded your complaint on to the proper authorities.
>
> *lean*
> We have forwarded your complaint to the proper authorities.

hand (one) herewith   This expression sounds inflated and can be replaced with leaner alternatives.

inflated
We are handing you herewith an invoice for the shipment of September 17.

leaner
We are enclosing an invoice for the shipment of September 17.
Enclosed is an invoice for the shipment of September 17.

have before me   This expression is superfluous. Obviously, the writer has previous correspondence at hand when responding to a letter.

not
I have before me your letter of June 1 . . .

but
In reply to your June 1 letter . . .

hereto   —*see* ATTACHED HERETO/ATTACHED HEREWITH

herewith   —*see* ATTACHED HERETO/ATTACHED HEREWITH; ENCLOSED HERE-WITH/ENCLOSED PLEASE FIND

hoping for the favor (*or* to hear)   These and other such participial-phrase endings for business letters are now outmoded and should be omitted.

not
Hoping for the favor of a reply, I remain

instead
I look forward to hearing from you.
I look forward to your reply.
May I hear from you soon?

I am/I remain   These expressions are outmoded when used as lead-ins to complimentary closes and should not be used. Instead, the writer may simply end the body of the letter on a cordial note and let the complimentary close stand on its own.

not
Looking forward to a speedy reply from you, I am (*or* remain)

instead
I look forward to your immediate reply.
I am looking forward to a reply from you soon.
May I please have an immediate reply?
Will you please reply soon?

immediately and at once   These terms are redundant when joined together; however, each element of the expression may be used separately.

May we hear from you immediately?
May we hear from you at once?

incumbent *it is incumbent upon (one)* The thought here is more easily expressed as *I/we must, you must,* or *he/she/they must.*

in re This expression should be avoided in the body of general business letters, although it is often used in the subject line of letters and in legal documents. It may be replaced with *regarding, concerning, in regard to,* or *about.*

> *stiff*
> In re our telephone conversation of . . .
>
> *easier*
> Concerning our telephone conversation of . . .

institute the necessary inquiries This expression is overlong and overformal, and may be reworded as follows:

> We shall inquire . . .
> We'll find out . . .
> We are inquiring . . .

in the amount of This is a long way of saying *for.*

> *longer*
> We are sending you a check in the amount of $50.95.
>
> *shorter*
> We are sending you a check for $50.95.
> We are sending you a $50.95 check.

in the course of This phrase may be more concisely expressed by *during* or *while.*

> *longer*
> In the course of the study . . .
>
> *shorter*
> During the study . . .
> While we were studying . . .

in the event that This phrase may be more concisely expressed by *if* or *in case.*

> *longer*
> In the event that you cannot meet with me next week, we shall . . .
>
> *shorter*
> If you cannot meet with me next week, we shall . . .

in view of the fact that This expression can be shortened to *because (of)* or *since.*

> *longer*
> In view of the fact that he is now president of . . .
> He was terminated in view of the fact that he had been negligent.
>
> *shorter*
> Since he is now president of . . .
> He was terminated because of negligence.

in view of the foregoing   This expression can be shortened to *therefore*.

> *longer*
> In view of the foregoing, we cannot accept the terms of the agreement.
> *shorter*
> Therefore, we cannot accept the terms of the agreement.

is because   —*see* REASON IS BECAUSE

it is incumbent upon   —*see* INCUMBENT

it is interesting to note that   This expression often constitutes padding and thus can be dropped or replaced with a transitional word or short phrase.

> *padded*
> It is interesting to note that by this time last year, all orders received in January had been met.
> *lean*
> By this time last year, all orders received in January had been met.
> Moreover, by this time last year, all orders received in January had been met.

it is within (one's) power   —*see* POWER

it may be said that   This phrase often constitutes padding and can be omitted.

> *padded*
> Indeed, it may be said that without the support of this department, this project would not have succeeded.
> *lean*
> Indeed, without the support of this department, this project would not have succeeded.

-ize   —*see* FINALIZE/PRIORITIZE

line   This word is a vague substitute for one of the following more explicit terms: *merchandise, line of goods* (or *merchandise*), *goods, product(s), service(s), system(s)*.

meet with (one's) approval   This is a stiff phrase more easily expressed as *is acceptable, I accept, we approve*.

> *stiff*
> If the plan meets with Mr. Doe's approval . . .
> *easier*
> If the plan is acceptable to Mr. Doe . . .
> If Mr. Doe accepts the plan . . .

note   *we note that, you will note that*   These expressions often constitute padding and thus should be dropped.

padded
We note that your prospectus states . . .
You will note that the amount in the fourth column . . .
lean
Your prospectus states . . .
The amount in the fourth column . . .

NOTE: If a word of this type is required, a more natural substitute is *see:*

We *see* that you have paid the bill in full.

oblige   This word is archaic when used in a sentence such as "Please reply to this letter and oblige." This sentence should be recast to read as follows: "Please reply to this letter immediately."

of the opinion that   This is a stiff way of saying, "We think (*or* believe) that," "Our opinion is that," "Our position is that."

our Mr., Ms., Miss, Mrs.   This phrasing is best avoided.

not
Our Mr. Lee will call on you next Tuesday.
but
Our sales representative, Mr. Lee, will call on you next Tuesday.
Mr. Lee, our sales representative, will call on you next Tuesday.

party   While idiomatic in legal documents, this word is nevertheless awkward in general business contexts when the meaning is "individual" or "person."

awkward
We understand that you are the party who called earlier.
smoother
We understand that you are the person (*or* individual *or* one) who called earlier.

pending receipt of   This phrase is used in legal documents, but in general contexts it is simply a stiff way of saying "until we receive."

stiff
We are holding your order, pending receipt of your check.
easier
We'll ship your order as soon as we receive your check.

permit me to remain   This expression is outmoded and should not be used as part of the last sentence in a business letter.

place an order for   This phrase takes 18 keystrokes, but the verb *order* takes only 5 strokes.

position   *be in a position to*   The phrase "We are not in a position to" is unnecessarily long and may be recast to shorter and more personal phrases, such as "We cannot" or "We are unable."

power *it is (not) within (one's) power to*   This is a lengthy way of saying "We can," "We are able to," "We cannot," or "We are unable to."

> *longer*
> It is not within our power to back such an expensive project.
>
> *shorter*
> We cannot back such an expensive project.

prepared to offer   This is a set phrase that can be reworded in a number of more original ways.

> *set*
> We are prepared to offer you the following discounts: . . .
>
> *varied*
> We can offer you these discounts: . . .
> We're ready to offer you these discounts: . . .
> We offer the following discounts: . . .

prioritize   —*see* FINALIZE/PRIORITIZE

prior to   This phrase is a stiff way to say *before.*

> *stiff*
> Prior to receipt of your letter of July 1, we . . .
>
> *easier*
> Before we received your July 1 letter, we . . .
> Before receipt of your July 1 letter, we . . .
> Before receiving your July 1 letter, we . . .

—*see also* SUBSEQUENT TO

pursuant to   This is a stiff phrase that unfortunately occurs in the very beginnings of many follow-up letters and memorandums. It can be replaced with *According to, Following up, As a follow-up to,* or *In accordance with.*

> *stiff*
> Pursuant to our telephone conversation of June 1, let me say . . .
>
> *easier*
> Following up our June 1 telephone conversation, I can say . . .

reason is because   This expression is often objected to as ungrammatical and redundant, despite the fact that it has been used by some well-known writers. While its use can be defended, it is liable to objection and is best replaced with one of the following: *The reason is, The reason is that, Because.*

receipt   —*see* PENDING RECEIPT OF

receipt is acknowledged   This is an unnecessarily impersonal passive construction more concisely expressed as *We received* or *We have received.*

recent date   *of recent date*   This is an unwieldy way to indicate an undated letter; the alternatives *your recent letter* or *your undated letter* are smoother. If the letter is dated, it is best to repeat the exact date.

reduce to a minimum   This phrase may be pared down to *minimize*.

> *wordy*
> This product reduces to a minimum the air pollution in work areas.
> *succinct*
> This product minimizes air pollution in work areas.

—*see also* AMPLIFY TO A MAXIMUM

refuse and decline   These words are redundant when used together; the use of one will suffice: *refuse* or *decline*.

> *redundant*
> We must refuse and decline any further dealings with your company.
> *lean*
> We must refuse any further dealings . . .
> We must decline to have any further dealings . . .

—*see also* DEMAND AND INSIST

regard   *in regard to, with regard to*   Both of these expressions can often be replaced with *because* for more concise wording.

> *wordy*
> We wrote to them in regard to their unpaid balance several times during this period.
> *concise*
> We wrote to them about their unpaid balance several times during this period.

reiterate again   The adverb *again* is redundant in this phrase, because the verb *reiterate* carries the total meaning by itself.

> *redundant*
> Let me reiterate our policy again.
> *succinct*
> Let me reiterate our policy.
> Let me restate our policy.
> Let me state our policy again.
> May I state our policy again?

said   This adjective is idiomatic in legal documents; however, it sounds stiff in general contexts.

> *stiff*
> a discussion of said matters
> *easier*
> a discussion of those matters

same   This word is an awkward substitute for the pronoun *it* or *them,* or for the applicable noun.

awkward
We have your check and we thank you for same.
Your July 2 inquiry has been received and same is being researched.

easier
Thank you for your check which arrived yesterday.
Your July 2 inquiry has been received and is being researched.

sells at a price of   This is a 19-keystroke phrase more concisely expressed as *costs*, *sells for*, or *is priced at*.

separate cover   *under separate cover*   This is an overlong and vague phrase. If a specific mailing method (such as Special Delivery) is not to be indicated, the adverb *separately* should be substituted.

subsequent to   This expression is longer than its synonyms *after* or *following*.

longer
Subsequent to the interview, she . . .

shorter
After the interview, she . . .

—*see also* PRIOR TO

thanking you in advance   This is an outmoded participial-phrase ending that should not be used in modern business letters. Writers who use this phrase are also presumptuous enough to assume that their requests will be honored.

not
Thanking you in advance for your help, I am

Sincerely yours

instead
Your help will be appreciated.
I'll appreciate your help.
Any help you may give me will be greatly appreciated.
I'll appreciate any help you may give.
If you can help me, I'll appreciate it.
I'll be grateful for your help.

therefor/therein/thereon   These words are commonly used in legal documents, but sound stiff in general business contexts.

stiff
The order is enclosed herewith with payment therefor.
The safe is in a secure area with the blueprints kept therein.
Enclosed please find Forms X, Y, and Z; please affix your signature thereon.

easier
We're enclosing a check with our order.
The blueprints are kept in the safe, which is located in a secure area.
Please sign Forms X, Y, and Z, which we have enclosed.

to all intents and purposes   This phrase can usually be shortened to *in effect*.

> *longer*
> Their response was, to all intents and purposes, no response at all.
> *shorter*
> Their response was, in effect, no response at all.

trusting you will   This is an outmoded participial-phrase ending that should not be used in business letters. Writers who use this phrase are also presumptuous enough to assume that their requests will be honored.

> *not*
> Trusting that you will inform me of your decision soon, I am
>
> Sincerely yours
>
> *but*
> I hope that you'll give me your decision soon.
> Will you please give me your decision soon?

under date of   This is an awkward phrase that should be omitted.

> *not*
> your letter under date of December 31
> *instead*
> your December 31 letter
> your letter of December 31

—*see also* DATED

under separate cover   —*see* SEPARATE COVER

(the) undersigned   While common in legal documents, this term is awkward and impersonal in general writing.

> *awkward*
> Please return these photographs to the undersigned.
> The undersigned believes that . . .
> *easier*
> Please return these photographs to me.
> I believe that . . .

up to the present writing   This expression is padding and should be omitted.

> *padded*
> Up to the present writing, we do not seem to have received your manuscript.
> *lean*
> We have not yet received your manuscript.
> As of now, we have not received your manuscript.
> We still haven't received your manuscript.
> We haven't received your manuscript.

valued   This word is redundant when used after the verb *appreciate* which means "to value or admire highly."

> *redundant*
> We appreciate your valued order of . . .
>
> *lean*
> We appreciate your order of . . .
> Your order is, of course, appreciated . . .

with the exception of   This phrase can usually be shortened to *except* or *except for.*

> *longer*
> We have completed planning for all of the stages of manufacturing with the exception of packaging.
>
> *shorter*
> We have completed planning for all of the stages of manufacturing except packaging.

would   When unnecessarily repeated, this word weakens the impact of a statement.

> *wordy*
> I would think that sales would improve if we hired her.
>
> *lean*
> I think that sales would improve if we hired her.
>
> *leaner*
> Sales would improve if we hired her.

Chapter 6

Composing Letters: Guidelines and Samples

CONTENTS

Many of the details concerning business correspondence are routine. The impact that a well-written business letter can have, however, is far from routine. A well-thought-out, precisely expressed letter delivers a positive impression on the reader and encourages cooperation.

The Writing of Letters: General Pointers

Getting Ready to Write

Good, clear business correspondence is not an accident. It is the result of careful planning and usually requires some pre-writing preparations. The following five steps, suggested for preparing a business letter or memorandum, can serve as a checklist for achieving optimum results with maximum efficiency.

1. **Assemble needed materials**   Frequently previous correspondence must be referred to before a meaningful or accurate reply can be sent. Tabular information, reports, printouts, catalogs, reference books, manuals, and other items also may have to be located and arranged for easy reference.

2. **Make marginal notes**   It is helpful to make marginal notes on letters to be answered. Jotting down information such as conference dates, appointments, and titles of brochures in advance will ensure a speedier reply.

3. **Underscore important facts**   It is useful to employ a yellow felt-tip pen or a red auditor's pen to underscore the significant facts in a letter

which are pertinent to the reply. Color will highlight this information and make it easy to identify when the response is later being written.

4. **Outline reply letter content**   Before beginning to draft a letter, put all the facts together. Have a clear-cut idea of what you want to say, jot down the major topics that will be treated in the reply letter, and examine examples of previous correspondence for guidance in drafting the reply.

5. **Compose the letter**   If careful plans and preparations are made before writing begins, the actual composition of the reply should be easier.

The Makeup of a Good Letter

The construction of good business correspondence is built on three key elements: creating the right opening, sending the right cues to the reader, and devising a friendly close to the letter. Each of these elements is discussed in the following paragraphs.

1. **Creating the opening**   Because a corporate image can be enhanced or diminished through word choice in a letter, the writer should make every effort to see that the right words are used. This statement is particularly applicable to the opening paragraph of a letter. The first paragraph should not only set the tone for the entire letter, it should capture the reader's attention. Openings that take into account the reader's point of view will elicit pleasure, satisfaction, and personal involvement in the matters being discussed. The following is an example of a good opening paragraph:

> We feel very fortunate that you have accepted our invitation to appear before a group of new secretaries at our annual "Get-Acquainted Day" on Thursday, October 1. I had the pleasure of hearing you address the CPS meeting last April, and I'm convinced that we couldn't find a better, more interesting speaker.

The reverse is also true. A stilted, cliché-ridden opening such as the following can actually create a negative impression on the recipient of the letter:

> Enclosed please find information regarding details of our annual "Get-Acquainted Day" on Thursday, October 1. We have noted with pleasure your acceptance to deliver a speech at the meeting as per our request.

2. **Cues to the reader**   The writer should regard every business-communication reader as a knowledgeable critic of corporate letter production. Thus, each communication to a client or to a potential customer provides an opportunity to epitomize the very best in company service, goodwill, and helpfulness. Here are some ways to create a positive impression on the reader:

A. Use tactful, easy-to-understand language. Short words, clear-cut and direct, are easier to read and to understand than lengthy words. Write as you speak, using natural, everyday expressions.

It is a real pleasure to know that you will lead our Transactional Analysis Seminar on May 14.

B. Organize your language carefully and concisely. Time is a precious commodity, and the busy reader wants to get the gist of the message on the first reading. Interesting messages contain sequences that vary in length and in internal structure. Coherence and continuity are other prime requisites of modern communications. (See also Chapter 4, "Composition and Grammar," pages 193–239, for sentence and paragraph strategy.)

C. Construct sentences correctly. Technical correctness in writing is a worthy goal for any writer. In order to attain it, proofread the material and make sure that none of the following infelicities—among many others—is present: misplaced commas, misspelled words, incorrect word division, numbers written incorrectly, hackneyed and stilted expressions, a lack of agreement between subjects and verbs, and other such grammatical and stylistic pitfalls. (Details concerning these elements of writing may be found in Chapters 3, 4, and 5.)

D. Give accurate, precise information. The omission of one important detail can spell the difference between order and confusion in the reader's mind. The following is an example of a letter written by a guest speaker accepting a speaking engagement for a sales conference (note the questions in paragraph two):

Thank you for your gracious invitation to participate in your secretarial conference on October 19 at Pine Manor. It is thoughtful of you to include me in your program.

Would you please send along a map showing the best driving route to your campus, and also mention the amount of time allotted for my message?

If the writer of the letter had checked the outgoing letter carefully for details, it would not have been necessary for the guest to politely request information on the length of the address and on conference location.

E. Write clearly to avoid any hint of double meaning. It has often been said that if a statement can be misunderstood, it will be! By going over all written messages for unintended hidden meanings, the writer can avoid many problems. Keep the reader's reaction always in mind. For example, the following statement raises several questions:

One and two-page photos are needed for this year's annual report.

The questions raised by this statement include the following: How many photos are actually needed? (The statement doesn't say.) Is the need for one one-page photo and one two-page photo? (The statement is ambiguous.) Is the reader expected to supply all of the photos needed? (The statement doesn't say.) The following rewording of the original statement will prevent any misunderstanding:

> Please prepare one full-page photo and one double-page photo for use in this year's annual report.

F. Respond to questions raised. It is frustrating to a correspondent when a question posed in a previous letter goes unanswered. The omission is also poor business practice, as it creates the need for more correspondence. Here is another safeguard that will help to ensure good business writing: double-check to see that no such omissions have been made, by rereading relevant previous correspondence and then comparing it with your response.

G. Introduce an unfavorable comment with a favorable one. It is helpful to present all the positive aspects of a situation first and then to lead into any negative or unfavorable comments. Find points of agreement with the reader and mention them before talking about an unfavorable aspect.

> Your complimentary copy of *Modular Office Units* is on its way to you. Your kind comments about the usefulness of this brochure are greatly appreciated.

> Popular demand for copies of the brochure within recent weeks has depleted our supply, unfortunately. However, please feel free to reproduce temporary copies for use by your staff. When our new shipment arrives, we'll speed a dozen copies to you.

3. **Devising a friendly way to close a letter**   Give the reader a pleasant closing thought in the final paragraph of the letter.

> Again, thank you for giving us permission to reprint the article on your company's research in the field of pollution control. This information will provide excellent material for next month's issue of *The Executive*.

Avoid thanking someone for something in advance. It is really rather impertinent to assume beforehand that a request will be honored. Wait until the service is rendered; then, make an appropriate acknowledgment for it. (See also Chapter 5, "Tone in Writing," pages 240–257, for a list of business clichés that should be avoided, especially in letters.)

The recipient of a letter of request should know exactly what is expected of him or her by the end of the letter. If a certain action is expected, it should be stated or restated in a clear and friendly manner in the last paragraph.

Composing Form Letters and Memorandums

Form Letter Construction

An expedient way to handle routine mail is through the use of guide letters or form letters to standardize responses. A ring binder might be used to categorize certain types of letters that are frequently written. By the use of appropriate index tabs on the various divisions of the ring binder, information can be quickly located. Thus, when such letters as those of announcement, acknowledgment, or apology must be written, the writer may refer to similar or prototypical letters—a shortcut that expedites composition. The notebook might also contain a stock of ready-made insertable paragraphs labeled as A, B, C, D, and so on. By referring to these, a writer might delegate to a secretary the responsibility of constructing certain letters. Form letters are often printed in advance. The secretary then adds the date and the inside address; sometimes other data are also added to the body of the form letter. When preprinted form letters are used, try to match the typeface as closely as possible. Automated letter production or word processing is a popular way to reproduce a form letter because it gives the letter the appearance of an original.

The Writing Of Office Memorandums

The office memorandum is another type of routine communication. Written for interoffice circulation only, it may include general messages (as notices, announcements, or inquiries). Memorandums are usually circulated freely among corporate branch offices located in distant cities. Large companies have standardized memorandum forms. There is a wide variety in the printed styling of memorandums; however, the basic parts of most memorandums are the headings (TO, FROM, SUBJECT, DATE) and the body (message). A memorandum has neither salutation nor complimentary close. It is not usually signed but it may be initialed by the author.

Preparing the heading of the memorandum The memorandum is a fast, economical, and efficient way to relay important news that should reach all or a significant fraction of the corporate staff. Today an office copier can, in a few minutes, reproduce multiple copies of a memorandum, thus making it ready for wide distribution to a large readership. On the other hand, a memorandum may also be addressed solely to one person. The TO line may be addressed to one individual, to several individuals, or to a group.

> TO: Frances Rummel, Customer Services Supervisor
> TO: Customer Services Personnel
> TO: Administrative Staff, School of Business

Typically, the other heading components consist of the following: the FROM line, which includes the name of the writer and his or her title or position; the DATE line; the SUBJECT line; and the optional LOCATION (floor, extension, or branch) line.

The subject line of the memorandum The SUBJECT line in the heading of the memorandum is very important, for it gives the reader an overview of the message content. A good SUBJECT line encapsulates the message, which makes it useful for filing purposes. Examples of typical SUBJECT lines are as follows:

      SUBJECT: April Meeting of the Advisory Council
      SUBJECT: NEED FOR A NEW ELECTRIC TYPEWRITER
      SUBJECT: Transportation Rates on Iron or Steel Bars

Composing the message (or body) of the memorandum Brevity courtesy, factualness, and tact are four requisites of message content in office memorandums. The main idea of the message is usually contained in the first paragraph, while additional or supporting data may be added in succeeding paragraphs. The final part of a memorandum may close with a courteous request for action or further information. In some instances the request for service, action, or specific information may be found in the opening paragraph with supporting data located in subsequent paragraphs.

Sample Letters

This section includes sample business letters that are appropriate for a wide range of situations and occasions. In each case the letter is preceded by a description of a situation in which it would be written and by a description of its elements.

Acceptance of an Invitation

SITUATION: Kathleen Simons, president of a small but fast-growing software-development company has been invited by a professor at a nearby university to speak to his marketing class. The professor particularly wants her to speak at this time because the subject his students are studying at present is one in which she has considerable expertise. She writes to the professor to accept the speaking engagement.

LETTER ELEMENTS: In writing a letter of acceptance to the professor, Simons does the following:

1. She opens by acknowledging the professor's request and by unambiguously accepting the invitation.
2. She repeats all of the details regarding the invitation. This serves as a way of confirming that the details have been communicated accurately.
3. She mentions the enclosed materials.
4. She closes by expressing appreciation for the invitation and her expectation that the event will be enjoyable.

DATAWARE Consultants

1287 West Liberty Avenue
Fort Caroline, ST 85348
406-937-1212

January 2, 19--

Dr. John C. Thomas
Associate Professor of Marketing
Department of Business Administration
State University
Stateville, ST 85364

Dear Dr. Thomas:

    Thank you very much for the kind invitation to lead an upcoming session of your senior seminar. I will be happy to do so. I understand that the seminar will be held from 2:30 to 5:30 p.m. on March 23, 19--, in Milton Hall, Room 1289. The topic—as you suggested in your letter—will be "Marketing the Services of the Emerging Growth Company."

    I am enclosing a list of references to recent articles on the subject that your students may want to acquaint themselves with before the seminar. Since your students are currently studying this topic, I think that these references will be valuable aids to them.

    I appreciate your thinking of me, and I look forward to working with your students.

Sincerely,

Kathleen C. Simons

Kathleen C. Simons
President

KCS/hg

Acknowledgment during an Employer's Absence

SITUATION: Barbara O'Toole is secretary to Arthur C. Roebling, president of Communications Media Corporation. Mr. Roebling has just received an invitation from Nancy Voelker, president of the Advertisers Club, to speak at the club's annual awards dinner. However, Mr. Roebling is in Europe on a business trip and therefore cannot reply promptly to the invitation. O'Toole has been instructed to reply to such letters with an acknowledgment letter that is friendly but noncommittal.

LETTER ELEMENTS: In writing her acknowledgment letter, O'Toole does the following:

1. She acknowledges receipt of the letter and thanks Ms. Voelker for it.
2. She explains the reason for the delay, and she gives Ms. Voelker some idea of when she can expect a reply from Mr. Roebling.
3. She closes in a courteous manner.

Communications Media Corporation/Hawthorne Building/Pierce and Fremont Streets/Houston, TX 77001

CMC

Telephone (713) 898-7642
898-2746

February 15, 19--

Ms. Nancy Voelker
President, Advertisers Club
Post Office Box 1234
Southfield, ST 77078

Dear Ms. Voelker:

Thank you for your gracious invitation to Mr. Arthur Roebling to be the speaker at the annual awards dinner of the Advertisers Club on May 26, 19--.

Mr. Roebling will be returning from a business trip in Europe next week. On his return, you can be sure that your letter will receive his prompt attention.

Cordially yours,

Barbara O'Toole

Barbara O'Toole
Secretary to Mr. Roebling

Adjustment Letter

—granting a claim

SITUATION: Thomas Sagarino is president of Sagarino Flower Company. A longtime customer of the company, Mrs. Katz, has just written to say that a shipment of roses she had recently received from the company included some that were noticeably wilted. Sagarino believes that Mrs. Katz has a legitimate complaint. He wants to rectify the current situation, and he wants to secure Mrs. Katz's goodwill and sense of confidence in the company.

LETTER ELEMENTS: In writing his reply to Mrs. Katz, Sagarino does the following:

1. He begins on a friendly and appreciative note by thanking her for calling the situation to his attention.
2. He acknowledges the error and explains the measures that will be taken to rectify the situation. He will send her a full refund.
3. He explains the reason for the error, extends an apology, and reassures her that it will not happen again.
4. He expresses appreciation for having her as a customer, and he closes with a friendly offer of future service.

Sagarino Flower Company
One Maywell Street
Palm Sands Beach, ST 56790
Telephone: 507-414-5252

August 15, 19--

Mrs. Richard Katz
425 Belmont Street
Smithville, ST 56789

Dear Mrs. Katz:

Thank you for letting us know about the roses that arrived at your home in less than perfect condition. We
have enclosed a check refunding your full purchase price.

An unexpected delay in the repair of our loaded delivery
van, coupled with an unusual rise in temperatures last
Thursday, caused the late delivery of your roses. Please
accept our apology and our assurance that steps will be
taken to prevent a repetition of such an occurrence.

During the past fifteen years, it has been our pleasure to
number you among our valued customers. Customer satisfaction is the goal we strive to achieve.

Please let us know how we may be of greater service to
you.

Yours sincerely,

Thomas Sagarino
President

jml

Enclosure: Check

Adjustment Letter
—refusing a claim

SITUATION: The Gem House sells high-quality jewelry through a mail-order catalog. A repeat customer, Ms. Wrightson, has returned an expensive pair of tourmaline earrings for pierced ears, because the stones' color did not match that pictured in the catalog. The Gem House's policy prohibits the return of earrings for pierced ears for hygienic reasons. The office manager, Lillian Ayala, must refuse the return without alienating the customer.

LETTER ELEMENTS: In writing the letter refusing this claim, Ayala does the following:

1. She reminds the customer in a pleasant way that the Gem House's return policy is clearly printed on every page of the catalog.
2. She acknowledges the fact that there is a slight difference between the shade of color of the earrings and the catalog's photograph.
3. She suggests a way that such a problem can be avoided in the future.
4. She expresses her regret that company policy prevents her from carrying out the customer's wishes. She concludes with the positive expectation that the customer will understand her decision without being alienated by it.

The Gem House

June 18, 19--

Ms. Emila Wrightson
123 Ambler Road
Everett, ST 56789

Dear Ms. Wrightson:

We are sending back to you the filigree tourmaline earrings ordered
through the Gem House catalog last month. We are happy to explain
the company's policy on returning earrings for pierced ears. Because we want our customers to be aware that for hygienic reasons
pierced earrings cannot be returned, we print a statement to that
effect at the top of each page in every catalog we print. We have
no intention of springing hidden or trick policies on our customers.

Since the Gem House is a mail-order company, our catalog is, in a
sense, our sales staff. Because of this, we expend a great deal of
time and effort on it. The colors of the gemstones pictured in the
catalog represent as accurately as possible the colors of our gems
in stock. However, colors are notoriously difficult to reproduce
exactly; and, in addition, the colors of gemstones do vary somewhat
from stone to stone. Because of these factors, it is true that the
tourmalines in your earrings do differ somewhat from the color
shown in our catalog.

If you are ordering jewelry to complement a specific garment, and
the exact shade is important, why not send us a sample of the material? Just a small swatch would be enough. Then a member of our
staff could match the color precisely.

I wish it were not necessary to return these earrings to you, but
unfortunately our company policy dictates that we must. I'm sure
that you can understand this necessity, and I hope we can serve you
in a less inconvenient way in the future.

Cordially,

Lillian Ayala

Lillian Ayala
Office Manager

LA:hg

Adjustment Letter

—granting a discount

SITUATION: Longville Art House, a wholesale art-supply store, has been running a promotional sale on a new line of brushes. A buyer, Mr. Arnaud, who has just received his invoiced order has called the store to complain about his total bill. His usual trade discount is 25%. However, he has been billed for a total that has been discounted 20%, the promotional-sale discount. He had thought, and hadn't been told otherwise by the sales staff of the store, that he would be getting a 45% discount. Since that appears to have been wrong, the buyer wants the trade discount of 25% instead of the promotional discount of 20%. The customer-service manager, William Moore, thinks the buyer has a legitimate complaint, and responds.

LETTER ELEMENTS: In composing his letter to the buyer, the customer-service manager does the following:

1. He begins by telling the buyer that the store was in the wrong. This is good news for the buyer, so Moore leads off with it.
2. He explains the situation without overdramatizing the store's error.
3. He tells the buyer precisely what adjustments will be made.
4. He closes on a positive note, without excessive apology.

multi-art suppliers

1440 Palmerstown Road : Haywood, ST 23555 : Telephone 416-835-1212

June 18, 19--

Mr. David P. Arnaud
Arnaud Arts
1100 Main Street
Longville, ST 23456

Dear Mr. Arnaud:

The invoiced order you were sent is indeed incorrect. Your
order should have been discounted 45%, instead of 20%.

Perhaps we've done our promotional job on those brushes too
well. Our billing staff is now so used to allowing the 20% discount that in your case they forgot to add on the 25% trade discount.

We're in the process of recalculating your order with the
correct 45% discount. The new invoice should be processed and
on its way to you by the end of this week. The new invoice
replaces the original, incorrect one in our files. Simply dis-
regard your copy of the original.

We do regret this slip, and are happy to have the chance to
set the matter straight. This month our store is featuring a
promotion on a new line of acrylics, and I can assure you that
it will be offered to you at a 45% discount, which we will make
sure you'll get!

Sincerely,

William T. Moore

William T. Moore
Customer-Service Manager

sgg

Adjustment Letter
—refusing a discount

SITUATION: Brandon-Rupert Inc. manufactures wall maps. They hold an annual January sale. They have just received a letter from James Maloney, the principal of Oak Hill School, and a good customer. He has complained that the six maps he ordered for the school were invoiced at the regular price. Oak Hill's order is found to have been received at Brandon-Rupert on February 19; the school is not entitled to the sale price.

LETTER ELEMENTS: In responding to Mr. Maloney, the president of Brandon-Rupert does the following:

1. He opens by thanking Mr. Maloney in a friendly way for bringing the matter to the company's attention. He does not immediately give his decision; a negative answer at the beginning of the letter may make Mr. Maloney ignore the rest.
2. He reviews the facts of the sale, and then, without assigning blame, compares them with his company's sales policy.
3. He states that while Brandon-Rupert is lenient in its policies, particularly when a good customer is involved, the discrepancy in this case between sales policy and the date of Oak Hill School's order is too great.
4. He concludes on a conciliatory note, promising that Brandon-Rupert's treatment of all its customers will be fair.

Brandon-Rupert Inc.

15519 Waterloo Road, Versailles, ST 44736
Telephone (514) 387-1551

March 3, 19--

Mr. James Maloney
Oak Hill School
P.O. Box 100
Manchester, ST 34679

Dear Mr. Maloney:

We can understand your distress when the maps that Oak Hill School ordered
from Brandon-Rupert Inc. arrived at the school invoiced at a price considerably higher than what you had anticipated. We appreciate your taking the
time to provide us with all the facts in this matter, and we welcome the
opportunity to explain this company's sale policy.

Oak Hill School ordered six wall maps from us in February. The order is
dated February 12, and it was received at Brandon-Rupert on February 19.
The maps were priced at $99.50 each, resulting in a total price of $597.00.
Oak Hill requested the January sale discount of 50%, which would have resulted in a total bill of $298.50. Instead, your school has been billed
for the full price of $597.00. Our problem here has to do with the date of
Oak Hill's order, both when it was written and when it was received here.
As the brochure advertising our annual January sale states, sale prices are
given on orders received here before February 1.

We do occasionally honor sale-price orders that reach us a few days after
February 1. We particularly try to give long-standing customers such as
Oak Hill School as much consideration as possible. Unfortunately, Oak Hill's
order wasn't made out until February 12, and we just can't fit it into this
extension period.

We hope you can understand our position. If we extend our February 1 cutoff
date to the middle of February or beyond, we would not only shortchange some
other customers, we would be creating a problematic precedent. We must abide
by guidelines that allow us to be as fair as possible to as many as possible.

Sincerely yours,

Harrison Takington
President

HT/hg

Application Letter

—for a franchise

SITUATION: Perretta and Sons Hardware Store wants to expand the variety of merchandise they offer. The store's president, Howard Perretta, has recently been to a trade show where he saw and was impressed by the Harkins Company line of gardening tools. Having decided that this would be a product line that the store could sell successfully, he writes to the credit manager, David Lindberg, to apply for a franchise to sell Harkins products.

LETTER ELEMENTS: In writing a letter of application for a new franchise, Perretta does the following:

1. He opens with a compliment to the manufacturer, and then he presents his request.
2. He provides the necessary supportive data.
3. He closes in an appreciative and courteous manner.

PERRETTA AND SONS HARDWARE STORE
1510 Long Street
Kansas City, ST 56777
Telephone (507) 877-3447

October 19, 19--

Mr. David Lindberg
Credit Manager
The Harkins Company
100 Lake Street
Smithville, ST 56789

Dear Mr. Lindberg:

After inspecting your recent exhibit of fine hardware
at the International Hardware Convention in San
Francisco last week, we should like to add your line
of merchandise.

Please consider this letter an application for a
charge account within the $1,000 to $1,200 range.
Credit references will be supplied upon request.

We should appreciate the opportunity to handle the
Harkins franchise in Kansas City.

Very truly yours,

Howard Perretta
President

jml

Appreciation

SITUATION: The Chen Lumber Company has received an order from Mr. and Mrs. Parent for all the lumber needed to build a new house. The order is considerable, and the president of the company writes a letter of appreciation to the Parents.

LETTER ELEMENTS: In writing to express his appreciation, Chen does the following:

1. He first focuses on the Parents, connecting with the excitement they must be feeling at the prospect of building a new house.
2. He expresses his appreciation for the order.
3. He reinforces the Parents' self-esteem with a compliment.
4. He offers further services that his company might provide.
5. He closes in a friendly but not overly effusive manner.

CHEN LUMBER COMPANY

650 Main Street
Manchester, ST 56717
Telephone (507) 643-2101

August 6, 19--

Mr. and Mrs. George Parent
68 Cottage Street
Smithville, ST 56789

Dear Mr. and Mrs. Parent:

Congratulations on your decision to become a new home
owner! Thank you for the confidence you have shown
in us through opening an account and placing your
order at the Chen Lumber Company.

It will be a pleasure to supply all the lumber and
millwork needs for your beautiful home. You can
build with confidence knowing that only quality lumber
materials and supplies are being used.

Mr. Ralph Fu will be glad to be of service to you in
any aspect of planning or designing your new home.

Please let us know if there is any way in which we
may be of further assistance.

Sincerely,

Larry Chen

Larry Chen
President

jml

Collection Letter

—reminder

SITUATION: Joseph Thomas has purchased a new car from Jamestown Auto Dealers. Up to now, he has been on time with his payments. At present, however, he is two months behind. Francine Hopkins, the credit manager, writes to remind him of the fact and to urge him to attend to his overdue payments.

LETTER ELEMENTS: In writing what is in essence a collection letter, Hopkins does the following:

1. She begins her letter in an unusual way, one that will catch her reader's attention immediately.
2. Before bringing up the problem, she mentions something positive, the fact that Mr. Thomas, up to now, has always met his payment deadlines.
3. She points out the problem tactfully but firmly.
4. She suggests possible alternatives, without being threatening.
5. She closes by asking politely for a response.

Jamestown Auto Dealers

36 Whipple Avenue
Jamestown, ST 58281
Telephone 303-666-2321 or 686-4897

November 5, 19--

Mr. Joseph R. Thomas
46 West Lincoln Street
Comptonville, ST 58201

Dear Mr. Thomas:

Have you ever had to write a reminder letter? We find
ourselves in that position now.

You have been sending your monthly installments to us
promptly for almost a year. However, we find that your
Jamestown Auto Dealers car payments of $215.00 for Sep-
tember 1 and October 1 have not as yet arrived here.

Perhaps your overdue payments are already on their way
to us. If this is the case, please overlook this letter. On the other hand, in the event that some difficulty has arisen, let us know. Perhaps we can offer
some helpful suggestions.

Won't you let us hear from you soon?

Sincerely yours,

Francine Hopkins

Francine Hopkins
Credit Manager

FH/jc

Collection Letter

—request for payment

SITUATION: Carol Derwinski is the treasurer for the advertising agency of Douglas and Alward. One of their clients is Quick Shop, Inc., which runs a chain of convenience stores and advertises on television and in the newspapers. Quick Shop's account with Douglas and Alward is now 90 days past due, and several reminders have already been sent. Quick Shop has been a client for many years and has always paid its bills promptly in the past; however, it now seems clear to Derwinski that failure to pay is no mere oversight. She writes to George Sebastian, director of advertising for Quick Shop, and once again requests payment. Her request to this valued client must be firm but still friendly and polite.

LETTER ELEMENTS: In writing to Quick Shop to request the overdue payment, Derwinski does the following:

1. She summarizes the situation and expresses her concern about it. Her opening is somewhat indirect, since she could have simply begun, "Your account with us is now more than 90 days past due." However, in light of this client's past history with the agency, she is trying to be as tactful as she can.
2. She makes a clear and simple request for immediate payment, and she reminds the client that his company's credit record is at risk. She is well within her rights to be doing this, so she employs no indirection at this point. Her praise for the client's past credit history is a polite gesture, but it is also a reminder that his company has something to lose.
3. She ends with a series of friendly gestures. She wants to maintain good relations with this company, especially if its failure to pay is the result of a temporary problem. However, she needs to know what the situation is, so her final request to Mr. Sebastian is that he make contact with her if something is still preventing payment.

Douglas and Alward

666 Euclid
New Pekin, ST 56151
Tel: 407-996-1438

October 6, 19--

Mr. George Sebastian
Advertising Director
Quick Shop, Inc.
7800 Stateville Road
Portland, ST 56891

Dear Mr. Sebastian:

Our records indicate that your account with us is now more than 90 days past due. We are very concerned that we have not yet heard from you about when we may receive payment, even though we have sent you three separate reminders about this matter.

We are requesting that you send your payment to us today. In this way you can preserve your excellent credit record with us.

Quick Shop has always been one of our best clients, and we value your business very much. If some special circumstances are preventing you from making payment, please call us now so we can discuss the situation with you.

Sincerely,

Carol Derwinski

Carol Derwinski
Treasurer

CD/hm

Collection Letter

—final notice

SITUATION: Anthony Legere is credit manager for Tri-State Building Supply Company, which sells hardware and building materials to retail customers and contractors. One of these contractors is Kirchoffer and Sons, and their account with Tri-State is now 120 days past due. Legere has written several times to Andrew Kirchoffer, requesting payment, and none of these letters has elicited a response. Legere has already suspended credit for Kirchoffer and Sons, and he now writes one last letter, with a stern ultimatum, before turning the account over to a collection agency.

LETTER ELEMENTS: In writing this final letter, Legere does the following:

1. He states the situation, and he delivers the ultimatum. This kind of ultimatum should never be an empty threat that the writer cannot go through with. In this case, Legere is completely prepared to call in a collection agency.
2. He explains some of the thinking that has gone into his decision. In doing this, he is trying to avoid alienating Mr. Kirchoffer any more than necessary. After all, he would still like to do business with him on a cash basis.
3. He makes one more attempt to try persuasion. He addresses Mr. Kirchoffer by name. This is a technique that should be used sparingly, but it usually does serve to get the reader's attention and add emphasis to a sentence. He ends by reminding Mr. Kirchoffer what can be gained and avoided by making a prompt payment.

Tri-State Building Supply Company
1264 Beaver Ruin Road
West Highlands, ST 09803
(111) 432-1236

February 20, 19--

Mr. Andrew N. Kirchoffer
President
Kirchoffer and Sons
P.O. Box 1200
East Highlands, ST 09809

Dear Mr. Kirchoffer:

Your account with us is now 120 days overdue. If payment in full is not received by March 2, 19--, we will be forced to turn your account over to a collection agency.

Up until now, we have been reluctant to take this step, as it will undoubtedly damage your credit rating. However, you have been given ample time to pay this bill, and since you have not responded to any of our reminders or letters to you, we feel we have no choice but to take this step.

Mr. Kirchoffer, I strongly urge you to settle this account with us immediately. In this way you can restore your credit standing with us and avoid any future unpleasantness.

Sincerely,

Anthony T. Legere
Credit Manager

ATL/jm

Collection Letter

—granting an extension

SITUATION: Albert Terranova, credit manager of Kelley Electrical Supply Shop, recently wrote a collection letter to Sarah Finnegan, owner of Modern Design Company, reminding her of her overdue account and requesting payment. In his letter, Terranova held out the offer that Kelley Electrical would be as cooperative as possible if Ms. Finnegan would get in touch with them and discuss the overdue payment. Ms. Finnegan has done so and has requested a 60-day extension, at the end of which time she has promised payment. Because Ms. Finnegan is a long-time customer who has always paid promptly in the past, Terranova agrees to the extension.

LETTER ELEMENTS: In writing this letter granting an extension, Terranova does the following:

1. He tells her that her request for an extension has been granted.
2. He lets her know that he understands and sympathizes with her situation.
3. He tells her the reasons why the extension is being granted. In doing so, he reminds her of the claims and commitments she has made.
4. He states the terms of the extension.
5. In a very polite way, he reminds her that this extension is an exception and she should not expect to receive any further extensions.
6. He closes in a friendly manner.

Kelley Electrical Supply Shop
6802 Eastern Highway
Smithville, ST 56789
Telephone (507) 841-3841

September 15, 19--

Ms. Sarah Finnegan
Modern Design Company
39 Harris Street
Marshaltown, ST 56759

Dear Ms. Finnegan:

I am happy to say that we have agreed to your request for a 60-day extension to pay the $875.60 due on your account.

We understand that you are currently having problems with your own collections, and we can certainly sympathize with that problem. We are pleased to hear you say that these conditions are temporary and that you feel certain that you will be able to meet the extended payment date of November 15, 19--. We are agreed that you will settle your account in full on or before that date.

We want to emphasize that granting this extension constitutes an exception to our usual credit terms. We are granting this exception because MDC has been a good and valued customer for many years, and we want to do whatever we reasonably can to maintain that good relationship; however, you should not expect that we will be able to grant any additional extensions in the future.

We thank you for your cooperation, and we wish you well.

Very sincerely,

Albert Terranova

Albert Terranova
Credit Manager

AT:jml

Complaint

SITUATION: Helen Davison owns and manages a small marina where she offers repair services to her docking guests. Recently she ordered a bilge pump from her usual parts supplier to replace one in the cabin cruiser of a guest who was staying at her marina. Although the supplier assured her the pump would arrive in seven working days, the pump did not actually arrive for more than three weeks, by which time the guest had left. Now Davison has discovered that the mounting arms are so badly bent that the pump would be very difficult to install. She writes to Barry Jacobs, the manager of the parts-supply house, to tell him why she is returning the pump and why she wants a full refund.

LETTER ELEMENTS: In making her complaint to the parts-supply house, Davison does the following:

1. Without being insulting or overly hostile, she gets directly to the point. The details will wait until the next paragraph. She uses the opening to tell the credit manager what he can expect, and why.
2. She goes on to explain the sequence of events, all of which lead in an orderly way to her demand that she receive a full refund for the pump.
3. She does not belabor her disappointment at not being able to complete the repairs for her guest. She does make clear, however, that she considers the supplier's performance below par in this instance and that she hopes they will try to improve their service.

```
                        DAVISON'S MARINA
                        5100 Harbor Drive
                     East Bay City, ST 76820
                        (505)-333-1111




                        July 28, 19--


Mr. Barry Jacobs
Manager
Oceanside Supply Company
129 Fulton Boulevard
Kingston Beach, ST 76842

Dear Mr. Jacobs:

     You will soon be receiving via UPS the Johnson II Bilge Pump
I ordered last month.  This pump is being returned by me both be-
cause it is defective and because it arrived too late to be used
in a repair for a customer.

     On June 30, three weeks prior to my guest's scheduled depar-
ture I telephoned Oceanside Supply and ordered the Johnson Pump
and was assured that the pump would arrive within seven working
days.  The pump actually arrived only after 16 working days, one
day after my guest's departure.  I had considered keeping the pump
in stock for a future repair, but the pump arrived with bent mount-
ing arms that would make installation very difficult and time-
consuming, leading to a labor cost that would have to be absorbed
by me or my customer.  Under these circumstances, I cannot accept
this pump, and I am returning it to you with the request that the
amount of the purchase price be removed from my account.

     Davison's Marina has been a regular customer of Oceanside Sup-
ply for several years, and I must say that we have been quite happy
with your service up to now.  I hope that in the future you will
pay a bit more attention both to customers' needs and your own as-
surances.  Then we all can avoid disappointment.

                         Sincerely,

                         Helen Davison

                         Helen Davison
                         Proprietor
```

Condolence Letter
—personal

SITUATION: James Artandi is the buyer for a furniture store. The wife of one of the manufacturer's representatives he works with has passed away after a long illness. The representative, Steve O'Donnell, is an acquaintance, not a close personal friend. Artandi writes to express his sympathy. The letter is on his own personal stationery, not on company stationery; and it is handwritten, not typed.

LETTER ELEMENTS: In writing a letter of sympathy that does not express an inappropriate degree of intimacy, Artandi does the following:

1. He gives his condolence right away. He avoids being maudlin, and he is careful to choose appropriate words. (Under these circumstances, for instance, it would be inappropriate to use the word *grief* to describe his feelings.)
2. He mentions the occasion when he met the deceased, recalling details that will be pleasant for Steve to remember.
3. He avoids closing the letter with an all-too-easy and not very meaningful expression such as "If there is anything I can do, don't hesitate to call." Instead, he suggests something specific that he can do for Steve.
4. He ends on a cheerful note and does not reiterate the condolence.

James Artandi
14 East Old Shakopee Road
Owen, ST 14398

June 8

Dear Steve,

I was very sorry to hear of Eileen's death. I extend to you my heartfelt sympathy.

I well remember meeting Eileen the evening you and she hosted a swimming party for local furniture buyers. I was new to the area at that time, and felt more than a little like an outsider. Eileen took the time to perform introductions and make me feel at home (she even provided me with a towel when George Harkness's four children and the basset hound were discovered playing tug-of-war with my own). I've never forgotten her way of making a stranger feel welcome.

You probably haven't made any definite plans yet, but if you should decide that you would like to get away for a while, I would be happy to keep an eye on the house for you. It would be no trouble at all to stop by each day, and I'd welcome the chance to come admire your garden.

Best personal regards,

Jim

Condolence Letter

—less personal

SITUATION: Randolph Parker, president of a textile mill, has heard that Gunnar Caroleen, president of a company that does business with Parker's firm, was recently widowed. The two men have met on business occasions, but not socially. Parker writes a short letter of sympathy which is typed on Executive-size company stationery.

LETTER ELEMENTS: In writing a letter of condolence to his business associate, Parker does the following:

1. He begins by offering sympathy simply and straightforwardly. He does so on behalf of both himself and his staff since others in his company have dealt with Mr. Caroleen in their work.
2. He offers business-related assistance that Mr. Caroleen might find helpful.
3. He ends on a less business-like, more comforting note.

PARKER MILLS

2605 Commerce Boulevard
Vestavia, ST 06548
Telephone 502-241-7425

Office of the President

September 9, 19--

Dear Gunnar:

My staff and I wish to extend our heartfelt sympathy to you
during this period of your bereavement since the passing
of your wife, Helen.

Your many friends here at Parker Mills join me in offering
assistance with special scheduling of your orders at this
time. Please do not hesitate to let us know how we may
help.

It must be a comfort to have your family so near. May the
memories of your years together sustain you all and bring you
strength and peace.

Sincerely,

Randolph Parker

Mr. Gunnar Caroleen
President
Universal Products, Inc.
Everett, ST 06789

Confirmation

—of oral information

SITUATION: Raymond Weese is the principal at Plainville Middle School. In the course of a telephone conversation, Charlene Rice, a textbook sales representative, has told him of an upcoming promotional sale her company is planning for the following month. A new science textbook that the school needs will be part of the promotion. Weese understood her to say that the books can be ordered from the company now, using a special ordering number, even though the promotion will not officially begin for 30 days. The principal wishes to confirm this information, and he writes to do so.

LETTER ELEMENTS: In writing to the sales representative to confirm oral information, Weese does the following:

1. He goes over the telephone conversation he held with the representative. He states the facts as he understands them.
2. He continues by asking in a friendly way if his information is correct. Without putting himself or the sales representative on the spot, he gives her an opening to tell him, if it is necessary, that his understanding is wrong.
3. He ends on a courteous and friendly note.

Plainville Middle School
Plainville Regional School District
1400 Olive Street
Plainville, ST 70707
(619) 135-7911

March 15, 19--

Ms. Charlene Rice
Charter Oaks Publishers,
 Educational Division
997 Hinsdale Road
Springfield, ST 65802

Dear Charlene:

When you and I spoke together on the telephone last Friday,
you described a promotional sale that Charter Oaks is planning for
next month. I pricked up my ears when I heard the titles that will
be featured in that sale, because one of them is a science text
that has been chosen by our science department. When I told you
I'd like to order the books as soon as possible so the text can be
used this semester, you gave me an ordering number (3507) for preferred customers. As I understand it, use of this number will allow me to order the text at the promotional-sale price now, even
though the sale will not begin until next month.

I'm about to order the science texts, but first I'd like to
check with you and make sure that my understanding of the situation
is correct. I'd also appreciate confirmation of the preferred-
customer ordering number.

I'm very pleased to have information of this sale in advance.
Buying the science texts on sale will be a big help to our budget,
and getting the books for next semester will be a big help to our
science department.

Sincerely yours,

Raymond Weese
Principal

RW:gad

Congratulation

SITUATION: Norman Langley is a newspaper reporter. Recently, Dick Maloney, a longtime friend and colleague on the same paper, was the Eastern Division's Reporter of the Year. Dick works mostly out of the paper's new bureau in another city, so Langley writes to extend his congratulations.

LETTER ELEMENTS: In writing a letter of congratulations to his colleague, Langley does the following:

1. He commends his friend on the honor, giving it its exact title (a courtesy gesture) and reflects on its meaning.
2. He makes additional comments on the nature of the achievement.
3. He closes with personal good wishes.

The Newark *Clarion*

Harcourt Building
Newark, ST 19711
109-340-5600

February 10, 19--

Mr. Richard Maloney
The Newark Clarion
Springton News Bureau
1413 Chestnut Street
Springton, ST 17101

Dear Dick:

A general announcement was made yesterday to the Clarion
staff of your selection as the Eastern Division's Reporter of
the Year. Congratulations! It is certainly a well-deserved
honor. It's also an honor that is well worth having, as you
and I and others here on the staff have frequently discussed.

If you had been in town, I would have extended these congratulations in person, of course. But since our schedules
seem to keep us at opposite ends of the state, I thought I'd
write and let you know how pleased I am for you.

I am very proud that you have received this honor, one of
the highest that can be bestowed in our field. I'm also proud
to be a colleague of yours. May you enjoy many years of continued success.

As always, please give my warmest wishes to Marcia and
the children.

Best wishes,

Norm

Consumer Relations Letter

—explaining a delay in service

SITUATION: Wright-Way Kitchen Supply finds itself in a predicament. Recently they began carrying a rarity—an all-metal mixer/blender at a price comparable to the same-size models made of plastic. The line sold out in a week, and the store is trying to get in more units. However, the factory that makes the mixer is unable to keep up with the demand, and there will be a shipping delay of at least three weeks. Meanwhile, customers continue to order the new product from Wright-Way. The products manager, Barney Cates, writes to each of them, explaining the situation.

LETTER ELEMENTS: In writing to the would-be customers, Cates develops a basic text that he can use for all of the letters. Each letter will, of course, be personalized with the name, address, and salutation of the recipient. In writing the basic text of the letter, Cates does the following:

1. He begins by acknowledging the new product's success, and goes on to explain that the line is presently sold out.
2. He keeps the second piece of bad news, the three-week delay in restocking, for the second paragraph—no need to hit the reader with two negative items in the first paragraph—and then puts the best face on it he can.
3. He gets to the question that the reader would ask if he and the products manager were face-to-face: What can be done in the meantime? He offers his solutions.
4. These solutions may or may not be agreeable to the reader, so the products manager does not push them. He closes by assuring the customer that he will be notified as soon as the new mixer units arrive at Wright-Way from the factory.

Wright-Way Kitchen Supply

1560 Wright Way, El Yuma, ST 89110
(717) 793-4118 / 795-8708

March 7, 19--

Mr. Hubert Johansson
Appleton Appliances
15 Appleton Way
Deep Springs, ST 89010

Dear Mr. Johansson:

We're pleased to hear that you are interested in the Speed-Mix Master Mixer 1500. This is truly a high-quality item at a reasonable price, and interest in this product has been very high. So high, in fact, that we sold out of this item in one week's time. As far as I know, that is a record for us.

As soon as we realized how quickly our stock of the Master Mixer was being depleted, we contacted the factory to order more. Unfortunately, this item is currently being manufactured at only one factory, and the factory's output cannot meet demand. I have been told that there will be a delay of at least three weeks before our order can be filled.

In the meantime we still do have available the smaller Speed-Mix model, the Master Mixer 1200. Like the 1500, it is made completely of metal and is an excellent value. Its disadvantage, of course, is that it lacks the blender attachment of the 1500. We also have in stock Brandwell's Model 30 all metal mixer/blender. That model does, however, sell at wholesale for $20.00 more than the Master Mixer 1500.

If either of these two options interests you, we'll be happy to fill your order. If, on the other hand, you prefer to wait for us to restock the Master Mixer, you may be assured that we will contact you as soon as our order comes from the factory.

Cordially,

Barney Cates

Barney Cates
Product Manager

BC/lar

Consumer Relations Letter

—to win back an inactive customer

SITUATION: Daniel McMillan is sales manager of the Hanson Company, an optical-supply wholesaler. He has recently noticed a fall-off in orders. The stores involved are located in several different areas, and the sales manager cannot attribute the drop in sales to any one factor. He writes to each inactive customer.

LETTER ELEMENTS: In writing to the inactive customers, McMillan does the following:

1. He briefly reviews the customer's past history with the company, arriving at his reason for writing—the customer is now inactive.
2. He gets right down to reasons for the letter. He wants to know why the customer is no longer ordering from his company, and the only way to find out is to ask straightforward questions.
3. He mentions a postage-paid questionnaire enclosed with the letter. This preprinted form indicates to the customer that the company is serious about regaining his business.
4. He brings up sales items that may interest the customer. He is taking advantage of having the attention of the reader, and he treats the situation as a selling opportunity.

October 14, 19--

Mr. Ralph Chauncey
The Camera Shop
1397 Rosemont Avenue
La Crosse, ST 54601

Dear Mr. Chauncey:

Every year for the past seven years our company has been pleased
to fill at least one order from your Camera Shop. Recently, however, I had the opportunity to go over our sales list, and I've
made the somewhat disquieting discovery that we've not received
an order from you in 14 months.

Given the Camera Shop's past relationship with the Hanson Company,
this may indicate a problem at our end. Have you encountered a
delay or dissatisfaction with an order? I can't find any evidence
in our files that you've written to us with a complaint. If you've
experienced any problems in ordering merchandise from us, I'd very
much like to know what they are.

A business owner with a crowded schedule doesn't have time to sit
down and write us a letter. However, we'd still like to hear from
you. I'm sending along a brief, postage-paid questionnaire, and I
do hope you'll take a moment to check off the questions on it.
This is one way of making your feelings known to us.

I'm also sending along something else that may be of interest to
you. We're currently offering the entire Monatrex autofocus line
of cameras at one-third off our usual price. This is one of our
best-selling lines, and we think you'll spot some excellent buys
in the enclosed brochure. You'll find a handy form inside the
brochure.

Sincerely,

Daniel McMillan
Daniel McMillan
Sales Manager

lvt

Hanson Company
P.O. Box 1435, Front Street, Wyanchochee, ST 37651
Telephone (101) 543-6660 or (101) 543-6503

Credit Letter

—canceling credit

SITUATION: Seven years ago, Howard Harris, owner of Universal Electrical Service, opened an account with Kelley Electrical Supply Shop. For some time he paid his store's bills within 30 days. For the past several months, however, his payments have been very late, necessitating letters of reminder from Albert Terranova, the credit manager of Kelley Electrical. Universal Electrical is now several months behind in its payments, and Terranova has decided to cancel the account.

LETTER ELEMENTS: In writing to Mr. Harris to cancel his account, Terranova does the following:

1. Before getting to the problem, he commends Mr. Harris for prompt payment in the past. An immediate negative or aggressive approach may prevent the letter from being read any further, and Terranova wants to avoid that.
2. When he brings up the current problem, he does so as tactfully and politely as possible.
3. Avoiding the negative, he suggests a solution.
4. He offers special assistance.
5. He requests a prompt response, keeping his wording polite but firm.

Kelley Electrical Supply Shop
6802 Eastern Highway
Smithville, ST 56789
Telephone (507) 841-3841

November 5, 19--

Mr. Howard Harris
Universal Electrical Service
4628 Southern Boulevard
Smithville, ST 56789

Dear Mr. Harris:

Over the past seven years, we have valued your account
with us and considered it one of our best.

Recently with the turndown in business, we have
noticed that your practice of discounting your bills
every thirty days has ceased. Your last payment was
ninety days late.

It is imperative that we keep current on our accounts
receivable; therefore, regretfully, it is necessary
to ask you to make future purchases on a cash only
basis until your account is cleared.

Please accept the enclosed Special Courtesy Discount
card for future cash purchases. It will entitle you
to a three percent cash discount to help you through
this transition period.

May we hear from you soon, Mr. Harris.

Very sincerely,

albert Terranova

Albert Terranova
Credit Manager

AT:jml

Enclosure

Credit Letter

—extending credit

SITUATION: Martin Goodson is credit manager of Craft's, a luggage wholesaler. He has received an order and request for commercial credit from Carry-on, a retail luggage shop now expanding its merchandise lines. A review of Carry-on's credit references shows that the store has a good track record of paying its bills on time. Goodson writes to Charles Gordon, the owner of the shop, to let him know that credit has been approved, and to establish a friendly relationship.

LETTER ELEMENTS: In writing to Mr. Gordon to extend him commercial credit, Goodson does the following:

1. He begins by giving the store owner the good news. He welcomes him as a new customer, and lets him know that the store's order is being taken care of. This letter should be kept informal, and credit terms should not be part of it. They can be sent in the same letter as an enclosure (which may be preprinted).
2. He winds up with a restrained sales pitch, combining it with a personal touch and an assurance of future service.

Craft's

800 Thunderbird Road
Myers, ST 88061
Telephone: 707-488-9322

September 5, 19--

Mr. Charles Gordon
Carry-on
Silver City, ST 88061

Dear Mr. Gordon:

Welcome aboard! Craft's is pleased to have you as a credit
customer. We are sending out your order of 25 all-in-one
suitcases and 10 garment bags (totaling $1500) by truck, and
you should have it by the time you read this. Our credit
terms are explained in detail on the enclosed form.

We've also enclosed a brochure describing a new line of overnight bags that we feel are an excellent buy. The bags have
proved to be best-selling items in markets similar to yours.
Congratulations on the expansion of your store, and if there
is any way we can be of service to you, please let us know.

Sincerely,

Martin Goodson

Martin Goodson
Credit Manager

MG/ph

Credit Letter

—requesting credit

SITUATION: Bret Atkins is the owner of The Pet Place, a large pet store, selling not only pets and pet supplies, but housing and fencing for large animals as well. A recent fencing innovation has been heavily advertised in specialty magazines. Atkins thinks it will sell well, even though it is a relatively expensive item. He writes to Gino Russo, the sales manager for the manufacturer, to request commercial credit terms.

LETTER ELEMENTS: In writing to Mr. Russo to request credit terms, the pet store owner does the following:

1. He opens by explaining how he came to hear of the new product. This information is helpful to the manufacturer.
2. He moves on to the heart of the letter—his order. His calculations are accurate, precise, and arranged in sequence so the manufacturer can see quickly how the store owner arrived at the total. He then requests credit terms.
3. He gives detailed, precise information on his business, and then supplies the names and addresses of credit references.
4. He also gives the name and address of a bank with which he does business. This may not be something the manufacturer will follow up on, but the store owner does give him the option. He closes by volunteering to give more information if the manufacturer wants it.

The Pet Place　South Carters Run Road　Fulton, ST 41823　Telephone 505-626-2626

June 15, 19--

Mr. Gino Russo, Sales Manager
William-Weeks Manufacturing, Inc.
4365 West LaSalle Street
Fairmont, ST 48790

Dear Mr. Russo:

This month's issue of <u>Pet World</u> features a full-page advertisement for your
company's Unseen Fencing. This "fenceless fencing" is something my customers
frequently inquire about, but up to now I've had to tell them there was no
such product. I'm very pleased at the reasonable cost, which is actually lower than the cost of conventional fencing.

According to <u>Pet World</u>'s ad, the Unseen Fencing kit wholesales for $400. I
would like to order 10 kits on sixty-day credit terms. I understand that
there is a $200.00 shipping charge for orders of 10 or more, so my order to-
tals $4,200. I would also like to establish sixty-day credit terms for the
future on purchases up to $5,000.

The Pet Place opened almost eight years ago, and it has proved to be a very
successful enterprise. The store is run in conjunction with a nearby board-
ing kennel owned by my parents. Consequently I have plenty of opportunities
to talk to pet owners and listen to their needs. The Pet Place is the only
store in this area to supply a wide variety of pet supplies, and I feel we
will continue to do well. Being able to provide innovative new products such
as your Unseen Fencing certainly helps.

I refer you to three businesses for information on our promptness in meeting
our financial obligations:

　　　　Ace Feed, 1211 Amity Street, Fulton, ST 41823
　　　　Biological Supplies, Inc., Winding Lane, Highland
　　　　　Park, ST 48203
　　　　Carter Carriers, 37 Hunter Boulevard, Everett,
　　　　　ST 41245

We do business with Fulton National Bank, 49 Parker Street, Fulton, ST 41801.
I will be happy to give you more financial information if you'd like it.

　　　　　　　　Very truly yours,

　　　　　　　　Bret Atkins
　　　　　　　　Bret Atkins

ga

Credit Letter

—refusing credit

SITUATION: Thomas Polani is the office manager for Ardmore Office Products, a retail office supply store. Margaret Allen, the owner of Interior Enterprises, a newly formed interior-design firm, has placed a sizable order for office equipment and has asked for 120-day credit terms. Interior Enterprises has been a good customer for the past year; however, a review of their financial statement and of the information supplied by credit references indicates that Interior Enterprises is in some financial difficulty. Polani decides to refuse the credit request, but he wants very much to keep Interior Enterprises as a cash customer.

LETTER ELEMENTS: In writing to refuse credit, Polani does the following:

1. He expresses appreciation for the order and for past patronage. He is letting Ms. Allen know that he sees their business relationship as an ongoing one and that he hopes it will continue in the future.
2. He states that the application for credit has not been accepted. He avoids the word *refuse,* and he expresses regret that this decision had to be made. At this point, he is neutral in tone and does not criticize or offer advice, which can often seem condescending. Nor does he say anything specific about the financial situation of Interior Enterprises; he simply says that the information provided does not warrant the decision to grant credit.
3. He holds out hope that the decision could be reversed if more information were provided. Most probably, such information is not available; however, he is making clear that he has not come to any negative conclusions about the company.
4. He reminds Ms. Allen that the order can still be filled on a cash basis. He adopts a cheerful tone here to encourage her not to cancel the order.

ardmore office products

136 John T. Slocum Street
Colquitt, ST 18282
Telephone (104)999-8115

September 27, 19--

Ms. Margaret Allen
Interior Enterprises
Suite 101
1700 Blanford Road
Kings Crossing, ST 18540

Dear Ms. Allen:

Thank you very much for the order you placed with us last week. We appreciate your patronage, and we hope we can continue to serve you in the future.

We have carefully considered your application for 120-day credit terms. We are sorry to say that, on the basis of the financial information we have seen so far, we are not able to approve your request. However, if there is any added financial information that you could send us that would allow us to reconsider this decision, we would be happy to do so.

In the meantime, we will be happy to fill this order on a cash basis, with our customary 3 percent cash discount.

Sincerely,

Thomas Polani
Office Manager

TP/mbs

Follow-up Letter

SITUATION: Claire Odom is office manager for Holliston and Beem Associates, a management consulting firm. Six weeks ago, she sent a check and a purchase order to Jenkins Press for a one-year subscription to their newsletter *Monthly Management Records*. The purchase order included a note saying that she wished the subscription to begin immediately. So far, she has received her canceled check, but no issues have arrived. She writes to urge them to begin delivery as requested.

LETTER ELEMENTS: In writing this follow-up letter, Odom does the following:

1. She states the date, amount, product, and other details involved in the original order.
2. She summarizes the current situation as she understands it, and she expresses her concern about it.
3. She renews her request for immediate delivery.
4. She requests notification if immediate delivery cannot be provided.

Holliston and Beem Associates

Faunce Building, Fourth Floor
Market Street
Tacoma Heights, ST 92614
Telephone: 916-484-0411

June 24, 19--

Subscription Department
Jenkins Press
95 High Ridge Road
Park City, ST 67890

Ladies and Gentlemen:

On May 9, 19--, we sent you a check for $52.50 and
a purchase order for a one-year subscription to
<u>Monthly Management Records</u>, and we asked that the
subscription begin immediately. A copy of the purchase order is enclosed.

To date, we have not received any copies of the
magazine, although we have received our canceled
check. We are concerned that somehow our order may
have gone astray, and so we would like to repeat
our request that we begin receiving our copies of
your newsletter immediately. If there is some reason why this cannot be done, please let us know as
soon as possible.

Sincerely,

Claire J. Odom

Claire T. Odom
Office Manager

CTO:kt
enclosure

Inquiry

SITUATION: Thomas Domizio is marketing manager for Acme Equipment Company, an equipment company that does a large proportion of its business through its catalog. The company plans to add a line of tractors to the equipment it currently leases, and it has chosen Laprade's Harris Tractors for the purpose. Domizio writes to Harold Thomas, sales manager of Laprade Industries, for specifications that can be used in the upcoming catalog.

LETTER ELEMENTS: In writing to Mr. Thomas, Domizio does the following:

1. He immediately gets to the point, while complimenting the manufacturer on its product.
2. He details his request in an easy-to-read way. He avoids the unhelpful request, "Please send me all the information you have on this particular product." He lists precisely what he needs, and he sets it up in such a way that it stands out from the surrounding text. Both things facilitate a helpful reply.
3. He mentions that he needs the requested information quickly, and he explains why.
4. He closes politely.

Acme Equipment Company
42 Grove Street
Johnsonville, ST 56855
507-327-0605

September 17, 19--

Mr. Harold Thomas
Sales Manager
Laprade Industries
1525 State Street
Smithville, ST 56789

Dear Mr. Thomas

Presently we are planning to add yard and garden tractors to our line of leased equipment. It is my pleasure
to announce that we shall feature Harris Tractors.

Would you please send us a complete list of models and
specifications for Harris Tractors. It would be helpful to have the following data as soon as possible:

  1. Horsepower/range of job function.
  2. Commercial/homeowner equipment.
  3. Contract samples/sale terms.

Since the publication date for our catalog is slated
for November, your early reply will be appreciated.

Sincerely yours

Thomas Domizio

Thomas Domizio
Marketing Manager

TD:jml

Introduction Letter

SITUATION: For eight years Anita Rothstein has worked as children's librarian at a library in a small town. Recently her husband has been transferred to a large city, and Anita intends to apply for a job at the city's main library. She has asked Diana Green, the head librarian at the small-town library, for a letter of introduction and recommendation to accompany her application. The head librarian responds.

LETTER ELEMENTS: In writing a combination letter of introduction and recommendation, the head librarian does the following:

1. She immediately makes the introduction.
2. She presents relevant professional information.
3. She gives her evaluation and a recommendation.
4. She offers more information upon request.

Carnegie Library of Munstead
510   10th Avenue
Munstead, ST 15120
(412)-461-0007

May 23, 19--

Mrs. Ruth Owens
Personnel Director
Atkins Memorial Library
47 Cooper Road
Montgomery, AL 36106

Dear Mrs. Owens:

    This is a letter of introduction and recommendation for Mrs. Anita N.
Rothstein, who has ably served as Children's Librarian here for eight years.
Mrs. Rothstein received her Bachelor of Arts degree in Comparative Literature just prior to coming to work here. She began studying for her Master's
in Library Science shortly after her arrival, and earned her degree two
years later.

    Mrs. Rothstein's main duties have been the reorganization of the chil-
dren's section, which was much in need of reorganization when she arrived
here, and the day-to-day running of this section, which has included the selection and ordering of new books and periodicals. In addition to her regular duties, she took on the added task of arranging special programming for
area children. She raised money for a wide variety of special speakers and
performers, and during her time here our children benefitted greatly from
her efforts. Because she so efficiently took over a multitude of duties
here, I don't feel that moving from a small establishment to a much larger
one will overwhelm her. She has been very quick to learn, to improvise when
necessary, and to accept responsibility.

    In short, I'm sorry to be losing Anita, but I do feel that our loss
will be your gain. If you'd like further comments regarding her, feel free
to give me a call.

Very truly yours,

Diana T. Green

Diana T. Green
Head Librarian

DTG:col

Invitation, Formal

SITUATION: The Friends of the Cheltenham Museum of Fine Arts invite members and honored guests to a Christmas ball with a formal printed invitation.

INVITATION ELEMENTS: The invitation should set out the pertinent information in a handsome, easy-to-read manner.

1. The invitation is printed in black on heavy cream paper. A small size, such as 4 by 5½ inches, is the usual choice for a good reason; large sizes, because of the heavy paper used, and because there is usually an insert (see item four below), may require extra postage. The envelope of the invitation is not mailable if it measures less than 3½ by 5 inches.
2. The information is separated by spaces. The lines are centered, not indented or placed flush left.
3. Typically the envelope of a formal invitation is handwritten, not typed.
4. The invitation is marked R.S.V.P. (the abbreviation for French *répondez s'il vous plaît*, "please reply"), and a name and telephone number are given. Alternatively, a formal invitation of this type may contain a card, printed in the same style as the invitation, that reads:

> I will _____ will not _____ attend the Christmas ball being given by the Cheltenham Museum Friends on Friday, December 15.
> Name _____

The card should be placed in a stamped envelope addressed in the same style as the envelope of the invitation.

The Friends of the Cheltenham Museum of Fine Arts

cordially invite you to their

Twenty-fifth Christmas Ball

on Friday, the fifteenth of December

Nineteen hundred and eighty-eight

at seven o'clock

at the Bradford Inn

Cheltenham, New Hampshire

R.S.V.P.

Roland Frasier

(603) 782-1864

Invitation, Informal

—to a business event

SITUATION: Wayne Thoren is sales manager for Global Hardware Associates, a sales promotion organization. They are hosting an exhibition of new industrial hardware products, and they are inviting leading retail and wholesale vendors to the show. The invitations will go out on business stationery and be individually signed by Thoren.

LETTER ELEMENTS: In writing this kind of invitation, Thoren does the following:

1. He opens in a cordial and attention-getting way.
2. He gives the date, time, and location of the event.
3. He describes the event and offers a motivation for attending.
4. He includes directions and other details.
5. He closes by encouraging the reader to attend.

GLOBAL HARDWARE ASSOCIATES

87 Highland Drive
Chicago, IL 60147
Telephone 312-120-0444

June 26, 19—

Mr. William Mann
Baker Company
14 Bank Street
Bartlett, IL 60432

YOU'RE CORDIALLY INVITED:

to come to our Industrial Hardware Exhibits to be
held on July 10, 19—, at the Civic Center, 25 High
Boulevard, Chicago, Illinois, from 9 a.m. to 3 p.m.

The newest industrial hardware will be on display.
Representatives from leading hardware manufacturers
will be on hand to answer your questions.

Parking facilities will be available at the Civic
Center Garage. Travel directions and a map are
enclosed for your convenience.

Won't you join your business associates for an
interesting and rewarding day at the Civic Center's
Industrial Hardware Exhibits on July 10.

Wayne D. Thoren, Sales Manager

jml

Enclosures (2)

Invitation, Informal

—to a social event

SITUATION: Sandra Wilhelm is president of Wilhelm and Cook, an industrial design and packaging firm. She has recently hired Jeffrey Nirenberg to be their new finance director. She has decided to give a dinner party so that Nirenberg and his wife can meet socially with the other executives of the company and their spouses, as well as with a few of the firm's most important clients. In all, ten couples are being invited. The wording for each couple's invitation may vary somewhat, but the basic text of the invitation remains the same. In this case, she is inviting Michael Rankin, the firm's design director, and his wife.

LETTER ELEMENTS: In issuing this invitation, Wilhelm does the following:

1. She has the letter typed on her own personal stationery. The typing is appropriate because this is in some respects a business event. If it were to be a purely social event, a handwritten note would have been appropriate. Because she knows the recipients very well, she addresses them by their first names. There is no need for an inside address on this letter.
2. She offers the invitation, giving the date, time, and a brief description of the event.
3. She offers a few more details about the event, and she encourages Sheila and Michael to accept the invitation.
4. She issues the invitation on a "regrets only" basis, and she gives her home phone number. For guests who don't work at Wilhelm and Cook, she may also include her work number.

Sandra B. Wilhelm
47 Bridgewater Road
Oxmoor, ST 21574

                              May 26, 19--

Dear Sheila and Michael,

     Sam and I would like to invite you to a dinner
party on June 28 at seven o'clock. The party is an
informal one to help welcome Jeffrey Nirenberg, our
new Finance Director, and his wife Christine to the
area.

     We are hoping all of the officers of the cor-
poration and their husbands or wives will attend.
In addition, we are inviting a few other friends
of Wilhelm and Cook to join us. We know that Jeffrey and Christine would be delighted if you would
accept.

     Please let us know only if you can't come. Our
home number is 987-8613. If we don't hear from you,
we'll be expecting you.

                    Best regards,

                    Sandy

Job Letter

—offering a job

SITUATION: Brandon Kiley is director of administration for Communications Media Corporation, a holding company that owns several radio stations, newspapers, and a television station. Kiley has recently been interviewing candidates for the position of assistant director of administration. He has now chosen one of the candidates, and he has called to give her the news. However, he also sends out a letter that confirms the offer and sets out other necessary details.

LETTER ELEMENTS: In writing this confirming letter to Ms. Reeve, Kiley does the following:

1.   He restates the offer of the job, giving the exact title of the position.
2.   He reviews pertinent aspects of the terms of employment.
3.   He gives a starting date for the job.
4.   He reviews the documents she will have to bring with her so that the company can remain in compliance with federal regulations regarding citizenship and residency status of new employees. He reminds her that it is mandatory that she bring these documents.
5.   He requests a formal acceptance of the offer.

Communications Media Corporation/Hawthorne Building/Pierce and Fremont Streets/Houston, TX 77001

CMC

Telephone (713) 898-7642
898-2746

July 15, 19--

Ms. Donna A. Reeve
4527 Van Dam Boulevard
Fairfield, ST 12321

Dear Ms. Reeve:

This letter constitutes our formal offer to you of the position of Assistant Director of Administration at Communications Media Corporation. Your duties will consist of assisting the Director of Administration in all professional areas of corporate administration and in carrying out special projects that relate to corporate communications and staff development, as assigned by the Director of Administration.

This is a full-time position, paying a salary of $27,500 a year less the deductions required by law for federal and state taxes and Social Security. You will receive a salary review after six months and annually thereafter. Increases will depend on the company's general policy and on your contributions to our administrative activities. Fringe benefits and other details regarding employment are explained in the employee manual that is being sent to you separately.

We have agreed that you will begin work on August 1, 19--. On that day, please bring with you proof of your U.S. citizenship or resident-alien status. A driver's license with photo (or a state-issued identification card with photo) and a Social Security card will suffice. If one of these is not available, you may bring alternative documents as explained on the enclosed form I-9. Unfortunately, if you do not bring the appropriate documents, you will not be able to begin work.

If this offer is acceptable to you, please sign and date the carbon copy of this letter and return it to us for our files.

Sincerely,

Brandon W. Kiley

Brandon W. Kiley
Director of Administration

BWK/hva
enclosure

Job Letter

—turning down an applicant

SITUATION: Gloria Markham is sales manager for Batterston Furniture Company, a retail furniture store. She has finished interviewing a group of applicants for a sales position in the store. She has chosen a candidate, and the candidate has accepted. She now writes to the other applicants to tell them that they did not get the job. Markham will use the same basic text for each letter.

LETTER ELEMENTS: In writing her letter to the unsuccessful applicants, Markham does the following:

1. She briefly thanks the applicants for applying and quickly moves on to the bad news, telling them that they were not selected.
2. She expresses her appreciation to them. Markham is being extra polite here, because she wants to do nothing to alienate the candidates. After all, they might be potential customers.
3. She tells them that she is keeping their applications on file in case she has a suitable opening in the near future. This is unlikely to happen, but it might. In addition, this is another polite gesture that she can make.

Batterston Furniture Company
16 Flower Street
Malvern, ST 23406
(300)-604-3232

August 16, 19--

Mr. John F. Zimmerman
628 Humphrey Street
Oakdale, ST 23412

Dear Mr. Zimmerman:

Thank you for giving us the opportunity to consider your application for the sales position that we advertised recently. We are sorry to say that we have chosen another candidate to fill this position; however, we want you to know that we appreciate your interest in the Batterston Furniture Company.

Your application will be kept on file. If we have an opening that is suitable for you in the near future, we will be in touch with you again.

Sincerely,

Gloria R. Markham
Gloria R. Markham
Sales Manager

GRM:pgk

Order

SITUATION: Paul Thomas is the purchasing agent of Rodriguez, Inc., a large home-products store. He has just been informed that the store has run out of two types of popular hardware. It is imperative that the store's stock be replenished as soon as possible. He writes a letter ordering more stock from his supplier.

LETTER ELEMENTS: In ordering replacement stock for his store, the purchasing agent does the following:

1. He makes known his store's urgent need for the order. He gives the shipping address that will best facilitate delivery.
2. He lists clearly the quantity, description, and price of the ordered items. By using a tabular approach, instead of inserting the item descriptions into the body of his letter, he makes clear what his store needs.
3. He closes by explaining why prompt delivery of these two items is necessary and by emphasizing that a rush order is needed.

Rodriguez, Inc.
2255 West 189th Street
New York, NY 11250
Telephone: 212-598-1534

November 13, 19--

Mr. George Holmes, Manager
Baxter and Halloway, Inc.
Smithville, ST 56789

Dear Mr. Holmes:

Please accept this order for immediate shipment to
Rodriguez, Inc., Wood Products Division, 2255 West
189th Street, New York, NY 11250.

Quantity	Description	Unit Price	Total
1800	No. 202 T. Hinges, Brass Plate	$1.50 pr.	$1,350
600	No. 78 Corner Braces, Brass Plate	1.75 ea.	1,050
		Total	$2,400

An unexpected flurry of orders has depleted our stock.
Therefore, any assistance that you can give in expe-
diting our order and delivery will be greatly
appreciated.

Sincerely,

Paul Thomas

Paul Thomas
Purchasing Agent

PT:jml

Price Quotation

SITUATION: Barry Zubroski, sales representative for Waterville Type-setting, Inc., has received a request for a price quotation for typesetting a new book from Nancy Bains, managing editor of Hampden Press, a local publishing company. He responds with a letter that supplies all of the pricing information that Ms. Bains has requested.

LETTER ELEMENTS: In submitting his price quotation, Zubroski does the following:

1. He begins in a polite and respectful way.
2. He supplies the requested information in a complete and detailed manner.
3. He provides additional information regarding the terms of sale.
4. He closes with an offer to provide additional information if it is needed.

Waterville Typesetting, Inc.
2965 James Street, Waterville, ST 21270
(101) 444-3131 or (101) 444-3003

December 30, 19--

Ms. Nancy L. Bains
Managing Editor
Hampden Press
44 Lincoln Street
Canton, ST 21212

Dear Ms. Bains:

Waterville Typesetting is pleased to submit the following quotation for The New Homeowner's Encyclopedia:

COMPOSITION: Baskerville, 40 x 50 text area, 8 x 10 trim

Quantity	Description	Unit Price	Total
10 pages	Front Matter	$24.50	$ 245.00
354 pages	Text	28.95	10,248.30
118 pages	Space Allowance for Art	6.00	708.00
30 pages	Index	26.00	780.00
200 pieces	Line Art to Shoot and Strip	4.50	900.00
512 pages	Negatives	3.00	1,536.00
512 pages	Proofs of Negatives	.75	384.00
			$14,801.30

These prices are FOB our plant in Waterville. The terms of sale are net 30 days, with a progress billing at the end of the galley stage.

Pricing is subject to review upon receipt of the fully edited manuscript, specifications, and scheduling requirements. Estimate is valid for 90 days.

Thank you for the opportunity to provide this quotation. If you have any further questions, please do not hesitate to call me.

Sincerely,

Barry Zubroski

Barry Zubroski
Sales Representative

BZ/gic

Refusal of an Invitation

SITUATION: Patricia Meacam is a partner in the law firm of Jenkins and Danforth. Recently she and her firm have been in the news for their efforts in negotiating some very important real-estate development projects in downtown Stateville. She has just been invited to speak at the annual banquet of Stateville United, a volunteer service that supports many charitable activities in the city. Meacam writes to Emilia Sheridan, the banquet organizer, to say that she cannot attend their banquet.

LETTER ELEMENTS: In writing to decline the invitation, Meacam does the following:

1. She thanks Ms. Sheridan for the invitation, and she expresses her regrets that she cannot accept the invitation. She offers a reason why she cannot, but she keeps the explanation very general.
2. She compliments the organization. The compliment is sincere, but it also helps maintain good feelings with the organization.
3. She ends on a friendly and cheerful note.

Jenkins and Danforth
Attorneys-at-law
One Court Street, Suite H
Stateville, ST 34533
Telephone: 512-507-1440

November 12, 19--

Ms. Emilia Sheridan
Stateville United
3700 Main Street
Stateville, ST 34534

Dear Ms. Sheridan:

Thank you very much for your invitation to
speak at your annual awards banquet. Unfortunately,
my responsibilities at Jenkins and Danforth prevent
me from accepting any outside speaking engagements
at this time.

I have always been a great admirer of the work
of your organization, and I am honored to have been
asked to speak to your group. I wish you well with
what I am sure will be a splendid evening.

Sincerely,

Patricia J. Meacam

Patricia J. Meacam

lol

Request

—for an appointment

SITUATION: Grace Diaz is a sales representative for Grayson Paper Company. She writes to set up a business appointment with Brian Watson, purchasing agent for the Pikeville School District. Diaz has done business with Mr. Watson in the past and is aware of at least one of his product needs that her company can now answer.

LETTER ELEMENTS: In writing to ask Mr. Watson for an appointment, Diaz does the following:

1. She opens by reminding her client in a low-key way that they have met before. She mentions one of her company's products that she feels will interest him.
2. She states her desire to meet with him, and she suggests a date and a time. She does this as a way of helping her own scheduling and also as a way of urging Mr. Watson to commit to a specific time for a meeting.
3. She says she will call later to confirm the appointment. This allows Mr. Watson the chance to suggest an alternate time or to decline the request entirely. It also allows Diaz the chance to speak to Mr. Watson before the actual appointment to get a better idea of his needs and to do some brief low-key preselling of her product.
4. She offers a number at which she can be reached. Whether or not the number is needed, it is a friendly gesture to offer it.
5. She closes in a mildly flattering way, saying that she is looking forward to the meeting.

GRAYSON PAPER COMPANY

12555 Berea Road
Fayette, ST 54778
Telephone: (123) 349-6200

March 3, 19--

Mr. Brian Watson, Purchasing Agent
Pikeville Township School District
Pikeville, ST 45101

Dear Mr. Watson:

Last year when I visited Pikeville, you found some essay paper in the Grayson line that you felt would suit several different needs within the district. At that time, you and I also discussed the problem you were having in finding multicolor file folders that would be large enough to accommodate your oversize record forms. Grayson was then in the midst of production planning for a new line of file folders, but manufacturing had not yet begun. Now I have samples of our new file folders, and I believe they will fill all your requirements.

I would like to call on you at your office later this month to show you samples of these folders and of some of our other new products that I think will be of interest to you. Perhaps sometime on the morning of Wednesday the 24th would be convenient for you. I will call you early in the week of March 15 to confirm this date or to set up an alternate time.

If you need to reach me before that time, please feel free to call me at Grayson headquarters in Fayette at (123) 349-6222.

I look forward to meeting with you and talking about the needs of the Pikeville School District.

Sincerely,

Grace Diaz

Grace Diaz
Sales Representative

GD/smb

Request

—for a price quotation

SITUATION: Nancy Bains is managing editor of Hampden Press, a small publishing company that produces a few new books each year. The company is about to begin work on another new title, and Bains wants to receive price quotations for the typesetting part of the project from several companies that she feels are qualified to do the job. One of the typesetting companies is Waterville Typesetting, and Barry Zubroski is their sales representative.

LETTER ELEMENTS: In writing to request a price quotation from Mr. Zubroski, Bains does the following:

1. She describes in detail the specifications of the product and services she is requesting.
2. She describes the particular way in which she wants the product delivered.
3. She provides additional information about other aspects of the project, including information about schedule requirements.
4. She gives a date by which time she expects to receive a quotation.
5. She offers to answer any questions that Zubroski may have.

HAMPDEN PRESS

44 Lincoln Street   Canton, ST 21212   Telephone: 101-555-6926

December 20, 19--

Mr. Barry Zubroski
Waterville Typesetting, Inc.
2965 James Street
Waterville, ST 21270

Dear Mr. Zubroski:

SUBJECT: The New Homeowner's Encyclopedia

We are writing to request a quotation for typesetting services for
the above new title.

The book will be 512 pages, composed of 10 pages of front matter,
472 pages of main text, and 30 pages of index. The text will include approximately 200 pieces of line art (equalling approximately 25% of the
text space), which we will ask you to shoot, reduce, and position in place.
The trim size will be 8" x 10". The text area will be 40 picas x 50 picas,
and the main text will be set in 10/11 Baskerville.

We will require one set of galleys, one set of page proofs, a set of
negatives, and a set of proofs of negatives.

The copy will be in the form of clean typed manuscript, which we expect to send in several batches, with the last of the copy arriving by
June 30, 19--. We would like to receive final negatives by December 30,
19--.

I hope to receive your quotation within two weeks. If you have any
questions, please do not hesitate to call.

Sincerely,

Nancy L. Bains

Nancy L. Bains
Managing Editor

NLB/rg

Request

—for a speaker

SITUATION: The program-committee chairman of the Altamont Conservation Club must find a speaker for the annual banquet. Several honored guests will be present at the banquet, and the club membership is anxious that the affair be a memorable one. Unfortunately funds are quite low this particular year. Elaine Goodrich, president of the club, writes to Susan Compton, the professional speaker mentioned by several club members as their first choice.

LETTER ELEMENTS: In asking Ms. Compton to speak at the club's annual banquet, Goodrich does the following:

1. She begins not by mentioning her club's event, but by complimenting the speaker. Only then does she bring up her group's banquet. She goes on to specify the date and location.
2. She continues with a description of the banquet and its setting and theme, using that to bring up the topic of the speech. She touches on the topic in a general way, leaving the specifics to the speaker. This is not only courteous to a professional speaker, but a compliment to Ms. Compton's judgment.
3. She does not offer a fee, but leaves it to the speaker to set one. Neither does she commit her club to something that may be too expensive for it. She waits to see the speaker's response before concluding the arrangements.
4. She closes with a courteous reminder that she is waiting to hear from the speaker.

Altamont Conservation Club/P.O. Box 60/Altamont, ST 72672

February 4, 19--

Ms. Susan Compton
29 Fairfax Lane
Jackson, ST 98499

Dear Ms. Compton:

You certainly do come highly recommended—every member of
our program committee has mentioned your name as a speaker for
the Altamont Conservation Club spring banquet. This year the
banquet will be held at the Marriott Hotel in downtown Jackson.
The date has been set for Thursday evening, May 30.

Our spring banquet is an annual event, and caps our year's
calendar of activities. Many of those activities are concerned
with environmental issues, both on the local and national level.
Because of our club's involvement with social issues, our past
speakers have tended to focus on that as a topic. I realize,
however, that is a broad area, and I leave the specific choice
of topic up to you. A length of thirty-five to forty minutes
for your talk, including time for a question-and-answer period,
would be ideal for us.

Could you let us know by the first of next month whether
or not you are available and what your fee will be. If you can
join us and if satisfactory financial arrangements can be made,
we will send along more information, including a map that shows
how to get to the Marriott.

I look forward to hearing from you!

Sincerely,

Elaine Goodrich
Elaine Goodrich

Sales Letter

SITUATION: Daniel Parsons is responsible for sales promotion at Parsons Office Management Services, a company that offers a monthly newsletter summarizing information on new office-supply equipment. Parsons wishes to increase the newsletter's circulation, and towards that end he has drawn up a list of the office-supply stores in his region that are not currently subscribing. He writes to each one individually to tell them about his company's product.

LETTER ELEMENTS: In writing a sales letter to the manager of Morris Office Supply, Parsons does the following:

1.   He writes a formal business letter on good-quality company stationery, and he addresses the store manager *by name*. This approach lessens the possibility that his letter will be dismissed as junk mail.
2.   He uses a unique opening that will catch the reader's attention immediately.
3.   He lists the advantages of his product, and describes his company's services.
4.   He provides the reader with a chance to look over the product and make a judgment. The implication here is that Parsons is fully confident of his product's appeal. He is not trying to trick the reader into paying for something that may be inferior or unsatisfactory.
5.   He uses a close that will encourage the reader to take positive action right away.

PARSONS OFFICE MANAGEMENT SERVICES
15 Evergreen Street
Jonesville, ST 02680
Telephone (108) 935-0246

October 24, 19--

Mr. James Huntwell
Morris Office Supply
250 Maple Street
Smithville, ST 56789

WHAT'S NEW FOR THE OFFICE?

Today's office manager is challenged to constantly seek information
on this question. Parsons Office Management Services is a recognized
authority on the subject.

Each month a newsletter entitled Office Products Update summarizes
new entries in the office supply and equipment arena to aid the be-
leaguered office manager in making the right decisions fast. This
month's edition is enclosed. Please accept it with our compliments.

Gain an edge on your competitors by obtaining the latest office products information in summary form each month. It won't take long
until your customers will recognize Morris Office Supply as a leader
in What's New for the Office.

Office Products Update may be yours each month for the new subscriber
fee of only $6 for the entire year. If you will make use of the en-
closed special subscriber's card before the end of this month, you
will receive two extra issues for the year at no extra cost. May
we hear from you soon?

Daniel B. Parsons

DANIEL B. PARSONS — VICE-PRESIDENT

jml

Enclosures

Thank-you Letter

—for hospitality

SITUATION: George Kinsey, plant manager for Fairfield Textiles Company, recently attended an out-of-town convention and trade show. During the convention, he was entertained by Fairfield's sales representative in the area, Barbara Raycroft, and her husband. When he gets back in his office, Kinsey writes a thank-you note to express his appreciation for the hospitality shown to him.

LETTER ELEMENTS: In writing his thank-you note, Kinsey does the following:

1. Because all his contacts with Ms. Raycroft are business-related, he has the letter typed on company stationery. He is on a first-name basis with her, and so he addresses her by her first name. This is, however, a business-related letter, and so the colon after the salutation is appropriate.
2. He thanks her for the hospitality he received, mentioning specifically each of the occasions on which he was entertained. Because Ms. Raycroft's husband Bill participated in the occasions, Kinsey refers to him as well in the letter.
3. He adds some friendly phrases that convey his good feelings and sense of appreciation.

Fairfield Textiles Company
2900 Northrup Way
Fairfield, ST 64380
Telephone: 505-555-9318

December 1, 19--

Ms. Barbara Raycroft
Fairfield Textiles Company
2100 Broadway, Suite 901
Silver City, ST 78920

Dear Barbara:

Thank you very much for all the kind hospitality that you and Bill showed to me during my stay in Silver City. I thoroughly enjoyed my tour of the city and the wonderful meal that you and Bill managed to put together on such short notice.

I certainly hope to see you again at this year's sales meeting. And again, many thanks to you both for making my trip such a pleasant one.

Sincerely,

George King

Thank-you Letter

—for information or service

SITUATION: Christopher Soule is a free-lance writer who writes mostly on local-history topics. Recently he asked for and was granted an interview with Barbara Chase, a librarian in a neighboring town who has amassed a collection of historical papers relating to that town's history. He writes to thank her for the interview.

LETTER ELEMENTS: In writing his thank-you letter to Mrs. Chase, Soule does the following:

1. He thanks her for the interview, and he specifically states what it is she did for him.
2. He describes the benefit he derived from the interview.
3. He expresses his appreciation for the time she gave him for the interview, and he offers a pertinent compliment.

1292 Park Street
Stateville, ST 46788
September 27, 19--

Mrs. Barbara Chase
Middleville Public Library
Middleville, ST 46712

Dear Mrs. Chase:

    Thank you very much for giving me the chance to speak
with you and to see your impressive collection of papers
relating to the history of Middleville. You not only helped
me with my current project, but you have also made me aware
of a valuable resource which I hope to be able to draw upon
in the future. I certainly appreciate the time you spent
with me, and I applaud the work that you and your staff are
doing to preserve these valuable materials.

        Sincerely,

        Christopher Soule
        Christopher Soule

Transmittal Letter

—for materials requiring no explanation

SITUATION: Jean Linamen is the public relations assistant for Fairmont Stainless Steel Corporation. James Wilhelm, a professor at a nearby university, has written to Fairmont Stainless, requesting copies of their annual report for use in his classroom. Linamen writes a letter to Professor Wilhelm, informing him that copies of the requested material are on the way.

LETTER ELEMENTS: In writing a letter of transmittal to Professor Wilhelm, Linamen does the following:

1.   She opens by acknowledging his interest in Fairmont's annual report.
2.   She gives precise details on the transmittal.
3.   She offers further assistance, and she closes in a friendly fashion.

Fairmont Stainless Steel Corporation
1480 Hamilton Road
Fairmont, ST 67890   Tel: 519-643-7899

March 18, 19--

Professor James Wilhelm
DePaul Technical College
Smithville, ST 56789

Dear Professor Wilhelm:

It is good to know of your interest in the <u>Annual</u> <u>Report</u> of
the Fairmont Stainless Steel Corporation for use by the
students in your research seminar.

As you requested, a dozen copies of Fairmont's <u>Annual</u> <u>Report</u>
were mailed to you today. Since these reports were labeled
Priority Mail, you will have them well in advance of the
target date for their use.

Each year, if you will let us know the number of these reports that you will need, it will be our pleasure to send
them. We feel that the material will be our contribution
to the business and economic understanding of your students.

Sincerely yours,

Jean Linamen

Jean Linamen
Public Relations Assistant

FSS

Transmittal Letter

—for materials requiring some explanation

SITUATION: James Santiago is president of Santiago and Nussbaum, an architectural firm specializing in restoration of historical buildings. William Demetrius, a real-estate developer, has asked the firm to develop a proposal for the restoration of a building that his company is considering for purchase. Santiago's firm has completed the proposal, and Santiago includes a cover letter with the proposal.

LETTER ELEMENTS: In writing his cover letter, Santiago does the following:

1.   He states clearly what it is that is being delivered.
2.   He points out some important details pertaining to the proposal.
3.   He adds a personal note, expressing his feelings about the proposal.
4.   He closes with an offer of additional assistance if it is needed.

Santiago & Nussbaum

The Arcade · Hillsborough, ST 64529 · Telephone 411-820-3333

August 27, 19--

Mr. William Demetrius
Demetrius Brothers, Inc.
1200 High Street
Hillsborough, ST 64501

Dear Mr. Demetrius:

Here is our proposal for the renovation of the McKay Building at 1300 State Street. In developing this proposal we have
kept in mind your stipulation that the result of this renovation
should be a multi-use commercial space. We have also developed
the proposal in such a way to ensure that it qualifies for favorable tax treatment as an historical restoration. The proposal
assumes that Demetrius Brothers will be acquiring the property
at 1308 State Street as well.

We think this is a very exciting project, and we look forward to hearing your reaction to our proposal. If you have any
questions about any aspect of the proposal, please do not hesitate to call.

Sincerely,

James Santiago
President

JS:gic

Chapter 7

Correspondence with United States Government Agencies

CONTENTS

Increasing government and private industry tie-ins have made it necessary for civilian contractors to be familiar with government agencies' special correspondence and security procedures. While it is true that letter format and security precautions vary with the policies of each government contracting agency, as well as with the nature of each contract, the following overview should serve as a general orientation for the person dealing with government correspondence for the first time.

The two most basic problems are the following: (1) ensuring that all material regardless of its classification be marked in such a way that it will be quickly delivered to its intended addressee and that copies of it are readily retrievable in company files and (2) ensuring that all classified material be safeguarded according to government guidelines so that unauthorized persons cannot gain access to it.

Correspondence Format

Letters to government agencies should conform to the guidelines of the agency with which one's firm is working. Letters incorrectly formatted and addressed may be delayed, lost, or even rejected and returned—any of which can result in costly delays or even to the loss of a contract, especially when bidding under a deadline is involved.

Correspondence with a nonmilitary government agency may be formatted in any of the generally accepted business-letter stylings discussed in Chapter 1. A subject line and a reference line are always included. These data are necessary for proper interagency routing of the letter. The correct forms of address for elected and appointed officials can be found in the Forms of Address Chart in Chapter 2.

The following general principles are applicable to correspondence directed to the Department of Defense:

1. A general Modified Block Letter style with numbered paragraphs is recommended.
2. If any section of the letter is classified, the highest classification category therein must be stamped at the top and the bottom of each page. This stamp is affixed above the printed letterhead and below the last line of the message on the first sheet, and above the heading and below the last notation on a second sheet. The CLASSIFIED BY and NATIONAL SECURITY INFORMATION stamps must be affixed at the bottom of the letterhead sheet (see the letter facsimile on pages 350–351).
3. A special mailing notation, if needed, is typically typed in all-capital letters or stamped in the upper left corner of the letterhead sheet and in the upper left corner of a continuation sheet or sheets.
4. The writer's courtesy title and surname, followed by a slash, followed left by the typist's initials and another slash, followed by the writer's telephone extension (if not already included in the printed letterhead) may be typed in the upper right corner of the first sheet.
5. An inverted date (day, month, year) forms the date line, blocked flush left about three lines from the last line of the letterhead. The date may be styled as 1 January 19— or 1 Jan — (last 2 digits of year), but one styling should be used consistently throughout the letter. Abbreviations for the twelve months are the following:

Jan	Feb	Mar	Apr
May	Jun	Jul	Aug
Sep	Oct	Nov	Dec

6. Companies contracted to the government for specific projects usually assign control numbers to files and correspondence related to the project. This number should be included in the date line block, one line below the date.
7. The next element of the letter—whether it be the SUBJECT block or the TO block (the order varies according to agency)—is typed about three lines below the last line of the date block and is blocked flush left. The SUBJECT block, shown first in this book, consists of the following elements:

   line 1. contract number
   line 2. name of program or project
   line 3. subject of the letter + appropriate security classification expressed as a parenthetical abbreviation, as (C) = Confidential, (S) = Secret, or (TS) = Top Secret.

8. The TO block, which is really the inside address, is typed about three lines below the date block or the SUBJECT block (order varies with agency policy). Its internal elements are the following:

   line 1. initials or name of office
   line 2. name of applicable administrator (the addressee)

CONFIDENTIAL

CERTIFIED MAIL

Mr. Exec/tp/413-734-4444

Merriam-Webster Inc.
America's first publisher of dictionaries
and fine reference books.

1 January 19—
76TRANS123

SUBJECT: Contract AF 45(100)-1147
            Foreign Technology Program
            Life Sciences Translation QC (C)

TO: Initials or Name of Office
            Name of Applicable Administrator
            Organization
            Geographical Address + ZIP Code

THROUGH: Applicable Channels
            and Addresses
            Listed and Blocked

REFERENCE: (a) WXYZ letter ABCD/EF dated 1 December 19—
            (b) EFGH letter IJKL/MN dated 1 November 19—

1. This is a typical format for letters directed to the Department of Defense.
    Styling varies with the agency or department one is writing to; thus, a
    format consensus is shown here.

2. In letters containing classified information, the highest classification
    category of any included information must be noted at the top and bottom
    of each page.

    a. Since the subject of this letter is supposed to be CONFIDENTIAL, it is
        so stamped above the letterhead and at the bottom of the page.

    b. The parenthetical abbreviation (C) for CONFIDENTIAL is typed at the end
        of the subject line.

    c. Appropriate classification stamps are affixed at the bottom of the first
        page.

3. Special mailing notations if required are typically typed in the upper left
    corner of the page.

CLASSIFIED BY: _____
EXEMPT FROM GENERAL DECLASSIFICATION
SCHEDULE OF EXECUTIVE ORDER 11652
EXEMPTION CATEGORY
DECLASSIFY on

CONFIDENTIAL

NATIONAL SECURITY INFORMATION
Unauthorized disclosure subject to
criminal sanctions.

47 FEDERAL STREET SPRINGFIELD MASSACHUSETTS 01101 TELEPHONE 413· 734 3134

Figure 7.1.   Letter styling for Department of Defense correspondence

CONFIDENTIAL

CERTIFIED MAIL

Contract AF 45(100)-1147   1 January 19—
Foreign Technology Program   76TRANS123
Life Sciences QC (C)   Page 2

4.   If the writer's name and telephone number are not on the printed letterhead,
     they may be typed with the typist's initials in the upper right corner of
     the first page.

5.   The date line featuring an inverted date and the company control number are
     flush left, with the date line three lines below the letterhead.

6.   The SUBJECT block, sometimes placed after the TO and/or THROUGH blocks
     depending on agency preference, contains the contract number, project name,
     and subject of the letter.

7.   The TO block is really the inside address. The THROUGH or VIA block lists
     the designated channels through which the letter must pass before it reaches
     the addressee.

8.   The REFERENCE block lists related material or previous correspondence that
     must be referred to before action can be taken.

9.   The SUBJECT, TO, THROUGH, and REFERENCE blocks are separated by triple-
     spacing, and are internally single-spaced.

10. There is no salutation. The message, comprising numbered paragraphs and
     alphabetized subparagraphs, begins two lines below the last line in the
     REFERENCE block.

11. Continuation-sheet headings begin six lines from the top edge of the page
     and contain subject data, date, pagination, and control number. The
     classification category must be stamped at the top and bottom of each
     continuation sheet.

12. There is no complimentary close. The company name is typed all in capitals
     two lines below the last message line, followed four lines down by the
     writer's name, title, and department in capitals and lowercase.

13. Typist's initials if not shown at the top of the first page may appear two
     lines below the signature block. Enclosures should be listed numerically
     and identified, as should carbon-copy recipients. Only external distribu-
     tion lists appear on the original.

MERRIAM-WEBSTER INC.

Executive Signature
Project Manager

Enclosures (1)   (C) 3 copies of Translation
                 Printout dated 30 December 19—

            (2) 1 copy of Contract AF 44(100)-1147

CONFIDENTIAL

line 3.   name of organization

line 4.   geographical address + zip code

9. The THROUGH or VIA block (caption varies with agency policy) is typed about three lines below any other blocks that precede it. This block is used in letters that must be sent through designated channels before reaching the addressee. Each agency, office, or individual should be named and addressed as in the TO block.

10. The REFERENCE block is typed about three lines below the last typed block. It contains a list of material or previous correspondence that must be consulted before the letter can be acted on by the addressee. This information is listed alphabetically or by Arabic numerals.

11. Regardless of the order of the items discussed above, the captions SUBJECT, TO, THROUGH, and REFERENCE should not be visible in the window area of a window envelope. Only the address in the TO block should be visible in such an envelope. The styling of these captions varies; they may be entirely in capitals, they may be in capitals and lowercase, or they may be abbreviated to SUBJ, THRU, etc. Use the styling recommended by the agency with which your company is dealing.

12. There is no salutation.

13. The message begins flush left, two lines below the last line of the REFERENCE block. Paragraphs are numbered consecutively and are single-spaced internally but double-spaced between each other. Subparagraphs are alphabetized, single-spaced internally, and double-spaced between each other. If there is a paragraph *1,* there must be a *2;* if there is an *a,* there must be a *b,* and so on.

   1. xxxxxxxxxxxxxxxxxxxxxxxxxxxxxxxxxxxxxxxxxxxx
      xxxxxxxxxxxxxxxxxxxxxxxxxxxxxxxxxxxxxxxxxxxx

      a. xxxxxxxxxxxxxxxxxxxxxxxxxxxxxxxxxxxxxxxxxxxx
         xxxxxxxxxxxxxxxxxxxxxxxxxxxxxxxxxxxxxxxxxxxx

      b. xxxxxxxxxxxxxxxxxxxxxxxxxxxxxxxxxxxxxxxxxxxx
         xxxxxxxxxxxxxxxxxxxxxxxxxxxxxxxxxxxxxxxxxxxx

         1. xxxxxxxxxxxxxxxxxxxxxxxxxxxxxxxxxxxxxxxxxx
            xxxxxxxxxxxxxxxxxxxxxxxxxxxxxxxxxxxxxxxxxx

         2. xxxxxxxxxxxxxxxxxxxxxxxxxxxxxxxxxxxxxxxxxx
            xxxxxxxxxxxxxxxxxxxxxxxxxxxxxxxxxxxxxxxxxx

   2. xxxxxxxxxxxxxxxxxxxxxxxxxxxxxxxxxxxxxxxxxxxx
      xxxxxxxxxxxxxxxxxxxxxxxxxxxxxxxxxxxxxxxxxxxx

14. There is no complimentary close.

15. The company name is typed flush left entirely in capital letters two lines beneath the last line of the message. The writer's name is typed in capitals and lowercase at least four lines below the company name, also flush left. The writer's title and department name, if not already appearing on the printed letterhead, may be included beneath his or her name in capitals and lowercase, also flush left.

16. The typist's initials, if not already included in the top right corner of the first sheet, may be typed flush left, two lines below the last element of the signature block.

17. Enclosures are listed and identified two lines below the typist's initials or two lines below the typewritten signature. The numeral stylings 1. or (1) may be used. The appropriate headings are *Enclosure(s), Encl.,* or *Enc.* for the Air Force and Navy; and *Inclosure(s), Inc.* for the Army. Classification categories should be noted at the beginning of each applicable enclosure description as shown in enclosure (3) below. If enclosures are to be mailed under separate cover, they still must be listed on the letter and their classification categories noted.

    Enc.:   (1) 3 copies of Test Procedure Report
             WXYzz dated 1 January 19—
          (2) 1 copy of Contract AF 45(100)-1147
          (3) (C) 2/c ea. specifications mentioned
             in paragraph 7

NOTE: Some government agencies require that enclosures be noted in a block two or three spaces below the REFERENCE block.

18. The carbon copy notation *cc:* or *Copy to* is typed flush left two lines below any other notations. It includes an alphabetical listing of all individuals or persons not associated with the company who will receive copies. Their addresses should be included. Internal copies should contain a complete list of both the external and internal recipients of copies.

    cc: COL John K. Walker, +address
          (w/enc. (1)—2 copies)

19. Continuation-sheet headings are typed six lines from the top edge of the page. The message is continued four lines beneath the heading. Continuation-sheet headings should include the SUBJECT block data as well as the company control number, the appropriate date, and the page number. See the following facsimile for setup.

20. In some correspondence, an approval line must be the last typed item on the page if the contracting agency must approve the material and return it to the contractor. In this case, two copies of the letter must be enclosed in the envelope.

    APPROVED:

    _____

    (addressee's title)

    date

This material may be typed two to four lines beneath the last notation and blocked with the left margin.

Classified Material

Both the United States government and its civilian contractors are responsible for the security of sensitive material passing between them—responsibility that specifically means the safeguarding of classified material against unlawful or unauthorized dissemination, duplication, or observation. Each employee of a firm that handles or has knowledge of classified material shares responsibility for protecting it while it is in use, in storage, or in transit. The Department of Defense has established an Information Security Program to implement its security regulations. These regulations are outlined in DoD 5200.1-R *Information Security Program Regulation* for sale through the National Technical Information Service, U.S. Department of Commerce, Springfield, VA 22161.

Classification in industrial operations is based on government security guidance. Private sector management does not make original security classification decisions or designations but does implement the decisions of the government contracting agency with respect to classified information and material developed, produced, or handled in the course of a project. Management also designates persons within the firm who will be responsible for assuring that government regulations are followed. Each system and program involving research, development, testing, and evaluation of technical information is supported by its own program security guide.

What is classified information and material? The following short glossary adapted from Department of Defense definitions should give some insight.

Classified information official information which requires, in the interest of national security, protection against unauthorized disclosure and which has been so designated

Declassify to determine that certain classified information no longer requires, in the interest of national security, any degree of protection against unauthorized disclosure, and to remove or cancel the classification designation

Document any recorded information (as written or printed material, data processing cards and tapes, graphics, and sound, voice, or electronic recordings in any form) regardless of its physical form or characteristics

Downgrade to determine that certain classified information requires, in the interest of national security, a lower degree of protection against unauthorized disclosure than is currently provided, and to change the classification designation to reflect this lower degree

Information knowledge which can be communicated by any means

Material any document, product, or substance on or in which information may be recorded or embodied

National Security a collective term encompassing both the national defense and the foreign relations of the United States

Official Information information which is owned by, produced for or by, or is subject to the control of the United States government

Regrade to determine that certain classified information requires, in the interest of national security, a different degree of protection against unauthorized disclosure than is currently provided, and to change the classification designation to one reflecting the new degree of protection

Upgrade to determine that certain classified information requires, in the interest of national security, a higher degree of protection against unauthorized disclosure than is currently provided, and to change the classification designation to reflect this higher degree

The following classification categories are designated on correspondence and other matter by the stamps (not less than ¼″ in height):

Unclassified referring to information or material requiring, in the interest of national security, no protection against unauthorized disclosure

Confidential referring to information or material requiring protection because its unauthorized disclosure could cause damage to the national security

Secret referring to information requiring a substantial degree of protection because its unauthorized disclosure could cause serious damage (as a serious disruption of foreign relations) to the national security

Top Secret referring to information or material requiring the highest degree of protection because its unauthorized disclosure could cause exceptionally grave damage (as armed hostilities against the U.S.) to the national security

These classification categories may also be represented before individual paragraphs, in subject lines, and in enclosure notations by the following parenthetical abbreviations:

(U)   (C)   (S)   (TS)

The phrases "For official use only" and "Limited official use" should not be used to identify classified information.

The following general marking procedures are required by the government:

1. The overall classification of a document, whether or not permanently

bound, or any copy or reproduction thereof must be conspicuously marked or stamped at the top and bottom on the outside of the front cover (if any), on the title page (if any), on the first page, on the last page, and on the outside of the back cover (if any). Each inside page of the document will be marked or stamped top and bottom with the highest classification category applicable to the information appearing there.

2. Each section, paragraph, subparagraph, or part of a document will be marked with the applicable parenthetical classification abbreviation (TS), (S), (C), or (U) when there are several degrees of classified information within the document.

3. Large components of complex documents which may be used separately should be appropriately marked. These components include: attachments and appendices to a memorandum or a letter, annexes or appendices to a plan or program, or a major part of a report.

4. Files, folders, or packets for classified documents should be conspicuously marked on both front and back covers with the highest category of classification occurring in documents they enclose.

5. Transmittal documents including endorsements and comments should carry the highest classification category applicable to the information attached to them.

Basic mailing procedures for classified documents are outlined below. For detailed information on mailing and on hand-carrying such documents, see DoD publication 5200.1-R:

1. Classified material must be enclosed in two sealed opaque envelopes or similar wrappings before it may be mailed through the U.S. Postal Service or by means of a commercial carrier.

2. Both envelopes must contain the names and addresses of the sender and the receiver.

3. The inner envelope must contain the appropriate classification category stamp, which must not be visible through the outer envelope.

4. The classified information should be protected from the inner envelope by being folded inward, or by use of a blank cover sheet.

5. The inner envelope must contain an appropriate classified-material receipt.

6. Confidential material is sent by CERTIFIED MAIL and Secret information is sent by REGISTERED MAIL. Top Secret documents require specialized transit procedures.

7. Classified material should be addressed to an official government agency and not to an individual.

Classified material is downgraded and declassified as soon as there is no longer any national-security reason for it to be classified. The Department of Defense makes these judgments. An automatic schedule of downgrading has been set up for the three categories.

1. TOP SECRET will be downgraded automatically to SECRET at the end of the second full calendar year following the year in which it was originated; downgraded to CONFIDENTIAL at the end of the fourth full calendar year following the year in which it was originated; and declassified at the end of the tenth full calendar year following the year in which it was originated.
2. SECRET will be downgraded automatically to CONFIDENTIAL at the end of the second full calendar year following the year in which it was originated, and will be declassified at the end of the eighth full calendar year following the year in which it was originated.
3. CONFIDENTIAL will be automatically declassified at the end of the sixth full calendar year following the year it was originated.

Classified documents therefore must be conspicuously marked or stamped to indicate the intended automatic downgrading schedule. This information is typed or stamped on the first or title page of a document immediately below or adjacent to the classification stamp.

Exemptions to the General Declassification Schedule will bear the following information affixed immediately below or adjacent to the classification stamp on the first or title page:

```
CLASSIFIED BY: _____
EXEMPT FROM GENERAL DECLASSIFICATION
SCHEDULE OF EXECUTIVE ORDER 11652
EXEMPTION CATEGORY
DECLASSIFY on
```

Figure 7.2.   General Declassification Schedule exemption stamp

See the letter facsimile in this section for the positioning of the above information on a confidential document.

Chapter 8

Using the Mail

CONTENTS

Successful business correspondence relies on efficient and reliable delivery of outgoing mail. The best way to ensure this kind of delivery is through effective office procedures for handling outgoing mail and an understanding of the requirements of and services offered by the U.S. Postal Service and by other delivery services. This chapter offers information and advice for office managers, secretaries, and small-business owners who wish to develop the necessary procedures and understanding.

For more information about preparing envelopes, see the section on Stylings for Envelope Addresses, beginning on page 49, in Chapter 1, "Style in Business Correspondence." For information about how to address special kinds of recipients, see Chapter 2, "Forms of Address."

Outgoing Office Mail

Who processes outgoing mail in a business office is usually related to the size of the business. A large office may have a special mailing department, including a messenger service. It may be necessary for a secretary to prepare mail for the mailing department. In a smaller office, one person may have to assume total responsibility for outgoing mail. The five most common checking tasks for both a large and a small office are discussed below.

Checking Addresses

The data in the inside address typed on the letter itself and that of the address on the envelope should be the same. To reduce the chance of error and to speed up the mailing process, some companies prefer to use window envelopes, thus eliminating the need for typing the address on the envelope. If a window envelope is used, it is imperative that the inside address be complete. It should include the complete name, street address, city, state, and zip code. The post office box and room number should also be included if applicable. If the letter is being mailed to a post office box, the zip code of the box number should be used and not that of the street address. The all-capitalized and unpunctuated two-letter state abbreviations are preferred by the post office. See page 52 for a table of two-letter state and dependency abbreviations.

Checking Mailing Notations

Two types of notations may be typewritten on an envelope: (1) on-arrival reminders such as CONFIDENTIAL or PERSONAL and (2) mailing-service reminders such as CERTIFIED MAIL or SPECIAL DELIVERY, all of which are typically typed entirely in capital letters. Every letter having an attention line, a special mailing notation, or an on-arrival notation should also have the same notation or notations on its envelope. On-arrival reminders or notations are typically typed four lines below the return address or nine lines below the top edge of the envelope, starting at least one-half inch in from the left edge of the envelope. On-arrival notations other than PERSONAL and CONFIDENTIAL (for example, Please Forward) are generally typed in capitals and lowercase letters and are underscored; however, their location on the envelope is the same as any other on-arrival notation. Postal directions or special mailing notations are placed on the same line as the on-arrival notations and are typed all in capital letters, one-half inch from the *right* edge of the envelope. See also the section on Stylings for Envelope Addresses, beginning on page 49, in Chapter 1, "Style in Business Correspondence," for detailed envelope addressing instructions.

An envelope should always include a return address. It is acceptable to type the sender's name on a line above the preprinted address and aligned at the left.

Checking Signatures

All outgoing mail must be checked for proper signatures. If a secretary is authorized to sign letters with an executive signature, the secretary's initials must be added (for examples, see page 33). A letter is invalid without a signature in ink.

Checking Enclosures

It is very important to check carefully to see that all enclosures cited in the enclosure notation at the bottom of the letter are included with the letter. It is frustrating for an addressee to receive a letter without the intended enclosure or to receive the wrong enclosure. Their inclusion, therefore, should always be double-checked.

If it is necessary to enclose coins or other small objects, they should be taped to a card or inserted in a coin card. In addition, the envelope should be marked, "Hand Stamp."

Checking Reference and Carbon Copy Notations

If you are answering a letter that is identified by a file number or policy number, you should be sure that the number is repeated in the reference line of your reply letter. The carbon copy notation (cc) or copy notation (c) indicates to whom additional copies of the letter should be sent. A careful check to see that envelopes have been addressed to the individuals mentioned in regular (cc) and blind carbon copy (bcc) notations is important. The blind carbon copy notation usually appears only on the carbon copies in the upper left-hand corner of the sheets; however, it may also be placed below reference and enclosure notations. These carbons should be checked for such notations. An extra carbon copy should be available for filing.

Folding and Inserting Letters into Envelopes

The diagrams in Figure 8.2 depict the correct procedures for folding and inserting letters. The following are some suggestions for sealing and stamping envelopes by hand:

1. Use a moist sponge or moistening device.
2. Never lick envelopes or stamps. This practice is unsanitary, and you can be cut by the sharp edge of the envelope flap.
3. Moisten envelopes and stamps over a blotter, which will absorb excess water.
4. A large quantity of envelopes can be moistened quickly by placing them one behind the other and pressing down the flap of each envelope as it is moistened.

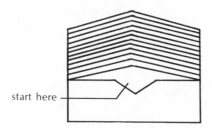

start here

Figure 8.1.   Arranging a large quantity of envelope flaps to be moistened

General Pointers

Sorting the mail Mail that must reach its destination the next day requires special separation and sorting from routine correspondence or mailings. (See pages 367–370 for information concerning special mail services such as Express Mail.) The Postal Service suggests that to receive faster service you should separate and presort your mail as follows:

1. Separate the mail. Your mail can skip an entire sorting operation at the post office if you separate it into major categories such as *local, out-of-town, state,* or *precanceled.* The mail is usually bundled with an identifying label indicating the applicable category.

Small Envelope

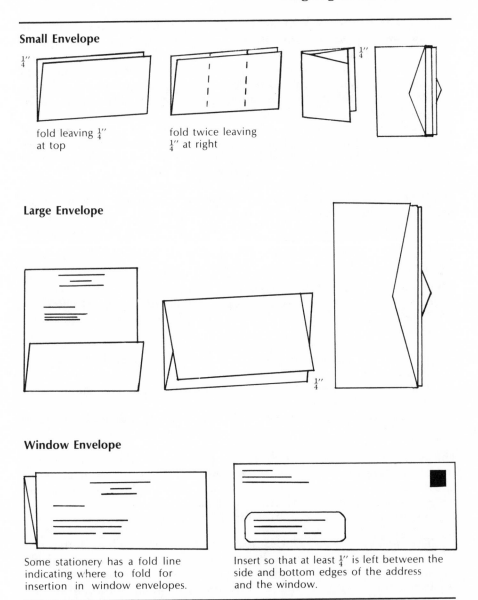

fold leaving ¼″
at top

fold twice leaving
¼″ at right

Large Envelope

Window Envelope

Some stationery has a fold line
indicating where to fold for
insertion in window envelopes.

Insert so that at least ¼″ is left between the
side and bottom edges of the address
and the window.

Figure 8.2.   Folding stationery for three kinds of envelopes

2. Use postage meters. Many businesses—both large and small—use postage meters to expedite the movement of mail. Five or more pieces of metered mail must be faced and bundled. The post office provides the needed printed bands. Large numbers of metered or permit mail may be placed in trays provided by the post office. Trayed mail should have addresses and postage faced in one direction to speed postal sorting and dispatching.
3. Presort your mail by zip code. Large mailings are further expedited if sequenced by zip code numbers with the lowest number first and the highest number last. Mail can be bundled by zip code number if there are ten or more pieces destined for a single zone.

When to mail The Postal Service suggests early mailings to alleviate the usual congestion at the close of the business day. If possible, mailings should be made throughout the day. One large mailing at the end of the business day is to be avoided.

Zip Codes

To handle the ever-increasing volume of mail, the Postal Service has automated mail handling by introducing optical character readers (OCRs) that can "read" a zip code—a five-digit number which encodes the following information:

1. The first digit designates one of ten national areas; each area is given a number (0–9).
2. The first three digits designate a large city or sectional center; there are 552 sectional centers in the United States.
3. The last two digits designate a delivery area or post office within a sectional center.

For example, in the zip code 06117, the first digit, *0*, indicates one of the states in the Northeast; the first three digits, *061*, indicate the area around Hartford, Connecticut; and the last two digits, *17*, indicate Bishops Corner Post Office in West Hartford, Connecticut.

There are three basic sources for zip code information:

1. The *National 5-Digit ZIP Code and Post Office Directory* lists all the five-digit numbers in use in the United States. The directory is available at many post offices for purchase. It may also be obtained from Superintendent of Documents, Government Printing Office, Washington, DC 20402.
2. The classified section of the telephone directory usually has a map indicating local postal zones and a complete listing of area zip code numbers.
3. The Postal Service will willingly answer questions concerning zip code numbers. Post offices in many cities have a special telephone listing for zip code information, found under "United States Government, United States Postal Service" in the telephone directory.

A piece of mail lacking a zip code can be delayed for a day or more. Business firms that address mail by computer may use without charge a magnetic computer tape providing zip code listings. Business offices can make application for the list through their main post office.

In 1981, the Postal Service introduced ZIP+4, a nine-digit code which further subdivides standard zip code areas into segments as small as a city block or even a particular building or a large company. The code consists of the standard zip code followed by a hyphen and four digits, as 06117-1234. The use of ZIP+4 is voluntary, but companies are being encouraged to use it in large mailings in order to save money and speed delivery of mail through the automated processing that the nine-digit code provides.

Metered Mail

Mail that bears an imprinted meter stamp is called *metered mail*. A postage meter is a useful convenience for many mailers. The postmark, date, and cancellation are imprinted by the meter directly onto the envelope or onto an adhesive strip that is then affixed to large envelopes or packages. The meter may also seal and stack envelopes. Sophisticated electronic mailing machines are now available that can even compute the most efficient way to send a particular piece of mail. Meters are leased or rented from the manufacturer, and the mailer must obtain a meter permit from the post office. Payment for postage is made in a lump sum to the post office. The meter is then set for that amount of postage in advance. For a fee, a Postal Service representative will set the postage meter at one's office. Some of the advantages of metered mail are the following: (1) accurate postage accounting that eliminates the theft of stamps; (2) speedier processing of mail in the office; (3) speedier processing of mail at the post office, since envelopes do not have to be turned to face in the same direction and stamps do not have to be canceled; (4) the option of using personalized meter ads; and (5) reduction in the number of trips to the post office.

The Postal Service

Determining the Mail Classification

If a business office does not have a mail room, it will be the responsibility of one person, often a secretary, to see to it that the mail is sent out efficiently and economically. Since postal rates change frequently, that person will need to write or call the post office for a brochure of current rates as well as brochures for all of the various classes of mail, the special services, and the rates for each class or service. The brochures are offered at no charge and contain a wealth of information on the preparation of mail, wrapping instructions, weight, zones, and rates. Since it is often necessary to determine the proper classification of the outgoing mail, the various classes are discussed below.

First-class mail This category includes handwritten and typewritten messages, bills and statements of account, postcards and postal cards (postal cards are the ones printed by the Postal Service), canceled and uncanceled checks, and business reply mail with a weight of 12 ounces or less. First-class mail is sealed and may not be opened for postal inspection. Within a local area, overnight delivery can ordinarily be expected. The post office will designate what constitutes your local area. To qualify for overnight delivery, letters must be deposited by 5 p.m., or at a mail processing facility by 6 p.m. Second-day delivery is standard for other points within specified adjacent states. Third-day delivery is standard for other points within the 48 contiguous states.

It should be noted that mailable envelopes, cards, and self-mailers can be no smaller than 3½" by 5" and should be at least .007 inches thick (about the thickness of a postal card). Also, to avoid a surcharge on first-class mail that is less than one ounce, the envelope should not exceed 11½" by 6⅛" by ¼". First-class postage is required for cards exceeding 4¼"×6". Large envelopes or packages sent as first-class mail should be stamped FIRST CLASS, just below the postage area, to avoid confusion with third-class mail at the post office. Manila envelopes with green diamond edging are useful because they immediately identify the contents as first-class mail.

First-class zone-rated (priority) mail All first-class mail exceeding 12 ounces is rated as priority mail. This type of mail is given full airmail handling. Rates are determined by weight and by the distance of the delivery zone. The maximum weight for priority mail is 70 pounds, and the maximum size is 100 inches in combined girth and length.

Second-class mail This category includes magazines and newspapers issued at least four times a year. A permit is required to mail material at the second-class rate. A mailer other than a publisher can mail individual, complete copies of a publication. The publication should be clearly marked SECOND CLASS.

Third-class mail This category consists of circulars, booklets, catalogs, and other printed materials (as newsletters or corrected proof sheets with manuscript copy). Merchandise, farm and factory products, photographs, keys, and printed drawings may be sent third class. Some people refer to third-class mail as "advertising mail." This mail class is limited in weight to less than 16 ounces; if it exceeds 16 ounces, it is classified as fourth-class mail or parcel post. The two categories of third-class mail are single piece and bulk; bulk mail costs less than single-piece but it requires a permit, a minimum number of separately addressed mailings (more than 200 pieces or more than 50 pounds), and presorted bundling. Third-class mail is usually not sealed so that it can be opened easily for postal inspection. It is generally slower than other types of mail, including fourth-class.

Fourth-class mail (parcel post) This category consists mainly of domestic parcel post. Also included in it are special catalog mailings, special fourth-class mailings, and library mailings. It is mostly used to send packages or parcels weighing 16 ounces or more. Parcels mailed at, and addressed for delivery to, a first-class post office in the 48 contiguous states may not exceed 40 pounds in weight or 84 inches in combined length and girth. The parcel post regulations specify that all other parcels may not be more than 70 pounds or 100 inches in combined length and girth. Parcel post postage rates are based on the weight of the package and the delivery distance. The minimum weight is 16 ounces per parcel. Parcels under 16 ounces are mailed according to third-class, first-class, or priority regulations.

Overnight delivery can be expected within the local area if parcels are mailed by 5 p.m. at post offices or receiving platforms. Second-day service can be expected for distances up to 150 miles. Service time depends on the distance the parcel must travel; for example, service time may be as long as eight days for distances beyond 1,800 miles.

A written message in an envelope may be taped to the outside of a parcel if first-class postage is affixed to the envelope. Another way to include a letter with a package is to enclose the letter in the package, mark "Letter Enclosed" on the package, and affix first-class letter postage in addition to the fourth-class mailing charge.

It is extremely important to wrap a parcel securely—in a strong container with the contents thoroughly cushioned—and to write or type the address label legibly. The Postal Service prefers that packages be secured with strong tape rather than twine, which can jam the machines that handle the parcels.

International mail This category includes letters, letter packages, printed matter, small packages of merchandise and samples, and parcel post destined for foreign countries. However, overseas military mail, i.e., APO (Army Post Office) and FPO (Fleet Post Office), is not classified as international mail. Aerogrammes are a convenient form of stationery for international correspondence. Their price includes prestamped stationery that folds into a self-enclosed envelope. International postal cards and parcel post service are available to most foreign countries.

Since there is a great deal of information concerning international mail too voluminous to include in this book, it is suggested that a copy of the *International Mail Manual* be obtained from the U.S. Government Printing Office, Superintendent of Documents, Washington, DC 20402. The publication is a handy reference source for those who must handle much outgoing office mail in this category.

The United States Postal Service also provides Publication 51, *International Postage Rates and Fees*. It includes an overview of international mail services as well as specific information about rates and fees, and it can be obtained without charge.

International mail consists of two sub-categories: postal union mail and parcel post. Postal union mail is divided into LC mail (letters and cards) and AO mail (other articles). LC mail consists of letters, letter packages, aerogrammes, and postcards; on the other hand, AO mail comprises printed matter, matter for the blind, and small packets. Postal union articles should be addressed legibly and completely. Roman letters and Arabic numerals should be used. The name of the post office and country of destination should appear entirely in capital letters. The sender should be sure to use the zip code or postal delivery zone if available. It is permissable to use a foreign-language address, provided that the names of the post office, province, and country are in English. The envelopes or wrappers of postal union mail should be marked ("Printed Matter," "Printed Matter—Catalogs," "Printed Matter—Books," "Letter," "Par Avion," or "Exprès") to show the mail classification. The maximum size permissible for articles not in the form of a roll is 36 inches in combined length, breadth, and thickness. The greatest length allowed is 24 inches. For articles in the form of a roll, the maximum length permitted is 36 inches. The maximum length plus twice the diameter permitted is 42 inches. Very small articles should have a strong, rectangular address tag attached.

All postal union articles except letters and letter packages must remain unsealed. The Postal Service requires that registered letters and registered letter packages be sealed. Neither insurance nor Certified Mail service is available for postal union mail. However, Special Delivery is available to most countries. It is possible to obtain a return receipt. Mail going to most countries can be registered. There is daily airmail delivery to practically all countries.

All articles should be correctly prepaid in relation to weight in order to avoid delays. The proper postage should be affixed. If an article is returned for additional postage, the proper amount should then be affixed and the words "Returned for postage" should be crossed out. A mailer can also send a correspondent international reply coupons that are used to prepay reply letters. Postal union mail is generally returned to the sender if delivery cannot be made.

Parcel post service is available to almost all countries. The greatest length allowed is 3½ feet. The greatest combined length and girth allowed is 6 feet. Parcels may measure 4 feet in length if not more than 16 inches in girth when mailed to some countries. Prohibited articles include items that may damage the mail or cause injury to postal employees, such as matches and most animals, alive or dead, and communications having the character of current correspondence (which means in effect that a letter cannot be enclosed in a parcel post package). There are restrictions on firearms that can be concealed, on flammable liquids, and on radioactive materials. In addition, any country may prohibit or restrict various articles that it wishes to control.

Parcels should be packed very securely in strong containers made of good quality material that will withstand often radical climatic changes and repeated or rough handling. Insured or registered parcels must be sealed. Some parcels, even though they may be unregistered and uninsured, must be either sealed or unsealed depending on the postal regulations of the countries to which they are sent.

Form 2966-B—a customs declaration—is required for parcel post packages mailed to other countries. A dispatch note (Form 2972 or Form 2966) may be required for mail going to some countries. Insurance is available for mail being sent to many countries; however, registration is available only for material being sent to a few countries. Although C.O.D. and Certified Mail are not available, air service and Special Handling are.

In conjunction with the foregoing discussion of international mail, it should be mentioned that there are private companies licensed by the U.S. government that help importers prepare the customs documents required for imported packages and articles. Other services that may be included are export crating, reforwarding, delivery to and from airports and ocean ports, and bonded warehouse marking and distribution. These companies are called *customhouse brokers*. They offer savings on import/export charges, and they expedite delivery.

Special Services

In addition to determining the mail classification (first class, second class, etc.), a secretary may have to select and use special services. The special services provided by the Postal Service are listed alphabetically and examined in detail below.

Aerogrammes An economical means of communicating abroad is the use of a combined letter and envelope called the *aerogramme*.

Business Reply Mail A business may wish to pay the postage for those responding to the company's mail—an important factor when something is being offered for sale through the mail. To use the Business Reply service, an application is made on Form 3614. This form can be obtained from a local post office. There is no charge for the permit; however, the business must guarantee that it will pay the postage for replies. Postage may be collected when the reply is delivered, and an advance deposit may be required under certain conditions. *Business Reply Mail* must be clearly written on the envelope. In addition, the permit number, the post office issuing the permit, the words "No Postage Stamp Necessary if Mailed in the United States," and the words "Postage Will be Paid by Addressee" (or "Postage Will be Paid by" over the name and address of the person or firm) must appear on the envelope.

Certificate of Mailing An original Certificate of Mailing for individual pieces of mail is issued for a fee. The post office keeps no record of such certificates. A Certificate of Mailing is used by a mailer to prove that an item was actually mailed.

Certified Mail This designation provides proof of both mailing and delivery. The carrier obtains a signature from the addressee on a receipt form which is kept by the post office for two years. There is a fee for this service. A return receipt (see below) will be provided the sender for an additional fee.

Collect-on-Delivery With Collect-on-Delivery—commonly referred to as C.O.D.—both the postage and the value of the contents of a parcel or letter are collected from the addressee. The maximum amount that can be collected is $300. The fee charged for C.O.D. includes insurance against loss or damage and failure to receive payment. First-, third-, and fourth-class mail can be sent C.O.D., the regular postage being paid in addition to a C.O.D. fee. The addressee may not examine the contents of the letter or parcel in advance of charges paid. Parcels sent must be based on bona fide orders or on agreement between the mailer and addressee. For an additional fee, the mailer of C.O.D. letters or parcels will be notified of nondelivery. First-class mail sent domestic C.O.D. may be registered at an additional charge.

Express Mail Express Mail is a fast intercity delivery system linking most major metropolitan areas in the United States. It is used for the reliable delivery of urgent mail weighing up to 70 pounds. Overnight delivery of letters and parcels is guaranteed. A 95 percent reliability record of on-time delivery for Express Mail has been established.

Regular Express Mail service requires that a shipment be taken to a post office by 5 p.m. The post office supplies a special address label. The package will then be delivered to the addressee by 3 p.m. the following day, or it may be picked up at the post office as early as 10 a.m. the next business day. Rates include insurance, a receipt for shipment, and a record of delivery at the destination post office.

The Postal Service also offers Express Mail Same-Day Airport Service between many major airports. To use this service, the mailer takes the shipment to the airport mail processing facility, and the addressee picks it up on arrival at his or her airport. You can even arrange to have Express Mail shipments picked up at a business office for an extra charge, but only if this is done on a regular basis.

Insured mail First-, third-, and fourth-class mail can be insured against loss and damage up to $400 if it is properly packaged. Items of greater value should be sent by Registered Mail. For an additional fee, a return receipt may be obtained as proof of delivery for insured mail exceeding $20 in value. Payment of another fee provides that the mail is delivered only to the addressee.

Mailgram The Mailgram is a special mail-via-satellite service offered jointly by the United States Postal Service and Western Union. These letter-telegrams are delivered the next business day by U.S. letter carriers to virtually any address within the 48 contiguous states. Small offices can use this service by supplying the Mailgram message to a Western Union office by telephone (toll-free) or in person. Fees are paid to Western Union for this service. Rates are based on 100-word units in the message.

Within larger firms, up to 50 common or variable-text messages can be typed directly from the company's teleprinter into the Western Union computer on a single connection. A basic fee is charged for each message, in addition to the telex/TWX usage charges. (Instructions may be found in the firm's telex/TWX directory.) Mailgrams in volume may be handled by putting mailing lists on computer tape, which can hold up to 10,000 address lines on a single tape. There is a basic fee for each message of 600 characters or less, and a fee for each additional 600 characters, plus a minimum charge for each tape. The most economical way to input a Mailgram is from the company's computer directly into Western Union's computer. In this case, a basic fee is charged for each message, in addition to a minimum fee for each tape.

An additional electronic mail system has been planned that will allow companies to transmit messages from their computers directly to post office computers, which will then print and deliver as many copies as are requested.

Money orders Money can be sent through the mail by purchasing Postal Money Orders up to $500 that are redeemable at any post office. International Money Orders can be purchased for amounts up to $500 at large, i.e., first-class, post offices.

Passport applications The Postal Service, working in conjunction with the United States Department of State, accepts applications for passports from those wishing to travel abroad.

Post office boxes Boxes and drawers may be rented in post offices. These boxes and drawers facilitate the receiving of mail, since mail can be obtained at any time that the post office lobby is open.

Registered Mail Domestic first-class and priority mail may be registered to protect valuable items. This is the safest way to mail valuables. The fee for this service is based on the declared value of the mail, and the indemnity limit is $25,000. The customer is given a receipt at the time of mailing; therefore, Registered Mail must be mailed from a post office. The post office keeps record of the mailing through the number it has been assigned. For an additional fee, a proof-of-delivery receipt will be returned to the mailer. Registered Mail is transported under lock and is kept separate from other mail.

Return receipts A mailer may request a return receipt that shows to whom and when a piece of certified, insured, or registered mail is delivered. If the request is made at the time of mailing, the fee is considerably lower than if the request is made later. The information is mailed to the sender on a postal card.

Self-service postal centers Self-service postal centers are located in convenient places such as post office lobbies, shopping centers, or automobile drive-ups. They supplement existing postal services by providing around-the-clock service seven days a week. Automatic vending machines dispense stamps, postal cards, stamped envelopes, and minimum parcel insurance. These stamps are sold at face value, unlike those from the private stamp vending machines.

Special Delivery This designation virtually assures delivery on the day mail is received at the destination post office. As soon as the mail is received there, it is delivered by Special Delivery messenger. An extra fee in addition to the regular postage is charged for this service. Special Delivery may be used for all classes of mail except Express. Although Special Delivery does not speed mail transportation from the post office of origin to the destination post office, it does assure rapid delivery from the destination post office to the intended addressee. However, the mailer must remember that mail cannot be specially delivered to post office boxes or on weekends to offices that are closed. Also, some small post offices provide this service only during post office hours.

Special Handling This designation assures preferential, separate handling for third- and fourth-class mail and normally speeds its delivery between post offices. It does not ensure speedy delivery after arrival at the destination post office. There is an extra fee for Special Handling.

Forwarding, Recalling, and Tracing Mail

First-class mail under 12 ounces (except for postal cards and postcards) may be forwarded without charge when the addressee's new address is known. When a piece of mail must be forwarded, the address on the original wrapper should be changed, and any required postage (as for second-, third-, or fourth-class mail) should be added. Undeliverable first-class mail, including priority mail but excluding postal cards and postcards, will be returned to the sender without charge. To ensure the return of other classes of mail, the sender must mark the envelope "Return Postage Guaranteed" and be willing to pay extra postage when the mail is returned.

It is wise to purge mailing lists occasionally to avoid paying for mail that cannot be delivered. This is done by printing "Address Correction Requested" on the envelope. If the addressee has moved to a known address, the post office will give the mailer the new address; or if the mail is undeliverable for any known reason, the post office will tell the mailer the reason. There is a fee for each address correction returned to the sender.

Occasionally it may be necessary to recall a piece of mail already delivered to the post office. To do this, the sender must fill out a request form at the post office as soon as possible. The sender must also be prepared to pay all costs of the recall, including telegrams and long-distance telephone calls. The sender will be notified if the mail has already been delivered. Other post office forms are available that allow either the sender or the addressee to request lost mail to be traced within a year of the mailing date.

Other Delivery Methods

Shipments to and from business offices are often made by means other than the post office. Shipments are made by air, rail, ship, bus, and truck. There are also delivery services such as United Parcel Service that use all of these methods of delivery. Check the Yellow Pages of the local telephone directory under "Delivery Services" or "Courier Services" for the names of other parcel delivery services in the area. Before preparing the package, be sure to find out what the carrier's regulations are concerning the size, weight, wrapping, and sealing of packages. United Parcel Service, for instance, does not allow the use of string, cellophane tape, or masking tape.

Messenger services may also be called upon to make local, same-day deliveries (as to banks) when the need occurs. Although some companies have their own messengers, many others prefer to use some of the commercial messenger services available for a nominal fee. These services are listed in the Yellow Pages of the telephone directory.

Express Service

Air express Air express is a fast-growing industry. While it is expensive, it is the fastest means of shipping letters and parcels to the larger cities in the United States. Some air express companies will also send a courier to make a delivery for you overseas. This service, too, is expensive, but there are many occasions in a business office where quick delivery is essential and it is worthwhile to bear the extra cost.

Bus express Most bus lines have a shipping service. This method of delivery is speedy and is especially suitable for delivery to small towns that are not served by airlines. Many items are insurable. The weight limit is 100 pounds per package, and the size of the package is limited to $24 \times 24 \times 45$ inches. There is an extra charge for pickup and delivery service.

Railway express The sender may either telephone the railroad to have the package picked up or deliver the package to the railroad station for shipping.

Freight Services

Freight, although slower than express, is the most economical way to ship large quantities of material in bulky packages. The various types of freight are railroad, motor, air, and water freight.

International Shipments

As the business dealings of corporations increase internationally, there is a greater need for international deliveries. Shipments may be made by boat or by air. Since foreign shipments involve special forms and special packaging, it is advisable to contact international airlines and steamship companies for instructions. They have personnel to assist with the preparation of the necessary forms and to furnish packing and shipping instructions.

Electronic Mail

Electronic mail is a new term that generally refers to the process by which a message or document is electronically transmitted in visual, as opposed to auditory, form. Thus the Mailgram described on pages 368–369, the telex, TWX, facsimile machines, intelligent communicating copiers, and communicating text-editing machines can all be considered as electronic mail systems. However, the term electronic mail is being used more specifically to refer to computer-based message systems that send digitally encoded documents directly from terminal to terminal and whose messages are displayed on a cathode-ray tube (CRT) terminal with the option of a printed hard copy. Many companies that communicate frequently with their branch offices have begun to take advantage of electronic mail. Through electronic mail systems, urgent correspondence can be transmitted in a matter of seconds to most major cities around the world.

Index

Index of Sample Letters